The Railroad and the City

Carl W. Condit

The Railroad and the City

A Technological and
Urbanistic History of Cincinnati

Ohio State University Press : Columbus

The frontispiece is a detail from figure 42.

Library of Congress Cataloguing in Publication Data

Condit, Carl W
  The railroad and the city.

  Bibliography: p. 307
  Includes index.
  1. Railroads—Cincinnati—History. 2. Cincinnati—History. I. Title.
HE2781.C5C65   385'.09771'78   76-55346
ISBN 0-8142-0265-9

Table of Contents

List of Illustrations

Preface

Although the railroad industry in general has given rise to an enormous body of naïve or vernacular literature, the serious history of railroad technology has begun to emerge only in recent years. Appropriately detailed analytical studies of American locomotives have been undertaken by Alfred Bruce and John H. White, Jr., but only the latter's book reflects an adequate level of scholarship. The major railroad bridges and train sheds are treated in various chapters of my books on American building techniques, and in David Plowden's *Bridges*, but in a highly selective way befitting the larger context. The history of railroad structures, line, track, and tunnels —railroad civil engineering *in toto*—has been largely neglected. The intricate and forbidding territory of communications, telegraphy, signaling, interlocking systems, and train control still awaits the historian with the courage to try his hand. And the same may be said of electric and diesel-electric motive power, since few qualified historians possess the scientific resources for the job. The architectural history of railroad stations constitutes the subject of an excellent study by Carroll Meeks, but it is limited to internal planning and formal design. The operating features of the metropolitan terminal are ably set forth in a work that was long standard, John Droege's *Passenger Terminals and Trains*, but it is a text that is restricted to the practices in existence when the book was published in 1916. The historical development of the terminal, conceived in terms of its total design, operational complexity, and its extensive role as a determinant of urban growth and character, deserves a thorough examination that it has yet to receive. There is a modest beginning, suggesting how this might be done, in Alan Jackson's *London's Termini*.

The evolution of the city with respect to urban circulation falls into three radically unequal periods that we might characterize respectively as the horse-and-pedestrian, the railroad, and the automotive phases. The second was decisive for the growth of the industrial city, since it was then that technology, for good and ill, became the chief determinant of urban form, with the rail pattern playing a major role. The constantly expanding station not only shaped the urban fabric and the pattern of land use but became a special kind of urbanistic institution, a microcity mirroring the urban life around it. The train became a mobile equivalent, a special kind of microcity moving over the ground. The station then served to unite the train with the city and the suburbs, and the metropolitan area with its larger milieu. The history of the railroad thus offers another means for comprehending the city through its growth around the new focal points, its arterial system, and through the pattern of movement in, out, and around it.

Americans generally believe that all this belongs irrevocably to the past, but I would like to show, with Cincinnati as a starting point, first, that even if this is the case, it is highly questionable whether the present offers any improvement on the past, and second, that the earlier arrangements offer valuable lessons for the future. I began with Cincinnati for various reasons of which the personal factor is admittedly an important one. I knew the city at first hand for the first thirty-one years of my life, gaining through my own explorations the kind of familiarity essential to writing effectively about any aspect of urban history. But there are objective justifications that are equally cogent. The city throughout the period of rail dominance was a strategic transfer point between the railroad systems of the Great Lakes and Ohio valley regions on the one hand and those of the Pocahontas area and the South on the other. The city was the gateway to the southeastern states, a position of fundamental importance both for its own development and that of the vast area beyond the Ohio. It was the foremost example among cities in its population range of the multi-terminal metropolis, so that the growth and special

Preface

character of its various parts were strongly affected by the expansion of its railroad pattern. Finally, there was a particular kind of interaction between growth and avenues of commerce arising first from earlier modes of transportation, but more decisively from its unique topography: no American city has been more profoundly shaped by its geological history than has Cincinnati. The aim of the present work has thus been twofold—first, to contribute a chapter to the history of railroad technology in its functioning whole, and second, to do so in terms of its interaction with the evolution of a particular city.

In the assembly of illustrations for this work, the gathering of data from drawings and printed sources, and investigations in the field I have been generously helped by a number of people associated with libraries, railroad companies, and other institutions. My foremost thanks must go to my friend John H. White, Jr., of the Smithsonian Institution, for his ready and useful responses to my many questions, for making available to me the resources of his archives at the Smithsonian's Department of Transportation, and finally, for reading and making valuable comments on portions of the manuscript, which were subsequently published in *Railroad History*. I am equally indebted to another old friend, John G. Brueggeman, of the University of Cincinnati, who acted as my guide, companion, automobile driver, and local topographer during my investigations in the field. Two local collectors of prints and documents relating to the Cincinnati rail scene, Gibson Yungblut and Otis Finchpaugh, have provided me with valuable information and prints that have disappeared from the public repositories. Mr. Yungblut has been particularly generous in making his voluminous collection of materials on the Union Terminal available to me. Members of various library staffs gave liberally of their time in providing essential material: particularly helpful were Carolyn Lea Mond, of the Cincinnati Historical Society; Janet Ayers, of the Technological Institute Library; and Mary Roy and Gertrude Lewis, of the Transportation Library, both at Northwestern University. Among members of railroad staffs I owe special thanks to William Pletz and J. E. Martin, of the Penn Central Company, for photographs and drawings of stations; to Joel De Valle and James Hall, of the Southern Railway System, for drawings of the company's bridge at Cincinnati and for permission to ride in a locomotive cab between Cincinnati and Danville, Kentucky; to J. H. Adams, J. R. Cary, L. F. Grabowski, Herbert Harwood, and Howard Skidmore, of the Chesapeake and

Ohio/Baltimore and Ohio railroads (now parts of the Chessie System) for drawings and valuation sheets of bridges and stations at Cincinnati and for an invitation to travel in an office car of the company from Chicago to Cincinnati.

The expenses of travel and illustrations were borne primarily by two grants respectively provided by the American Philosophical Society of Philadelphia and the Office of Research Coordination at Northwestern University. These are the most recent in a long series of similar occasions when I have been happy to express my gratitude for their support.

Carl W. Condit

The Railroad and the City

1

The Pioneer Roads and Their Stations
From the Beginning to the Time
Of the Civil War

The City and Its Natural Setting

The prominent and in places rugged hills of the Cincinnati area
are the eroded remains of a gentle upfolding of marine sediments
that forms a broad anticline with its axis roughly on the north-
south line. Shaped mainly in the Middle and Upper Ordovician
periods and designated by the geologists as the Cincinnati Arch
or Dome, the uplifted mass consists of relatively thin beds of
heavily fossiliferous limestone interspersed with thinner beds of
soft, friable shale. The exposed strata of the Cincinnati series extend east and west at the maximum from around Peebles, Ohio, to
Madison, Indiana, for a distance of about 115 miles, measured on
the straight line. The average depth of these strata in the immediate area of Cincinnati is about 250 feet, but the maximum
reaches 570 feet at various locations outside the city. The rock is
of great interest to paleontologists, but it is an inferior building
stone with a very limited bearing capacity. The upper surface of
this limestone arch was eroded down to a relatively level state
and then deeply dissected by the many streams of the region, so
that the separate hills and ridges now stand from 250 to 450 feet
above mean water level in the Ohio River. The chief tributaries
of the main river are, from west to east, the Great Miami River,
Mill Creek, the Licking River, and the Little Miami River, three of
them flowing generally southward and southwestward on the

Facing page: Detail from figure 1.

Ohio side, and the Licking flowing northward on the Kentucky side. These natural waterways constitute the primary bounding and defining features of the city's metropolitan area.[1]

For the first seventy-five years of its history the city of Cincinnati occupied the roughly triangular alluvial plain standing at an average of 108 feet above the mean water level of the Ohio and defined chiefly by the lower river terraces on the south, steep hills along its diagonal boundary to the northeast, and the broad, level-floored, easily flooded valley of Mill Creek on the west, in turn bounded on its western side by other ranges of hills. The lower alluvial bench, which has been entirely covered in the most extreme Ohio River floods, extends from the upper edge of the original river bank, approximately at the south side of Front Street, northward to Third Street, where it rises rather sharply to Fourth Street, then more gently to Fifth; the upper plain constitutes the remainder of the old city area, penetrating at the deepest to a point about two miles north of the river. The rest of the city's present area is distributed over the tops and the more gently sloping flanks of hills.

The presence of this topographic configuration of main river, hills, and subsidiary valleys meant that the chief avenues of commerce, both water and rail, and the first of the main roads extending to outlying communities, would be confined to the river banks and the tributary valleys. The canals and railroad lines had for the most part to be located on the level valley floors, and the main streets were gradually extended along the sloping valleys of the smaller creeks. The chief natural obstacles to the full economic and physical development of Cincinnati, as we shall learn in detail in the appropriate places, were, first, the need to knit together the old city on its alluvial plain with the spreading hilltop communities and, second, to bridge the barrier of the Ohio River in order to link the city with the South and the Pocahontas regions.[2] The entire canal, rail, and street pattern of Cincinnati, and hence the form and distribution of its residential, commercial, and industrial areas, have probably been shaped to a greater degree than those of any other American city by topographic and geological features.[3]

The history of urban growth in Cincinnati began in the late eighteenth century: in 1788 settlements were established at the mouth of the Little Miami and opposite the mouth of the Licking River, the latter suggesting to the surveyor John Filson the odd and short-lived name of Losantiville, a Latin derivative the vari-

4

ous elements of which mean in reverse order "the city opposite
the mouth of the L[icking]." This community was incorporated
as a town in 1802, when its population numbered about 700, and
grew at a rate sufficient to include by 1820 about 10,000 inhabi-
tants within the general area comprehending the Kentucky, Little
Miami, and North Bend settlements as well as the city itself.[4]
The first steamboat on western streams passed Cincinnati en
route from Pittsburgh to New Orleans in 1811, and within the
next fifteen years river shipping and the construction of steamboats were to rank as major industries. By 1842 Cincinnati had
become the leading slaughtering and meat-packing center of the
nation, processing among other animals about one-quarter of all
the hogs slaughtered in the United States. By mid-century it was
the fourth city in the land, a manufacturing center of first-rank
importance, its population growing at a rate sufficient to double
the total at all but one census prior to the Civil War, and its wealth
expanding even more rapidly. These were the characteristics that
quite understandably made the city and the railroad-builders of
its region objects of the greatest mutual attraction, the city sup-
plying substantial proportions of the capital necessary to finance
construction, and the railroads building the lines to carry the
products of its busy stockyards and factories.

Aside from steamboat traffic on the Ohio River, the history
of organized transportation in Cincinnati began on 21 July 1825,
when local and visiting dignitaries took a hand in turning the
first shovelful of earth for the construction of the Miami Canal.
Water was diverted into the bed in July 1827, and the first boats
made the passage from Cincinnati to Middletown in the fall of
the same year. The waterway was extended to Dayton, its originally projected terminus, in 1828-29, and southward from its
lower end at East Eleventh and Main streets in Cincinnati to the
Ohio River in 1831-34. The extension to the river involved a rapid
descent from the upper flood plain to the water surface, requiring
an unprecedented flight of ten locks in continuous series. The
course of the canal within the corporate limits of Cincinnati lay
along the far south and east sides of Mill Creek Valley, but it
diverged further from the natural stream both in horizontal distance and elevation as it approached the inner area of the city (the
canal appears on the city map of 1855; see fig. 9). The length of
the original waterway and its Miami and Mad River feeders was
sixty-seven miles, and its total cost was $881,447, a heavy invest-
ment for a city of 20,000, equivalent at the 1975 building cost level

to at least $23,000,000.[5] It was renamed the Miami and Erie Canal after its extension to Toledo in 1840, and thus became the first artery of transport to unite the Ohio River and the Great Lakes. For a few years traffic increased rapidly, but rail competition soon put an end to the upward climb: tonnage and tolls began to decline from the high point of 1851, and by 1895 the company was compelled to abandon operations. Even in its defunct state, however, the canal repeatedly proved to be a potent factor in shaping the circulatory system of Cincinnati.

The second of the city's canals struggled through an even shorter life, and it too was to play a more decisive role dead and largely obliterated than alive. The Whitewater Canal, designed to serve the Ohio and Indiana communities west and northwest of Cincinnati, was placed under construction in 1839, opened to Brookville, Indiana, for its first traffic in 1843, and extended for its full length to Connersville, Indiana, in 1848.[6] Three obstacles along the way required costly solutions: an aqueduct supported by an arch-and-truss combination of the Burr patent had to be built to carry the canal over the Whitewater River at Metamora, Indiana; another of probably similar construction had to be thrown across Mill Creek in Cincinnati; and a 1,900-foot tunnel had to be dug to admit the water through the low, narrow ridge at Cleves, Ohio, where the unbroken chain of high, steep-faced hills along the Ohio River was interrupted by a saddle-like formation somewhat lower than the surrounding hilltops. East of Cleves the canal lay close to the riverbank, diverging from it at an increasing distance for the straight-line Mill Creek crossing, then turning through an elongated S-curve to reach its eastern terminus at West Pearl and Plum streets. The expenses of construction, light traffic, the static character of the rural Indiana economy, and repeated damage from the floods of the Whitewater River quickly drove the company to bankruptcy: the canal survived only twelve years; and when it was abandoned in 1860, the railroad that would have been its mortal competitor quickly snapped it up.[7]

Little Miami Railroad

The canals found their way through hills along the natural waterways by physical necessity, and the railroad-builders bent every effort to follow the same principle in order to minimize the grades that greatly add to the cost of operating trains, both in time and money. This close interdependency between right of

6

The Pioneer Roads and Their Stations

way and water level appears in the very name of the first railroad line to serve the city of Cincinnati. The Little Miami Railroad was chartered on 11 March 1836 to build a line from Cincinnati to Springfield, Ohio, for the purpose of connecting at the latter point with the Mad River and Lake Erie Railroad and thus providing a through route from the Ohio River to Lake Erie at Sandusky, which was expected to be a major lake port because of the harbor potential of Sandusky Bay.[8] The fortunes of the new company lay in a different direction, however, and the Springfield line eventually declined to the status of a minor branch. The Little Miami reached Loveland, Ohio, in 1843, when it operated its first train, extended its tracks to Xenia the following year, and rounded out its system with the completion of the Springfield line in 1846. The rapid construction was made possible in part by a loan of $200,000 from the city of Cincinnati, the first act of municipal generosity that was to be repeated many times in the building up of the regional rail pattern. The extension of the Miami company to Xenia promised a connection to Columbus and the east, and in little more than twenty years the railroad was part of a flourishing system that joined Cincinnati with Pittsburgh to mount a mortal threat to the steamboat interests.[9]

The first terminal facilities in the Cincinnati area were built in Pendleton, somewhat east of the city limit at the time, in 1843–46 (fig. 1). They included a semicircular enginehouse properly designed with classical pilasters in the mode of the Greek Revival, a freighthouse, a shop building, and a passenger depot, the last of which appears in the only surviving print to have westward-facing track openings and hence to require backing of loaded trains in and out of the enclosure. All these structures were of brick and timber construction, and the two-track passenger station was built according to the customary practice of the time of incorporating the track and platform area within the station building, so that waiting room, ticket offices, and other passenger facilities lay along the outer platforms. To and from this primitive depot the company operated a single passenger train in each direction, one leaving Cincinnati at 9:00 A.M., and the other arriving on the return trip at 10:15 A.M., the journey requiring four and one-half hours to Xenia and five and one-half to Springfield.

But the Little Miami Railroad enjoyed several advantages that led to immediate financial success, and the loan from the city was soon repaid. As the first Cincinnati line, it was the first to exploit the traffic potentialities of the region; and since it had no rail

7

Fig. 1. Terminal facilities of the Little Miami Railroad at Pendleton, 1843-46. *Ohio State Railroad Guide, Illustrated.*

competitor east of the city for nearly the first decade of its existence, whatever traffic flowed in from the hinterland was carried over its own rails. The fairly rapid piecing together of the lines extending east and west of Xenia brought an equally rapid expansion of traffic through connecting lines, of which that portion originating in the flourishing Pittsburgh economy virtually guaranteed prosperity. From the standpoint of operations the Little Miami was one of the most favorably located among the Cincinnati lines: following the valley of the Little Miami River for very nearly the entire length of its main line to Xenia, the track lay on a fairly uniform grade of easy ascent, although the numerous curves in the hilly setting that made for superior scenic attractions formed a minor nuisance for the movement of freight trains. In addition to its own operations the company soon acquired a tenant that provided a modest rental income: in 1853 the Cincinnati, Wilmington and Zanesville began to operate its four daily trains by trackage rights over the older road from Morrow, Ohio, to the Cincinnati terminal. The consequence of all these factors was a high level of prosperity accompanied by a rapid and continuing expansion of traffic, revenues, and net income. In the first year in which all lines were in service (1847), operating expenses were little more than half the revenues, for an enviable operating ratio of 50.8 percent. In the nine years between the completion of the Xenia line and the opening of the last independent passenger station in Cincinnati, the number of passengers increased 550 percent and total revenues, 1,342 percent.[10]

The growth of traffic soon compelled the expansion of the Little Miami's terminal properties in the city. By 1848 the company had enlarged the repair facilities at Pendleton to include car, machine, and blacksmith shops, replaced the existing freight station with two new depots divided between inbound and outbound freight, added a small office building, and constructed a new passenger station at East Front and Kilgore streets, some three miles closer to the business center of the city but still at a discouraging distance for horse-drawn vehicles (fig. 2).[11] All the structures were brick-walled enclosures under gable roofs probably supported by timber trusses of the traditional braced king-post form. The passenger depot measured 60 × 154 feet in overall dimensions, a size sufficient to enclose four tracks and their associated platforms and with a clear span possibly great enough to dictate the use of wrought-iron tension members in the roof trusses, but neither drawings nor descriptions exist in enough detail to confirm such conjectures.

Fig. 2. Little Miami Station, East Front and Kilgore streets, 1848. Reprinted with the permission of the Cincinnati Railroad Club.

The Pioneer Roads and Their Stations

The last passenger station built by the Little Miami before it was leased to the Pittsburgh, Cincinnati and Saint Louis Railroad was a structure with enough pretense to elegance to reflect the company's prosperity far better than its comparatively crude predecessors. Constructed in 1853-54 on East Front Street near the point where both Deer Creek and the Miami Canal flowed into the river (about one block east of Butler Street and the line of the future Newport bridge), the building was a single vaulted enclosure measuring 90 × 465 feet in plan and standing 60 feet high to the crown of the light monitor (figs. 3, 4, 5).[12] Designed by the architect William McCammon in a vaguely "early Italian" style, it was built to accommodate the three tracks, associated platforms, and all public and service spaces within the tightly bound enclosure. The side and end walls were brick, but the generous windows —nineteen in each of the long elevations—were surmounted by cast-iron arches. Trains entered through two arched openings in the east end wall, and found themselves snugly fitted into the interior along with the locomotive smoke, provisions for the dissipation of which were virtually nonexistent.

The segmental vault of the roof was supported by means of the one unusual structural feature of the building (fig. 5). The conventional arrangement of tin-sheathed wood planking on purlins rested on twenty-six laminated arch ribs built up of twelve thicknesses of 1 × 12-inch pine boards. The ends of the ribs were set in cast-iron shoes fixed to the top of the brick walls, each shoe centered over the crown of the arched opening below it. The lateral thrust of the arch was translated into tension in a wrought-iron tie rod suspended from hangers, the assemblage of ties and hangers made fairly rigid by longitudinal ties and double-diagonal bracing in the rectangles formed by the two sets of horizontal rods. The entire system represented a considerable advance over previous wide-span enclosures in wood, and the only possible precedent may have been the roof structure of the first Philadelphia, Wilmington and Baltimore station in Philadelphia (1842).[13]

The interior plan of the station revealed the tight longitudinal arrangement of facilities that existed by necessity before the headhouse was separated from the track area (fig. 5). The three tracks lay adjacent to one another, with a single twenty-four-foot platform running the length of the north wall for the ticket office, baggage room, and "parlors" for men and women. A curious feature of the internal layout was the presence of a short length of track carried on a wheeled platform by means of which locomo-

11

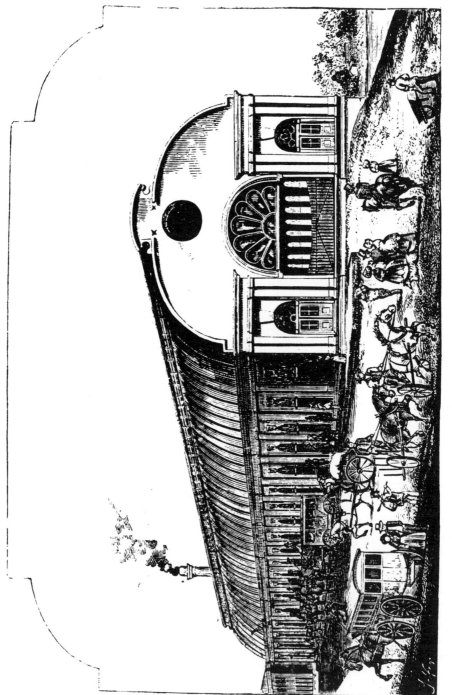

Fig. 3. Little Miami Station, Front Street near the Miami and Erie Canal, 1853-54; William McCammon, architect. *Ohio State Railroad Guide, Illustrated*; photograph courtesy of the Smithsonian Institution.

Fig. 4. Little Miami Station of 1854 after its conversion to a freight house in 1881, shown during the flood of spring 1883. The Cincinnati and Newport Bridge appears in the background. Reproduced with the permission of the Cincinnati Historical Society.

Fig. 5. Little Miami Station of 1854, interior view. Culver Pictures, Inc.

tives and cars could be transferred from one track to another. Invented by D. M. Carhart of Cleveland, this device was necessary in a cramped area that allowed insufficient space for the crossover tracks that soon became standard. In this thoroughly creditable work of contemporary building art, constructed at a cost of $60,000 and claimed to be capable of accommodating 10,000 people, the Little Miami Railroad operated six scheduled trains per day, and its tenant, the Zanesville company, four trains; but such announcements of train schedules as one can find before the *Official Railway Guide* appeared in 1868 are highly unreliable. The depot survived until its destruction by fire in 1889, but it had already been reduced to the status of a freight station in 1881, when the PC&StL, lessee of the Miami company, built a new terminal, which was to survive for better than half a century (fig. 4).

The earlier work was so far superior to anything else in the city at the time that it excited understandable local pride. The *Cincinnati Enquirer*'s correspondent undoubtedly reflected the prevailing view in his enthusiastic description.

> Whether viewed from the river or from the street, it is a building well calculated to give a favorable impression to a stranger visiting our city, and to call out a feeling of pride in those of us who claim something more than a temporary interest in the Queen City. . . . The visitor cannot but pronounce it a magnificent structure.[14]

Seen from a different vantage point, however, the station in its total setting may have offered a less-pleasing prospect to the traveler, as another contemporary commentator pointed out.

> At the head of [Deer Creek] about a mile above the Depot are the principle slaughtering establishments; and . . . I have seen the creek running with blood, from the hogs killed upon it. In the cold weather of December and January, thousands of these animals are slaughtered each day, and the stream is crimsoned till it mingles with the Ohio.[15]

Other Ohio Lines

Within a radius of 100 miles of Cincinnati, or roughly half a day's journey by rail at the mid-century, there lay a number of communities with some promise of future prosperity, two of which, Dayton, Ohio, and Lexington, Kentucky, respectively paralleled and antedated the larger city in their foundation. The presence of the Miami Canal, the early manufacturing establishments, and the extension of the National Road across Ohio and Indiana between 1822 and 1838 brought prosperity to Dayton and in a lesser degree to its smaller neighbors Hamilton and Middletown. At the very time that the Little Miami Railroad was close to completion, the railroad-builders made plans to link the Ohio River city with the communities to the north. The immediate consequence was the incorporation of the Cincinnati and Hamilton Railroad in March 1846 and the expansion at least of its title to Cincinnati, Hamilton and Dayton within the ensuing year. The new line was opened to Hamilton before the end of the earlier year but did not reach Dayton until the late summer of 1851. The fortunes of the CH&D lay in its connections at Hamilton and Dayton, and the promise seemed most inviting even in the early years of its construction. The builders appeared uninterested in seeking state and municipal aid and relied instead entirely on the sale of stock, which was subscribed mainly by Cincinnatians, who completed payment of $750,000 on the first subscription by October 1850. The company became the second to link the Ohio River with the Great Lakes through various operating and leasing arrangements with other lines, and though these eventually brought prosperity, they also brought burdens in its youth that the new road could not sustain.

The CH&D line in the Cincinnati area occupied the entire length of the north and west sides of Mill Creek Valley, from the confluence of its northern tributaries in upper Hamilton County to close to its mouth at the Ohio. The consequence was a nearly level track from the upper flood plain of the main river to the north city limit at the suburb of Wyoming, where a noticeable though modest upgrade begins that extends very nearly to Hamilton. The company's first station, claimed to be a combined passenger and freight facility, was erected at West Fifth near Baymiller Street in 1851, on a site where its terminal properties were to remain for more than a century. It was about as far from the eventual focal point of the core area as the Little Miami depot, both about twelve of the city's irregular blocks east and west of Fifth Street at what was later to become Fountain Square. Neither drawings nor adequate descriptions survive, but the general character can be reconstructed with some reliability. Measuring 103 × 500 feet in plan, the big enclosure was covered by a tin-sheathed plank roof carried on timber trusses (probably the multipanel king-post form) that were in turn supported by exterior walls of brick and interior wooden posts. The great size and the unencumbered space excited favorable attention at the time, as the correspondent of the *Railroad Journal* enthusiastically indicated in his description of the structure. "A friend of ours, who has recently traveled through Europe and Great Britain, speaking of this building remarked that

16

it was the largest and most perfectly planned depot he had ever seen, and he believed larger than any other in the world."[16] But this naïvely lavish praise merely underscored the irony of its design, and the company was finally compelled to admit it in their annual report for 1862. "To this period, we have received and delivered our passengers in the freight depot at Cincinnati, very much to their annoyance, as they have sometimes had to walk through and climb over the freight."[17] In the first full year in which this nuisance was maintained (1852), the CH&D operated three trains in each direction between Cincinnati and Dayton, the 66-mile run requiring two and one-half hours, for the quite creditable average speed of 26.4 miles per hour. In the following year through service to Sandusky was inaugurated as a joint operation with the Mad River and Lake Erie Railroad, to provide the second rail link and the first through trains between the Ohio River and the Great Lakes.

By 1860 the growth of traffic had resulted in intolerable confusion, errors, discomforts, and congestion at the Cincinnati depot; and in the succeeding two years the company initiated planning and gathered its resources for the erection of an entirely new passenger station wholly separated from the earlier structure, which was to be retained exclusively as a freight house. The new terminal was placed under construction in 1863 and opened in the following year on West Fifth Street at the corner of Baymiller, immediately alongside the earlier building, where nearly the whole complex was destined to stand until 1933, and parts of it until 1963. It was far more sumptuous than anything the city had previously seen, a conspicuous extravagance that was reflected in its high cost of $136,000 (about $2,500,000 at the 1975 building cost level). Fronting 50 feet on Fifth Street and extending 475 feet along Baymiller to Sixth, the two-and-a-half-story headhouse surmounted by a corner tower was another work in the ubiquitous Italian style, with exterior walls of brick trimmed in stone and an interior structure of iron and timber framing (fig. 6). The main entrance, facing Fifth Street under a lofty arch, was reached by a stairway of sufficient grandeur to prove discouraging to the passenger heavily laden with luggage. The first floor was given over to the usual station facilities—ticket offices, baggage, waiting and dressing rooms, toilets, a newsroom, and a restaurant, and the second contained the offices of the railroad company. The four tracks were originally covered by a gable shed of timber construction, although this was later replaced by wooden platform

17

Fig. 6. Baymiller Street Station, 1863–64, West Fifth and Baymiller streets, Cincinnati, Hamilton and Dayton Railroad. Reproduced with the permission of the Cincinnati Historical Society.

canopies, and all switches were operated manually throughout the long life of the station. The CH&D and its tenant, the Marietta and Cincinnati, operated a total of ten regularly scheduled trains in each direction in 1864, but the well-established residential community of Glendale north of Cincinnati and the proximity of the manufacturing center of Hamilton in the same direction guaranteed a rapidly expanding local traffic for the first half-century of the Baymiller station's existence.

The construction of the Cincinnati depot coincided with a considerable expansion of owned properties, leasing arrangements, and trackage rights, all of which were aimed at greatly increasing the Hamilton company's traffic, but which also aided in its financial collapse. A chain of small roads built end-to-end along a diagonal line through Indiana during the 1850s led to the inauguration in 1861 of a through operation between Cincinnati and Chicago over what was called either the Chicago Short Line or the Chicago Air Line, and which was, in fact, the shortest distance, at 276 miles, between the two cities.[18] The next step came in 1863: the lease of the Dayton and Michigan Railroad in that year gave the CH&D entry to Toledo and a connection to Detroit over lines that were eventually to become parts of the Pere Marquette and the Wabash railroads. This north-south line was important not only for Cincinnati but ultimately for the South and the railroads that were going to be built to serve it. The small companies destined to become parts of the great east-west trunk lines were being pieced out in the general westward direction from Buffalo, Pittsburgh, and Wheeling ultimately to link the seaboard with the Great Lakes and the Mississippi, so that a route turned to the other cardinal directions was a vital necessity if Cincinnati was to become the entrepôt of the South, a status it was rightfully to achieve and share with Saint Louis if only by virtue of its geographical position. The expected increase in freight traffic made the expansion of the CH&D's Cincinnati facilities seem essential, and before the passenger depot was opened, the company began construction of a three-story freight station and warehouse extending 440 feet from Fifth to Sixth streets somewhat to the west of the Baymiller station.

In 1865 it completed an equally ambitious undertaking that made the CH&D a curiosity among American railroads: a third rail was laid at a six-foot gauge for the entire length of the main line from Cincinnati to Dayton in order to provide trackage rights for the trains of the broad-gauge Atlantic and Great Western Railroad. This arrangement grew out of one of those grand schemes of the nineteenth century that proved historically misdirected because the economic growth of the nation followed a pattern contrary to entrepreneurial expectations. The Great Western was built as a central piece in a through route aimed at joining the New York and Erie Railroad at Salamanca, New York, with the Mississippi

19

River at East Saint Louis via Dayton and Cincinnati, but the construction of trunk lines across the central and northern parts of Ohio and Indiana, along with the explosive growth of Chicago, effectively nullified the potentialities of this circuitous route.[19] The three-rail arrangement of the CH&D over the double-track line to Dayton was costly and awkward enough, but in the increasingly extensive railroad tangle at the lower end of Mill Creek Valley it must have been a nightmare. In spite of the possibilities of eastern and western connections and the company's strategic position in a coming Great Lakes-Gulf system, the traffic around the time of the Civil War offered too little nourishment for the Cincinnati line. Although its Huguenot president, S. S. L'Hommedieu, who held the reins for the two decades from 1848 to 1868, strove mightily to keep it afloat, it could not avoid eventual bankruptcy and reorganization.

The last of the strictly Ohio lines to be built before the Civil War was the Marietta and Cincinnati, which secured its original charter as early as 1845 but was not placed under construction until 1851. As originally projected, the line united two Ohio River towns of which the eastern lay wholly isolated from any form of land transportation, and the outpouring of financial assistance from towns and counties along its route was essential to maintain the construction program but did nothing to save it from the financial disaster that eventually overtook it.[20] The initial line was opened in 1857 between Marietta and Loveland, Ohio, whence the new railroad operated by trackage rights over the Little Miami into Cincinnati at a discouraging annual rental to the Marietta of $60,000. The simultaneous construction during the same year of the Parkersburg, West Virginia, branches of the Baltimore and Ohio and the M&C at least put the latter on a through route, but Cincinnati seemed as far away as ever. The reorganization of 1860 made most of the capital available for the westward extension, which was built down the Little Miami valley, through the hills along Sycamore Creek to Madisonville, just east of the main city, and thence on a near tangent through the Norwood trough to Mill Creek Valley at the west edge of Saint Bernard, where the exhaustion of funds made it advisable to pause once again. The hapless company finally reached the downtown terminal area in 1861 by building a connecting track from the south side of Mill Creek Valley across what was then called Ludlow Grove (later Spring Grove) to a junction with the CH&D line on the north side

20

of the valley, over whose tracks it again operated by rental agreement.[21]

The Marietta trains entered and departed from the CH&D station for only four years, at which time the company made arrangements with the Indianapolis, Cincinnati, and Lafayette Railroad to use the latter's new Plum Street Station following its opening in December 1865. Through service from Cincinnati to Baltimore and Jersey City via Parkersburg and the Baltimore and Ohio was established shortly before the end of the year, but the construction of the Marietta's own line into the Cincinnati terminal area did not come until 1872, and then only after the continuing shortage of capital required the incorporation of a separate building company that was then leased to the M&C.[22] The entry into the Cincinnati core, however, did little to improve the fortunes of a line that was crippled from the beginning: grossly over-capitalized, with annual revenues only one-tenth of those of the far from healthy CH&D, depending almost entirely on connection traffic, the Marietta had no meaning as a separate entity, and only its acquisition by the B&O in 1882 preserved it as a going concern.

Among the many abortive railroad schemes for which Cincinnati was to be the chief terminus, none began with more utopian ambitions, offered what seemed to be greater promises for the economic development of the city's business center, and ended in a more profound anticlimax than the Dayton Short Line. The program began with the incorporation of the Dayton, Lebanon and Deerfield Railroad in 1847, but this unaspiring name was changed officially to the Dayton and Cincinnati and given the popular designation of Dayton Short Line in 1852. The plan was to construct a double-track railroad on a direct line of 51 miles from Cincinnati to Dayton, which included the fantastic project of digging a 10,011-foot tunnel with an internal clearance of 25 feet in width × 19 feet in maximum height under Walnut Hills in order to bring the railroad line straight through the city to an east-side terminal in the vicinity of Broadway and Hunt Street (later Reading Road), where the company had acquired fifteen acres of land for station facilities (fig. 20). The authors of this remarkable scheme appear to have been S. H. Goodin, the president of the company, and Erasmus Gest, the engineer of the tunnel and the original contractor for its construction. The initial contract was let in January 1853, with expected completion in twenty-two months, but by October Gest had exhausted his resources and abandoned operations. A second contractor, after spending nearly $2,000,000, gave up in the spring of 1854; and in spite of the local excitement, the whole project reached final collapse in 1860. The air line to Dayton, with its unbroken succession of cuts and fills, was a masterpiece of surveying, but it lay entirely on paper.

The insurmountable difficulties that stood in the way of realizing this plan in no way diminished the enthusiasm of its proponents, among whom the editors of the Cincinnati *Railroad Record* were the most vociferous. The logical outcome of their years of reflection on the idea was the first proposal for a union station in the city, and they thought of the Short Line depot on the upper flood plain yet "almost in the very heart of the city," together with the tunnel approach, as giving the projected road a "decided advantage over all others entering the city."[23] Five years later, when the project was dying, the *Record* editors saw in it the potentiality of a far-reaching revision of the existing railroad pattern that could only provide great benefits to the city and to the carriers that would bring it to reality.

> It is obvious enough that a depot at the corner of Broadway and Hunt Streets will accommodate three-fourths of the people and business of Cincinnati far better [than the existing stations]. From that point to the corner of Sixth and Walnut is not very far [actually eight blocks], with the great advantage of *not going uphill*, and, therefore, rendering the transportation of freight less costly. . . . But, there is another motive of the strongest kind, which acts on a large number of persons, and a vast amount of capital. This is the immense amount of railroad property, which must derive a profit, if any, from *the mode in which they can transport products through Cincinnati*. This property is . . . invested in the *N. Y. Central*, the *Pennsylvania Central*, the *Baltimore and Ohio*, and the *New York and Erie*; the Marietta Road, the *Wilmington and Zanesville*, and the *Delaware and Steubenville Road*. . . . The competition between these lines with each other, and with other lines north of them *turns upon just such an advantage as the tunnel will give*. . . . If either one of the Great Central Roads were to possess and control a connection with the Tunnel, at Cincinnati, and that were completed, all competition of other roads with it would be at an end. . . . The road which can control the [tunnel] route, has *a decisive advantage over any other* . . . [in] a superior point of distribution [and] a diminution of costs.[24]

One is immediately struck in this somewhat opaque and syntactically confused passage from the hand of the *Record*'s editor by the contrast between the exaggerated claims and the reality of this ambitious tunnel scheme. The railroad line was eventually built on a much reduced scale and ultimately dwindled to the status of an unproductive branch, but behind the fervor of the editorial lay a valid if defective vision of Cincinnati as a great transportation focus and of its increasingly tangled railroad web being drawn by means of a union station into a unified and co-herent whole.[25] There were other proponents who expressed similar hopes, as the local historian Charles Cist, for example, was writing at the same time. "The Railway . . . has afforded interior cities a power far greater than those on the ocean coast, by giving them the means of creating artificial radii . . . to every point of the great circumference, by which they are surrounded. . . . In this respect, Cincinnati stands pre-eminent. . . . [She enjoys] superiority in centrality of position, in the vast area of which she is the metropolis, and in possessing the shortest radial lines to the great ports."[26] Before the subject of a rail hub and rail unification can be pursued any further, however, it is necessary to describe the additions to the station circuit made by the new western roads, to which the editors of the *Record* paid too little attention. As for the tunnel, construction of the long twenty-five-foot bore was never resumed after the abandonment of 1860, and the one that was finally built by a short and unpretentious railroad was a modest enterprise by comparison.[27]

Westward toward Chicago and the Mississippi

The first railroad company to build directly west from Cincinnati soon became a candidate for bankruptcy to balance the Marietta line to the east. The aim of the promoters was to link the city and its river commerce with the waterborne economy of Saint Louis, the importance of the waterways in both cases indicated by the corporate title of Ohio and Mississippi Railroad. The business communities of the two terminal cities had discussed the enterprise as early as 1847, but the three state charters, from Indiana, Ohio, and Illinois, were granted respectively in 1848, 1849, and 1851. The line was placed under construction in 1851, opened for service to the river town of Aurora, Indiana, three years later, and to East Saint Louis in 1857, but this far from impressive construction program was realized only because the municipal government of Cincinnati loaned the company $600,000 in return for a first mortgage and the citizens raised another half-million through a stock subscription.[28] The O&M was built with a six-foot gauge to take the rolling stock of the Great Western, although the missing link of the CH&D's third rail still lay a few years in the future, and the high cost of construction on top of heavy overcapitalization was enough to make the company financially sick from the beginning. A well-qualified president, James C. Hall of Cincinnati, and an able chief engineer, Simeon S. Post, inventor of the Post truss, had to struggle against discouraging odds for years. The only favorable element was that the rail was laid in easy country, and the surveyors followed the natural path west of Cincinnati by locating the track along the Ohio River until they were compelled to leave it at Aurora in order to strike upgrade along a small stream to reach the higher interior land of Indiana. At Cincinnati the track lay across Mill Creek Valley on a long tangent that penetrated well into the West End, where portions of the original line still remain (1975).

With service established at least to Aurora—the extension to Jeffersonville, Indiana, opposite Louisville, was to come in a few months—the O&M had to find the means to build a depot in Cincinnati. Both the appearance and the location of the 1854 structure clearly implied the unhealthy financial state of the road, and its successor of twenty years later revealed that no improvement had occurred in the intervening period (fig. 7). The tangent track across Mill Creek Valley was so located as to lie on the line of Front Street, and the company built its little wooden depot at the intersection with Mill, at the very edge of the city's built-up area. All that one can now discover from surviving drawings of the station is a two-story building of timber framing and crude wood siding standing at the end of a platform protected by what appears to be a gable roof of planking carried on heavy squared posts. (The print reproduced in figure 7 also shows the peculiar size and proportions of the broad-gauge cars.) The structure that replaced this primitive work was erected on the same site in 1873 in a manner that suggests a little more skill on the part of the carpenter and a somewhat higher aesthetic sense (fig. 8). It had the merit, at least, of looking like the conventional railroad way station, although it was a terminal facility. Henry C. Lord, once president of the Indianapolis, Cincinnati and Lafayette Railroad, Cincinnati's first railroad historian, and something of a local wit, summed the matter up very well thirty years after the O&M first offered service. "At last . . . the rails were all laid, the necessary ballast unprovided, and terminal facilities simply in the future. The same old rickety depot remains looking more like a horse market than a retreat for passengers and the court still holds possession."[29] The conversion of the O&M to standard gauge in 1871 offered the advantages of being part of the railroad family, but it was the turn of the century before rescue came.

For the four years between its opening to East Saint Louis and the Civil War, the Mississippi line had the territory between

Fig. 7. Ohio and Mississippi Station, Front and Mill streets, 1854. Culver Pictures, Inc.

Fig. 8. Ohio and Mississippi Station, Front and Mill streets, 1873. From D. J. Kenny, *Illustrated Cincinnati.*

The Pioneer Roads and Their Stations

Cincinnati and the Indiana border to itself, but a potent competitor was not long in coming. In 1861 the Cincinnati and Indiana Railroad was granted a charter to construct a track westward from Cincinnati to the state line as the Ohio extension of the Indianapolis and Cincinnati, and in the following year the company acquired an independent entry into the city by the remarkably far-sighted act of buying the properties of the abandoned Whitewater Canal. At one stroke the new road gained several advantages—a nearly level line of generous width extending from the lower Whitewater River to the inner city, ample space for a downtown terminal relatively close to the urban core, and a ready-made pass through the narrow ridge at Cleves, Ohio, opened up from the tunnel that the canal company had dug through the shale and limestone barrier. The loss of the canal was mourned by a few nostalgic souls, for it had come to be regarded by 1860 either with sentimental attachment or as a quaint joke. Henry Lord, looking back more than twenty years later, expressed the prevailing view very nicely. "[The Whitewater Canal] was a beautiful, although sluggish stream, whose waters were only disturbed by a boat once or twice every month and the occasional plunge of a schoolboy who always came out of his bath to be made clean at home with honest water. Yet it was always white with the frosts of winter and ever green in summer and was regarded as a sacred stream by the medical faculty."[30]

The new Indiana line followed the bed of the canal, which lay immediately contiguous to the Ohio and Mississippi right of way to North Bend, Ohio, and continued as far as the west edge of the Whitewater valley, very nearly at the state boundary, then turned sharply away from its long, level tangent over the combined Whitewater-Great Miami flood plains to follow the narrow and tortuous valley of Tanner's Creek through the hills to the Indiana upland. The winding nineteen-mile grade proved to be the steepest that any of the pioneer companies had to negotiate in their escape from the valley complex that converged in the Cincinnati region. Within the city itself the C&I location offered opportunities with extensive urbanistic implications, for the future as well as for its own time. It penetrated the city through the walled cut of the canal that lay in a long **S**-curve the floor of which had been depressed well enough below street grade to provide ample clearance for trains (fig. 9). The editor of *Railroad Record* was the first to suggest the economic possibilities of the right of way in a prophetic sentence. The company, he suggested, could "erect buildings on the

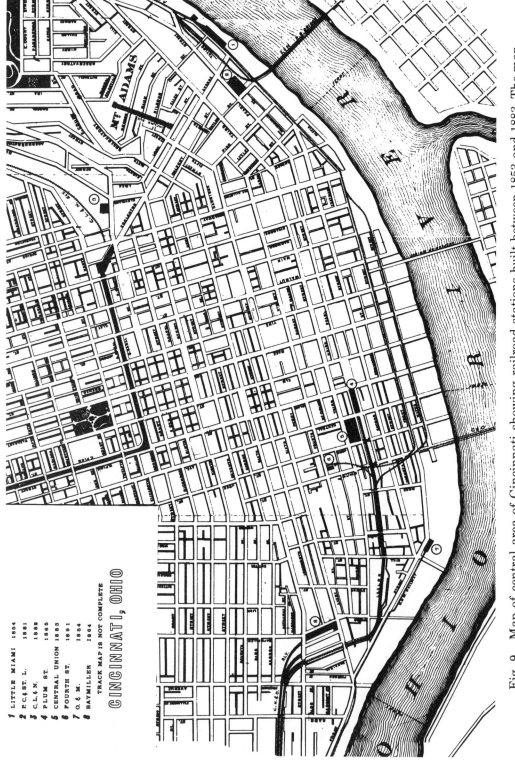

Fig. 9. Map of central area of Cincinnati showing railroad stations built between 1853 and 1883. The map indicates how the approach of the IC&L Railroad to the Plum Street Depot and later to Central Union Depot followed the long S-curve of the Whitewater Canal. A small part of the Miami and Erie Canal appears in the upper center, but the extension to the river along Eggleston Avenue is not shown. From the private collection of John H. White, Jr.

cross streets over their line. They could be used for manufacturing and other purposes, and their rental would make the valuable property now owned by the railroad remunerative."[31] Although the original road and its successors appear never to have taken advantage of the opportunity, the passage represents the first proposal in the United States for air-rights construction, a concept that was not to be implemented until the completion of the Grand Central project in New York in 1913.

With the opening of the line to Lawrenceburg, Indiana, promised by the end of 1863, and substantial segments in the direction of Greensburg and Indianapolis already in existence, the C&I's successor, the Indianapolis and Cincinnati, began to plan a Cincinnati terminal. It was in this respect that the acquisition of the canal property proved its value to the city as well as the railroad, and the whole construction program provided a compelling demonstration of how transportation technology at the mid-nineteenth century shaped urban growth. The company presented a petition to the City Council of Cincinnati in 1863 requesting authority to lease the Pearl Street Market House and the surrounding market space extending over the two narrow blocks from Central Avenue to Elm Street mainly between Pearl and Third for station facilities, since the structure and the open areas had never been used for their intended purpose. The part of this area lying along the south side of Pearl Street had been the 1,200-foot-long terminal basin of the Whitewater Canal, the presence of which was one factor in the rapid expansion of the wholesale produce business in the West Pearl Street area (the map of figure 9 shows the relations of streets to the canal). The railroad company's plan was to rebuild the market house as a passenger depot if the foundations were adequate and to construct a freight station and warehouse in the remaining space. Backed vigorously by the merchants of the area, the railroad petition was granted by the council and the lease drawn up before the end of 1863. The freight station was the first structure planned, and it was erected along Pearl between John Street and Central Avenue in 1863-64. The passenger depot, facing Plum Street at Pearl and destined to last for nearly a century (until 1961), was opened in December 1865 (fig. 10).

Three full stories in height, designed in the Italianate manner, the sturdy brick-walled timber-framed structure under a mansard roof excited nearly rhapsodic comments from the *Record*'s correspondent. He called it "one of the finest railroad depots in the country." The east half of the main floor was given over to ticket

Fig. 10. Plum Street Station, IC&L Railroad, West Pearl and Plum streets, 1864-65. The station later became the Plum Street Warehouse of the Big Four, in which state it survived until 1961. From D. J. Kenny, *Illustrated Cincinnati.*

offices, parlors, toilets, lavatories, and a saloon. "The ladies' parlor adjoins on the north side, the carpet is a fine and beautiful Brussels, while the furniture is the best of Walnut; mirrors, chandeliers, &c., add greatly to the elegance of the room. . . . The dining department is certainly the finest in the United States. The imposing display [of food?] fronting to each parlor is very tempting; for the weary passenger can indulge in a hot or cold meal equal to any restaurant in the land, and then can go on his way rejoicing."[32] Train service in 1866 offered him a limited choice of destinations, and given the schedules of the time, he needed to fortify himself with substantial quantities of food and drink before setting out. The I&C operated five trains in each direction, and the Marietta and Cincinnati three, for a total of sixteen in and out, or one quarter of the city's passenger service at the time.

The Plum Street Depot, as it was called before it came to be regarded as Cincinnati's original union station, was in every respect a typical structure of its time, insofar as this can be inferred from surviving drawings. It was nearly square in plan, measuring 61 feet 6 inches out-to-out along the Plum Street (front) elevation, the 24-inch brick walls rising from a stone foundation and terminating in a mansard carried on truss-like frames reputed to have been built up of massive walnut timbers. The rest of the interior structure was the heavy timber frame known as mill construction. The train shed was a segmental vault of planking supported by timber purlins and possibly timber ribs like those of its Little Miami predecessor, but nothing survives to provide a positive clue. The outside span of the roof was about fifty-three feet, sufficient for two or three tracks, the number dependent on the platform area; and the broad canal-way provided comfortable space for a double-track approach with service and industrial sidings along the way, although the space proved to be none too generous for the expansion of railroad properties and traffic that followed the Civil War. The Indianapolis and Cincinnati was leased to the Indianapolis, Cincinnati and Layfayette Railroad in 1866, and the larger road was consolidated with other companies in the same year to form the Cincinnati, Indianapolis, Saint Louis and Chicago Railroad, which reached Kankakee, Illinois, and a connection for Chicago with the Illinois Central through acquisitions made in 1874. The president of these companies was Henry C. Lord, who seems to have been more adept at commenting on the railroad scene than he was at directing railroad operations.

Meanwhile, north and east of Cincinnati another Ohio system was in the making to swell the traffic at Plum Street and eventually to place the city at the focal point of a powerful rail empire. In 1868 a number of companies, of which the Mad River and Lake Erie was the pioneer, were merged to form the Cleveland, Columbus, Cincinnati and Indianapolis Railroad. Three years later this company acquired through lease the Cincinnati and Springfield, which began operations between the two cities in 1872. The new company had built a somewhat indirect line in order to serve Dayton and Middletown, but it came straight down the length of Mill Creek Valley with only two curves and a gentle descending grade to reach the recently completed extension of the Marietta and Cincinnati at what was soon to be called Ivorydale Junction after the chief product made in the neighboring factories of the Procter and Gamble Company. Trackage rights over the M&C allowed the Springfield line to use the Plum Street Depot as a tenant, which suggested the possibilities of expanding Plum Street into a union station. Ferocious competition on one side and mutually beneficent trackage-rights agreements on the other found H. C. Lord ready with another waggish comment. "The Cleveland company had eventually, but at an unexpected outlay of credit, secured a new route to Cincinnati, and the Cincinnati, Hamilton and Dayton had gotten a parallel road so near to her line that a well-drilled base-ball player could have pitched his ball from one track to the other almost anywhere between Dayton and Cincinnati."[33] The construction of Central Union Depot in 1883 ended the role of Plum Street as a station, but it became the center of a great complex of warehouses built over the years by the proprietary company, in which state it survived intact until it was partly destroyed by fire in July 1944, and then continued in a rebuilt form until the demolition for the downtown extension of the Mill Creek Expressway in 1961.

Multiplying railroads, expanding traffic, the distribution of existing stations, and the rental arrangements in effect at Plum Street again suggested the idea of a union station, and other events of the Civil War decade were strongly to reinforce it. The four stations in existence at the end of the war stood at varying and mostly inconvenient distances from the urban core—the Little Miami was the easternmost of the group, eleven blocks from the intersection of Fourth and Vine streets; the CH&D and the O&M lay well to the west, at twelve and thirteen blocks respectively; Plum Street, at a distance of five blocks, was the only one that could be said to stand contiguous to the core area; the Kentucky Central station in Covington, which we will consider in the next chapter, was no farther away in distance than the Little Miami, but until 1867 the passenger could reach it only by ferry transfer over the Ohio River.[34] At the end of 1862 the Cincinnati railroad companies operated forty-four daily trains to and from these stations to various destinations along the routes to the terminal points of the existing lines, which were then Dayton, Toledo, Sandusky, Cleveland, Pittsburgh, Wheeling, Lexington, East Saint Louis, and Chicago, if we take them in roughly clockwise direction. The total length of main and secondary lines within this circle had passed 3,200 miles in 1860 and was rapidly approaching 5,000 in 1862. The location of the four stations and their associated freight-handling facilities was in no way dictated by considerations of rational urban planning but rather by topography, the availability of land, and the financial resources of the companies. In the age of the horse-and-pedestrian city this distribution of terminals offered serious inconveniences and obstacles to orderly development; yet if the problem of local transportation could be solved, it is possible to support the claim that in certain respects the stations in their size, function, and location were right for Cincinnati in the sense that they were natural consequences of the city's own organic growth. At the time, however, it was the inconvenience of scattered sites at the outer edges of the city's working area and the absence of a station in the northeast part of the urban core (where the Dayton Short Line planned its terminal) that formed the prominent aggravations. The editors of *Railroad Record* had made a careful analysis of the disadvantages as early as the fall of 1859.

> The depots of all our roads are far apart, on the borders of the city, and unconnected. . . . While Street Railroads may lessen this inconvenience, it does not wholly take it away. There must be a Depot *on the upper plain of the city*, accessible to the great body of the inhabitants, who now nearly all live on that plain, or the *distribution* of business from the depots will always be inconvenient and costly. Passengers must not only go a greater distance, but must go through unpleasant and uncomfortable streets, and lose time. Let us take an example or two, and illustrate the amount of this inconvenience. Take the Little Miami depot. There is not one in one hundred of the passengers from that depot stop *short* of Broadway, and not ten in one hundred stop below Third Street. The consequence is that they lose unnecessarily a half a mile in distance, and much more proportionably in time and comfort. Go now to the Hamilton and Dayton depot, and it is further yet to come up to Vine and Walnut Streets. Then go to the Ohio and Mississippi depot, and that is the least convenient of either. Each is on the outer limits, and unconnected with each other. If we look now to the transportation of freight, the cost is greater yet, and the tax on commerce by no means inconsiderable. . . . If any of the citizens and gentlemen who own property north of Fourth and east of Vine Streets, . . . will examine a city map, they will see, first, a great deal of business (and, therefore, values of property also) has been drawn off south and west by the influence of railroads. The assessors' appraisements show that lands and lots on the north side of Cincinnati, are *not worth as much in 1859 as they were in 1853*; certainly a most admonitory fact to all concerned in the rise and fall of property, is that extensive region. There can not be a doubt that this is owing chiefly to two facts: 1. To what we said above, the *drawing off* of business; and 2. To the *want* of facilities for reaching dwellings in that region. The latter will, in some degree, be obviated by Street Railroads; but, the first and most important can only be obviated by concentrating . . . passenger and retail business on the *upper plain of the city*, where the great body of people live. It is not necessary for this purpose, that business should actually be in the streets around the depot; but, the effect of such a central depot will be to give activity and concentration and value to business and property, in the *upper center* of the city, and this will at once act on that great body of property which lies north.[35]

The editorial reflects certain aspects of nineteenth-century urban life throughout the United States, but in the form, of course, that they were taking in Cincinnati. The scattering of stations was most obvious to the passenger and the merchant, since local rail service was the only means of physical connection between the metropolitan center and the market as well as the agricultural produce of its hinterland. Less obvious but increasingly compelling in its effect on urban form was the accelerating growth of railroad facilities—passenger and freight stations, coach and freight yards, coal and water facilities, engine terminals, and appurtenant structures—in the areas beyond the stations, on the lower flood plain of the Ohio River east and west of the terminal outposts and in the lower end of Mill Creek Valley. The area, density, and complexity of these rail facilities were to expand at an increasing rate until they reached their maximum extent at the end of World War I, when even the federal government became concerned about the movement of traffic through the Cincinnati gateway. The dirt and chaos and the "unpleasant streets" were growing nineteenth-century manifestations of the fundamental fact of modern community life, namely, the failure to make technology subservient to the human and the civic order. Yet Cincinnati, like other industrial cities, was wholly dependent on these lifelines, and the need to impose some rational organization on them was increasingly apparent through the decade of the 1860s.

Several events of the period gave further impetus to the idea of unification. The first of these was the presence, even in an unfinished state, of the Dayton Short Line's costly Walnut Hills tunnel, which the editors of *Railroad Record* tirelessly promoted from 1859 to the end of the journal's existence in 1872 as the natural access way not only for the abortive Short Line but equally for the Little Miami, the CH&D, the Marietta, and later, the Cincinnati and Springfield. The proposal editorially advanced in 1865 was that the tunnel be extended southwestward to Sixth Street, then westward to the Sixth Street Market at Elm where the new union station was to be built.[36] More important than the tunnel, if only because it came to exist in a finished state, was the waterfront belt line. The Cincinnati Street Connection Railway, jointly sponsored by the Little Miami and the Indianapolis and Cincinnati, was authorized by the city council in December 1863 to construct a transfer line in Front Street to connect the properties of the two companies, then separated by an interval of 2.5 miles.[37] The completion of this line in 1864 suggested the proposal offered two years later by various business interests as well as the *Record* editors for a union freight depot near Front and Vine streets, which was to be made available to the cars of the Kentucky Central Railroad by placing tracks on the newly completed Covington Suspension Bridge.[38]

The *Record* editors were the most vociferous proponents of this scheme, but in urging their Sixth Street tunnel plan, they were downright passionate. They advanced the full program in September 1867, then enlarged it with exact quantitative details in November 1872, following a survey and an estimate of costs made by Erasmus Gest (fig. 11). The double-track approach tunnel on the east side was to be placed under Fifth or Sixth Street, but preferably under the latter at an elevation sufficiently far above the highest flood stage to allow the track to be depressed thirty feet below grade, which would have been 9.4 feet above the record high water (January 1937). The editors cited as precedents the tunnel approach and core-area station in Edinburgh, Scotland, and the first Thames River subway tunnel, completed in 1869. Since the grade of West Sixth Street drops toward Mill Creek Valley, the western approach tunnel would have been considerably shorter than its eastern counterpart. The eastern approach was to be reserved for the Little Miami, the Cincinnati and Zanesville, and the Dayton Short Line, and the western for the Indianapolis and Cincinnati, the CH&D, the Marietta, the O&M, and the Atlantic and Great Western. The trains of the Kentucky lines terminating at Covington were to reach the east-west tunnel by means of a subsidiary tunnel and a short viaduct that would extend from the Suspension Bridge immediately below Third Street between Vine and Walnut northward to Sixth Street; for those lines terminating at Newport, the accessway would be a new Ohio River bridge, which was placed under construction in 1868.[39] Descriptions of the tunnels do not specify the manner of construction, but because of the shallow depth and the limestone and shale beds of the Cincinnati outcroppings, a cut-and-cover technique would have been the most feasible.

The depot proper was to extend as a through station for two blocks along Sixth Street from Elm to Central. The twelve-track facility was to embrace a total gross area, including headhouse, track-platform space, and vehicular drives, of 246 feet 6 inches × 845 feet in overall dimensions. The cost of construction was estimated to be $393,125, that of land $560,000, and the total investment, apparently exclusive of the tunnel approaches, coach yard, and engine terminals, was calculated to be $1,677,434, the equivalent of at least $25,000,000 at the 1975 building-cost level. A general conference of railroad officials, the local chamber of commerce, the board of trade, and the city council's committee on

35

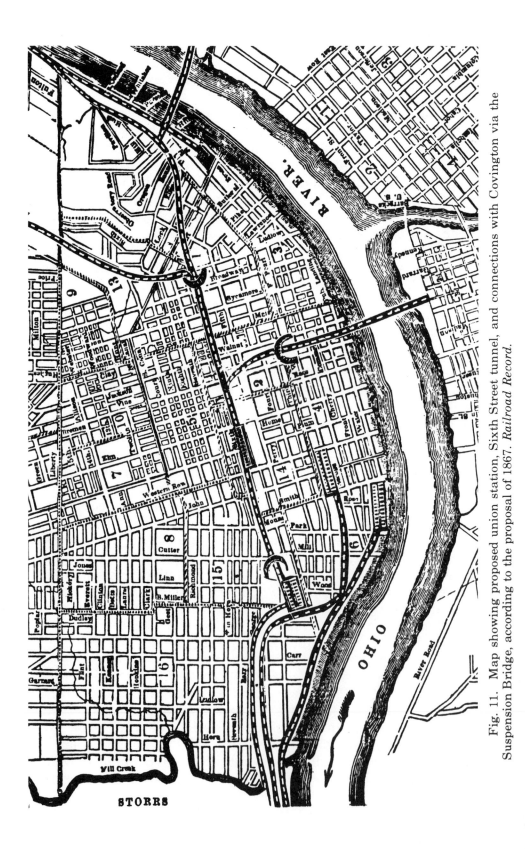

Fig. 11. Map showing proposed union station, Sixth Street tunnel, and connections with Covington via the Suspension Bridge, according to the proposal of 1867. *Railroad Record.*

railroads was convened in December 1872 to consider the implementation of this program, or another comparable to it, but that was as far as the scheme was destined to go. The high cost, the precarious financial state of two of the participating railroads, the failure of the tunnel project, the engineering difficulties, the problems of condemning and assembling property, the question whether the city had need of a terminal planned on this scale, the further question of sacrificing space at the edge of the inner core area—all these quickly and understandably inhibited further action. The next phase in the history of rail unification in Cincinnati was not to come until the turn of the century.

Locomotives and Trains in the Early Years

The operation of trains before 1870 was a highly informal and strictly handicraft affair, and the fundamental inventions that eventually guaranteed within the limits of human frailty the safe as well as the efficient operation of trains all fell in the last third of the nineteenth century. The consequence was that the railroads were ill-prepared to handle the rapid increase in freight and passenger traffic that came in the fifty years between the beginning of the decline of canal transportation around 1850 and the end of the century. Eli H. Janney was granted his initial patent for the automatic coupler in 1868, but not until the Master Car Builders Association adopted a standard model in 1887 did the railroads begin a wholesale abandonment of the dangerous link-and-pin variety. George Westinghouse received his first patent for the air brake in 1869, but the railroads showed little interest in dropping the hand brake for the air-operated form until the state legislature of Iowa passed a law compelling its use following extensive tests on the Burlington Railroad in 1887. The control of train movements by means of continuous systems of wayside signals was nearly as slow in spreading: Ashbel Welch invented the manual block signal in 1865, and William Robinson acquired a patent on the automatic electric block signal in 1871, but the impetus to general applications on heavily traveled main lines came only after the Boston and Albany Railroad first equipped a continuous section of track with automatic signals in 1874. Everywhere else trains were operated in accordance with timetables and handwritten train orders, techniques still in effect on branch lines and only a little less primitive than the voice directions given to airplane pilots for landing and take-off. Robinson's crude signal system, involving a red flag dropped over a white board (the "clear board" of railroad argot), lasted undisputed until 1893, when J. W. Lattig of the Central Railroad of New Jersey invented the automatic sema- phore signal. The interlocking machine for the control of switches and signals at junctions, crossings, and terminal throat tracks ap- peared almost simultaneously with the block signal: Welch in- vented the mechanical variety in 1870 (fourteen years after John Saxby's pioneer machine appeared in England), and the engineers of the Westinghouse Company developed the electropneumatic type in 1883; but again the railroads showed great reluctance to spend money on this particular improvement until the Pennsylvania Railroad made the initial installation on the scale of the big metropolitan terminal for its Jersey City station (1888-92).

The form of the Cincinnati railroad pattern was established in its initial outline and likely future development by 1854, when the first three stations were in operation. The four railroad com- panies serving the city in that year operated eleven passenger trains per weekday in each direction, for a total of twenty-two, with the Little Miami Railroad accounting for at least eight of the total, and its station, because of the Zanesville tenant, accommo- dating a daily average of twelve. When the Marietta and Cincinnati began service in 1857 as another tenant of the Little Miami, the traffic at the company's station increased to sixteen daily trains and the total for the city to twenty-six.[40] It would be hazardous to try to estimate the total number of passengers: a likely weekday average of 50 passengers per train would suggest a total of 1,100 in 1854 and something more than 1,300 in 1857, possibly as high as 1,600, if we assume that all roads enjoyed the rate of increase of the Little Miami.

By the spring of 1863, with the Indianapolis and Cincinnati now providing service into and out of the city from a makeshift station on West Pearl Street, the number of trains had risen to thirty- six per weekday for the city proper, or forty for the metropolitan area if we include the two round trips of the Kentucky Central, terminating at Covington. The Baymiller Street Station had be- come the busiest terminal, its sixteen trains made up of ten operated by the CH&D, four by the Marietta and Cincinnati, and two operated as connections for the Atlantic and Great Western at Dayton (although the local timetable designated this as an A&GW train). At the end of the year the volume of traffic increased to fifty-six trains per weekday, and the winter of 1865-66, following the conclusion of the war, saw the total rise to thirty-two trains inbound and thirty-two outbound, for a total of sixty-four, with the division of traffic among the stations remaining approximately what it had been during the previous few years. The great majority of these trains were operated on local, or accommodation, schedules (the latter term being the common expression of the time), and their runs at the maximum length extended only to the terminals of the various Cincinnati companies. The one exception, inaugurated before the end of the war, was prophetic of the extensive system of long-distance rail service that was to come with the operation of sleeping cars following George M. Pullman's introduction of the costly but successful *Pioneer* in 1864. The first through train operated from Jersey City to Saint Louis via Cincinnati by the B&O, the Marietta, and the O&M was placed in service in August 1864; the run of 1,200 miles was covered in forty-seven hours, for an average speed of 25.5 miles per hour. In the following year the A&GW–CH&D connection was established at Dayton, with the promise in the very near future of another through train connecting Cincinnati with the New York area.[41]

The publication of the first issue of the *Official Guide of the Railway and Steam Navigation Lines*, in June 1868, provided more extensive and more reliable timetables of railroad passenger trains; but at the same time it could be misleading on the total traffic accommodated at a given station because of the absence of trains operated exclusively for mail and express and of any kind of special train (and, one might add parenthetically, because for years the material in the *Guide* was arranged and indexed in ways guaranteed to yield maximum confusion). The number of trains serving Cincinnati passengers reached a total of sixty-five per weekday in the spring of 1868, to which must be added at least eight mail and express trains not listed in the public timetables, for a total of seventy-three. Excursion specials, extra sections of regularly scheduled trains, and trains operated exclusively for employees probably increased the daily average to seventy-five or eighty trains.[42]

For the first time in the quarter-century of rail operations at Cincinnati, the CH&D dropped from the front rank to a position second to the newly organized Indianapolis, Cincinnati and Lafayette Railroad because of the latter company's inauguration of train service to the numerous communities lying west and northwest of Cincinnati in the Ohio, Miami, and Whitewater valleys. The Baymiller Street Station, however, continued to accommodate the heaviest traffic, at twenty-one trains per day, through the tenancy of the Marietta and the Atlantic and Great Western. There was no specific identification in the 1868 timetables of through service between Jersey City and Saint Louis via the Marietta and the O&M, but two other interline runs appeared for the first time. The A&GW established through service to Jersey City over its own line to Salamanca, New York, and over the New York and Erie Railroad east thereof; and the Little Miami offered through service to Philadelphia over the Columbus and Xenia, the PC&StL, and the Pennsylvania east of Pittsburgh. The Great Western train required 34 hours 40 minutes to cover the 862 miles to Jersey City for an average speed of 24.9 miles per hour, a creditable performance in view of the frequency with which locomotives had to be changed on long runs in the nineteenth and early twentieth century. The Philadelphia train, on the other hand, was so much slower as to suggest connecting rather than through service: the thoroughly puzzling timetables indicate a time of 33 hours 30 minutes for the 668 miles to Philadelphia, yielding an average speed of 19.9 miles per hour.[43]

The freight trains of the heroic age at Cincinnati (roughly the twenty-five years from 1845 to 1870) were operated in much the same manner as passenger trains, with the same locomotives, and from stations immediately contiguous to the passenger facilities, although by 1870 the differences in weight and speed between the two classes were beginning to widen rapidly. With very few exceptions before 1870 all trains of whatever kind were drawn by the ubiquitous 4-4-0 locomotives, so nearly universal for so long a period in the nineteenth century as to earn the designation of the American type. The only other motive power to appear in Cincinnati at the time was the 4-6-0 locomotive, more familiarly known as the Ten-wheel type, or simply Ten-wheeler, in spite of the fact that the 2-8-0 or Consolidation type has an identical total number of wheels. A high proportion of the locomotives used by the Cincinnati companies in the early years were manufactured by local builders, who once constituted a flourishing though extremely short-lived industry. The first of the seven companies that came and went over a twenty-three-year period was Anthony Harkness and Sons, which established a factory on East Front Street between Lawrence and Pike in 1845 that lasted until 1851, when a new organization acquired the property. The Harkness plant flourished at so early a date that the great majority of its engines were built for the Little Miami, but a few were produced for the CH&D in that company's inaugural year. By 1868 the manufacture of locomotives had ended at Cincinnati, the small firms having been unable to weather the economic vicissitudes of the age and the competition of the larger and older eastern manufacturers. The last engines produced in the city were destined for the Union Pacific Railroad and shipped nearly two years before the completion of the first transcontinental rail line on 10 May 1869.[44]

A typical engine used around the beginning of Cincinnati rail history was the 4-4-0 Hamilton, manufactured in 1847 by the Harkness firm for the Little Miami, with a driving wheel diameter of fifty-four inches and a total weight without the tender of sixteen tons. Its counterpart toward the end of the period of local manufacture was a 4-4-0 turned out by Moore and Richardson for the Indianapolis and Cincinnati in 1864, the weight now grown to 32 tons, the driving wheel diameter to 62 inches, and the cylinder dimensions to 16 × 22 inches. An early Ten-wheeler of the time was a 24-ton machine produced by Moore and Richardson in 1853 for the CH&D. Within this twenty-two-year period the weight of the engines increased from the twelve tons of a little 4-4-0 manufactured for the Mad River and Lake Erie in 1845 to the forty-three tons of a standard 4-6-0 delivered to the Union Pacific in 1867. Implied in these simple figures indicating dimensional expansion over the years is a great basic fact of railroad technology, one with extensive implications for the economy, the environment, and the energy resources that it can provide. Although the size, weight, and power of locomotives have increased continuously through the years, that increase has always remained within the clearance envelope that became standard on American railroads around the turn of the century; and in spite of the overall growth in all dimensions, the weight per horsepower has constantly decreased, and the efficiency as a consequence steadily increased. These and other factors, which we will consider in their appropriate places, ultimately gave the railroad an endless expansibility of capacity without expanding the scope of its intrusion into the natural and the civic environments.

1. In addition to the more prominent waterways, the Cincinnati area was once marked by a dense network of small streams the downward cutting of which left the many troughs, depressions, and defiles that characterize the city's topography, but most of these were placed underground over the years as parts of the expanding sewer system. The few streams still remaining within the city more or less in a state of nature are the several forks of Mill Creek in the north-central part of the metropolitan area, Duck Creek to the east, Muddy Creek on the west, and a short stretch of Bloody Run in the north-central part of the city proper.

41

Deer Creek and its tributaries, which formed the broad troughs occupied by Gilbert Avenue, Eggleston Avenue, and Reading Road, have entirely disappeared, as have Ross Run and its tributaries in the north-central area. The valley of former Lick Run, a western tributary of Mill Creek, divides the high range of the Western Hills into two strongly separated masses.

2. On uniting the hilltops with the lower city, see pp. 52-55; on bridging the Ohio River, pp. 55-56.

3. The following table showing the elevations above sea level of the river surface and various points in the city gives some idea of the extreme vertical dimensions of the local topography:

Mean water level, Ohio River, 1972	455.00 ft.
High water, Ohio River, 1913	500.42 ft.
High water, Ohio River, 1937	508.90 ft.
Elevation of Fifth Street at Race	548.30 ft.
Highest point on a railroad line (C&O)	870.00 ft.
Highest point in city (Mt. Airy)	956.30 ft.

(Sources: CNO&TP Ry. Drawing no. 36828; Office of Division Engineer, C&O Ry., Cincinnati; U. S. Geological Survey, *West Cincinnati Quadrangle* and *East Cincinnati Quadrangle* [1914]; Frederick Kock, Cincinnati architect.)

4. For the population growth of Cincinnati and its Standard Metropolitan area, see Appendix C, table 1.

5. The Miami Canal was in many respects a model of waterway technology for its frontier milieu. It was expertly surveyed, and the original length from Dayton to Main and Eleventh streets in Cincinnati fell on a continuous descent of 188 feet, requiring 22 locks with an average lift of 8.55 feet. The rapid drop from Eleventh Street to the Ohio River involved a more formidable challenge: the difference in elevation of grade between upper and lower ends of this stretch was 106.27 feet, and the depth of 3.73 feet in the lowermost lock raised this figure to a total of 110 feet, requiring a continuous flight of 10 locks with an average lift of 11 feet (a similar flight of eight locks still exists at the lower end of the Rideau Canal in Ottawa, Canada). The canal entered the river at the point where the Little Miami Railroad station of 1854 and its successor were later to be erected near the intersection of East Pearl and Butler streets. The narrow roadway lying immediately contiguous to the flight of locks was called Lock Street, the name and the street surviving until 1974. There were several aqueducts along the route of the canal, one crossing Mitchell Avenue in Cincinnati.

6. Historians have paid little attention to the short-lived Whitewater Canal, and the most reliable timetable of construction is apparently that placed on a historical plaque at Connersville. I am indebted to John G. Brueggeman for recording the information on it and making it available to me.

7. The Metamora aqueduct was restored by the Indiana State Historical Society and stands in good condition with the water still flowing through it. The tunnel at Cleves was later opened into a cut when the railroad replaced the waterway.

8. The Mad River line was the first rail company chartered in Ohio and the original nucleus of the potent Big Four system that was put together in 1889. Although the through line to Sandusky was established in 1848, the city was soon eclipsed in volume of water-borne commerce by the ports of Cleveland, Ashtabula, and Lorain.

9. The chief corporate expansions and mergers that established the Pittsburgh route were the following: (1) consolidated operations of the Little Miami and the Columbus and Xenia, 1854; (2) Little Miami acquisition of the Dayton,

The Pioneer Roads and Their Stations

Xenia and Belpré, 1865; (3) lease of the Dayton and Western to the LM, 1865; (4) lease of the Columbus and Xenia to the LM, 1868; (5) formation of the Pittsburgh, Cincinnati and St. Louis, 1868, by merger of three smaller companies lying between Pittsburgh and Columbus; (6) lease of the entire Little Miami system to the PC&StL, 1 December 1869. The Pennsylvania Railroad had acquired a controlling interest in the PC&StL the previous year.

10. The following table shows the annual increase in number of passengers and revenues of the Little Miami Railroad for the nine years preceding joint operation with the Columbus and Xenia:

Year	Revenues	Percent Increase	Number of Passengers	Percent Increase
1845	$ 46,297	...	44,760	...
1846	116,052	150	54,265	24
1847	221,133	90	78,342	45
1848	280,085	27	87,555	12
1849	321,328	15	100,970	15
1850	405,696	25	144,486	44
1851	487,845	20	174,089	21
1852	526,745	8	212,687	22
1853	667,558	27	291,375	40

Source: "Annual Report and Results of the Little Miami Railroad," *Railroad Record* 48:1 (26 January 1854) pp. 754–55.

The Cincinnati, Wilmington and Zanesville Railroad was later reorganized as the Cincinnati and Muskingum Valley and was eventually acquired by the Pennsylvania Railroad.

11. I am indebted to Daniel Frinfrock of the Cincinnati Railroad Club for the precise location of this station. The photograph of the building is one of a series of daguerreotypes made by Carl Vitz in 1848 and published under the title, *The Cincinnati Waterfront, 1848*.

12. For the Newport bridge see pp. 58-61.

13. The surviving description of the Philadelphia station does not indicate whether the primary supports were laminated ribs or trusses; the wider span of the 1851-52 replacement dictated what has been regarded heretofore as the initial installation of arched roof trusses in the United States. Early examples in Europe of train shed roofs on timber ribs were the Hauptbahnhof in Munich (1847-49) and King's Cross Station in London (1851-52).

14. "Little Miami Passenger Depot," *Cincinnati Daily Enquirer*, 27 August 1854, p. 3.

15. *Ohio State Railroad Guide, Illustrated*, p. 6.

16. "Cincinnati, Hamilton and Dayton Railroad," *American Railroad Journal* 24:812 (8 November 1851), p. 711.

17. Annual Report for the year ended 31 March 1863; reprinted in "Cincinnati, Hamilton and Dayton Railroad," *American Railroad Journal* 36:1,415 (30 May 1863), p. 503.

18. Among these railroads the line between Hamilton and Indianapolis (the Cincinnati and Indianapolis Junction, later the Cincinnati, Hamilton and Indianapolis) was acquired by the CH&D in 1872 but later relinquished as part of the reorganization program. It became an independent company with the title of Cincinnati, Indianapolis and Western. The remaining lines over the years in which this arrangement was in effect were the Cincinnati, Richmond and Chicago (originally Hamilton and Eaton) and the Chicago, Saint Louis and Pittsburgh (originally Cincinnati and Chicago Air Line between Richmond and Logansport.)

19. For the Cincinnati-Mississippi River link in this system (the Ohio and Mississippi Railroad), see pp. 23-25.

20. Few railroads enjoyed the financial support that public bodies provided the M&C. During the early years of construction Chillicothe contributed $50,000, Athens County $200,000, and Ross County (of which Chillicothe is the county seat) $300,000. When money ran out with the end of the line a few miles west of Athens, other counties and municipalities came to the rescue: Cincinnati dipped into a fund of $150,000 established to assist all ailing railroad lines building toward the city; Washington County contributed $200,000; and the town of Marietta the astonishing sum of $1,000,000.

21. The place where the connecting track turned away from the long Norwood-Saint Bernard tangent was later called Ivorydale Junction. The S-shaped connecting track that crossed Spring Grove Avenue at grade was a fixture of the area for 109 years: it was not finally straightened, elevated, and turned in the right direction for later operating practices until 1970. The junction still remains under its original name, since it was here that the predecessor of the Big Four's Cincinnati Division joined the M&C (pp. 31-32).

22. The title of this little railroad, only six miles long, was the Cincinnati and Baltimore Railway Company, reflecting the true function of the Marietta line as a link in the B&O chain, which it eventually became. The new line from Ludlow Grove lay along the south and east sides of Mill Creek Valley, rounding the elbow close to the flank of Mt. Storm, which was later to be the site of one of Cincinnati's spectacular hilltop parks. The construction of this city line led to the building of another local landmark, the little wood-sheathed and timber-framed suburban station at Winton Place, which was abandoned by the railroad in 1970 and transported by the city to Sharon Woods Park in 1971, close to its 100th anniversary.

23. "The Dayton and Cincinnati Short Line R. R.," *Railroad Record* 2:7 (13 April 1854), p. 99. The total sum of money spent on the tunnel in the 15 months between January 1853 and April 1854 was $2,437,996 (ibid.), or about $53,600,000 at the 1975 building cost level.

24. "The Tunnel and Its Railroads," *Railroad Record* 7:30 (15 September 1859), pp. 349-50.

25. For the union station plans, see pp. 33-37; for the history of the railroad line in the Walnut Hills tunnel, see pp. 78-82.

26. Charles Cist, *Sketches and Statistics of Cincinnati*, p. 230.

27. Contractors excavating the right of way for the I-71 expressway in Cincinnati discovered in 1966 portions of the stone lining of Gest's long-forgotten tunnel. Photographs of the masonry now in the collection of the Cincinnati Historical Society suggest an elliptical upper section with long axis horizontal, a shape that supports the claim of the 25-foot width.

28. There were good reasons for Cincinnati's generosity toward the O&M. Much of the city's prosperity had come from its location on the river and its construction of the Miami Canal, but by mid-century the railroads were making deep inroads into the waterborne traffic. The city, accordingly, wanted a railroad connection to the west, first, so that freight destined for the Saint Louis gateway, originating either in Cincinnati or east thereof, would have to pass through the city and, second, so that it could compete with Pittsburgh and Cleveland in reaching a western market. These economic concerns explain the interest in the A&GW-CH&D-O&M chain; but the long, indirect route never flourished because of more direct routes to the north, especially the PC&StL-Vandalia route extending west from Pittsburgh on a straight line via Columbus, Dayton, Rich-

mond, and Indianapolis. The city's loan to the O&M meant that the road was the only one up to 1880 with close financial ties to Cincinnati and with its interests primarily in the city.

29. Henry C. Lord, "History of the Ohio and Mississippi Road, with Some Reflections," *Railway Age* 8:28 (12 July 1883), p. 413.

30. Henry C. Lord, "The Cincinnati, Indianapolis, St. Louis and Chicago," *Railway Age* 8:32 (9 August 1883), p. 482. (I have uncovered no local myth to explain the obscure allusion to the medical faculty.) The original ancestor of the Indianapolis and Cincinnati and the Cincinnati and Indiana companies was apparently the Cincinnati and Indianapolis Short Line Railroad, which was incorporated in 1853 to build a line from Greensburg, Indiana, to Cincinnati. The line was pushed west to Indianapolis and east to the Ohio state boundary during the succeeding seven years.

31. "Indianapolis and Cincinnati Railroad," *Railroad Record* 11 (7 January 1864): 544. By 1863 the Cincinnati and Indiana Railroad had been so completely absorbed by the Indianapolis and Cincinnati as to lose its separate identity, which was purely titular to begin with.

32. "The New I. and C. Railroad Depot," *Railroad Record* 13 (14 December 1865): 518.

33. Henry C. Lord, "The Cincinnati, Indianapolis, St. Louis and Chicago," *Railway Age* 8:34 (23 August 1883), p. 518. One may appreciate the humor, but he would be compelled to admit that the exaggeration is extreme: only for a short stretch within the city limits of Dayton are the two roads within sight of each other.

34. I have determined the distances of these stations from the intersection of Fourth and Vine streets by counting blocks equivalent in length to that extending from Vine Street to Walnut or Race along Fourth, as shown in the 1855 map of Cincinnati (fig. 9).

35. "The Tunnel and Its Railroads," *Railroad Record* 7:30 (15 September 1859), p. 349.

36. The dimensions of Erasmus Gest's tunnel were sufficient to provide space for a double-track railroad line: the width was 25 feet (a little under the 28 feet that eventually became the railroad standard), and the height to the crown 19 feet, leaving very tight clearances at the sides even with the flattened elliptical section. The originally planned length of 10,000 feet had been cut back to 6,200 before construction began.

The idea of a union station with a single approach line had apparently originated during the previous decade in a city close enough to Cincinnati for the local proponents to be influenced by the earlier plan. The first line designed to be used jointly by all railroads entering the city was constructed in Indianapolis in 1850, when there were four companies serving the capital. The first union station followed in the same city in 1853. (This facility was replaced in 1886 by a much larger station, the headhouse of which still remains [1975], having been rescued as a local landmark.) The second was probably the Union Depot of Chattanooga, originally constructed in 1858 and surviving in part until 1971.

37. The Cincinnati, Indianapolis, Saint Louis and Chicago (successor to the I&C and the IC&L) repudiated the bonds of the transfer company in 1877, so that the ownership passed entirely to the Little Miami and its successors.

38. A corporation with the curious title of Storrs Township, New Richmond and Union Depot Company was formed in 1866 to build the union freight station and approach tracks, which, as the name suggests, were to extend some distance east and west of the city.

The idea of placing railroad tracks on John Roebling's Covington bridge was undoubtedly suggested by the same engineer's Niagara River bridge (1851-55), which was expressly designed for rail traffic. The Cincinnati span, however, would have had to be considerably strengthened, as was the case when streetcar tracks were laid in the deck in 1898.

39. The Kentucky Central, terminating at Covington, began operations in 1856, but the Louisville, Cincinnati and Lexington did not reach the Cincinnati area until 1867. Since these lines constitute a development sharply separated from that of the Ohio and Indiana companies, I have treated their history and the associated construction of the Cincinnati-Newport bridge in chapter 2.

40. The distribution of trains in 1857 was as follows (the figures indicate the number for both directions, inbound and outbound): Little Miami, 8; CH&D, 6; Cincinnati, Wilmington and Zanesville, Marietta, and O&M, 4 each; total, 26. There is a discrepancy in the number given for the Little Miami between the *Railroad Record's* weekly timetables, which list eight trains, and the local news account of the station opening, which gives 10.

41. The following table lists departures from Cincinnati in the spring of 1863, or half the total of inbound and outbound trains:

Little Miami Station
   Little Miami Railroad

Cincinnati Express	7:00 A.M.
Mail and Express	8:30 A.M.
Columbus Accomodation	4:00 P.M.
Morrow Accomodation	6:00 P.M.
Cincinnati, Wilmington and Zanesville	
Morning Express	8:30 A.M.
Accomodation[a]	6:00 P.M.
Baymiller Street Station	
Cincinnati, Hamilton and Dayton	
Dayton, Sandusky, Toledo[b]	7:00 A.M.
Cincinnati and Chicago Air Line	
Mail and Express[c]	8:00 A.M.
Dayton Accommodation	3:15 P.M.
Dayton and Toledo[d]	5:20 P.M.
Hamilton Accommodation, Cincinnati	
and Chicago Air Line Express	7:00 P.M.
Marietta and Cincinnati	
Mail	7:45 A.M.
Marietta Accommodation	3:30 P.M.
Independent Stations	
Indianapolis and Cincinnati	
Mail	5:00 A.M.
Chicago Express[e]	5:00 P.M.
Ohio and Mississippi	
Mail	6:15 A.M.
Saint Louis Express	7:00 P.M.
Kentucky Central (Covington)	
First Train	6:45 A.M.
Second Train[f]	2:10 P.M.

SOURCE: "Arrival and Departure of Trains," *Railroad Record* 11 (1863): passim. For illustrations of early trains and sleeping cars, see Arthur Dubin, *Some Classic Trains*, passim, but especially pp. 14-19.

[a] This train may have been combined with the Little Miami's Morrow train between Cincinnati and the latter community.

The Pioneer Roads and Their Stations

^b The Sandusky train was operated by the Sandusky, Dayton and Cincinnati Railroad north of Dayton, and the Toledo train by the Dayton and Michigan north of Dayton.

^c The Cincinnati and Chicago Air Line was originally a separate corporation and later an operating association formed by the CH&D, the Cincinnati and Indianapolis Junction, the Cincinnati and Chicago Air Line, and the Chicago, Columbus and Indiana Central (Chicago, Saint Louis and Pittsburgh after 1874).

^d The Dayton and Michigan operated this train north of Dayton.

^e The Chicago Express was probably not a through train at that time but a series of end-to-end connections provided, in south to north order, by the Indianapolis and Cincinnati, the Lafayette and Indianapolis, the Cincinnati, Lafayette and Chicago, and the Illinois Central railroads. The first three companies were among those merged in 1866 to form successively the Indianapolis, Cincinnati and Lafayette and the Cincinnati, Indianapolis, Saint Louis and Chicago railroads.

^f One Kentucky Central train ran through to Lexington, but the other probably terminated at Falmouth, as suggested by the 1868 timetable.

42. As rail passenger traffic grew, the total number of trains actually operated exceeded to an increasing degree the number listed in the public timetables as a consequence of the more frequent operation of special trains, extra sections of regularly scheduled trains, and all-mail-and-express trains, which were operated on passenger-train schedules to and from passenger terminals. The number of such additional trains varied considerably among the various railroads: the smaller companies providing little more than local service ordinarily operated special trains only on weekends during the warm-weather months to the picnic grounds and resorts of the immediate area, and customarily operated a single mail train in either direction on the main line; the big through carriers, on the other hand, operated a steadily increasing number of extra sections of leading trains on weekends and around major holidays, and transported the lion's share of mail and express tonnage. The volume of service additional to the scheduled trains never reached the proportion at Cincinnati that it did at Chicago, New York, Philadelphia, Washington, or Boston; but the trains destined for these larger cities were frequently operated in extra sections, especially during the great period of Pullman travel that extended over the thirty years from 1900 to 1930. A convenient rule-of-thumb for determining the total number of daily trains actually operated is to add 10 percent to the number shown in the public timetables.

The chief sources of confusion in the early years of the *Official Guide* were the following: absence of numbers or names in the designation of trains; failure to list short-run accommodation trains (they would later become surburban trains with schedules shown in special timetables); inconsistent practice in listing trains of a given railroad originating on, or running over, the tracks of other roads, or running by trackage rights on the lines of other roads.

43. The distribution of trains by station and railroad company in the spring of 1868 is shown in the following table:

Little Miami Station
  Little Miami Railroad
    8 trains to and from Columbus
    2 trains to and from Morrow
  Cincinnati, Wilmington and Zanesville
    2 trains to and from Zanesville
    2 trains to and from Morrow

Baymiller Street Station
  Cincinnati, Hamilton and Dayton
    5 trains to and from Dayton
    4 trains to and from Toledo
    3 trains to and from Hamilton
    2 trains to and from New Castle, Indiana
    1 train to Lima
  Atlantic and Great Western
    2 trains to and from Jersey City
Plum Street Station
  Indianapolis, Cincinnati and Lafayette
    5 trains to and from Lafayette
    4 trains to and from Lawrenceburg, Indiana
    4 trains to and from Hagerstown, Indiana
    2 trains to and from Brookville, Indiana
    1 train to Indianapolis
  Marietta and Cincinnati
    4 trains to and from Marietta
    2 trains to and from Loveland
Independent Stations
  Ohio and Mississippi
    4 trains to and from East Saint Louis
    2 trains to and from Seymour, Indiana
  Kentucky Central (Covington)
    4 trains to and from Nicholasville and Lexington
    2 trains to and from Falmouth, Kentucky

SOURCE: *Official Guide of the Railway and Steam Navigation Lines of the United States, Mexico and Canada.*

44. The seven Cincinnati and Covington locomotive-builders, with the dates of founding and the locations of factories, were the following: Anthony Harkness and Sons, 1845-51, East Front Street between Lawrence and Pike; Harkness, Moore, and Company, 1852, same location; Moore and Richardson (Cincinnati Locomotive Works), 1853-64, same location; Robert Moore and Son, successor to the previous firm, 1867, same location; Niles and Company, 1852-58, two plants along the Miami Canal at East Front and Congress streets; George Escol Sellers (the best known mechanical inventor among the group), 1851-52, West Sixth Street between Cutter and Linn; Covington Locomotive Works, 1853-57, foot of Smith Street. (For details of the company histories, descriptions, and illustrations of their products, see John H. White, Jr., *Cincinnati Locomotive Builders*, passim.)

2

Links with the South

By the decade of the 1870s there were signs that Cincinnati was entering into a period of decline relative to the rapid expansion of wealth and population that had characterized its growth up to the Civil War and that had left the unshakable conviction that it would always be the Queen City at least of the Northwest Territory. In the ten years of 1870–79 the increase of its population fell to 18 percent from the 34 percent of the previous decade, and the rate of increase was never again to reach even the lower figure.[1] The river and canal traffic that was once a major factor in its economy was falling steadily before rail competition, but the rapidly expanding railroad tonnage was being carried to an increasing degree over routes that bypassed Cincinnati in favor of more direct lines of movement. And where the railroad ran, trade and manufacture went also, in a mutual cause and effect relationship. The city itself, trapped by steep hills on its narrow alluvial plain, suffered from extreme overcrowding, a feature of its physical life that provided a particularly striking example of the intense interstitial building characteristic of all industrial cities in the horse-and-pedestrian age. The little enclaves of the wealthy stood out in a sea of tightly packed shops and row houses that either had always been, or were rapidly deteriorating into, slums. As an anonymous citizen of the time commented, "Within a stone's throw of the most aristocratic

Facing page: Detail from figure 53.

portions of the city, there is another civilization, or rather absence of it, where thousands of human beings are crowded like cattle in pens, and lose all the sympathies of humanity in a greedy struggle for the common pittance of air, and light and water."[2] Worse than the excessive density was the dirt: soot, ashes, and sulfurous gases arising from the combustion of bituminous coal in houses, public buildings, factories, steamboats, and locomotives gave Cincinnati the reputation of having the most concentrated atmospheric pollution in the world.

If the city was to realize the economic and civic potentiality that it still possessed, it had first to expand its own physical fabric in ways that made it possible to break out of the trap of river plains, and it had also to expand its trading sphere in the direction necessary to open the former Confederate South and the Pocahontas region into markets and resource bases. Two natural barriers, however, stood in the way of satisfying these needs: one was the circuit of steep hills that surrounded the triangular pocket on which the city lay; the other was the river itself, a prime commercial artery along its length, but one that had to be bridged by structures suitable for heavy rail traffic to reach the land below its south bank. The solutions to both the problems were to involve novel and even daring technological feats along with the unprecedented action of constructing a municipally owned railroad system south of the river when private capital appeared unable or unwilling to tackle the job.

The assault on the hills was the simpler task in both the financial and the technical sense, and it had to be undertaken in order to bring the hilltop communities into contact with the city proper and to open the hills to recreational possibilities as well as to allow the city to expand its physical fabric. Before the advent of streetcars driven by electric motors and of properly scaled streets carved out of hillsides, the only way to make the higher hilltops accessible was to adopt the novel expedient of constructing steeply inclined rail viaducts against the flanks of the more rugged hills and operating cars on the viaduct tracks by means of cables. Called variously inclined-plane railways, inclined railways, or in vernacular usage simply inclines, the American variety had been constructed originally by the Delaware and Hudson Canal Company in 1825–29 east and west of Carbondale, Pennsylvania, for the transportation of anthracite coal from the mines around Scranton to the head of the canal at Honesdale. The first inclined plane designed expressly for carrying passengers was built in 1870 up the face of Mount

Links with the South

Washington in Pittsburgh, where it still survives as a local curiosity. The structural system and the motive power involved no great problems, and both were undoubtedly derived from various aspects of subsurface mining technology. The viaduct itself was a conventional timber framework of stringers, primary transverse girders, and braced bents resting on masonry piers, although iron girders or trusses were used for the longer spans over streets. Timber deck beams carried the rail, which was laid at an extremely broad gauge so that the cars would be wide enough to accommodate wagons and teams, and the floor of the car was maintained in the horizontal position by building the undercarriage and the trucks at the same angle with the horizontal as that of the viaduct (in side elevation the car thus showed a trapezoidal profile). The motive power consisted of a battery of steam-operated drums around which the wire-rope cables that pulled or lowered the cars were wound. The cables were maintained in a nearly straight line by beds of sheaves located at intervals along the length of the plane, and the movement of the cables was controlled by an automatic braking device that was brought into action in the event that the car began to descend at an excessive speed. For certain inclined planes economy of operation was much increased by the device of using the kinetic energy of the descending car as part of the motive power expended in raising its ascending counterpart. Aside from the danger of a cable break, which was a rarity, the inclines were safe, inexpensive, quiet in operation, efficient in moving loads rapidly up and down the steep hillsides, and offered spectacular vistas of the lower city and the river. Like all such decent and useful devices, they long ago disappeared in Cincinnati.

The first of the city's inclined railways had the shortest life, in part because it suffered the only major disaster. The Cincinnati Inclined Plane Company, established in 1872, constructed a viaduct in the same year from the head of Main Street to the brow of Mount Auburn at what was then called Jackson Hill Park. In 1889 a ruptured cable released a descending car, which then rolled free and crashed into the lower abutment, taking six lives along the way. The accident did nothing to improve the company's already precarious traffic, and it abandoned operations in 1898. The second line, the Price Hill Inclined Railway, fared much better. Constructed in 1875 from the west end of Eighth Street to the Lookout House at the top of Price Hill, it operated parallel freight and passenger tracks, the former until 1929 and the latter until 1943. The Clifton or Elm Street Inclined Railway followed in a year, its viaduct constructed against the cliff-like face of Fairview hill between the intersection of West McMicken Avenue and Elm Street at the foot and the end of Ohio Avenue at the head. The property was acquired by the Cincinnati Street Railway in 1880 and operated for the conveyance of street cars and miscellaneous vehicles until 1926. The best-known and the longest to survive among the Cincinnati structures was the Mount Adams plane, constructed in 1876 by the Mount Adams and Eden Park Inclined Railway from Lock Street near the lower end of the canal to the top of the prominent hill from which it took its name. The viaduct was rebuilt in 1879–80 and again in 1891, the second time in order to carry the cars of the Cincinnati Street Railway, in which capacity it continued to operate until its closure in 1948. The last incline to be built was the second Fairview line, constructed in 1894 by the street railway company to unite the old west end of McMillan Street with the upper end of McMicken Avenue and hence with Mill Creek Valley and the western hills. Until McMillan was extended westward into the valley in 1923, the Fairview incline was necessary to transfer passengers between Clifton and the western areas of the city, but the extension of the main crosstown thoroughfare led to its abandonment in the same year. Only fragments of masonry piers survive today to remind us of the once remarkable sight of cars gliding up and down incredibly steep grades as though they were suspended in midair.

The inclined railways were essential to the outward extensions of the first street railway lines, and as a consequence the great period of expansion and consolidation coincided in part with the construction of the inclines. The original streetcars of Cincinnati were horsedrawn vehicles, as they were in all cities where they supplanted the earlier omnibuses, and they dominated local public transportation until they began to be progressively replaced by cable cars in 1885 and by the electrically operated motor-driven variety in 1888. The initial horsecar line in Cincinnati, one of five authorized by the ordinance of 1 July 1859, was opened to service in September of that year, its route extending from Fourth and Walnut streets in the core area northward to Ninth and westward to Freeman Avenue close to the far edge of the West End. The wrought-iron rails were laid in the street paving at the conventional wagon gauge, which probably fixed the standard railroad gauge of 4 feet 8-1/2 inches but which was later widened for Cincinnati streetcar lines to 5 feet 2-1/2 inches. The multiplication of horsecar routes began in 1864, and by 1880 thirteen had been

Links with the South

added to the original five for a total of eighteen with an aggregate length of more than a hundred miles. Most of these lines were constructed and operated by separate companies, but these were merged mainly in two stages into the Consolidated Railway Company (1873) and the Cincinnati Street Railway Company (1880), the latter of which subsequently acquired or built all the electric-traction lines of the city. The combination of a radial system of horsecar routes with inclined-plane links meant that by the decade of the eighties there was a reliable if slow-moving public transit extending from the core to the major hilltop neighborhoods, such as Price Hill, Westwood, Clifton, Mount Auburn, Avondale, Walnut Hills, and Mount Adams, and to the chief Mill Creek Valley residential communities of Cumminsville and Winton Place. The presence of these early car lines helps explain why the great bulk of the housing in the inner-hill circuit belongs to the "old" category, built at the turn of the century or earlier.[3]

The barrier of the Ohio River offered more serious difficulties than the hills and required far greater outlays of talent and capital to surmount it. As a matter of fact, the construction of the four multispan truss bridges necessary to unify the railroad systems terminating at Cincinnati with the new lines of Kentucky brought the art of designing and constructing long-span iron truss bridges to its maturity. The idea of drawing together the economies of Cincinnati and Covington had been a matter of discussion among the business interests of Lexington as well as of the two river communities as early as 1839, and the eventual issue of these plans for the future was Roebling's celebrated Suspension Bridge, which was designed only for roadway vehicles until the Cincinnati, Newport and Covington Railway laid streetcar lines in the deck following the reconstruction of 1895–98 (figs. 12, 13). With the vehicular span as a precedent, at least one of the Kentucky railroads that had come into existence prior to the decade of the Civil War was prepared to build a rail counterpart. The first company to lay track directly south of Cincinnati was the Covington and Lexington Railroad, having been chartered as early as 1849. The difficulties of raising capital in the sparsely inhabited hinterland of Kentucky led to the usual delays in construction: the struggling company could show only twenty miles of track extending up the valley of the Licking River by 1853 but managed to reach the little town of Paris, Kentucky, by 1856. Merger with the equally slow-moving Maysville and Lexington Railroad in 1859 at last provided a through line from Covington to the flourishing community that

Fig. 12.   Cincinnati-Covington Suspension Bridge, as originally constructed, 1856–57. *Engineering.*

Fig. 13. Cincinnati-Covington Suspension Bridge as it now appears, following the reconstruction of 1895-98. Photograph by F. T. Kihlstedt; reproduced with permission.

had been established in the eighteenth century and that was already the financial, social, and cultural capital of Kentucky's agricultural heartland. The corporation created by the merger of the two smaller railroads was the Kentucky Central Railroad; but for the directors of the lightly traveled eighty-five-mile line the idea of bridging the Ohio River remained a hopeless dream, and it was not until the Chesapeake and Ohio Railway opened its own bridge into Cincinnati in 1888 that the KC could gain an entry into the city.

Meanwhile, a second Kentucky company with a much longer history and greater resources was on the way. The Lexington and Ohio Railroad was chartered in 1831 as the oldest line west of the Allegheny Mountains and opened a track between Lexington and the state capital of Frankfort in 1832, relying at the time on horses for motive power. The company operated its first steam locomotive in 1835, but it was another twenty-two years before the track reached the Ohio River at Louisville. Reorganized through merger with the Louisville and Cincinnati as the Louisville, Cincinnati and Lexington Railroad, the larger line was prevented chiefly by the war from building toward the Cincinnati area until 1867, and it was another two years before it began to operate trains into Newport, opposite Cincinnati on the east side of the Licking River. Because of the absence of an alluvial terrace at a sufficient elevation above ordinary floods along the south bank of the Ohio River below the city, the LC&L laid its track well inland through the unbroken ranges of hills flanking the narrow river valley on both sides. Masterful surveying kept it free of any but minor grades, but only at the expense of an almost continuous succession of curves, so that it came to be described by train crews and travelers alike as having no more than fifty feet of tangent track between Louisville and Cincinnati. It was so much shorter than the Ohio and Mississippi route, however, that its directors thought the company was entitled to the favorite designation of nineteenth-century railroads and adopted the unofficial name of Louisville Short Line, or Louisville and Cincinnati Short Line. They also exhibited the daring, or possibly recklessness, of deciding equally quickly to carry the line into Cincinnati by building the city's first railroad bridge over the Ohio River.

The initial proposal for such a structure had been suggested by the editors of *Railroad Record* as early as September 1867, in connection with their plan for a union depot and a Sixth Street tunnel; but the location adopted by the Louisville directors suggested an understandable indifference to the *Record*'s brave hopes, as the name of the new corporation indicated. The Newport and Cincinnati Bridge Company was incorporated early in 1868 to construct a combined rail and roadway bridge over the Ohio River at an estimated cost of $1,000,000 and with an expected completion date of 1870. The decision to undertake this costly and risky enterprise was motivated in good part by the successful completion of the Pittsburgh and Steubenville Railroad's bridge at Steubenville, Ohio (1863–65), the first railroad bridge over the Ohio River and the first long-span iron bridge; and it was undoubtedly reinforced by the nearly simultaneous construction of the second and third Ohio River bridges, the Louisville and Nashville span at Louisville (1867–70) and the B&O crossing between Bellaire, Ohio, and Benwood, West Virginia (1868–71).[4] The location of the Cincinnati bridge was established on the line of Butler Street in Cincinnati and Saratoga Street in Newport, in order to connect the track of the LC&L with the Little Miami Railroad almost exactly at the site of its passenger depot. The design of the structure was completed under the direction of Jacob H. Linville as chief engineer, and the contract for construction was awarded to the Keystone Bridge Company, both before December 1868.

The superstructure of the Cincinnati bridge as designed consisted of seven simple spans of Whipple-Murphy trusses (distinguished from the standard Whipple form chiefly by the double diagonals in the center panels), their particular web system derived directly from the trusses of the Steubenville bridge; the total length between shore piers was apparently to be 1,640 feet, and that of the channel span a little more than 400 feet, or nearly 100 feet longer than the equivalent span of its Steubenville predecessor. The piers were composed of dressed limestone ashlar up to the high-water line and local freestone above (figs. 4, 14).[5] The rail line at the Cincinnati end constituted another remarkable feature of this impressive structure. Since the Little Miami tracks lay parallel to the river bank and hence at right angles to the axis of the bridge, the approach viaduct had to be turned through a right angle and inclined at a marked grade to bring it down to the level of the station approach, which lay only a little distance east of the bridge (a short length of this inclined approach trestle appears in the foreground of figure 4). Since the junction point of the track leaving this viaduct and the station approach tracks thus had to be located still further east of the platform area, the Kentucky trains could enter the station only by backing into the track area, or leave it

Fig. 14. Cincinnati-Newport Bridge, LM and LC&L railroads, 1868–72; Jacob H. Linville, chief engineer. The Whipple trusses are incorrectly drawn; see fig. 4 for their true appearance, *Railroad Record.*

only by backing out, an awkward mode of operation that continued for the sixty-one years until the station and its successor were abandoned.

Construction of the Louisville Short Line's bridge was expected to be, and very likely would have been, completed before the end of 1870 were it not for the fact that a well-established partnership of railroad opponents suddenly asserted itself. In the fall of 1870 the Corps of Engineers decided that the structure was unacceptable. They objected to the design on two grounds, one that the deck was too low to clear steamboats at high water (that is, normal or navigable high water rather than flood stage), and the other that the piers were turned at two degrees to the current vector, thus reducing the effective opening of the channel span to 390 feet. The Engineers' adverse report induced the United States Congress to revoke the War Department's original permit and to require that the bridge be rebuilt according to the Engineers' criteria. Exactly what this reconstruction entailed is not clear from contemporary descriptions, but the chief results appear to have been the raising of the deck by thirty feet, which then required a partial rebuilding of the Cincinnati approach, and the lengthening of the channel span to 418 feet. These expensive changes delayed the opening of the bridge until March 1872 and the entry of the Louisville company's eight daily passenger trains into the Little Miami depot until the summer of that year. In 1881 the Louisville, Cincinnati and Lexington was acquired by the Louisville and Nashville Railroad to put Cincinnati on a unified route to the Gulf Coast, and traffic grew so rapidly as a consequence that the replacement of the Newport span had to be undertaken in fifteen years following the merger of the two rail lines.[6]

The establishment of the second railroad line linking Cincinnati with the South followed the creation of a municipal enterprise embracing elements of the greatest importance in American technological as well as urban history. The first proposal for the construction of a railroad between Lexington and Cincinnati with the associated Ohio River bridge was introduced at a public meeting of representatives of the two communities convened at what was then called Cincinnati College on 5 April 1839. Thirty years of intermittent discussion, the initiation of the Newport bridge, and the threat of a competitive north-south rail route following the completion of Fink's Louisville bridge finally persuaded the Cincinnati authorities to act on their own. Overtures to the General Assembly at Columbus led to the passage on 4 May 1869 of an act authorizing the city to construct a railroad line over the staggering distance and topography from the north bank of the Ohio River to Chattanooga, Tennessee. The Cincinnati City Council passed the necessary resolution one month later for a popular referendum on the matter, and at the special election of 26 June 1869 the question of constructing the railroad and issuing the bonds to cover the costs thereof received a favorable vote of slightly better than ten to one. The legislature of Tennessee acted with dispatch by granting the municipal corporation a charter on 20 January 1870, but the Kentucky assembly did not act for more than two years, delaying its final authorization until 13 February 1872. Meanwhile, the city of Cincinnati issued revenue bonds in the amount of $18,000,000 to cover the estimated costs of building the rail line and its many expensive structures, a sum that proved, as we shall see, to fall only a little short of the actual total investment. The official title of the municipal corporation was the Cincinnati Southern Railway Company, and its municipally appointed trustees were answerable to the mayor and the council of the city. Construction was initiated at Kings Mountain, in Lincoln County, Kentucky, on 23 December 1873, and completed throughout its 336-mile length to Chattanooga on 8 March 1880, although the first train had been operated over a portion of the road on 3 July 1877.[7]

The question of whether the city was to enter into competition with private carriers by operating a municipally owned railroad corporation was soon and probably wisely resolved in favor of the traditional practice within little more than a year after its completion. The trustees decided to lease the property for operating purposes to a privately financed corporation expressly organized to that end, and they awarded the lease on 3 September 1881 to an association of the New York financier Frederick Wolffe and the Erlanger family of Cincinnati, who presented the seventh of ten bids for what the more farseeing clearly recognized as a plum of very generous proportions. The Wolffe-Erlanger group conveyed the lease on 12 October 1881 to a newly established corporation named the Cincinnati, New Orleans and Texas Pacific Railway Company, whose proud title nicely summarized the full implications of this remarkable enterprise. The initial lease was to run for twenty-five years and to be renewable at similar intervals thereafter. The terms were obviously advantageous to the city: rentals were to be $800,000 per annum for the first five years, $900,000 for the second five, and $1,000,000 for the remaining fifteen. In addition the lessee agreed to spend $8,000,000 on permanent improvements as directed by the trustees, and to maintain, repair, and operate motive power, rolling stock, structures, shop facilities, and associated equipment in every respect in a first-class manner.[8] There were good reasons for this magnanimity on the part of the lessee. Although the railroad sometimes experienced discouraging vicissitudes of fortune in its early years, it began operations at a level of profit that must have aroused the envy of the Cincinnati railroad lines that served the prosperous manufacturing towns north of the city, where they were concentrated in an area far more densely populated than any part of Kentucky and Tennessee was ever to be. In its first year of operating the completed line the Cincinnati Southern reported total operating expenses equal to little more than one-third of the gross revenues and hence a net operating income of better than 60 percent of its revenues.[9]

It was enough to excite the lusts of any capitalist, but there was more than that, as the Erlangers knew very well. The family held a controlling interest through stock ownership in the Alabama Great Southern Railway, which extended from Chattanooga southwestward through Birmingham to Meridian, Mississippi, where it connected with the New Orleans and Northeastern for an entry into New Orleans and westward into Texas. In addition to these a connection at Meridian with the Alabama and Vicksburg, joined in turn to the Vicksburg, Shreveport and Pacific Railroad, provided a through line to Shreveport, Louisiana, and a secondary route into Texas. The Cincinnati Southern was the northern link in a chain that united the Ohio River with the Gulf coast, the lower Mississippi valley, and east Texas, a strategic succession of railroad lines that came to be known after the nicknames of the terminal cities as the Queen and Crescent Route and that made the title of the CNO&TP neither an idle boast nor a vain dream. Moreover, the new company connected at Chattanooga with the East Tennessee, Virginia and Georgia Railroad, which, with the Georgia Southern and Florida, composed a route to Jacksonville and hence into the peninsula itself. Cincinnati had become at last and without immediate competitor the entrepôt to the South, a position that has guaranteed through the years the handsome profits and the generous rentals that both the operating and the proprietary companies continue to enjoy.

But the Cincinnati Southern was built at a high cost in talent, energy, and resources: there were formidable barriers to be surmounted along the entire route, and the first appeared at the very threshold of the city. The river crossing was the major challenge, but the irregular and in places rugged topography through the two southern states placed obstacles before builders and operating crews alike. Ludlow, Kentucky, on the south bank of the Ohio, marked the beginning of the discouraging Erlanger hill, a long, steep, winding up-grade extending over and along deeply cut ravines that had to be climbed to bring the track to the top of the Kentucky highlands below the river. Through the northern part of Tennessee the line cut obliquely across the parallel ranges of the Clinch and Cumberland mountains, requiring so many tunnels that the lower portion of the route came to be known among trainmen as the Rat Hole Division. As for the Ohio River bridge, it was a structural triumph that was matched only by the same company's Kentucky River bridge at Dixville, both built simultaneously in 1876-77 and both immediately destined to give the new railroad an international prominence (figs. 15, 53). With a total length, including approaches, of nearly half a mile and a river crossing of just under 1,500 feet, the reputation of the Cincinnati bridge rested not only on its overall size but even more on the 515-foot length of its channel span, the longest truss span in the world at the time.[10]

The creators of this masterpiece were Jacob H. Linville of the Keystone Bridge Company, who was chief engineer of the structural design, and Louis Ferdinand Gustave Bouscaren, chief engineer of the railroad company, supervisor of the whole construction enterprise and author of the specifications on the basis of which the design was prepared. These specifications were the first of the now universal form in which the kind and the quality of materials, the criteria of performance and workmanship, the obligations of the contractor, the loading factors, allowable stresses, wind pressure, and the testing procedures are given in full and precise terms allowing no ambiguity of interpretation and no deviation from the standards set forth. This document together with the exact proportioning of each truss as a whole and of the individual elements of which it is composed, all set forth in great detail in the working drawings, indicated that the art of bridge design had by that date reached the level of rigorous scientific analysis. The somewhat smaller though more celebrated span over the Kentucky River was taking form at the same time in the Kentucky wilderness at Dixville, the creation of Bouscaren and Charles Shaler Smith, who adopted the novel device of introducing hinges at the points of contraflexure in the end spans to transform the continuous truss into the first railroad cantilever bridge. In this way the engineers

64

CINCINNATI SOUTHERN RAILWAY BRIDGE ACROSS THE OHIO RIVER, CONNECTING CINCINNATI AND LUDLOW.

Fig. 15. Ohio River Bridge, CS Railway, 1876–77; Jacob H. Linville, chief engineer. The system of web members is again incorrectly drawn; see fig. 53 for a better indication of their appearance. Reproduced with the permission of the Cincinnati Historical Society.

combined the same standards of scientific exactitude with a more daring structural innovation.[11]

The Cincinnati Southern Railway must be judged a resounding success, whether measured in immediate financial or long-range economic terms, and the city enjoyed a steady and handsome return on its investment. In the first thirteen years of operations under the lease agreement (1881-94) the total rental paid to the city amounted to more than $11,000,000 which came to roughly one-quarter of the total operating revenues but consumed a high proportion of the total net operating income for the same period. The improvements to the physical property and in the efficiency of conducting railroad operations were probably without parallel among the Cincinnati companies. The original iron rail in the 336 miles of main track between the termini was entirely replaced by steel rail at greater weight; all original ballast was replaced by varying lengths of gravel, slag, and broken rock; and the earlier timber bridges were entirely removed in favor of iron and steel structures. The company laid out a manual-block system with semaphore signals at all operator's stations and distance signals (giving advance warning of the indication of the block signal) at a large majority of them, and it was soon to inaugurate a program of installing automatic electric block signals. The number of locomotives and passenger-train cars nearly doubled, and the number of freight cars increased about 2 1/2 times. It was in all respects a model enterprise, permanently beneficial to the economy of Cincinnati, and it has continued in this flourishing state down through the years.[12]

1. See table 1, Appendix C.

2. Quoted in John Brinckerhoff Jackson, *American Space: The Centennial Years, 1865-1876* (New York: W. W. Norton & Co., 1972), p. 71.

3. At their maximum extent the 18 horsecar lines embraced 122.8 route miles and operated 203 cars with 995 horses, of which 65 were kept in reserve. (for a map showing the horsecar lines, see Wagner and Wright, *Cincinnati Streetcars*, 1:17.)

4. The channel span of the Steubenville bridge was carried by Whipple-Murphy trusses over the then unprecedented length of 320 feet (for an illustration of this span, see Carl W. Condit, *American Building: Materials and Techniques*, fig. 50). The 400-foot channel span of Albert Fink's mile-long Louisville bridge was supported by the first subdivided Warren trusses (for an illustration, see Condit, *American Building Art: The Nineteenth Century*, fig. 75).

5. The seven spans of the Cincinnati-Newport bridge, from the Ohio to the Kentucky bank, were as follows: channel span, 418 feet; adjacent span at Ohio end, 240 feet; remaining five spans, 200 feet each. The long channel span

was dictated by the Corps of Engineers, who so blatantly represented the steamboat interests as to constitute their chief lobbying agent. The overall width of 42 feet embraced a single-track rail line at the center flanked by a roadway and a walkway on each side. This multi-purpose traffic way and the unusual width required four parallel trusses to carry each span, characteristics of the present bridge that replaced the original. The local freestone would have been limestone slabs broken in any direction to form roughly prismatic blocks.

6. The editors of *Railroad Record*, in their unquenchable enthusiasm for the Dayton Short Line's forlorn tunnel, proposed that the Dayton company's projected Broadway station be connected with the new bridge by means of a tunnel under Eggleston Avenue, which lay along the old bed of Deer Creek adjacent to the lowermost flight of locks in the Miami and Erie Canal. Something like the proposed connection was established in the decade following the opening of the Newport bridge, but it was located on the surface of Eggleston Avenue rather than in a tunnel underneath.

7. The city constructed the entire line from Cincinnati to Chattanooga except for the 13 miles from Lexington to Nicholasville, Kentucky, which was acquired in 1873 from the Lexington and Southern Kentucky Railroad, the company that first proposed the bridging of the Kentucky River at Dixville, to be accomplished by means of a suspension bridge designed by John Roebling. No more than the masonry towers was ever constructed.

8. The total rental under the original lease was $23,500,000. This lease was renegotiated in 1902, four years before its expiration date, to cover the 60 years from 1906 to 1966, and rentals were increased to $1,050,000 per annum for the first 20 years, $1,100,000 for the second 20, and $1,200,000 for the third 20-year period, but the final figure was raised in 1950 to $1,350,000 plus a varying percentage of the net income. By the end of 1974 the rentals paid to the city had reached a total of $156,000,000.

9. The Cincinnati Southern Railway's annual report for the first full year of operation (1880-81) is summarized in the following table:

Freight revenue	$1,062,416
Passenger revenue	345,918
Express revenue	83,098
Mail revenue	22,029
Miscellaneous revenue	22,865
Total revenues	1,536,326
Total operating expenses	586,900
Net operating income	949,426
Interest charges	67,121
Net income	882,305
Operating ratio	38.2%

This substantial income of nearly a million dollars was not in fact available to the company treasury: since the total cost of construction came to $18,960,429, or $960,429 more than the funds provided by the bond issue, the excess was taken from revenues and charged to operating expenses, so that the net operating income actually turned into a deficit of $11,403. But this is typical of a newly opened company, and the operating results in themselves promised a flourishing state in the future, which proved to be the case after the flow of traffic was stabilized.

The nearly $19,000,000 cost of construction would indicate a replacement value of the original property of at least $320,000,000 in 1975.

10. The various parts of the Cincinnati bridge and their lengths were as follows: four river spans, Ludlow to Cincinnati, respectively 365 feet 4 inches,

515 feet, 295 feet 4 inches, and 295 feet 10 inches, for a total length of 1,471 feet 6 inches over water; one Kentucky approach and six Cincinnati approach spans, average length 150 feet 4 inches; total end-to-end length, 2,524 feet.

The single-track spans were carried on masonry piers founded on bedrock, and the trusses of the river spans were the Whipple-Murphy form, at the time the ruling type for long-span iron bridges but destined to give way during the next 15 years to Pratt and Warren trusses. A connecting track between the Cincinnati approach and the tracks of the Cincinnati, Indianapolis, Saint Louis and Chicago Railroad in Mill Creek Valley made it possible for the Cincinnati Southern passenger trains to use the Plum Street Station until the opening of Central Union Depot in 1883. The north approach line of the bridge extended directly into the new company's Mill Creek freight yards.

11. For the specifications prepared by Bouscaren for bridges and trestles of the Cincinnati Southern Railway, see Appendix A.

Since working drawings and the results of tests of the Ohio River bridge have not, so far as I know, survived, we can approximate the likely total load and the bending moment on the long channel span by basing our calculations on the live-load factor derived from actual load tests of the Dixville span and on the dead-load factor of the same structure with 25 percent of this load added to make allowance for the increased length and hence increased depth of the Ohio River span. The maximum live load would be 2,073 pounds per lineal foot (253 pounds greater than the specified load of 1,820 pounds per lineal foot imposed by two coupled 4-6-0 locomotives followed by loaded freight cars weighing 20 tons each and occupying a 22-foot length of span per car) and the dead load $1.25 \times 3,840$, or 4,800 pounds per lineal foot, yielding a total dead and live load of 6,873 pounds per lineal foot. The total weight of structure and train for the channel span would then be $6,873 \times 515$, or 3,539,595 pounds, and the maximum bending moment would be given by the formula $M = wl^2/8$, or $[6,873 \times (515)^2]/8$, which would yield a moment of 227,861,428 foot pounds.

12. The improvements and expansion of the company's property in the period 1881-94 were set forth in Bouscaren's report to the trustees dated 30 June 1894, the essential data of which are the following:

Length of main line: 336 miles
Weight of steel rail in place of iron: 60, 75, and 85 pounds per yard.
Ballast: gravel, 75 miles; slag, 86 miles; broken rock, 175 miles.
Interlocking machines installed at all crossings and junctions with other railroads.
Manual block system installed throughout, with semaphores at all operators' stations.
All timber bridges replaced by iron or steel structures.
All timber trestles replaced by iron or masonry structures or earth fill.
Number of intermediate stations increased to 53, for an average spacing of 6.22 miles (an index to the extent of good local service).
Number of locomotives: 55 in 1881; 104 in 1894.
Number of passenger-train cars: 38 in 1881; 66 in 1894.
Number of freight-train cars: 1,482 in 1881; 3,877 in 1894.
Total cost of improvements in the 13 1/2 years from 1 January 1881, to 30 June 1894: $2,204,497.
Summary of operating results for the same 13 1/2-year period:

Gross revenues	$43,635,363
Operating expenses	29,941,044
Net operating income	13,694,319
Rental to city	11,370,480
Operating ratio	69%

3

The Terminal Pattern of
Half a Century

The Pan Handle and the Court Street Stations

If Cincinnati seemed to be suffering during the 1870s from the economic doldrums and felt trapped on its river terraces, it was at the same time undergoing a civic and cultural renaissance that eloquently expressed the expansive spirit of the city. The Chattanooga railroad was, as we have seen, one manifestation of this new birth, but other aspects of urban life were to reveal in their way the same outpouring of creative vigor. The city's most famous monument, the Tyler-Davidson Fountain, was erected in 1871 on the Fifth Street square that took its name from the sculptural group, which was the work of the German sculptor August von Kreling and the gift to the municipality of Henry Probasco. The old Cincinnati College advanced to the status of a municipal university in 1873, at the time the only institution of its kind in the United States. The city's long-established families, vigorously aided by the growing German population, laid the foundations of its great musical tradition with the incorporation of the Cincinnati Musical Festival Association in 1872 and the production of the first May Festival in the following year. Since this celebrated choral and symphonic event proved successful, it seemed entirely fitting that the city should have a new auditorium for such performances of the musical arts. With a bequest from Reuben R. Springer and a donation of land from the municipal government, Cincinnati built

Facing page: Detail from figure 5.

the huge Music Hall in 1875–78, a gauntly forbidding work of Gothic revivalism that included among its numerous facilities a concert hall of superb acoustical quality. In the year the hall was opened the local musical interests also established the Cincinnati College of Music. The federal government contributed its share to the civic revival on an equally lavish scale when it placed the Post Office and Federal Building under construction in 1874, although it was not to complete this final masterpiece from the hand of Arthur B. Mullet until 1885. The impetus to build in the interests of both art and the material life continued into the next decade, when the Rookwood Pottery (1880) and the Art Museum (1886) were opened on Mount Adams, and Henry Hobson Richardson's once celebrated Chamber of Commerce Building was completed in the commercial core (1889).

The major railroads of the city, their directors spurred by steeply rising traffic as well as civic ambitions, were prepared to act in keeping with this generous spirit, which was most impressively demonstrated by the opening of three terminal stations in a four-year period. The first line to build was the young company that had taken over the operations of the prosperous Little Miami Railroad. As we noted earlier, a series of corporate maneuvers led to the creation in 1868 of the Pittsburgh, Cincinnati and Saint Louis Railroad, to which the Little Miami and its affiliate, the Columbus and Xenia, were leased in 1869.[1] The new name of the Pittsburgh and Steubenville Railroad, the Pan Handle Railway Company, seemed so appropriate and was obviously so much more convenient than the awkward Pittsburgh, Cincinnati and Saint Louis that its usage in advertisements quickly became fixed in the popular mind. The new company was at the time essentially a Pittsburgh-Cincinnati line, and the volume of traffic that moved between the terminals, from intermediate points to the Cincinnati gateway, and through the gateway to the Kentucky connection, soon compelled the replacement of the Cincinnati terminal facilities. Both the freight and passenger traffic nearly doubled in the decade of the seventies, and the rate of increase rose even higher in the succeeding years.[2] It was obvious that the station that attracted so much attention in 1854 would have to be replaced, and the decision to make the investment was adopted by the directors in 1879.

The new station was designed by the architect S. J. Hall under the direction of M. J. Becker, the railroad company's chief engineer. It was placed under construction in 1880 and was completed in the following year exactly at the corner of East Pearl and Butler streets and thus stood a full block north and another west of the 1854 structure, which was retained as a freight house (figs. 16, 17). The station building and its train shed were to stand in active use for fifty-two years, until the Union Terminal was completed in 1933. The headhouse rose through two stories and an attic under a narrow central gable, its floors and roof supported on interior bearing partitions and exterior bearing walls of red brick, with the low base, the lintels, and the quoins of local freestone. At the street corner a massive clock tower rose through another one and one-half stories under a steeply pitched, outwardly flaring pyramidal roof. The whole work was done in a kind of free-wheeling Gothic Revival style in which openings formed the dominant features—the high grouped windows, the three entrance doorways on Butler Street, and the skylights that admitted light through a second-floor well to the waiting room and flanking ticket offices on the main floor. A telegraph center, dining room, baggage room, toilets, and other service facilities occupied the remaining space on the first floor, and the company offices were distributed around a peripheral balcony on the second. It was a serviceable plan that had been developed in the major rail centers of Europe and the eastern United States over the years during which the rail terminal was progressively divided into two distinct parts, one the headhouse, or station building, and the other the train shed over the track-platform area.

The Pan Handle Station, as it was officially designated for many years, was noteworthy more for its traffic pattern and rail connections than for the architectural design of its headhouse, although this possessed a kind of dignified gaiety that stood in absolute contrast to the black-painted sobriety of the train shed (fig. 17). The roof of this structure was a greatly flattened segmental vault slightly recurved at the edges that carried a longitudinal light monitor running the length of the crown. Spanning six tracks within its 85-foot width and only 360 feet long, the roof was sustained by a series of tin-sheathed timber ribs that rested on two rows of iron columns near the outer edges and were braced and tied by wrought-iron rods, the system of rods under each rib being arranged in the form of the Polonceau truss. A similar construction was used by the Philadelphia, Wilmington and Baltimore Railroad for its first Broad Street Station in Philadelphia, also constructed in 1880–81, but the Little Miami station of 1854 may also have provided a precedent.[3]

The track and platform system of the Pan Handle Station was

distinguished by several features that set it apart from most of its contemporaries. The track area was open along Pearl Street except for an ornamented black-painted iron fence of the kind that marked every rail terminal in the days of all-covering sheds, and the concourse or midway between the headhouse and the platforms was entirely open to public access from the street. The consequence was that passengers—or any curious visitor, for that matter—could walk directly from the street to the trains without passing through the station building, as he would if he was en route from its true front entrance on Butler Street. But there was also an aesthetic element in this plan that may well have flowed from deliberate intention on the part of the architect. The open-sided shed immediately adjacent to the sidewalk meant that the lively drama of the terminal tracks—passengers, crews, baggage trucks, cars, locomotives—was clearly visible to spectators on the walk or in passing streetcars. The station thus offered an exciting extension of street images, either as backdrop or as a compelling yet slightly forbidding world of much larger scale that powerfully suggested the adventure of travel.

The track pattern, though conventional for stub-end terminals and even primitive by twentieth-century standards, also included certain novel features that revealed how Cincinnati's growth as a major transfer point had to be adapted to the exigencies imposed by topography and waterways. As we noted in an earlier chapter, the Newport bridge of the Louisville, Cincinnati and Lexington Railroad (1868–72) was located and constructed in such a way as to provide a physical connection with the Little Miami tracks. When the site of the new station was moved northwestward to the Pearl and Butler corner, the sharply curved and steeply graded connecting viaduct had to be relocated along the south side of the station, with the consequence that one could enjoy the arresting spectacle of trains descending from an elevation conspicuously above the top of the train shed to the approach tracks, from which they backed into the shed (all these movements, of course, would be reversed for outbound trains). When the rapidly expanding Louisville and Nashville Railroad acquired the LC&L in 1881, this connection took on a new and vital importance. Another similar

Opposite: Fig. 16.   Passenger station, PC&StL Railroad, East Pearl and Butler streets, 1880–81; S. J. Hall, architect. This terminal was for some years known as the Pan Handle Station and eventually as the Pennsylvania Station, following the merger of the PCC&StL Railroad with the larger company. Reproduced with the permission of the Cincinnati Historical Society.

Fig. 17. Train shed, PC&StL Railroad, 1880–81, Pearl and Butler streets. Reproduced with the permission of the Cincinnati Historical Society.

though less spectacular connection on the north side of the station came into existence more by fortuitous circumstance than by design. The Little Miami in 1876 had laid a track in Eggleston Avenue, which lay parallel and close to the lowermost reach of the Miami and Erie Canal, at first to serve the numerous industries and warehouses along the two arteries. The opening of the Court Street Station in 1885, however, and the subsequent entry of the Norfolk and Western Railway into Cincinnati turned an industrial spur into another of those useful connectors that served to unify the intricate pattern of the city's rail lines.

The whole complex of the Pan Handle Station formed the most compact association of rail facilities in the city. The station tracks, the approach, junctions on either side, the bridge connection, merchandise freighthouses adjacent to the station throat, the coach yard and the engine terminal extending eastward along the approach tracks—these stretched out east and west in the narrow corridor between Pearl Street and the riverbank. The station accommodated about twenty-two trains per day when it was opened in 1881, but the total was to rise to more than fifty by the time of World War I. Regular train movements and interchange traffic were handled for half a century without an interlocking system or overhead signals, all switches being thrown by hand at the trackside. It is questionable, however, whether the capacity of the station was ever strained by the traffic that its participating railroads normally handled, although the owning company could easily have afforded more spacious accommodations. (The tenant companies continued to be the L&N and the Cincinnati and Muskingum Valley, but two more were to be added before the end of the decade.) The traffic and the net income of the PC&StL continued to rise: in the first full year after the opening of the station the company enjoyed an operating ratio of little more than 67 percent, on the basis of total revenues of more than $4,000,000, of which 30 percent came from the transportation of mail, express, and passengers.[4]

The construction of the second of the three stations to be opened within the four years of 1881 to 1885 was originally associated with another of those ambitious and even fantastic projects with which the nineteenth century abounded. Narrow-gauge railroads (ordinarily three feet in distance between rails) were widely regarded after the Civil War as offering the most satisfactory solutions to the numerous problems arising from the construction of necessary railroad lines where traffic was light, capital inadequate,

and the engineering exigencies dictated by topography and waterways formidable. Cincinnati railroad-builders, intending to take
the lead in such enterprises, planned a chain of three-foot lines
to extend throughout the western part of Ohio to Toledo and called
a convention of interested and hopefully cooperative entrepreneurs
that was held at the Grand Hotel in July 1878. Among the early
constituents of this projected system was the Miami Valley Narrow
Gauge Railway Company, which passed rapidly into bankruptcy
following the partial construction of a line from Norwood to
Waynesfield, Ohio, in 1876–78. Reorganized as the Cincinnati
Northern Railway in 1880, the new company inaugurated operations between Lebanon and a connection with the Marietta and
Cincinnati at Norwood in 1881. The directors had already looked
toward a Cincinnati extension, especially since the road had acquired among other properties of the Miami Valley the unfinished
10,000-foot tunnel of Erasmus Gest and fifteen acres of land on
East Court Street near Broadway (ten blocks from the focal point
of the city's core).

The completion of this monstrous tunnel by a narrow-gauge
road with no more than fifty miles of line was quickly seen to
be chimerical, and the directors chose instead to dig a short high-
level tunnel through Walnut Hills from McMillan to Oak Street,
which was completed in 1878 (figs. 18, 19). In order to reduce the
tunnel to a financially manageable length, however, the company
paid a high price in operating costs. The line from Court to McMillan Street had to be built at the very steep grade of 3.4 percent along
the east side of Deer Creek Valley and through a deep limestone
and shale cut at the top of the hill lying between the two northeastern arteries of Reading Road and Gilbert Avenue (fig. 19), and
the grade of the north approach in places rose to 2 percent. It was
hilly Cincinnati's only railroad tunnel, and it survived for ninety
years before it was excavated out of existence for the inevitable
expressway. The trains of the Cincinnati Northern terminated at
Norwood for at least two years, then began a progressively deeper
penetration into Cincinnati during 1881 and 1882 by means of a
succession of temporary stations first at Oak Street, later at the
west edge of Eden Park, and eventually to temporary quarters on
Court Street. This makeshift arrangement ended when the company put together a permanent facility in the form of its little two-
story station and office building on East Court Street between June
and December of 1885 (figs. 20, 21).[5] This homely structure,
timber-framed and covered with board-and-batten sheathing, had

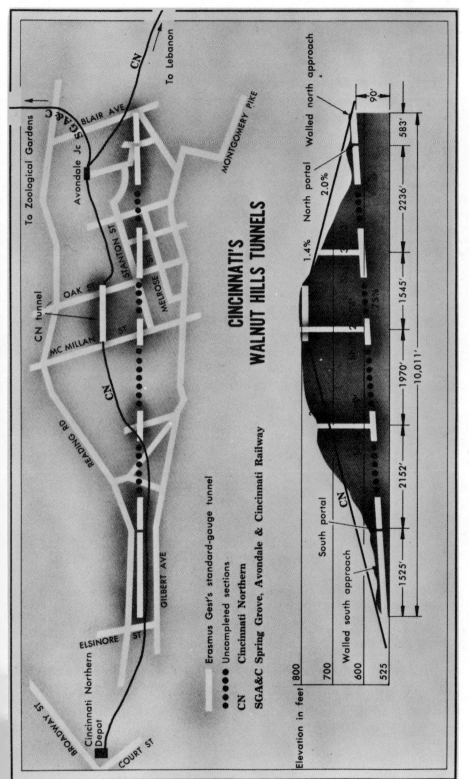

Fig. 18. Map and profile drawing showing the Walnut Hills tunnel of the Cincinnati Northern Railway, 1878, and the uncompleted low-grade tunnel of Erasmus Gest. The Spring Grove, Avondale and Cincinnati Railway was a Cincinnati Northern branch that was built only to the city's Zoological Garden in Avondale and was abandoned when the street railway was extended to that point. John A. Rehor, *The Nickel Plate Story* (Milwaukee: Kalmbach Publishing Company, 1965); reprinted with permission.

Fig. 19.   Walnut Hills tunnel, south portal. Reproduced with permission of the Cincinnati Railroad Club.

Fig. 20. Court Street Station, Cincinnati Northern Railway, East Court Street near Broadway, 1885. From the private collection of William C. Pletz; reproduced with permission.

Fig. 21. Court Street Station, platform and canopy. From the private collection of William C. Pletz; reproduced with permission.

a kind of primitive charm that seemed appropriate to the local and even bucolic character of its owner.

For about forty years the miniature terminal saw a fairly lively traffic: the CN inaugurated through service to Lebanon and Dayton in the year of its completion and took on a tenant in the following year when it granted trackage rights to the narrow-gauge Cincinnati and Eastern, an undernourished little company that was then embarked on a long struggle to reach Portsmouth, Ohio.[6] The flow of freight and passengers, however, was not lively enough to prevent the reorganization of the proprietary company in 1885 and the subsequent adoption of the title of Cincinnati, Lebanon and Northern Railroad. The dreams of a narrow-gauge empire evaporated in less than twenty years, and the road was compelled to adopt standard gauge in 1894 as the condition of survival. Two years later the Pennsylvania Railroad acquired a controlling interest in the property. Its location gave it a measure of importance in the economy of Cincinnati during the years of its ascendancy. The metropolitan communities lying to the north of Norwood, which eventually came to be nearly surrounded by the city of Cincinnati, and the rural businesses and farms among the small towns en route to Lebanon were wholly dependent on the line. Moreover, the route of the CL&N offered one great advantage over all other Cincinnati roads: its tracks lay far enough above the floodwaters of the Ohio River and its tributaries to be untouched even by the disasters of 1913 and 1937.

Central Union Depot

Some years before the Pan Handle lines and the Little Miami decided to build their new station, various railroads on the western side of the city began to set grander schemes in motion. By 1873 three passenger and as many freight depots lay scattered along Front, Pearl, Fifth, and Sixth streets in the West End, their multiplying tracks even at that early date threatening to become an impassable tangle. The first step toward unification came in February 1873, when a committee drawn from the directors of the Indianapolis and Cincinnati, the Ohio and Mississippi, the Marietta and Cincinnati, and the Dayton Short Line railroads met to consider the construction of a single station to be used jointly by the four companies.[7] The directors at first entertained the idea of a true union station but quickly "decided that a Union Depot, for the accommodation of all the railroads entering the city, is impracticable; that is to say, it could not be so located as to accommodate

82

the East and West roads."[8] The site that the planners selected lay immediately west of the Plum Street Station, along Pearl from Central Avenue to Smith Street. These plans appear to have been shelved at the conclusion of the meetings at which they were advanced, for no further step was taken during the next eight years. Meanwhile, other corporate developments occurred that offered the promise of effective action.

In 1866 a number of small Indiana companies, among them the Indianapolis and Cincinnati, had been merged to form the Cincinnati, Indianapolis, Saint Louis and Chicago Railroad under the presidency of Henry C. Lord. Neither the directors nor the president of this road seem to have recognized the full extent of its resources until it came under the presidency of a youthful, ambitious, and clever Boston attorney named Melvil Ezra Ingalls. His first step in the direction of implementing the terminal plans of 1873 came in the spring of 1881, when the directors authorized him to acquire additional property in the West End, extending westward from Central Avenue to Smith Street between Pearl and Third, for a new and hopefully union station and to offer a stock issue of $1,000,000 in 1882 to pay the costs of construction. The enthusiastic comment of the *Railroad Gazette* was no very great exaggeration: the company plans to erect "the largest passenger depot west of the Alleghany [*sic*] Mountains. . . . the finest and largest passenger depot in the West."[9] The original plans for this monumental work were prepared in the summer of 1881 by the Chicago architect William W. Boyington, but they proved too grand even for the free-spending company that commissioned them and were extensively scaled down before construction was initiated in the following year.

The station building that Boyington designed was said to be in the "Eastlake style" decorated with Queen Anne details (fig. 22).[10] The exterior walls were to be constructed of red pressed brick on a stone foundation, and interior floor and roof loads were to be carried probably on timber frames supported by iron columns. The handsome building, marked by a strong vertical accent and vigorous articulation, consisted of three distinct though well-unified parts. The main block was to rise at the corner of Third Street and Central Avenue, its interior spaces intended mainly for the offices of the participating railroad companies. The lower wing, extending west along Third Street, was to contain the main waiting room, ticket offices, and the numerous service facilities, and the long single-story extension stretching still further to the west was

Fig. 22. Central Union Depot, original design of 1881, West Third Street and Central avenue; William W. Boyington, architect. *Railway Review*; reproduced from the collections of the Library of Congress.

to house the baggage rooms and the postal terminal, the main floors of which would have been at track level, one story, or fifteen feet, below the Third Street grade. The main elevation would have extended 233 feet along Central Avenue, and the west wing of the now standard L-shaped plan 475 feet along Third Street. The track layout was planned with unusual generosity: there were to be ten tracks (two for each of the five companies expected to participate in the program) and five platforms with a length of 700 feet, the whole said to be more commodious than the similar spaces of the new Grand Central Terminal in New York (1869-71).

It was unfortunate from the historical and operational as well as the civic standpoints that this impressive design was never built, since the actual work that was begun in the spring of 1882 and opened on 9 April 1883 was inferior to it in formal and spatial characteristics (figs. 23, 24).[11] The headhouse was much reduced in floor area and height; the separation of waiting room and concourse levels was abandoned in favor of a single-level plan in which everything necessary to the convenience of the passenger was disposed on one floor set fifteen feet below the natural entrance on Third Street; and the formal treatment of the building was so much inferior to that of the original as to suggest that Boyington's work was redone by the heavy hand of a company architect. The decision to place the waiting room, dining room, concourse, and baggage room on one level offered certain advantages to the passenger in ease of access but nullified these to some extent by the greatly reduced floor areas available to the various facilities. The headhouse, reduced to three stories and a much-contracted office space, was a brick-walled structure stand-

Fig. 23. Central Union Depot as constructed, 1881–83. Reproduced with the permission of the Cincinnati Historical Society.

Fig. 24. Central Union Depot train shed during flood of 1883. Reproduced with the permission of the Cincinnati Historical Society.

ing on a high base of irregular stone masonry and capped by a mansard roof. Surviving illustrations indicate that the interior loads were supported by cast-iron columns that in turn probably carried floor and roof frames of timber. The oddly mixed and proportioned treatment of the exterior walls and openings suggests elements of the Gothic, Italian, and French Renaissance revivals composed into what would most conveniently be designated simply as "Victorian."

The train shed was a homely work representing a mode of construction that was fast disappearing in the 1880s for roofs of such great area (fig. 24). The segmental vault of the shed, with recurved or flaring edges, covered eight tracks and five platforms in a single span of 215 feet, a dimension that did in fact exceed the span of the far more sophisticated roof of the Grand Central Terminal train shed in New York. The Cincinnati shed was carried by deep-arched trusses of timber in the conventional Howe form, their ends resting on two rows of iron columns located near the outer edges of the roof. The horizontal thrust of the trusses was taken by the familiar wrought-iron tie rods carried by hangers suspended from the bottom chords of the arched members. The length of the four passenger platforms was originally probably no more than the 565 feet of number two, but the three to the south of it were progressively lengthened over the years to a maximum of 910 feet for number five (fig. 25). Platform number one on the north side, reserved for mail and express, was cut off by service tracks and reduced to 240 feet in length.[12] The average elevation of the tracks was 484 feet above sea level or a little below the grade of the main tracks in Mill Creek Valley and well below the water level of serious floods (twenty-five feet below it in the case of the record flood of 1937).

When Central Union Depot opened in the early spring of 1883, it accommodated the trains of only two railroads, the proprietary company and a single tenant, the Cleveland, Columbus, Cincinnati and Indianapolis, but before the mid-year two more tenants entered the premises, namely, the Ohio and Mississippi and the Cincinnati, Washington and Baltimore, the successor to the Marietta and Cincinnati.[13] The trains of the four roads used the approach tracks that the I&C had laid down for Plum Street Station and thus continued to take advantage of the relatively broad, nearly level, crossing-free access route provided by the bed of the old Whitewater Canal (figs. 9, 26). This double-track line paralleled by a continuous siding was wholly owned by the CIStL&C approximately to the intersection of Sixth and Carr streets, where two

87

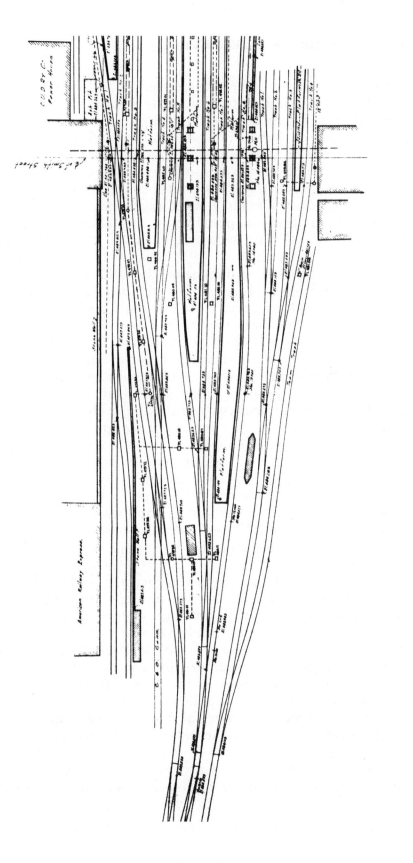

Fig. 25. Central Union Depot track plan, 1883. CCC&StL Railway drawing; reproduced through the courtesy of the Penn Central Transportation Company.

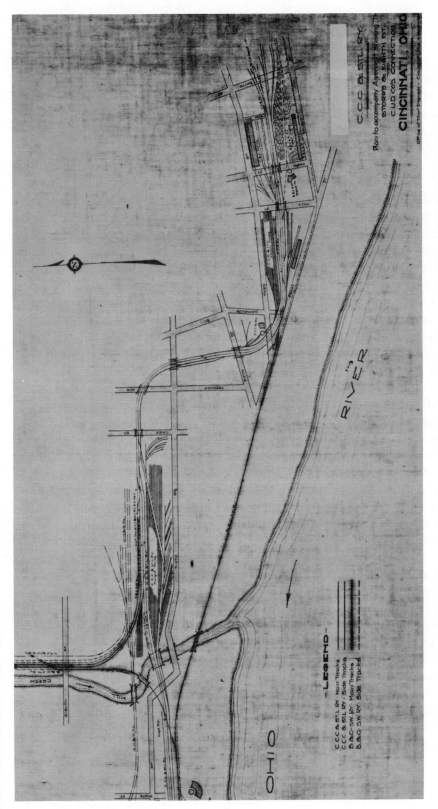

Fig. 26. Central Union Depot, plan of approach tracks and coach yards as they existed from the turn of the century to 1933. The Big Four owned the entire approach line and had located its coach yard on the north side of these tracks, along Third Street west of Mill. The B&O's coach yard and engine terminal lay on the south side of the approach near the union depot, roughly on the line of the O&M's long tangent across the lower end of Mill Creek Valley. CCC&StL Railway drawing; reproduced through the courtesy of the Penn Central Transportation company.

more main tracks extending to Mill Creek had been added by the Baltimore line. The coach yards, engine terminals, freight stations, and warehouses of the four participating lines lay to the west of the station throat, forming a tight linear succession along the approach tracks. This compact arrangement, dictated largely by the densely built mass of tracks, warehouses, factories, and river facilities in the West End, offered the advantage of reducing to a minimum the movements of empty trains and light engines, but it also produced the inevitable delays arising from growing traffic congestion and from the fact that all switches at the throat and along the approach tracks were hand-thrown at the trackside throughout the life of the station.

The location of the depot had much to recommend it from an urbanistic standpoint, contrary to the attacks increasingly leveled against it by local citizens. If we regard the major focal point of the city center as the intersection of Fourth and Vine streets, the station headhouse stood only four blocks to the west of this point and one to the south. Even in the days of horse-drawn vehicles it was no great distance, and when the electrically operated street-car was introduced in Cincinnati, a car stop was established no further than the width of the sidewalk from the concourse entrance. No arrangement involving taxis and private automobiles has improved on this either at rail or air terminals. The location of the station posed a problem for passengers transferring to or from the trains of the two eastern stations, since both of them were a good mile and a half away; but the evidence suggests that there never were a great many travelers involved in such east-to-west connections for the chief reason that the PC&StL and its connecting lines had already established a through route by-passing Cincinnati from Columbus and Dayton westward to Richmond, Indianapolis, Chicago, and Saint Louis. There was ample space within the depot to accommodate both trains and passengers, and the approach line and the various terminal facilities stretched along it served well enough until additions to the Cincinnati rail pattern that came before the end of the decade greatly complicated terminal operations. The arrival of three new tenants from the south and the inauguration of sleeping-car service requiring that Pullmans be operated through the city not only increased total traffic but introduced a great many awkward reverse movements. The remarkable thing is that a stub-end terminal without interlocking controls and automatic signals served as well as it did.

The Terminal Pattern of Half a Century

Rounding Out the Cincinnati System

Local Lines and Street Railways

The three depots that were opened in the early years of the eighties, and the Baymiller Street Station of twenty years before very nearly closed the ring of the Cincinnati terminals and fixed the pattern of rail operations in all the succeeding years of their history. But an enormous volume of new construction was to come before the rail network was filled out. Three new trunk lines, two more terminal stations, new bridges, extensive additions to freight yards and stations, the introduction and spread of automatic block signaling, new forms of motive power, suburban rail lines, the electric street railway, the rise and rapid expansion of an entirely new form of rail transportation—all these were to appear virtually on top of each other in the quarter century following the opening of Central Union Depot; together they brought the Cincinnati railroad system to its maturity and laid the groundwork for the peak of operating capacity that was to come with World War II.[14] The task of describing this multidimensional development presents difficult organizational problems, and perhaps the best—or at least most convenient—solution is to separate the major phases of rail construction from organization and operation and to arrange them according to a straightforward chronological plan. This has the additional virtue of taking us roughly from the establishment of the small local or suburban roads to the extensions of great trunk-line systems.

Until the building-up of the electrified street railway system in the years following 1888, the hilltop communities lay isolated from the city on its alluvial plain. The nearer of such communities, those overlooking the city itself, could be reached by the inclined-plane railways that were built largely in the decade of the 1870s; but the more distant towns and suburbs in the hills were beyond the reach of public transportation, their distances in miles often increased in effect by rugged topography. The initial attempt to break down this isolation and the one that offered for some years the only feasible means was the construction of local railroad lines designed to unite the city with once separate communities that were in some cases later incorporated within its expanding limits. The first of these strictly local lines was the Cincinnati and Columbia Street Railroad, chartered in 1863 and built over the succeeding three years along Eastern Avenue (then Wooster Pike)

91

from Pendleton, at the foot of Delta Avenue, to Columbia on the Little Miami River. The inner terminal at Pendleton was chosen in order to provide a connection with a long horsecar line that extended into the city core at what was later to be Fountain Square. The railroad was operated by steam locomotives of a kind called dummy engines, a type of motive power in which the engine proper was entirely hidden within the forward part of a passenger-car body. Traffic on the Columbia line expanded rapidly with the opening of a branch to Mount Lookout, near the easternmost hills of Cincinnati, in 1873. The aim of the builder, Charles H. Kilgour, was the development of his real estate holdings, and in this respect the little railroad proved a great success. The community flourished to the point where the residents objected to the noise of the dummy engines that provided their transportation, but a solution that met with everyone's satisfaction was ready at hand. The traffic level on the Mount Lookout line was such as to attract the attention of the Cincinnati Street Railway Company, which acquired the entire Columbia property piecemeal over the years 1891-96 and converted it to electrical operation in 1897.

Two similar and nearly simultaneous developments took place in the hills west and northwest of the city. The earlier of the two was the College Hill Railroad Company, incorporated in 1873, opened for service initially from Winton Place to College Hill in 1876, and extended to Mount Healthy in the following year. Both the hilltop terminals stand among the highest elevations in the Cincinnati area, and College Hill rises fairly abruptly from the north side of Mill Creek Valley. As a consequence of these topographic exigencies, the railroad had to be built at narrow gauge on a winding 4 percent grade along the wooded, deeply dissected east flank of College Hill. The company was reincorporated as the Cincinnati-Northwestern Railway in 1883, when it shifted its tracks to standard gauge and began to operate by trackage rights over the Cincinnati, Hamilton and Dayton from its crossing with that company's line at the edge of Spring Grove Cemetery to Baymiller Street Station. The C-NW was acquired by the Southern Ohio Traction Company in 1901 and converted to an electric interurban line in the following year. By 1895, however, the street railway company had extended an electrically operated car line to College Hill by way of Hamilton Avenue, and the rail line, as a consequence, quickly lost its traffic within the city limits.

The third of the city's local roads was also involved in operations on a steep grade. The Cincinnati and Westwood Railroad was incorporated in 1874 to build a narrow-gauge line from the west edge of Mill Creek Valley to the top of the lofty hill on which the community of Westwood is located. The distance was less than five miles, but only a few hundred feet on the valley floor was level right of way. The track was converted to standard gauge in 1891 to allow the interchange of freight with the trunk lines, and for a few years the little company enjoyed a remunerative traffic of both freight and passengers transported to its totally isolated terminal neighborhood. The opening of the Westwood car line, however, killed the passenger business, and the coming of the motor truck took what little freight remained, chiefly coal to serve the local yards. It survived precariously until 1926, when it abandoned its operations *in toto*, leaving only a stored locomotive to stand idle in an abandoned enginehouse for a few more years. The last vestiges—even graded rights of way—of these local railroads have disappeared, but there was a time when they too possessed a kind of bucolic charm that arose chiefly from their unhurried if somewhat noisy pace along the flanks and in the ravines of Cincinnati's once densely wooded hillsides.

The last of the short lines that sprang up in the days before electricity radically changed the whole pattern of urban life was the Cincinnati, Georgetown and Portsmouth, which was incorporated as the Cincinnati and Portsmouth in 1873. The line did not reach the Cincinnati periphery until the company extended its narrow-gauge track to Columbia on the Little Miami River from Hamersville, Ohio, in 1883. Within the Cincinnati area the CG&P provided service to Mount Washington, another isolated hilltop community that lay east of the broad Little Miami valley. The original plan of the Georgetown builders was to enter the city by means of trackage rights over the Cincinnati Northern, probably via the Cincinnati and Eastern's new line; but this idea was abandoned in 1886, when the road was converted to standard gauge. The change made possible a more satisfactory arrangement with the PC&StL whereby the CG&P used the tracks of the larger company into the station at Pearl and Butler streets. This agreement seems to have been repeatedly terminated and reestablished during the next decade, but the short line eventually constructed its own terminal at Carrel Street in Pendleton. In 1902 it was converted to an electric interurban road with the same corporate title.

The street railway system was the chief factor in the decline of the local railroad and to some degree of local metropolitan service on the trunk-line railroads. The newer mode of transportation was cleaner, faster, vastly more flexible in scheduling, and more efficient in terms of energy consumption than any of its predecessors (or successors, for that matter). Indeed, without it, cities like Cincinnati not possessed of a rapid transit system could never have grown beyond the bounds of their commercial nuclei. The first power-operated form was the cable car, which was introduced in Cincinnati in the summer of 1885 for the movement of cars on the long Gilbert Avenue hill. The second line was opened two years later to negotiate the forbidding Sycamore Street hill to Mount Auburn, and the third and last came shortly thereafter to provide service to Clifton via Vine Street and Jefferson Avenue.[15] The movement of the cable that provided the immediate motive power for these car lines was originally accomplished by steam-operated drums, but electricity was substituted for steam as a source of power in 1898. The transition had scarcely been made when the accelerating expansion of the electric-traction streetcar lines ended the life of the cable-drawn variety in Cincinnati and every other city except San Francisco.

The reliable traction motor was scarcely ten years old when the first electrically operated street railway service was inaugurated in Frankfurt, Germany, in 1884. The first successful urban line in the United States was built by Frank J. Sprague at Richmond, Virginia, in 1887–88. The initial installation at Cincinnati appeared at almost the same time: the Mount Adams and Eden Park Inclined Railway Company operated the first electric cars in June 1888 on McMillan Street from Gilbert Avenue westward to Reading Road. The Cincinnati Street Railway Company began the operation of electric cars a year later, its directors selecting the level Colerain Avenue from Brighton to Cumminsville for the route (lying wholly in Mill Creek Valley). The basic Cincinnati system of streetcar lines was built up in twenty-two years, from 1889 to 1911, at a gauge of 5 feet 2 1/2 inches, the 6 inches beyond the standard figure apparently adopted to prevent the operation of steam railroad and interurban cars on the company's tracks (see fig. 43). The street railway mileage was filled out to its maximum extent with the construction of McMillan Street and its associated car line westward from near the top of Clifton Hill down into Mill Creek Valley in 1923. The Kentucky lines of the Cincinnati, Newport and Covington Railway were built largely at the same time, construction having been initiated in 1890. The establishment of this cross-river system greatly stimulated the unification and interdependency of the various parts of what was becoming a two-state metropolitan area. The beginnings of this long-hoped-for union waited on the completion of the Suspension Bridge of 1867 (figs. 12, 13).[16]

The first permanent addition to the rail mileage of Cincinnati following the opening of the three new terminals revived once more the dream of Gest's 10,000-foot Walnut Hills tunnel. The Cincinnati and Eastern Railroad was placed under construction as a narrow-gauge line in 1882, but in little more than a year the track was widened to standard gauge, in which form it was pushed to its intended terminal of Portsmouth, Ohio, in 1884. The Cincinnati end was at Idlewild, the old and now forgotten name of the community lying roughly between Walnut Hills and the separate city of Norwood. From this point the builders of the C&E planned to extend the track to a terminal in lower Deer Creek Valley most likely on Court Street by completing the unfinished low-grade tunnel. No proposal was more irrational than this: construction of the Portsmouth line was carried out on a day-to-day basis as the intermittent flow of inadequate capital dictated, and the usual reorganization came soon after its completion. At the same time there was an element of farsighted intelligence in certain aspects of its program. The new company planned to extend its line below Court Street to join the industrial spur of the PC&StL in Eggleston Avenue and thus to provide a small but useful link in the growing network of Cincinnati rail lines.

The C&E emerged from the reorganization of 1887 as the Ohio and Northwestern Railroad, but precisely what ambitions on the part of the directors suggested a northwestern horizon is now difficult to determine. Whatever the case, the new name had no magic to raise new traffic, and a second reorganization was carried out in 1891, from which the company emerged as the Cincinnati, Portsmouth and Virginia Railroad. The third title contained the suggestion of a valuable idea: Portsmouth lay on the main line of the Norfolk and Western Railway, a rich and powerful coal-carrying road the directors of which saw the possibility of picking up a Cincinnati entry at a bargain price. The larger company acquired control of the Portsmouth line in 1901 and merged it in the following year. The next step filled out another strand in the continuous web of the city's railroad lines. The Cincinnati Connecting Belt Railway, the only such property in the local rail system, was opened between Idlewild and a connection with the recently formed Baltimore and Ohio Southwestern at Bond Hill in 1899, and with the Big Four at Ivorydale in 1900. The CP&V acquired the belt line in

95

1901 and transferred title to the N&W in the following year. The larger company rebuilt the various lines into a low-grade, largely tangent track extending directly through the eastern and north-central portions of the city to the outlying Mill Creek yard of the Big Four. The whole program put Cincinnati on the line of another trunk-line carrier, even though it is a single-track branch west of Portsmouth.

Corporate Mergers

The connection of the belt line with the B&OSW at Bond Hill indicates that the older trunk lines were involved in numerous changes of corporate character, organization, and fortune in the last two decades of the nineteenth century. The Baltimore and Ohio acquired a controlling interest in the Marietta and Cincinnati Railroad in 1882 and reorganized it under the title of the Cincinnati, Washington and Baltimore. The new company was renamed the Baltimore and Ohio Southwestern in 1889, which still exists as a separate entity (in reality, a paper corporation) though controlled by the B&O and merged with the larger company since 1900. These changes in corporate status meant salvation for the hapless Marietta road, which had no *raison d'être* in an economic sense as an independent line.

A similar series of events made up the end-of-the-century history of the Ohio and Mississippi: the Baltimore and Ohio Southwestern acquired the Saint Louis road in 1893, so that it also became part of the B&O system with the merger of 1900. The much enlarged B&O then expanded the Cincinnati portions of its empire still further with the acquisition of the Cincinnati, Hamilton and Dayton Railroad over a period of years from 1909 to 1917. This move made the B&O the primary carrier for a few years of the heavy volume of traffic (chiefly coal) originated by the Southern and Pocahontas roads and destined for Toledo, Detroit, and other Great Lakes ports.[17] The whole series of mergers had important consequences for the B&O and the Cincinnati economy: the railroad had put together a single trunk line extending from Baltimore to Saint Louis through the West Virginia and eastern Ohio coalfields, thus making Cincinnati in effect a way station on the newly formed system; further, in the absence of a true belt or transfer company in the Cincinnati terminal district, the B&O, with its multitude of connections that missed only the L&N, took over this essential function.

Equally decisive for the city's economy was the consolidation in

The Terminal Pattern of Half a Century

June 1889 of the Cincinnati, Indianapolis, Saint Louis and Chicago and the Cleveland, Columbus, Cincinnati and Indianapolis into the Cleveland, Cincinnati, Chicago and Saint Louis Railway—a staggering combination of four-city names that probably put all other corporate titles to shame. This already extensive system was enlarged still further in the following year through the merger of eight small companies that extended the lines north to Benton Harbor, Michigan, and south to a potential Louisville connection. But the new name, like the old, although certainly impressive and suggestive of the financial power of its possessor, was an obvious barrier to easy communication, and a popular nickname had already been coined for the CIStL&C—the Big Four. Its application to the CCC&StL was to fix it so deeply in common usage as to give it and its variations the status of a common expression in the English language. The whole matter called forth another display of Henry C. Lord's wit.

> The two roads having the longest and hardest-to-remember names in the country—the Cleveland, Columbus, Cincinnati and Indianapolis and the Cincinnati, Indianapolis, Saint Louis and Chicago, are to be fused into one with a new name just half as long as the two old ones—namely, Cleveland, Cincinnati, Chicago and Saint Louis. That is, the C. C. C. & I. and the C. I. St. L. and C. became the C. C. C. & St. L. As these initials represent four of the great cities of the interior, the system can still be called, "The Big Four," although "The Three C.'s and St. L." will also be in order. The wear and tear of memory in attempting to keep the initials straight in cases like these are fearful and would seem in the public interest to call for legislation compelling railway companies to adopt short names. Perhaps the interstate commerce commission will take the matter up.[18]

A controlling interest in the new company was rapidly acquired by the New York Central and Hudson River, its board chairman Cornelius Vanderbilt and his successors having already embarked on a program of conquest among numerous smaller lines west of Buffalo.

The establishment of the enlarged Big Four proved to be only a part of Ingalls's ambition in the creation of a rail empire. As president of both the CIStL&C and the Kentucky Central, he proposed possibly as early as December 1882 the construction of a railroad line from a connection with the Ohio and Mississippi at Aurora, Indiana, to Louisville along the north bank of the Ohio River via the Indiana towns of Rising Sun, Madison, Jeffersonville, and New Albany. Associated with him in drawing up the blueprint for this scheme was the Indiana rail entrepreneur W. Horace Scott. The only rail line that touched the river between these terminal points was the Jeffersonville, Madison and Indianapolis, which as the name indicates reached the river at Madison, at the foot of what is still the steepest standard railroad grade in the United States (as opposed to cog railways). The other two lines connecting Cincinnati and Louisville lay a considerable distance from the Ohio River: the O&M extended directly west from Cincinnati via North Vernon, Indiana, and the Louisville, Cincinnati and Lexington followed a shorter route at an average though highly variable distance of some fifteen miles south of the waterway. As the editors of *Railway Age* commented, "A wide and fertile region is thus left with no transportation except by river. . . . The new line . . . would command all the business on both sides of the river, or so much of its as any line could take away from the steamboats. . . . Mr. Ingalls believes that the proposed line will be an important feeder of the Big Four (C. I. St. L. and C.) and the Kentucky Central system, and that it would also do a good local business."[19]

The idea lay dormant until it was revived in the summer of 1889, when the directors of the newly established CCC&StL Railway ordered a survey of a potential route. They tentatively adopted the name Louisville, Cincinnati and Dayton for the planned company, then quickly dropped it in favor of the more accurate Louisville, Madison and Cincinnati Railroad. But the projected line was never built, chiefly because the Big Four gained access to Louisville by the far more economical method of acquiring trackage rights over the Ohio and Mississippi from North Vernon to Jeffersonville in July 1895.[20] Even with this bargain, however, the new route was expensive enough: the Louisville end, beyond the tracks of the O&M, required the construction of an enormous Ohio River bridge that cost years of heroic effort (1889–95) and thirty-seven lives along the way. The 547-foot length of each of the three river spans established a new record at the time for a succession of simple truss forms.

The plan of building a rail line downriver from Cincinnati became active once more when various entrepreneurs incorporated the Cincinnati, Indiana and Louisville Railroad in April 1914 and went so far as to order a survey in the summer of that year. That turned out to be the end, however: the former river traffic had long ago been taken by the L&N, the B&O, and the Big Four, and there was none left for a fourth line. The failure of these schemes meant that the steep wooded hills along both banks of the Ohio River were to remain isolated and economically forgotten to this day, which is the chief factor, perhaps, in the preservation of the nineteenth-century charm of Madison, Indiana.

The Terminal Pattern of Half a Century

The greatly expanded Big Four had scarcely been called into being when similar mergers brought forth another Ohio and Indiana system very much like the earlier company in size, location, traffic, and cumbersome four-city name. In September 1890 the Pittsburgh, Cincinnati, Chicago and Saint Louis Railroad was created by consolidation of five smaller companies of which the PC&StL and the Chicago, Saint Louis and Pittsburgh were the dominant roads. Among the remaining three (Cincinnati and Richmond, Cincinnati, Richmond and Chicago, and Jeffersonville, Madison and Indianapolis) the little 24.5-mile Cincinnati and Richmond, incorporated in 1881 and opened in 1889, connected Cincinnati with Hamilton to form the southernmost segment in another series of end-to-end links that brought through routes from the Ohio River to Chicago and Grand Rapids. Since the Pennsylvania Railroad already held a controlling interest in the Pan Handle company, it was a foregone conclusion that the eastern road would extend its dominion over the newly created system. The PCC&StL was eventually leased to the Pennsylvania and merged with it to form part of a unified system. The strands in the great web of Cincinnati rail lines were nearing completion, and one of the anchor members was at that very time being put into place.

New Southern Lines

The last of the trunk lines to enter the city was involved in new construction of a magnitude that was not to be seen again until the terminal complex and its associated structures were launched in 1928. Under the presidency of the California railroad organizer Collis P. Huntington, the Chesapeake and Ohio Railway was pushed westward from its previous terminal at Huntington, West Virginia, to Cincinnati through a combination of acquisitions and new constructions. The line was laid down on the south bank of the Ohio River at what was for all practical purposes a level grade and brought into Cincinnati through the erection of a record-breaking double-track bridge in 1886–88 (figs. 27, 28).[21] Designed under the direction of William H. Burr as a combined rail and highway structure, this once celebrated work was the forerunner of the long-span steel railroad bridge of the twentieth century. Of the three spans in the river crossing, the one over the channel extended 550 feet from center to center of bearings and thus became the longest simple truss span in the world at the time. The superstructure consisted of subdivided Pratt trusses in which all chord and web members of the truss proper were steel and all members of the top and bottom chords with associated lateral frames were

99

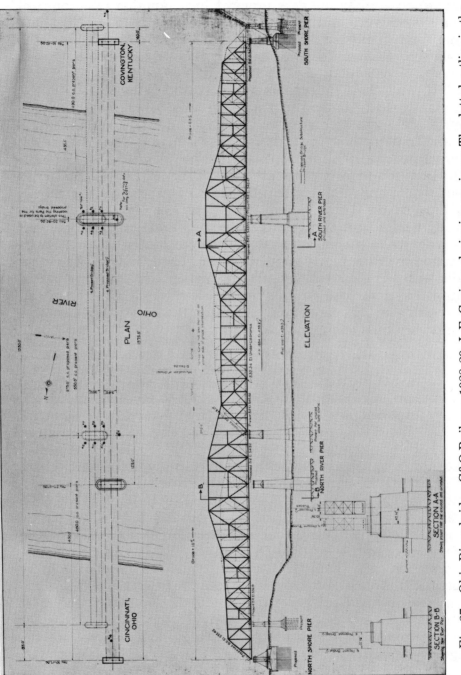

Fig. 27. Ohio River bridge, C&O Railway, 1928-29; J. E. Greiner, designing engineer. The dotted outline in the background represents the original bridge, 1886-88; William H. Burr, designing engineer. C&O Railway drawing; reproduced through the courtesy of the C&O/B&O Railroads (now the Chessie System).

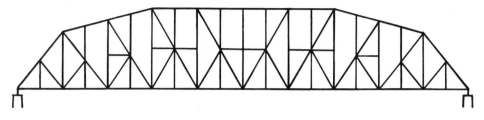

Fig. 28. Ohio River bridge, C&O Railway, 1886-88, elevation of the channel span. Author's drawing.

wrought iron. The calculation of forces in the truss was rendered difficult to an unparalleled degree by the complex pattern of eccentric loading arising from the different kinds of traffic, rail and vehicular. Construction of the bridge progressed nicely and without interruption until 26 August 1888, when a sudden late-summer flood brought down floating debris that destroyed the timber falsework, so that the steel of partly completed trusses collapsed into the river. The bridge was opened before the end of the year, and the C&O inaugurated service into the city on 1 January 1889. Steadily increasing train and locomotive weights, however, compelled the replacement of the structure forty years later.[22]

The obvious choice of terminal for the passenger trains of the C&O was Central Union Depot, but ironically enough, its very proximity to the new line made for operating difficulties. The Cincinnati end of the bridge stood almost directly above the depot throat, as the third level of transportation in the immediate area (the Smith Street bridge over the approach tracks was the second). For freight traffic it was simply a matter of making the necessary end-to-end connections with the grade-level lines of the Big Four, over which cars could move in a continuous direction. In the case of passenger trains, however, since the distribution of buildings, streets, and tracks required that the approach viaduct be turned westward, in the opposite direction from the depot, it was necessary to move incoming trains down the steep grade of the bridge approach, then back them into the station. The reverse pattern of movements, of course, would be followed by outbound trains. These cumbersome reverse movements, together with the addition of the Cincinnati Southern and the Kentucky Central trains to the union depot roster, led to predictable results: the station that had been generously planned for the traffic of 1883 suddenly found itself hard-pressed to accommodate the greatly increased flow that came at the end of the decade. The number of trains and the num-

101

ber of cars per train continued to increase throughout the remainder of the nineteenth century and into the twentieth, and hand-thrown switches, a two-track approach, severe limitations on the space for coach yards and engine terminals, long reverse movements of the empty trains of roads with distant yard facilities—all these made the operation of trains at Central Union Depot a very tight squeeze.

To the operating departments of the C&O these immediately obvious difficulties were compounded by the location of the coach yard in Covington, several blocks from the end of the south bridge approach. The officers of the company, accordingly, soon made plans to relieve the north approach and the union station of some of their burdens. The actual results of these originally extensive plans, however, proved to be anticlimactic, suggesting that the officers lost much of their enthusiasm as the estimated costs mounted. In 1889–90 the road planned to build new terminal facilities in the block bounded by Third and Fourth streets on the south and north, and John and Smith streets on the east and west, immediately north of the union depot track area. The program included a four-track freight station along Third Street, with its entrance facing John, and a two-track passenger station with a gable train shed on iron trusses, the entrance of the headhouse to face Fourth Street. Since Fourth Street lies at a conspicuously higher elevation than Third, its grade nearly coincided with the track level in the railroad's Ohio River bridge, so that by placing the tracks of the freight station on a viaduct structure the whole complex of tracks and platforms could have been reached by a nearly level connecting line diverging from the north bridge approach. It was the first time in Cincinnati rail history that terminal trackage and access lines were to be entirely elevated above the natural grade. The passenger station was to be used exclusively for local trains. The plan had a number of features to recommend it, but the high cost of constructing extensive steel viaducts and elevated station facilities discouraged the company from carrying out the program as it was originally conceived.

The freight station was built on a much-reduced scale in 1890, but the passenger station was never placed under construction because the company substituted a makeshift arrangement that promised to work well enough. Standing very nearly on the site of the proposed station was a dwelling that had been built in 1869; it was a narrow three-story structure with exterior brick walls carrying timber joists and floor planking, the whole a conventional piece of residential construction that is still common. The C&O acquired the property in 1891, extended the approach for the freight station, laid down a track on either side of the house, converted the parlor into a waiting room, the dining room into a ticket office, the kitchen into a toilet and lavatory, and the upstairs bedrooms into company offices, and in this way inexpensively and instantaneously produced the Fourth Street Station (figs. 29, 30). The time was to come when this little curiosity would be regarded as something of a joke, but in 1890 the railroad's plan for a separate station rested on a good understanding of the situation at the union depot. Compared with the long intercity trains composed of the standard assortment of sleeping cars, coaches, mail and express cars, and dining car, the assembly and emplacement of which is a slow and cumbersome operation, local or suburban trains are short, homogeneous in equipment, and can be loaded, emptied, and moved in and out of stations quickly and under close headway. If they can be separated from the long through trains that must stand at platforms for extended periods of time, the efficiency of the whole operation can be greatly improved. Where suburban traffic is extremely heavy, complete separation of the two classes of traffic, as at Grand Central Terminal in New York, is very nearly a matter of necessity. The officers of the C&O saw clear advantages in constructing a separate station on the level of the bridge deck; the only reason the homely little structure on Fourth Street seldom saw more than four trains in a day was that the expected local traffic never materialized.[23]

The improvement and expansion of the Louisville and Nashville facilities followed soon after the construction program of the C&O. The first step was the acquistion by the L&N of the Kentucky Central Railroad in December 1890, a move that gave the large and rapidly growing southern carrier a second direct entry into Cincinnati. The earlier merger of the Louisville, Cincinnati and Lexington, or Louisville Short Line, gave the L&N a continuous line through Louisville to Nashville, Memphis, Birmingham, and connections to New Orleans. The KC at first offered no such promise, since it terminated not far south of Lexington; but through the purchase of other Kentucky roads and the extension of its own line to Knoxville and Chattanooga, the L&N penetrated the eastern Kentucky coalfields and opened a through line to Atlanta shortly after the turn of the century. Since the northern terminus of the KC was at Covington, the construction of the C&O bridge offered a convenient access route into Cincinnati, and the L&N began to operate trains by trackage rights into Central Union Depot in Feb-

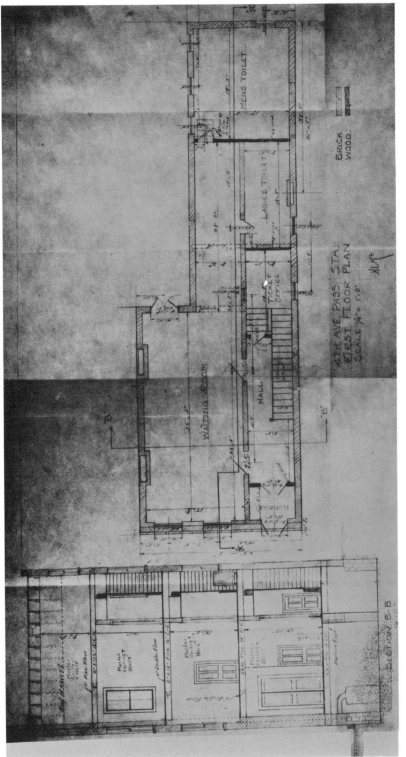

Fig. 29. Fourth Street Station, C&O Railway, West Fourth Street near John, 1869. Left: transverse section; right: main-floor plan. C&O Railway drawing; reproduced through the courtesy of the C&O/B&O Railroads (now the Chessie System).

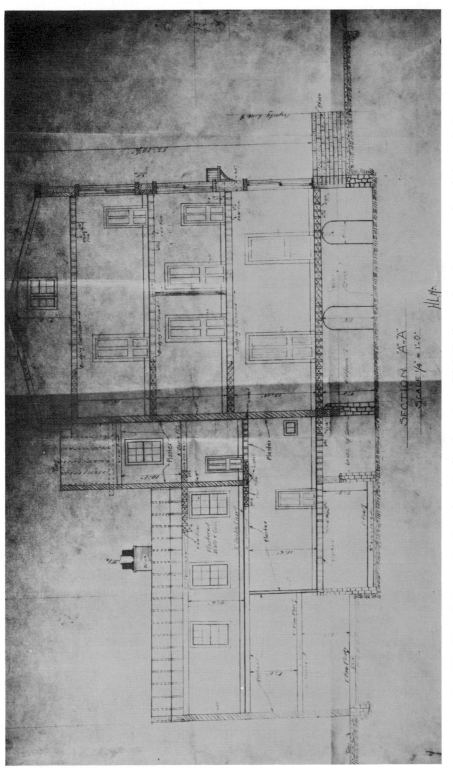

Fig. 30. Fourth Street Station, longitudinal section. C&O Railway drawing; reproduced through the courtesy of the C&O/B&O Railroads (now the Chessie System).

ruary 1891. The point where the two roads join in Covington has retained the designation of KC Junction down to the present time.[24]

The freight tonnage of the L&N increased 20.5 percent in the two years following the acquisition of the KC and very likely would have continued to climb at this rate for the remainder of the century had it not been for the prolonged business depression that followed the panic of 1893. In the first decade following 1900, however, the increase in tonnage was spectacular, amounting to nearly 100 percent by 1910, and it made the L&N the envy of all other railroad directors (see Appendix C, table 5, part 6). Since a substantial part of both freight and passenger traffic was destined for terminals or connecting lines of the PCC&StL, the Newport bridge of 1872 was approaching the limits of its capacity. The decision to replace the existing structure was made in 1895, and construction was carried out in the astonishingly short period of six months, from August 1896 to February 1897, by the Newport and Cincinnati Bridge Company, a subsidiary of the Pittsburgh road, which sold the span to the L&N in 1904 (figs. 31, 32). Designed under the direction of M. J. Becker as chief engineer, the bridge is a straightforward work that evolved from forms introduced by Burr for the C&O bridge. The Newport structure originally carried a single-track rail line, a roadway with two streetcar tracks, and a walkway (the car tracks have been removed), a complex that required four parallel trusses for each of the six spans. These trusses are the subdivided Pratt form, in which the tension members (all diagonals, lower halves of intermediate posts, and bottom chords) are composed of multiple eyebars arranged in parallel series for any one panel (figure 32 shows the distribution of tensile and compressive stresses in the truss members). The bridge deck over the full length of its river crossing was bowed upward in order to provide maximum clearance for the channel span and at the same time to bring the ends down at approximately the same grades of the approaches that descend to the Pan Handle tracks in Cincinnati and Saratoga Street in Newport.[25]

The same necessities that compelled the replacement of the Newport bridge dictated a comparable program of reconstruction on the part of the CNO&TP Railway. The company's Ohio River bridge (opened in 1877) consisted from end to end of a total of thirty-one spans, of which only four constituted the river crossing, all but one of the balance forming the long Cincinnati approach that had to be built to clear the numerous rail lines near the lower

Fig. 31. Ohio River bridge, L&N Railroad, 1896-97; M. J. Becker, chief engineer. Photograph by William C. Tayse; reproduced through the courtesy of the L&N Railroad.

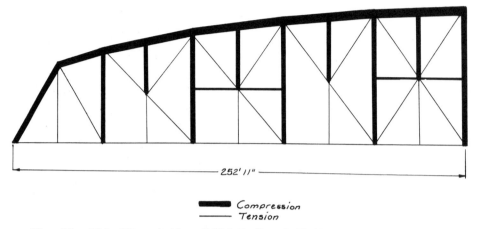

Compression
Tension

Fig. 32. Ohio River bridge, L&N Railroad. Half-elevation of the channel span showing the distribution of tensile and compressive stresses, which corresponds to the distribution of the slender eyebars and the heavier built-up box members. Author's drawing.

end of Mill Creek Valley. Over the twenty-one years from 1890 to 1911 the railroad replaced all the approach spans, using steel plate-girder forms for the 30-foot spans of the Cincinnati viaduct and Warren trusses for the remainder of the approach spans, all of which exceeded 100 feet in length. The Whipple trusses of the river crossing remained until the reconstruction of 1920.[26]

A few scattered additions to the railroad plant and to corporate plans served to round out the great program of new construction that filled the decade of the 1880s. The Cincinnati, Hamilton and Dayton Railroad built a way station in 1888–89 for transfer passengers at Cincinnati Transfer, or Cincinnati Junction, as it was later called, which remains to this day the inner heart of the whole metropolitan system, lying at the center of the huge ganglion that occupies the lower end of Mill Creek Valley and the alluvial plains on either side. All companies using both Central Union Depot and Baymiller Street Station had interconnecting lines, and the CH&D built the structure for the convenience of passengers who had to transfer from one terminal to another. The road somehow managed to squeeze a respectable little depot, complete with dining room and lunch counter, into this jungle of interweaving rail lines. There was some justification for it at the time: when the station was opened in 1889, the railroads that entered the city through the junction operated a total of 137 scheduled trains per day. Four

108

years later the CH&D greatly expanded its freight-handling facilities in the neighborhood of its passenger terminal by adding a
new l.-c.-l. (less-than-carload) station on George Street between
Baymiller and Freeman Avenue in 1893–94. It was probably the
largest in-town station at the time, with a capacity of 106 cars.
The numerous freighthouses of the other roads were located along
main lines close to the passenger depots, resulting in a concentration of facilities that was useful as well as economical in the
early years but that eventually led to chaos during World War I.
The troublesome, expensive, and ever-growing classification yards
were already at the turn of the century being located at the periphery of the metropolitan area, where land was available and both
prices and taxes lower than in the densely built city.

There was no question about Cincinnati's importance as a rail
hub and a manufacturing center in this period of almost explosive
industrial expansion. The city was still first in Ohio, ahead of sec-
ond-place Cleveland, in the volume of manufactured goods an-
nually produced in local factories. It stood behind only Chicago
and Saint Louis in the number of freight cars passing through the
switching district. When the C&O inaugurated service to and from
the city in January 1889, the fifteen railroad companies using its
six stations operated a minimum of 196 scheduled passenger trains
per weekday; and if we include the various kinds of extra trains
and mail trains not shown in the public timetables, the total was
about 220 on a normal weekday. The number was to increase by a
third in the next three years, before the depression of 1893 called
a temporary halt to this expansive prosperity. One indication of
the importance of the city as a commercial center was the fact
that between June 1868, when the first *Official Railway Guide* was
issued, and the end of the century at least 142 steam railroads
were incorporated with the name *Cincinnati* in their official corporate titles.[27] Given the city's dependence on the railroads in
this age of their dominance and ascendancy, the legal adoption
of standard time by the municipal government in December 1889
was a long overdue symbolic as well as practical step.

Final Strands in the Cincinnati Network

The Chesapeake and Ohio was destined once more to play the
major role in completing the steam railroad system of Cincinnati,
but the ultimate step in the process was neither originally planned
nor even foreseen by the road's directors. Because the C&O entered
Cincinnati on a viaduct that was designed to connect with the Big

Four tracks along the union depot approach, its line was effectively separated from the CH&D even though the sheer density of rail lines placed all of them within easy reach of each other. The C&O viaduct at one point lay only 1,226 feet on a direct line from the Hamilton trackage in the neighborhood of Fifth and Baymiller streets, but in order to move cars from one road to the other, the C&O had to make the connection at Cincinnati Transfer and to use the tracks of the Big Four and the B&OSW for a total distance of 2 1/2 miles. The plan, to which the L&N was a party because of its trackage rights over the Chesapeake company, was to build an elevated structure that would in effect unite physically the freight-handling facilities of the West End lines. The Cincinnati Inter-Terminal Company was chartered in the summer of 1903 to implement this program; construction of the viaduct began the following year and was completed in 1905. This was the first link in the great viaduct complex that was to come with the new Ohio River bridge and the union terminal.

The building program that was to round out the Cincinnati system was already under way among the fields and towns of Indiana. The Cincinnati, Richmond and Muncie Railroad was incorporated in March 1900 with the express intention of building a new line between Cincinnati and Chicago along the shortest route between the two cities. Two other companies were formed to carry out the planned construction, and the three together completed the line from Cincinnati to Griffith, Indiana, in June 1904, at which time the three were merged to form the Chicago, Cincinnati and Louisville Railroad. The new road had already operated its first train into Cincinnati in February of the same year, having constructed a small combined freight and passenger station in 1903–4 on McLean Avenue near Eighth Street, at furthest remove from the city's core (fig. 33). The announcement of the building of what was the last Cincinnati station before Union Terminal reported that the company "is having plans prepared for a large passenger station and freight houses" and the company itself claimed that the remote terminal was provided with "the best street car facilities of any station in Cincinnati." Both statements stood considerably at odds with the facts, but the assertion of the shortest distance to Chicago (284.5 miles) was the unvarnished truth.[28] The company negotiated several trackage-rights agreements for access to a Chicago terminal, eventually settling on the Erie Railroad via Griffith and Hammond, Indiana.

The direct line of the CC&L proved to be a double irony: the

Fig. 33. Passenger and freight station, CC&L Railroad, 1903–4, West Eighth Street at McLean Avenue. Reproduced with the permission of the Cincinnati Historical Society.

through traffic was insufficient to provide adequate financial nourishment, since most of the available through business had long ago been preempted by the established companies, and to lay the line on the promising short route to Chicago came to be prohibitive in costs of construction and operation. Moreover, if the CC&L had extended itself to the limits that were originally planned, it would have fulfilled a twenty-year dream and undoubtedly would have suffered even greater financial misfortunes. The "Louisville" of the corporate title arose from the intention of its builders, chiefly William R. Bradford, to construct a line from Cincinnati to Louisville via Madison, Indiana, along the route previously envisioned by Melvil Ingalls. Inadequate capital and poor traffic expectation, however, led to the shelving of what once seemed a promising idea.[29]

The poor traffic of the CC&L, yielding revenues insufficient to pay even operating costs, made the helpless road an easy target for larger railroads with ambition, capital, and hopefully remunerative schemes for generating new traffic. In July 1904 the CH&D acquired control of the Chicago line and made it the middle link in a "Great Central Route" of which the third was the Pere Marquette. The volume of traffic derived from this tripartite arrangement, however, fell short of expectations and proved too little to overcome chronic deficits; as a consequence, the CC&L passed into receivership in 1908 and was sold at foreclosure to the C&O in July 1910. For a number of years afterward it was operated as a separate subsidiary known as the Chesapeake and Ohio of Indiana.

Spectacular railroad engineering is always expensive, and the leading illustration of this rule in Cincinnati is the line of the CC&L Railroad. Since all the valley routes had been occupied by the older roads, the new company had the alternatives either of acquiring local trackage rights, which would have threatened its short-line mileage, or of making a direct assault on the hills that surrounded the river plains and valley floors of Cincinnati. The directors chose the latter course. The range of lofty hills that bounds the Mill Creek flood plain on the west is broken by the relatively narrow, steep-sided valley of Lick Run, lying between Westwood and Price Hill. The CC&L track was built along the south flank of this valley at an average grade of 1.6 percent and a maximum of 1.91 percent from Brighton to the hilltop at Cheviot over a succession of timber trestles required to cross the numerous ravines in the steep slope along Price Hill. Since the rail line lay across the axes of the main tributary valleys of the Ohio River, all the elevation gained in the

The Terminal Pattern of Half a Century

Cheviot crossing was immediately lost in the descent into the Great Miami valley and had to be regained in the climb through the hills toward Richmond. Moreover, the initial cost of building what is virtually a mountain railroad line was increased still further by the need to construct a 680-foot bridge to escape from Mill Creek Valley and another of 480 feet to cross the Great Miami River. These bridges and the Lick Run trestles were originally timber but were later replaced by steel structures.[30] What the company was compelled to spend on right of way it attempted to save on a penny-pinching station: the little two-story timber-framed structure under a gable roof served both passengers and shippers, and its two tracks provided coach yard facilities as well as terminal trackage (fig. 33). When the CC&L lost its independent status, passenger trains were transferred to Baymiller Street Station and eventually to the C&O's Fourth Street Station.

The construction of the CC&L and the Eighth Street depot closed the ring of terminal stations and filled out the pattern of Cincinnati railroads. As we will note in chapter 4, plans were already being advanced for a union station; and they were to be made, unmade, and remade repeatedly in the coming years. Such activity suggested dissatisfaction with the existing arrangement, but since the plans were not to bear fruit for nearly thirty years, we may assume that whatever the defects and the popular view, the arrangements were working well enough. The stations comfortably accommodated a traffic of 250 scheduled trains per weekday around the turn of the century, the total varying from 276 to 243 over the twenty years from 1890 to 1910. They were smoky, homely, inefficient, and strictly hand-operated (airports, we must remember in this context, are voice-operated), but in their urbanistic character they and their associated rail lines were exactly appropriate to the topography and land-use patterns of Cincinnati (figs. 34, 39). The Cincinnati stations, like those everywhere, played a complex role in the functioning of the city and in the image of the city that takes shape in the minds of all who dwell in it or pass through it. They were not only utilitarian structures, places where one boarded or left trains, they were also essential visual and psychological elements, simultaneously serving as nodal points, gateways, and boundaries.[31]

The gateway character of the railroad station has long been recognized and early became a motif in the formal design of the headhouse, appearing in such details as arched entranceways and portes-cocheres, colonnades, lofty windows, vaults, domes, and

Fig. 34. Panoramic view of Cincinnati, 1900. The bridges, from left to right, are the CS, the C&O, the Suspension, the Broadway, and the Ohio end of the L&N. Mill Creek Valley and the upper alluvial plain of the Ohio River occupy the central portion of the picture; Price Hill and Westwood flank it on the left, and Clifton, Mount Auburn, and Walnut Hills on the right. Reproduced with the permission of the Cincinnati Historical Society.

The Terminal Pattern of Half a Century

clock towers. The rail traveler passes through this gateway to enter into the city, or to leave it for places near or far, to conduct business, to return to home, to visit family or friends, or to enjoy holiday and summertime pleasures. The three Cincinnati stations possessed of some architectural distinction (Baymiller Street, Pan Handle, and Central Union) were also visual focal points where the two forms of transportation, urban and intercity, met; and in the case of the Baymiller and the Pan Handle, the headhouse was consciously designed to compel attention, to establish its presence, its function, and its importance to the community. The Baymiller was clearly meant to have a monumental quality, with its corner tower and deeply penetrating double-arched entranceway (fig. 6). The Pan Handle offered a similar experience by means of its massive tower, but its unique feature was the open train shed along Pearl Street, which made it possible for the trains themselves to add drama to the visual experience without in any way interferring with the traffic on surrounding arteries (fig. 16). The design of Central Union Depot, on the other hand, was visually disappointing, the architect of the revised plan having failed to provide any expressive accents except for the entrance to the carriage drive (fig. 23). The two nearer stations (Union and the PC&StL) were close enough to the urban core for the traveler to sense the presence of the city center and to participate immediately in its highly mobile activities. The passage into the core area was made successively by horse-drawn omnibus, streetcar, and automobile; but for the suburbanite traveling to office or store or theater, the penetration into the city was frequently made by foot, so that he was simultaneously actor and spectator in the urban scene. The CH&D station unfortunately lay remote from the commercial heart of the city in a deteriorating neighborhood that was later to become the West End ghetto. After the B&O acquired the Hamilton line, the station declined in importance as the larger company steadily shifted its trains to the union depot.

The two nearer of the large stations and the little Court Street facility also functioned in a physical and a psychological sense as boundaries, a characteristic that was most strongly marked in the case of the union depot. We have taken the focal point of the core area in the days of rail ascendancy as the intersection of Fourth and Vine streets; east and west of it the prestige office buildings, hotels, theaters, and department stores gave way in a few blocks to older office structures, lofts, smaller commercial enterprises, and, in the case of Second and Third streets, to warehouses, old

115

flat buildings, and row houses. This mixture suddenly ended along the lines of Central Avenue and John Street, where the eastern edge of the great complex of passenger stations, freight-handling facilities, warehouses, and tracks announced unmistakably that one had passed from the world of ordinary day-to-day urban activities to an extensive railroad jungle that spread in increasing size, density, and complexity as one moved westward to Mill Creek Valley, the lower end of which has always been the site of the chief rail ganglion of Cincinnati. It was a world of tracks, bridges, viaducts, coach yards, engine terminals, and appurtenant structures that seemed to the urban layman to be impenetrable and forbidding though obviously necessary to the city's material life. On the east side the relations of tracks and streets were a little different because the ranges of eastern hills come down so close to the river as to leave only a narrow corridor for the tracks of the Pennsylvania Railroad and its predecessors. Moreover, Eastern Avenue for much of its length lies contiguous to the rail lines, so that tracks and trains were clearly visible from passing streetcars, and one thus had striking evidence of the railroad as a major urban pathway. Court Street Station was surrounded by yard tracks two of which continued through along the Eggleston Avenue connection, the whole once forming a dense mass of freight tracks, canal, industries, and warehouses that East Court Street cut across to emerge at the foot of the wooded hill under Mount Adams and Eden Park.

The pattern of neighborhoods, communities, and suburbs in and around Cincinnati was decisively fixed by topography and the distribution of metropolitan railroad lines. Mill Creek Valley early became and remained a huge belt of rail yards, main lines, factories, and grain elevators that gradually gave way to a long chain of communities established in a linear series along the lines of the CH&D, the B&O, the Big Four, and their predecessors— Cumminsville, North Side, Winton Place, and Hartwell within the city; Saint Bernard, Elmwood, Wyoming, Woodlawn, Lockland, and Glendale outside it. These railroad arteries have been the chief factor to this day in the great expansion of industrial property throughout the northern part of the valley following World War II (figs. 34, 39). Similar chains of commercial-residential nuclei grew up along the other main lines: Fernbank, Sayler Park, Addyston, North Bend, and Cleves lie in westward succession along the river and the parallel lines of the O&M and the Big Four; Norwood, Oakley, Madisonville, and Madeira extend eastward along the B&O; Pendleton, Wooster, Milford, Loveland, and Morrow were stations on the Little Miami; Pleasant Ridge, Kennedy Heights, Silverton, and Blue Ash lie to the north along the CL&N. Between these strands or chains, until well into the twentieth century, only Mount Adams, Mount Auburn, Walnut Hills, and Clifton could be described as solidly built-up hilltop communities. The consequence was that the city had a unique form and a special kind of urban beauty: between the rail corridors, outside the older neighborhoods on the hills, and everywhere on their steep flanks there were unbroken woodlands dissected by numerous streams, through and along which the streetcars passed on their way to the outlying communities. Such peripheral areas as Westwood, College Hill, and Mount Lookout, as we have seen, would never have grown beyond minor rural settlements without the little railroads that once bound them to the inner city. Even with the coming of the electric street railway, the streetcars for years passed through or along extensive forested hillsides and ravines to reach these distant places.

Train Operations and Locomotives to World War I

Operating Characteristics

When the C&O Railway inaugurated train operations into Cincinnati in January 1889, the various companies that served the city faced the happy prospect of a rapidly rising traffic, measured both in freight tonnage and number of passengers, moving over already busy main and yard tracks (see Appendix C, tables 4 and 5). On the opening of Central Union Depot in 1883 the railroads operated about 120 passenger trains per weekday to transport approximately 8,000 daily passengers in and out of the city. By the early months of 1889, with the coming of the C&O trains and those of its tenant, the Kentucky Central, the totals had risen to 196 scheduled trains and about 12,000 passengers; but the daily average of loaded trains moving into and out of the various stations probably ranged from 210 to 220, depending on the season (summer excursions accounted for a high proportion of extra runs). Central Union Depot, having six participating railroads on its property, enjoyed the lion's share, with a total of ninety-nine trains shown in the public timetables; Baymiller Street came second with fifty-two; the Pan Handle third with thirty-three; and the little Court Street Station at the bottom with eight.[32]

The overwhelming majority of these trains operated on what

were long called accommodation schedules. They ordinarily consisted entirely of coaches, although mail, express, and milk cars were often included in the equipment, and they provided all the metropolitan suburban and short-run intercity local service that existed until the rise of the electric interurban car shortly after the turn of the century. The average number of passengers per train on the local runs was about seventy-five throughout the decade of the 1880s, but the average for all trains was no more than sixty as late as 1889. These figures imply that though the local day coach of the late nineteenth century was scarcely a model of comfort and cleanliness, the frequency of service and the number of seats available guaranteed everyone a tolerable ride from suburb or rural town to city. The great advantage offered by the railroad was reliability: only serious wrecks and floods and blizzards of uncommon magnitude prevented the daily maintenance of schedules. Accidents were common enough, and wooden coaches offered little protection in the event of high-impact collisions, but the truth is that the railroads, even before the adoption of the air brake and the automatic coupler, were progressing rapidly in safety of operations in the ten years of 1880-89. The precise figures for fatalities at Cincinnati do not exist, but the experience of the heavily traveled Boston railroads may offer a guide. The various companies serving the city carried a total of 27,800,197 passengers for the year 1882 with only eight fatalities, of which seven occurred as a consequence of carelessness on the part of the passengers who met their ends.

The most rapidly growing form of rail service at the end of the century was sleeping-car operation, and by 1890 Cincinnati had become the focus of a constantly enlarging web of overnight and long-distance Pullman runs, of which there were seventeen scheduled in each direction in 1889. The location of the city placed it at the center of a ring of major cities all of which lay within a night's trip on the sleeper, and during the sixty years of Pullman ascendancy the night train, departing between nine o'clock in the evening and midnight and arriving between seven and eight in the morning, was the dominant feature of Cincinnati sleeping-car traffic. The cities of the inner or overnight ring, in clockwise order, were Saint Louis, Chicago, Toledo, Detroit, Cleveland, Pittsburgh, Charleston, Knoxville, Louisville, and Nashville. Beyond these the more distant terminals—Washington, Richmond, Baltimore, and New York in the East, Atlanta, Jacksonville, Memphis, and New Orleans in the South—required schedules of sixteen to thirty-six hours. Until the various affiliates of the New York Central and Hudson River Railroad established through service to Boston in 1891, the longest sleeping-car run originating at Cincinnati was the New Orleans route via the L&N. The average of all average speeds of the fastest trains (almost invariably those providing sleeping-car service) operating exclusively over railroads terminating at Cincinnati (as opposed to through sleeping cars running over connecting lines) was 30.01 miles per hour in 1889. The fastest was PC&StL Number 20 (predecessor of the *Cincinnati Limited*) between Cincinnati and Columbus, with an average speed of 34.3 miles per hour, and the slowest was C&O Number Four to Richmond, its 25.1 mile-per-hour average setting a leisurely precedent for mountain railroading that the Chesapeake company has followed throughout its history.[33]

Rail passenger traffic increased at an extremely high rate throughout the decade of the 1880s, the average for the single year being 8.8 percent, sufficient nearly to double the total volume over the ten-year period. This rate of increase continued into the last decade up to 1892, but the panic of the next year and the subsequent severe depression drastically curtailed both freight and passenger traffic, so that generous annual increases turned into the reverse for the mid-portion of the decade, although the World's Columbian Exposition in Chicago (1893) powerfully stimulated midwestern traffic (see Appendix C, table 5). The terminal stations of Cincinnati served at least 14,000 passengers per day in 1892, but the number dropped thereafter and was not regained until the beginning of the new century. The increase in the total number of passengers carried throughout the nation was only 12.3 percent between 1890 and 1900, and we may assume that the Cincinnati volume fell and rose in the same proportion. To accommodate the lively pre-depression business of 1892, the Cincinnati roads operated a total of 272 regularly scheduled trains per weekday, but the actual total of scheduled and extra was very likely an average of about 299 trains. Much of the increase over the three years from 1889 to 1892 came from the inauguration of passenger service by the little Cincinnati and Westwood Railroad. Central Union Depot accounted for nearly half the total, with a minimum of 128 trains per day, and the Baymiller and PCC&StL terminals trailed far behind in second and third positions. The total of nearly 300 daily trains proved to be the largest number operated in and out of Cincinnati stations throughout the entire history of the city's rail service, in spite of the fact that the total passenger traffic, both local and national, continued to climb irregularly but rapidly to the high point of 1920.[34]

The volume of rail transportation at Cincinnati, measured in terms of number of trains, fell during the depression years of the mid-nineties, rose again at the turn of the century, then began a very slow decline, as the electric interurban car quickly attracted a growing share of the vulnerable local traffic (see chapter 4, "Interurban and Rapid Transit Plans"). The great number of regularly scheduled trains that persisted up to the early years of the new century was a consequence of the combined demand for accommodation service outside the limits of the expanding street-car system, and for sleeping-car service on runs of 200 miles or more (the shortest distance for a sleeping-car run was the 128 miles between Cincinnati and Louisville via the O&M). In the three years following 1889 the minimum number of scheduled sleeping-car runs had increased from seventeen to thirty-one per day, or a round-trip total of sixty-two. In 1892 the Big Four moved into the commanding position in this respect, operating a minimum of eight sleepers in each direction on its lines terminating at Cincinnati, and it was to hold the lead until the general collapse of rail passenger service in the decade of the 1960s. The combination of early-morning Pullman arrivals (their departures were spread out through the afternoon and evening) and incoming suburban and rural locals gave the two busiest stations at Cincinnati an extremely high passenger-train density in the morning rush. The railroads at Central Union Depot operated a minimum of twenty-seven weekday trains between the hours of 7:00 and 8:30 A.M., and those at Baymiller Street operated a minimum total of fifteen in the same period of time. The usual number, however, was generally higher; and in the periods of peak travel—Christmas holidays, for example—the union depot was called upon to handle as many as four trains per track per hour. When we recall that no Cincinnati station was equipped with an interlocking system or had an approach of more than two tracks, we realize how much reserve capacity even the seemingly primitive facilities of the 1890s possessed.[35]

The through trains of the larger roads, especially those carrying sleeping cars over highly competitive routes, were operated at steadily increasing speeds in the last decade of the century, when the enthusiasm for fast movement was beginning to become a national mania. Railroads with the necessary motive power and reasonably level, well-maintained track regularly ran trains at

sixty miles per hour, and it was well known though not publicly
admitted that there were frequent unauthorized bursts far above
that figure. The New York Central and Hudson River Railroad
established a record of 112.5 miles per hour in 1893, and there
were other roads that claimed to have operated trains at speeds
reaching and even exceeding two miles per minute shortly after
the turn of the century, but these assertions have not always been
reliably documented. The overall average of average speeds for
representative Cincinnati trains remained well down in the thirties, the maximum of 39.4 miles per hour held by the Big Four's
Southwestern Limited (another kind of preeminence that the
company was to maintain throughout the years), and the minimum of 24.5 established by the Ohio and Northwestern's bucolic
Portsmouth Express. The low averages of the time were chiefly
a consequence of numerous engine changes on long runs and of
minor servicing of train and motive power en route.[36]

The precise effects of all the determinants operating at the
turn of the century formed a complex pattern of changes: local
traffic began to level off and on some lines actually fell as the result of interurban competition; at the same time, the expanding
metropolitan area greatly stimulated local metropolitan traffic,
and the extremely rapid increase in the demand for sleeping-car
service led to increases in the length and number of through
trains. The so-called accommodation trains, however, constituted
the most numerous class in both freight and passenger service,
so that the net result of all these changes was a slight reduction
in the number of trains after 1900 accompanied by a rapid expansion in the total number of cars, passengers, and tons of freight.
Traffic at the terminal stations of Cincinnati reached about 23,800
passengers per weekday by 1910, but the number of trains listed
in the public timetables dropped to 243 per day, a reduction of
twenty-nine trains below the level of 1892, the decrease coming
almost entirely because of the cancellation of passenger service
in 1902 by the Cincinnati-Northwestern (ten daily trains) and the
Cincinnati and Westwood (sixteen trains). The loss was a consequence of the opening of streetcar service to College Hill and
Westwood before the turn of the century.

Central Union Depot continued to accommodate more trains
than the other five stations combined, its 139 scheduled daily
trains representing 57.2 percent of the total. The aging Baymiller
Street Station had entered into its long decline, its total of 31
trains fewer than half the number of 1892, and the PCC&StL

Station thus rose to second place. What continues to be impressive and most important for an assessment of transportation capacity was the ability of the union depot to handle high concentrations of traffic: in the period of 1908-10 the average of scheduled movements was forty-eight trains in the hour and a half between 7:00 and 8:30 A.M. In all the stations together the various railroads operated an average of seventy-four trains within the same hour and a half of a typical weekday morning. A high proportion of these morning arrivals were the premier Pullman trains, the average speed of which had risen to 36.9 miles per hour at the end of the first decade, with the spectacular 50-mile-per-hour average of the *New York Central Limited* at the top (this Big Four–Lake Shore–NYC&HR train was operated as a second section of the *Twentieth Century Limited* east of Cleveland).[37]

Passenger traffic in the nation as a whole and at Cincinnati grew relatively slowly in the years between 1910 and the beginning of World War I, so that passenger service measured in number of trains remained nearly static during this period. In 1913 (traditionally regarded by economists as the last year of normalcy and the base for many changing indices) the Cincinnati lines carried about 24,000 daily passengers in and out of the terminal stations in a likely total of 265 trains, of which 241 were listed in the public timetables. This slight change from the period of 1908-10 followed the establishment of through service by the Erie Railroad, using trackage rights over the former CH&D, to offset the small contractions in service made by the B&O and the L&N. The Erie added four trains to the shrinking traffic at Baymiller Street, while reductions came at the near-capacity Central Union Depot. The station accommodated 136 trains per weekday in 1913 and an average of 145 for the five years of 1908-13, a volume of traffic representing 60 percent of the total at Cincinnati. Yet Central Union was one of the very few metropolitan terminals in the United States to be operated without an interlocking system. Since it had frequently accommodated more than 150 daily trains, it seems reasonable to conclude that with the addition of an interlocking plant, a third approach track to serve coach yard and engine terminal leads, and a fifth 600-foot platform, the station could have comfortably handled a maximum of 240 trains per day. The twin problems, which we shall consider further in subsequent chapters, were floods and restrictions on yard space.[38]

The only noteworthy addition to Cincinnati sleeping-car service in the years immediately preceding World War I came with the inauguration by the Chesapeake and Ohio Railway of a through train operated between Chicago and Old Point Comfort, Virginia, in July 1911. Running over the recently acquired CC&L line between Chicago and Cincinnati and known for most of its short life as the *Old Dominion Limited*, the service survived for six years as the only train other than the B&O's New York–Saint Louis and Detroit-Louisville runs to be operated *through* Cincinnati, which like Chicago and Saint Louis had always been conceived as a terminal and transfer point rather than a way station. The fact that the union depot was a stub-end terminal meant that the C&O train had to be backed into or out of the station, depending on the direction, from or to the foot of the approach to the Ohio River bridge. The company ended the service in July 1917 and returned to its previously established practice of transferring Saint Louis and Chicago Pullmans to the Big Four at Cincinnati.[39]

In the years around the turn of the century the chief freight yards and freight stations of the Cincinnati railroads were located close to the core area, except in cases where transfer points dictated a more distant location. The big classification yards on the periphery of the metropolitan area still lay in the future, although the locations of some were fixed in earlier years. Since the railroads in 1910 handled 95 percent of all tonnage transported, they carried all the l.-c.-l. freight, virtually all single carload lots, and most of the bulk cargo. The first category required freight stations, or houses, as they were usually called, and their efficient operation for the urban economy dictated their location as close to the passenger terminals or to the core area as possible. The houses of the Big Four, B&OSW, C&O, CH&D, and L&N were densely clustered around the union and Baymiller depots; and their counterparts of the eastern lines, CL&N, N&W, and PCC&StL, were located along the river south of Pearl Street or along East Court. The CNO&TP moved close to the urban core in 1906 when it opened a handsome new freight station on Vine Street at Front. In addition to the Cincinnati freighthouses there were smaller stations operated by the C&O and the L&N in Covington and Newport, and there were great numbers of sidings, team tracks, and industrial spurs scattered throughout the industrial areas of the city and its suburbs, where consignees could unload freight directly from car to factory, warehouse, or wagon and, later, truck. The major freight yards served a triple end, as they continue to do at the present time—the making-up or taking-apart of trains, the classification of loaded cars in terms of forwarding road or destination, and the assembly of transfer cars (usually designated yard or transfer cuts). The western roads had packed lower Mill Creek Valley and the West End flood plain so densely with yards and appurtenant structures as to turn the whole area into a sea of freight cars. This growing congestion compelled a number of roads to move out to the metropolitan periphery or to expand facilities already located there—the Big Four to Ivorydale, the L&N to De Coursey, Kentucky, the N&W to Bond Hill, the PCC&StL to East End in the Little Miami valley, and the C&O as far as Silver Grove, a little Kentucky town fifteen miles up the winding river.

Locomotives and Signaling

The increasing weight of rolling stock and freight-car loads, together with the increasing length and speed of freight as well as passenger trains, compelled a rapid and progressive evolution of railroad motive power that was concentrated in the years around the turn of the century. The universal 4-4-0 locomotive, which had served American railroads since their beginnings in the decade of the 1830s, began to give way around 1885 to heavier and more powerful forms. The last of the earlier type to be built for Cincinnati roads was manufactured in 1910 at the Juniata (Altoona) Shops of the Pennsylvania Railroad for the PCC&StL. With a tractive effort of 17,491 pounds, the locomotive clearly outdistanced all of its predecessors and probably carried the 4-4-0 to the peak of its capacity.[40] The first step in the direction of greater power and speed was the return to the forgotten Ten-wheel, or 4-6-0, locomotive, which had been invented in primitive form as long ago as 1836. The additional pair of driving wheels allowed a considerable increase in weight with a corresponding increase in capacity, so that before the end of the century tractive force had been stepped up to double the best that the 4-4-0 could produce. It is difficult to determine when the Ten-wheeler first appeared at Cincinnati: the L&N adopted the form as early as 1870, but the most likely candidates for local use were probably the CH&D 4-6-0s manufactured in 1881 by the Pittsburgh Locomotive Works. Other Cincinnati roads adopted the type mainly during the last decade of the century, the CNO&TP in 1889, the Big Four in 1890, and the PCC&StL in 1889.[41] A slow-speed equivalent of the Ten-wheeler designed expressly for freight service was the Consolidation, or 2-8-0, locomotive. Originally built in 1866 for the Lehigh Valley, it came to Cincinnati via the CNO&TP in 1882.

The Terminal Pattern of Half a Century

A characteristic of all American motive power began to assume the proportions of a serious defect by the mid-nineties. The demand for both speed and power required the rapid generation of steam at pressures of 180 pounds per square inch or more, but the narrow and shallow firebox of locomotives without trailing trucks—that is, without supporting wheels behind the drivers—greatly restricted the rate of combustion and hence the generation of steam. The solution was the introduction of a trailing pair of wheels to support a much enlarged firebox. The new form appeared in 1894 as the Atlantic-type locomotive, with a wheel arrangement of 4-4-2. The most numerous of this type, the most celebrated, and the most spectacular in their performance were the Class E Atlantics of the Pennsylvania Railroad and its western affiliates. They appeared on the PCC&StL in 1899, products of the Juniata Shops at Altoona, and for thirty years the various companies of the Pennsylvania family depended on them for through as well as local service.[42] Atlantics were also common on the B&O, the C&O, and the Big Four, all of them coming shortly after 1900. They were progressively restricted to local service over the years except on the C&O, which retained them on the eastern main line up to 1930 and on the Chicago Division as long as passenger trains survived.[43]

As driving wheels were added to the Ten-wheeler and the Mogul (2-6-0) to increase their length, weight, and power, so a similar step was taken in expanding the Atlantic type (4-4-2) into the Pacific (4-6-2), for forty years the mainstay of passenger motive power in the United States. This useful machine, which saw service on every Class I railroad, was introduced at Cincinnati by the C&O in 1902 in the form of a special design created by W. S. Morris, the company's superintendent of motive power. Similar engines came in the next eight years, with variations developed to suit the conditions of individual roads—on the Big Four and L&N in 1905, the Pennsylvania subsidiaries and the CNO&TP in 1907, and the CH&D in 1910.[44] The addition of the trailing truck to engines designed strictly for freight service came shortly after the creation of the Pacific. The 2-8-0 locomotive was expanded to the 2-8-2, or Mikado type, in 1903, but it was not to appear in Cincinnati until 1911, when the C&O once again acted as the pioneer in introducing the new form.

The appearance of new locomotive types of much increased power coincided with a period of fundamental technological innovations that drastically improved the performance and efficiency of the steam engine. The superheater and the mechanical

125

stoker were developed almost simultaneously in a series of experiments carried on by various inventors over the years from 1905 to 1911. A leading experimenter in the creation of a practical power-driven stoker was W. T. Hanna of Cincinnati. The feedwater heater, a device for preheating boiler water by means of exhaust gases, appeared in primitive form around 1910 but did not become common on American railroads until the decade of the 20s. At the same time the outside valve gear—that is, located outside the driving wheels and the driving rods—began to be installed on newly manufactured locomotives in 1910, a seemingly minor innovation that greatly improved the accessibility of this complex mechanism while reducing wear and damage.

The rapid increase in the length, number, and speed of trains around 1900 made the manual block-signal system for controlling the speed and spacing of trains a necessity on heavily traveled lines, and made the far more reliable form of the electric automatic block signal at least highly desirable for economy as well as safety. The manual block signal was invented in the United States by Ashbel Welch in 1865, and its automatic electrical counterpart by William Robinson in 1871, although the electrically operated semaphore that dominated railroad signaling until 1930 did not appear until 1893. The mechanical interlocking type came as early as 1870 and the electropneumatic type in 1883, but neither kind was to be built for a terminal station in Cincinnati until the opening of the new union terminal in 1933. The railroads used a considerable variety of signals during the last years of the nineteenth century, the great majority of the manually operated form, but the different types began to disappear around 1890 in favor of the lower-quadrant semaphore signal. By 1898, however, a few roads had begun to experiment with the much superior upper-quadrant form, which was more easily read and less ambiguous than the lower quadrant and which made possible the showing of three clearly distinct indications with a single blade (clear, approach, and stop) in place of only two for the older signal. The adoption of the newer form came rapidly after 1905, when a committee of the American Railroad Signal Association recommended its installation.

By the decade of the nineties the C&O, the Big Four, and the PCC&StL railroads had placed varying lengths of manual block systems into service on main lines, but the leading company among the Cincinnati group in this respect was the CNO&TP. The enterprising officers of this road began the installation of electric automatic signals in 1891, and by the turn of the century they had placed nearly 80 percent of its main line under similar protection and progressively extended this length to 100 percent by 1909. Two forms of signals were dominant on the CNO&TP in 1900, the lower-quadrant semaphore and the so-called Hall banjo signal, in which a banjo-shaped box at the top of the wayside mast contained a lens covering automatically operated red and white discs, but both these types were gradually superseded by upper-quadrant semaphores after 1905. The rest of the Cincinnati roads favored the manual-block form, which spread rapidly after 1900 on all the lines other than the CH&D and the L&N, but except for the CNO&TP the local companies were slow to adopt automatic signaling until 1910. Although three of the Cincinnati roads had by that year placed more than 90 percent of their passenger-carrying lines under block-signal control, and a fourth had come close to 80 percent, the proportion of automatic block was only 9.9 percent of the total. By 1914 the mileage under automatic block signals had climbed to 21 percent of the total, and by 1920 virtually 100 percent of the passenger-carrying main lines radiating from Cincinnati were operated under block-signal control, with only the L&N acting as something of a laggard. The introduction of automatic signaling in some cases nearly doubled track capacity over what it had been under operation by timetable and train order, an increase in capacity that was gained without any increase in the volume of space and the area of ground occupied by the right of way, the trains, and the associated structures. One sees, in this phenomenon, a genuine example of technical progress measured in human as well as economic terms.[45]

1. The four companies involved in this merger were the Pittsburgh and Steubenville, the Holliday's Cove, the Central Ohio, and the Steubenville and Indiana, the completion of which in 1865 opened a continuous line of railroad from Pittsburgh through Columbus and Dayton to the Indiana state line near Richmond. The merger of 1868 was accompanied by the reorganization of the Pittsburgh and Steubenville into the Pan Handle Railway Company, whose homely name was derived from the popular designation of the narrow northward extension of West Virginia between the Ohio River and the western boundary of Pennsylvania. The expression has survived to the present day: after the various roads were leased to, and merged with, the Pennsylvania Railroad, the company retained the name in the designation of its Pittsburgh-Columbus line as the Pan Handle Division. The term was later applied to the broad northward extension of Texas between the states of Oklahoma and New Mexico and

to the similar westward extension of Oklahoma itself. The Texas designation also found its way into railroad names, in this case as a single word in the official corporate title of the Panhandle and Santa Fe Railroad (later merged with the Atchison, Topeka and Santa Fe).

2. In the two years of 1880 and 1881 the number of passengers increased 11.1 percent (from 888,791 in 1880 to 987,314 in 1881) and the freight tonnage 13.3 percent (from 782,495 tons to 886,415, respectively, in the same years). For the passenger and freight traffic of Cincinnati railroads from 1885 to the present, see Appendix C, table 5.

3. For an illustration of the Broad Street Station train shed and supporting frame, see Carl W. Condit, *American Building Art: The Nineteenth Century*, fig. 114. No drawings or photographs of the supporting structure under the Cincinnati shed appear to have survived, so that we are compelled to rely on descriptions in various company histories. The Polonceau truss was named from its French inventor, Remi Polonceau, who was granted a patent for the form in 1845. The Pennsylvania Railroad had acquired a controlling interest in both the PC&StL and the PW&B by 1880.

4. Although the vicissitudes of the highly unstable American economy often brought disaster to the most prosperous of railroads, the annual report of the PC&StL for the year ended 31 December 1882 was fairly typical of the larger Ohio Valley and Great Lakes roads with a stable as well as expanding traffic base:

Freight revenues	$2,927,997.70
Passenger revenues	994,220.27
Mail revenues	174,175.76
Express revenues	100,240.86
Non-operating income	18,288.49
Total revenues	$4,214,923.08
Total operating expenses	2,830,999.80
Net operating income	$1,383,923.28
Operating ratio	67.17%

(Total revenue derived from the operation of passenger and mail trains was $1,268,636.89, or 30.1 percent of the total of all revenues.)

5. I am indebted to John W. Hauck for details of the chronology of Cincinnati Northern stations.

6. For a short period after January 1883 control of the Cincinnati Northern passed to the Toledo, Cincinnati and Saint Louis Railroad.

7. We have followed the history of these roads in chapter 1, but the Dayton Short Line requires further identification. The original Dayton and Cincinnati Railroad, which was popularly known as the Dayton Short Line and had planned the abortive Walnut Hills tunnel, was reorganized as the Dayton and Cincinnati Short Line in 1871, and again as the Cincinnati Railway Tunnel Company in 1877. Like the huge tunnel, however, it was destined to die unfinished and unused, its properties finally acquired by the Cincinnati, Lebanon and Northern Railroad in 1902. (I am again indebted to John W. Hauck for the details of these corporate transformations.)

8. "Union Depot at Cincinnati," *Railroad Gazette* 5:8 (22 February 1873), p. 79.

9. "Cincinnati Union Depot," *Railroad Gazette* 13 (8 July 1881): 379, and 14 (16 June 1882): 367.

10. The Eastlake style was a popular Gothic Revival mode of the time that was characterized by great attenuation of vertical elements such as mullions,

door posts, finials, and other decorative details. An alternative designation is "Stick style," a term coined by the architectural historian Vincent Scully.

11. The available photographs (see, for example, fig. 24) suggest that the opening of the station was fixed by the recession of the 1883 flood and that the headhouse was in an unfinished state when operations began.

12. Changes in station design during the great building period that extended from about 1880 to World War I arose not only from constantly increasing traffic but from drastic increases in the length of trains. In the earlier part of this period the overwhelming majority of trains were the local or accommodation variety consisting of three or four cars and seldom carrying more than 100 passengers. The sleeping and parlor car trains were as a rule similar in length though less well patronized. The latter kind of traffic, however, grew rapidly in volume, with the consequence that train length had grown to eight or ten cars by the time of World War I. The expansion of Pullman traffic following the war and the continuing increase in the volume of mail and express resulted in train lengths of 12–14 cars, which was sometimes increased still further by the consolidations of schedules compelled by depression-born economies. The consequences of all these changes were revisions in station track plans, the lengthening of certain platforms, and the extensions of train-shed protection by means of separate platform canopies. The history of these changes and their causes could be clearly read through the long life of Central Union Depot.

I am using the name *Pullman* as synonymous with sleeping and parlor car service. Although there were at one time a number of different companies providing equipment of this kind, the Pullman Company had gained a near-monopoly by the beginning of World War I. The only roads in the United States that continued to operate their own sleeping cars were the Chicago, Milwaukee and Saint Paul ("Pacific" was added to the title following the reorganization of 1927) and the Minneapolis, Saint Paul and Sault Sainte Marie (Soo Line).

13. Unlike the financially ailing latecomers, either of the two original users of the union depot could have afforded the million-dollar cost of the new terminal: for the six months of 1 July–31 December 1882 the operating ratio of the proprietary company (CIStL&C) was only 61 percent, leaving a net operating income of $550,068 from revenues of $1,410,780; for the calendar year of 1882 the operating ratio of the initial tenant (CCC&I) was 66.7 percent, the net operating income having been $1,477,822 from gross revenues of $4,441,601.

14. The high point of steam railroad mileage in the United States (as distinct from electric interurban) came in 1916, when the total reached 254,037 miles; and the peak year for passenger traffic was 1920, when Class I railroads (originally line-haul roads with total revenues above $1,000,000, later $3,000,000) carried 1,234,862,000 passengers. It is difficult to choose a year for maximum freight traffic, since the total volume of both tons and ton-miles reached successively higher levels in the years following World War II, but the railroads' proportion of freight traffic had shrunk to 39.83 percent of the total by 1970. In 1910 the figure was 95 percent, most of the remainder going by water. The rounding-out of the Cincinnati rail complex thus coincided with the distinguishable phases in the evolution of the national system. (For the traffic of Cincinnati railroads, see Appendix C, table 5.)

15. The respective corporate titles of the three cable-car lines were the following: Walnut Hills Cable Road (terminating at Woodburn Avenue in Walnut Hills); Mount Auburn Cable Railway; property of the Cincinnati Street Railway Company.

16. John Roebling's masterpiece had to be drastically strengthened and reconstructed in 1895–98 to support the new streetcar loads on top of a wagon

traffic that was alone approaching the limit of the allowable load (fig. 13). The reconstruction included the following additions: new Cincinnati approach viaduct from Second Street to the Ohio tower; two new cables and associated anchorages; new and much deepened stiffening trusses; new wind stays. The reconstruction more than doubled the allowable loading of the bridge: the combined capacity of the original cables was 8,400 tons; the combined capacity of the new set is 12,000 tons, for a new total of the four cables of 20,400 tons. The traffic at the time of reconstruction comprised 1,000 carts and wagons, 1,200 streetcars, and 6,000 pedestrians per day.

17. The completion of the C&O bridge over the Ohio River at Sciotoville, Ohio, in 1917 allowed the road to move the bulk of the Pocahontas-Great Lakes traffic over its own line to Columbus and thence over the line of the C&O-controlled Hocking Valley Railroad north thereof. The larger road acquired and merged the Hocking company in 1930.

18. Editorial, *Railway Age* 14:14 (5 April 1889), p. 217.

19. "Miscellaneous Projects," *Railway Age* 8:4 (25 January 1883), p. 53.

20. This trackage-rights agreement became feasible only because of the prior acquisition in 1890 of the Cincinnati, Wabash and Michigan Railway, one of the eight smaller lines that were consolidated with the CCC&I and the CIStL&C to form the Big Four system. The Wabash company extended down the length of eastern Indiana, with its southernmost segment lying between Greensburg and North Vernon.

21. C. P. Huntington, after whom the city of Huntington was named, is chiefly famous for organizing, controlling, and guiding the construction of the Central Pacific and the Southern Pacific railroads.

The C&O's big Cincinnati bridge was built by a subsidiary with another long-winded corporate title, the Covington and Cincinnati Elevated Railroad and Transfer and Bridge Company.

By locating the line along the south bank of the Ohio River, on the upper alluvial terrace out of reach of floods, the builders of the C&O made the eastern main line the only one of the Cincinnati group over which trains do not have to operate on an ascending grade in leaving the metropolitan area.

22. The C&O's Cincinnati bridge marked a number of important advances in long-span bridge construction through the initial application of recent theoretical developments to a bridge of great size and heavy loadings. The rail line occupied the center corridor of the bridge, between the trusses, and the roadways flanked by outer sidewalks lay outside the trusses. This distribution of arteries accounts for the extreme eccentricities of loading. The three river spans were respectively 476, 550, and 476 feet in length, for a total of 1,502 feet, and were carried by trusses with polygonal top chords and a maximum depth of 84 feet. The subdivided Pratt truss introduced by Burr superseded the dominant Whipple truss for long-span bridges, and the earlier form was soon permanently eclipsed. The masonry piers of the C&O structure rested on foundations built up of solid blocks of concrete supported by timber cribbing. The extremely generous loading factors made it possible for the bridge to carry engine loads 55 percent higher and train loads 100 percent higher than those that were the rule when it was completed. By the time of World War I, however, it was clearly approaching its limit, and only severe restrictions on train speeds kept it in use until it was replaced in 1928-29.

23. To the best of my knowledge the junction point on the C&O approach viaduct where the lines to the freight and passenger stations diverged was the first in Cincinnati in which switches were controlled by an interlocking plant. I have seen no documents to support this assertion, but it is unlikely that switches would have been hand-thrown at trackside on a high, narrow iron bridge.

The Terminal Pattern of Half a Century

24. The merger of both the KC and the LC&L into the L&N system produced one of the more absurd irrationalities in the pattern of Cincinnati rail lines. Of the two L&N routes, the one extending westward and southward to Louisville terminated at the Pan Handle Station, on the east side of the city, whereas the line extending south and southeastward to Knoxville and Atlanta in effect entered the union depot, on the west side. The two lines still intersect at Latonia, Kentucky. To compound the difficulties, the L&N from time to time operated various local trains to and from the C&O's Fourth Street Station and thus earned the possibily unique distinction of using three separate passenger terminals in a single city. Since travelers were understandably confused, the company tried to be helpful by means of the costly device of operating a connection train between Central Union Depot and Latonia for every through train operated at the Pan Handle Station.

25. The overall length of the L&N bridge between approaches is 1,649 feet, and the river crossing is divided into six spans of which one is 133 feet in clear length, four are 198 feet 6 inches each, and one (channel) 505 feet 10 inches, for a total of 1,432 feet 10 inches. The maximum depth of the channel trusses (scaled from drawings) is about 110 feet. The sharp curve of the rail deck at the Cincinnati end, necessary to turn the track to a direction parallel to the railroad lines lying along the river bank, is carried on a series of brick vaults that are still standing; beyond these, however, the connection is a steel-girder viaduct. The presence of the railroad track on a city street in Newport represents a surviving example of a once common practice in the South, the combining of the railroad right of way with a traffic artery of the town. A number of communities in Kentucky revealed this questionable symbiosis until recent years.

26. The schedule of this long-drawn-out program of replacements was as follows: one span, Cincinnati approach, 1890; three more, Cincinnati, 1895–96; two more, Cincinnati, 1896; remaining 20, Cincinnati, 1902; one span, Ludlow approach, 1911. The loading factors indicate how locomotive and car weight had increased in the 13 years since the original span was completed (1877–90): the allowable loads were two 2-8-0 locomotives with individual driving axle loads of 41,000 pounds, followed by a unit train load of 4,000 pounds per lineal foot. The total allowable maximum load on the Dixville bridge, by comparison, was 2,073 pounds per lineal foot.

27. The list I have culled from the *Official Guide*, railroad journals, and the publications of investment services, is, I am sure, far from definitive, but at least it provides an index to the importance of the city in the minds of entrepreneurs. In addition to the number of railroads with "Cincinnati" titles, there were ten companies that served the city over the years that did not include the name of the city in their corporate designations. Two of the 142 companies had identical names, Cincinnati Northern: the first was the narrow-gauge predecessor of the Cincinnati, Lebanon and Northern, and the second eventually became the Jackson, Michigan, Branch of the Big Four. Among the Cincinnati group the Dayton and Cincinnati Terminal was incorporated in June 1894 to pursue once again the vain dream of a high-speed short line connecting the two cities via the long tunnel under Walnut Hills. The project died, and its demise seems to have brought down the curtain on these abortive schemes for the last time.

It is a revealing commentary on changing fortunes, perhaps, that the name *Cincinnati* would eventually disappear from the titles of the roads serving the city, although many of the earlier corporations have continued a legal existence to the present time under their original names.

28. The first quotation in the preceding sentence is from "Cincinnati, Ohio," under "Other Structures," *Railroad Gazette* 35:34 (28 August 1903), p. 610; the second, from a company advertisement, *Official Railway Guide*, March 1909, p. 539.

The comparative distances between Cincinnati and Chicago of the four remaining through passenger routes in 1904 were the following: PCC&StL via Richmond and Logansport, 299.7 miles; Big Four-Illinois Central via Indianapolis and Kankakee, 303.8; CH&D-Monon via Indianapolis and Monon, 308.0; PCC&StL-Pittsburgh, Fort Wayne, and Chicago via Richmond and Fort Wayne, 315.0.

29. The persistent dream of a Louisville line via the north bank of the Ohio River reached the stage of incorporation in this case but never progressed beyond it. The state of Indiana granted a charter to the Cincinnati and Louisville Railroad in the fall of 1902 to build a line southwestward from a junction with the existing CC&L track in the Great Miami valley, but apparently not even the survey was started.

30. The elevations of successive stations on the CC&L between Cincinnati and Richmond clearly indicate the roller-coaster character of the line:

Station	Elevation (feet)	Miles
Cincinnati (Fourth Street)	ca. 530	0.0
Cincinnati (Eighth Street)	510	. . .
Cincinnati (Brighton)	557	3.2
Cheviot	870	6.9
Miami	524	16.1
Fernald	529	20.7
Shandon	629	24.0
Okeana	670	27.5
Peoria	1,005	34.6
Cottage Grove	1,042	46.5
Kitchell	1,108	52.4
Boston	1,122	56.4
Richmond	948	64.5

31. I have here adopted the useful terminology formulated by Kevin Lynch in his book *The Image of the City.*

32. For the total number of rail passengers carried in the United States at five-year intervals, an estimate of the number using Cincinnati stations per weekday, and the total freight and passenger traffic of Cincinnati railroads at five-year intervals, see Appendix C, tables 4 and 5.

The distribution of listed daily trains by station and railroad company for the year 1889 is given in the following table:

Central Union Depot
CCC&I	24
CIStL&C	20
CNO&TP	14
O&M	14
CW&B	13
KC	8
C&O	6

New York, Pennsylvania and Ohio (Erie) [a]

Total	99
Total plus 10 percent	109

Baymiller Street Station
CH&D	42
Cincinnati-Northwestern	10

Total	52
Total plus 10 percent	57
Pan Handle Station	
PC&StL 10	
L&N 8	
Cincinnati and Richmond 7	
Cincinnati and Muskingum Valley 4	
Ohio and Northwestern 4	
Total	33
Total plus 10 percent	37
Court Street Station	
CL&N 6	
Ohio and Northwestern[b] 2	
Total	8
Total plus 10 percent	9
Columbia (Pendleton)	
Cincinnati, Georgetown, and Portsmouth 4	
Total, all stations	196
Total plus 10 percent	216

[a] The NYP&O was one of several of the Erie's transformations following receiverships (new corporate title of Atlantic and Great Western following control by Erie). One of the most puzzling details of Cincinnati rail operations was the disposition of the Erie trains. The company's predecessor in the middle area (Atlantic and Great Western) never completed the Cincinnati branch beyond Dayton. Since early issues of the *Official Railway Guide* do not indicate stations used in multi-station cities, and since company timetables disappear as fast as they are issued, it is frequently a matter of speculation to determine how the Erie flock was stabled. In 1889 it seems clear that the CCC&I provided connection service and carried through sleeping cars.

[b] The Ohio and Northwestern and its successors, the Cincinnati, Portsmouth and Virginia and the N&W, split their schedules between the Pan Handle and the Court Street stations until 1928, to the predictable confusion of passengers. This practice was a Cincinnati railroad disease until the opening of Union Terminal in 1933.

With an estimated daily traffic at Cincinnati of 12,400 passengers (see Appendix C, table 4), the average number of passengers per train was about 60.

33. Through sleeping-car runs and representative schedules of Cincinnati trains for the year 1889 are given in the following tables:

THROUGH SLEEPING-CAR RUNS

Railroad	Destination
C&O	Richmond
Chicago, Saint Louis, and Pittsburgh [a]	Chicago
CH&D	Detroit
CIStL&C	Chicago
CNO&TP	Atlanta
	Jacksonville
	New Orleans
	Shreveport
CW&B	Jersey City
CCC&I	Cleveland
	New York
L&N	Nashville
	New Orleans
O&M	Louisville
	Saint Louis
PC&StL	New York

133

AVERAGE SPEED OF THROUGH TRAINS

Railroad	Train	Destination	Time (Hrs. - Min.)		Distance (Miles)	Average Speed (MPH)
C&O	No. 4	Richmond	23	30	590	25.1
Chicago, Saint Louis and Pittsburgh [a]	No. 1	Chicago	10	35	298	28.2
CH&D	No. 16	Detroit	9	20	262	28.1
CIStL&C	No. 1	Chicago	10	10	304	29.9
CNO&TP	No. 1	Chattanooga	10	45	335	31.2
CNO&TP-Q&C	No. 1	New Orleans	27	05	826	30.5
CW&B	N.Y. Express	Parkersburg	6	15	195	31.2
CCC&I	No. 12	Cleveland	7	15	244	33.7
L&N	No. 3	New Orleans	35	10	921	26.2
O&M	No. 1	Saint Louis	10	35	341	32.2
PC&StL	No. 20	Columbus	3	30	120	34.3
Average Speed						30.01

SOURCE: *Official Railway Guide.*

[a] Through line with Cincinnati and Richmond Railroad.

34. The distribution of listed daily trains by station and railroad company for the year 1892 is given in the following table:

Central Union Depot
CCC&StL	42	
B&OSW	39	
O&M	14	
CNO&TP	13	
C&O	8	
L&N [a]	8	
KC [b]	4	
Total		128
Total plus 10 percent		141

Baymiller Street Station
CH&D	50	
Cincinnati and Westwood	16	
Cincinnati-Northwestern	10	
Total		76
Total plus 10 percent		83

PCC&StL Station
PCC&StL	34	
L&N	8	
Cincinnati, Georgetown and Portsmouth	4	
Cincinnati and Muskingum Valley	2	
Total		48
Total plus 10 percent		53

Court Street Station
CL&N	6	
Cincinnati, Portsmouth and Virginia	6	
Total		12
Total plus 10 percent		13

Fourth Street Station
KC	6	
Total		6
Total plus 10 percent		7

Cincinnati and Westwood Brighton Station
Cincinnati and Westwood	2	
Total		2

Total all stations   272
Total plus 10 percent   299

^a The L&N trains using Central Union Depot were shuttle trains operated to and from Latonia to connect with the L&N trains arriving at, and departing from, the PCC&StL Station.

^b The Kentucky Central had come under the control of the L&N by 1892.

35. Special movements of passengers, occurring under the conditions of normal peacetime travel, reached astonishing proportions in the days of low-fare excursions. A possible record for Cincinnati before the turn of the century came on 1 August 1899, when the CH&D participated in a Niagara Falls excursion that carried 3,199 passengers, requiring a total of 37 sleeping cars, 34 coaches, and 9 parlor cars, which were moved in a special train operated in seven sections.

36. The average speed of through trains for the years 1891-92 is given in the following table:

Railroad	Train	Destination	Time (Hrs. - Min.)		Distance (Miles)	Average Speed (MPH)
B&OSW	No. 2	Saint Louis-Jersey City	34	25	1,119.0	32.5
C&O	Fast Flying Virginian	Washington	19	18	596.0	30.9
CH&D	No. 32	Chicago	9	15	307.3	33.2
CNO&TP	No. 1	New Orleans	27	05	826.0	30.5
CCC&StL	Southwestern Limited	New York	22	35	892.1	39.4
CCC&StL	No. 17	Chicago	9	16	305.6	33.0
L&N	No. 1	New Orleans	29	10	921.0	31.5
O&NW	Portsmouth Express	Portsmouth	4	20	106.0	24.5
PCC&StL	No. 2	Jersey City	21	52	758.0	34.7
Average Speed						32.24

37. The distribution of listed daily trains by station and railroad and representative schedules of 1908-10 are given in the following tables:

DISTRIBUTION OF TRAINS

Central Union Depot
B&OSW   52
CCC&StL   52
L&N   16
CNO&TP   14
C&O   5
Total   139
Total plus 10 percent   153
PCC&StL Station
PCC&StL (including C&MV
connections)   36
L&N   10
N&W   4
Total   50
Total plus 10 percent   55
Baymiller Street Station
CH&D (including Erie cars)   31
Total   31
Total plus 10 percent   34
Court Street Station
CL&N   6
N&W   4
Total   10
Total plus 10 percent   11

135

Fourth Street Station
C&O	5	
L&N	4	
Total		9
Total plus 10 percent		10

Eighth Street Station
CC&L	4	
Total		4
Total all stations		243
Total plus 10 percent		267

AVERAGE SPEED OF THROUGH TRAINS
(1910)

Railroad	Train	Destination	Time (Hrs. - Min.)		Distance (Miles)	Average Speed (MPH)
B&OSW	No. 1	Jersey City-Saint Louis	32	14	1,118.2	34.7
C&O	C&O Limited	Washington	17	05	598.1	35.0
CC&L	No. 1	Chicago	10	00	284.5	28.5
CH&D-CI&L	No. 33	Chicago	8	00	308.0	38.5
CNO&TP	Queen and Crescent Special	New Orleans	24	45	835.7	33.8
CCC&StL	NYC Limited	New York	17	45	885.9	49.9
CCC&StL	White City Special	Chicago	8	20	305.6	36.7
L&N	No. 34	Atlanta	16	20	489.0	30.0
PCC&StL	Cincinnati and N.Y. Express	Jersey City	16	41	757.1	45.4
Average Speed						36.9

SOURCE: *Official Guide of the Steam Railways,* etc.

38. A study of terminal capacities conducted by the American Railway Engineering Association for its convention of March 1913 produced the following data on actual and potential traffic at Central Union Depot:

Number of tracks	8
Number of platforms (width 13-15 feet)	4
Length of platforms	1 @ 600 feet
	3 @ 650 feet
Number of trains arriving per day	67
Number of trains departing per day	69
Total number of daily trains	136
Number of trains in peak hour	28
Number of trains using one track in peak hour	4
Estimated potential number of trains, peak hour	30
Estimated potential number of trains using one track, peak hour	5

SOURCE: Droege, *Passenger Terminals and Trains,* p. 198.

These estimates suggest that the station could accommodate no more than 138 daily trains without delays, unless additional trains were conveniently spread over vacant midday hours. Other investigations carried out in 1908-11, however, revealed that the station regularly accommodated 153 trains per weekday, and that there were many occasions of heavy summertime and holiday travel when the total reached 160, but there is no question that this volume gave rise to delays that became increasingly exasperating as train lengths grew and schedules shortened. To understand the capacity of a rail terminal, it must be recalled that for every loaded train movement there must be a corresponding empty or reverse movement of the train to and from the coach yard and a cor-

The Terminal Pattern of Half a Century

responding movement of the road engine running light to and from the engine terminal (empty trains are handled by yard engines). The 136 scheduled trains at Central Union Depot would thus require an additional 136 empty-train movements and 136 light-engine movements, for a total of 408 movements per day. In the case of the peak-hour traffic, there would be 84 such movements, or an average of something below 1.4 per minute passing through the throat, the precise number depending on the number of empty passes that would have been made outside the hour.

A comparative study of terminal capacities over the years 1908-13 yielded the following data for leading metropolitan stations in the United States:

Station	Year Opened	Number of Tracks	Number of Trains Per Day	Number of Trains Per Track Per Day
Boston, North	1894	23	607	26.4
Boston, South	1899	28	786	28.1
Chicago, La Salle Street	1903	11	210	19.1
Chicago, North Western	1911	16	300	18.8
Chicago, Union	1880	9	270	30.0 [a]
Cincinnati, Central Union [b]	1883	8	153	19.1
Cincinnati, PCC&StL [b]	1881	6	55	9.1
Hoboken, Lackawanna	1906	14	263	18.8
Jersey City, Pennsylvania	1892	12	334	27.8
Kansas City, Union	1913	16	313	19.6
New York, Grand Central	1913	66	479	7.3
New York, Pennsylvania	1910	21	392	18.7
Philadelphia, Broad Street	1893	16	574	35.9 [c]
Saint Louis, Union	1894	32	322	10.1
Washington, Union	1907	26	244	9.4

SOURCES: A. S. Baldwin, "Factors Governing the Design of Passenger Terminals" [see Bibliography]; Droege, op. cit., pp. 198-99.

[a] The figures for Chicago Union Station are somewhat misleading because it was operated as two stub-end stations placed back-to-back, theoretically doubling its track capacity.

[b] The Cincinnati stations were the only facilities in this group to be operated without interlocking systems. This defect required a corps of switchmen who threw all switches by hand at the trackside and provided manual signals to all enginemen for governing train movements.

[c] Broad Street Station had the highest traffic density of any terminal in the United States, with 35.9 trains per track per day and a peak-hour traffic of 66 trains (the maximum for peak hour of 90 was reached at South Station, Boston, for years after its opening in 1899). The high Broad Street total was possible chiefly because of the spacious approach line, which consisted of seven tracks serving the terminal proper and two serving a local freight house (Philadelphia's notorious "Chinese Wall," which for 60 years prevented the orderly development of the Market Street blocks west of Broad).

It is instructive to compare the American traffic with that at the leading London terminals for 1967-68, when through passenger service had come close to disappearing in the United States:

Station	Number of Tracks	Number of Trains Per Day	Number of Trains Per Track Per Day
Liverpool Street	18	1,001	55.6
Waterloo	21	1,214	57.8
Victoria	17	1,031	60.6

SOURCE: Alan Jackson, *London's Termini* (New York: Augustus M. Kelley, 1969), p. 348.

39. Although the C&O was free of direct competition on the Chicago-Cincinnati-Tidewater runs, it operated the *Old Dominion Limited* on a schedule that outclassed those of the company's other premier trains. The long run of 950.3 miles was covered, according to the 1913 timetables, in 26 hours 55 minutes, for an average speed of 35.3 miles per hour. Even in the heyday of Big Four service on the Indiana lines, the overall time to the eastern Chesapeake terminals was never reduced below 24 hours. The Old Dominion had various names in its short

137

life: it was originally the *Eastern and Western Express* and then finally the *C&O Limited*.

The existence of such through trains as the *Old Dominion* pointed up another problem in the operation of Central Union Depot, namely, the need to make reverse movements for trains running through the city. The reverse movements of the C&O trains were relatively short, since the foot of the approach viaduct lay near Mill Street, a little more than three blocks from the rear end of the train shed. The B&O lines, however, lay in Mill Creek Valley, and through trains running between Saint Louis and the East and between Detroit and Louisville had to back for about a mile over the old Ohio and Mississippi track along the line of Front Street. The only alternative to this tedious procedure was the parking of Cincinnati sleeping cars at Cincinnati Transfer (in the case of all-Pullman trains), where they were cut into trains passing through the busy ganglion. This practice was followed between World War I and the opening of Union Terminal for the B&O's premier train, the *National Limited*, which was, until the depression of 1930, made up only of Pullman sleeping and club cars and a dining car.

40. The essential physical data for the Pennsylvania Lines 4-4-0 (Class D-16) were the following: driving wheel diameter, 80 inches; cylinder dimensions, 18 1/2 × 26 inches; weight of locomotive, 134,500 pounds; boiler pressure, 185 pounds per square inch; tractive force, 17,491 pounds. The large driving-wheel diameter indicates an engine designed for high-speed service. (For illustrations of these and similar locomotives, see Alvin F. Staufer, *Pennsy Power*, pp. 107-8.)

41. A typical freight-handling machine at the turn of the century was the CH&D Class B-54 4-6-0, manufactured by the Pittsburgh Locomotive Works in 1902-3. The physical data were the following: driving wheel diameter, 57 inches; cylinder dimensions, 19 × 26 inches; weight of locomotive, 136,000 pounds; boiler pressure, 180 pounds per square inch; tractive force, 25,019 pounds. (For illustrations, see Lawrence W. Sagle, *B & O Power*, pp. 70-71.)

The most powerful Ten-wheelers of the time appear to have been those operated by the CNO&TP, several of which developed a tractive force of 35,800 pounds.

The Big Four order of 1890 came at the beginning of one of the largest programs of motive power acquisition in the history of American railroads. The growth of the company's traffic was so rapid that it was compelled to purchase 900 locomotives in the first 25 years of its existence (1890–1915). (For Big Four traffic volume, see Appendix C, table 5, part 5.)

42. Physical data for the culminating design of the Pennsylvania 4-4-2 locomotives were the following: driving wheel diameter, 80 inches; cylinder dimensions, 23 1/2 × 26 inches; weight of locomotive, 240,000 pounds; tractive force, 31,300 pounds. (For illustrations, see Staufer, *Pennsy Power*, pp. 125–29.) One of these locomotives (Number 7002) established a speed record that stood until the mid-century: on 11 June 1905, hauling the Pennsylvania Special, the engine covered three miles near Crestline, Ohio, at an average speed of 127.5 miles per hour.

43. For illustrations of the Big Four and the C&O Atlantic locomotives that were used at Cincinnati, see Alvin F. Staufer, *New York Central Early Power*, pp. 270, 280–81, and Philip Shuster et al., *C & O Power*, p. 217.

44. Physical data for the C&O 4-6-2 were the following: driving wheel diameter, 73 inches; cylinder dimensions, 23 1/2 × 28 inches; weight of locomotive, 243,000 pounds; boiler pressure, 180 pounds per square inch; tractive force, 32,400 pounds. (For numerous illustrations over many years of development, see Shuster et al., *C & O Power*, pp. 230–53.)

The Terminal Pattern of Half a Century

45. The following tables giving mileage of track operated under block signals as of 1 January 1910 and 1 January 1914 indicate how rapidly this form of operation was expanding on trunk lines:

1 JANUARY 1910

Railroad	Miles of Track Operated by Automatic Block	Miles of Track Operated by Manual Block	Total Miles of Track Under Block Signals	Percent of Miles of Track Operated in Passenger Service
B&OSW		60	60	6.0
C&O	48	1,465	1,513	100.0
CH&D	8	93	101	11.1
CNO&TP	335	1	336	100.0
CCC&StL		867	867	49.0
L&N	35	135	170	4.0
N&W	138	1,507	1,645	95.0
PCC&StL	9	1,103	1,112	78.0
Total	573	5,231	5,804	48.9
% of Grand Total	9.9	90.1	100.0	

1 JANUARY 1914

Railroad	Miles of Track Operated by Automatic Block	Miles of Track Operated by Manual Block	Total Miles of Track Under Block Signals	Percent of Miles of Track Operated in Passenger Service
B&O	372	2,730	3,102	100.0
C&O	455	1,133	1,588	98.0
C&O of Indiana		262	262	100.0
CH&D	145	557	702	79.0
CNO&TP	332	4	336	100.0
CCC&StL	101	826	927	49.0
L&N	177	242	419	9.0
N&W	563	1,051	1,614	89.0
PCC&StL	30	1,362	1,392	98.0
Total	2,175	8,167	10,342	64.7
% of Grand Total	21.0	79.0	100.0	

SOURCE: *Railroad Gazette.*

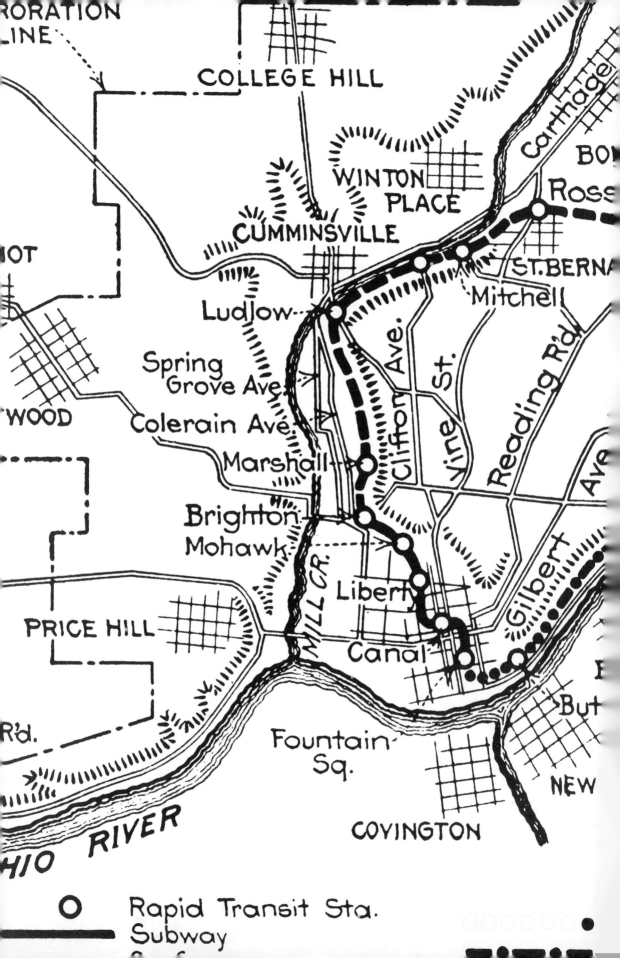

RORATION
LINE

COLLEGE HILL

Carthage

WINTON
PLACE

BO

Ross

CUMMINSVILLE

St. BERNA

Mitchell

OT

Ludlow

Spring
Grove Ave.

Clifton Ave.

Vine St.

Reading R'd.

WOOD

Colerain Ave.

Marshall

Brighton
Mohawk

MILL CR.

Liberty

Gilbert Ave.

PRICE HILL

Canal

But

NEW

R'd.

Fountain
Sq.

COVINGTON

HIO RIVER

O   Rapid Transit Sta.
     Subway

4

Grand Schemes for the
New Century

Proposals for a Union Terminal

When the nation finally shook off the effects of the depression that had begun with the panic of 1893, the accumulated backlog of unsatisfied demands proved an enormously potent stimulus to manufacturing expansion. With the growth of industrial production went the increasing requirements for the transportation of raw materials and finished goods, while expanding wealth attended by growing social mobility led to similar increases in travel for commercial and pleasure-time purposes. The overall consequence for the rail network of the United States was a rate of growth in both freight and passenger traffic during the first two decades of the new century far in excess of that of the national population. The total number of passengers and the total tonnage more than doubled in the twenty-year period, whereas the population of the country increased by little more than one-third.[1] The nine railroad companies serving Cincinnati shared in this prosperity well beyond the proportion one might expect from their mileage. Passenger traffic kept an almost identical pace with that of the rail system as a whole, but the freight tonnage rose at a considerably higher rate: the number of passengers somewhat more than doubled between 1900 and 1920, while the volume of freight increased more than three times, an indication of the extraordinary and rising

Facing page: Detail from figure 40.

economic vitality of the Great Lakes–Pittsburgh–Ohio valley triangle.[2]

In the case of the great coal-hauling railroads, the expansion of tonnage was spectacular to a degree possibly unparalleled in the history of American transportation. With serious waterway competition still largely in the future, since the Corps of Engineers' progressive canalization of the Ohio River was not to be completed until 1929, and with the near absolute dependence of industry on bituminous coal as a source of energy, freight tonnage on the prosperous L&N Railroad tripled in twenty years, and on the equally profitable C&O it quadrupled. The expansion continued at nearly the same rate after 1920, and by the peak years of 1928 and 1930 the respective increases for the two roads reached four and seven and a half times.[3] The revenues produced by the yearly increases in passengers and tonnage meant profitable operations for all but two of the Cincinnati roads, at least until the wartime year of 1918 brought burdens the railroads could not carry and with them the necessary control by the federal government. The average operating ratio of the nine companies was 67.3 percent for the fiscal year ended 30 June 1910, and only for the CH&D and the CC&L were operating expenses so high as to leave either barely enough or too little to pay the interest and other fixed charges. The former managed to get by until the B&O ended the precarious financial state that had plagued it from the beginning, but the latter fell so far short of making ends meet that only the rescue by the C&O brought survival. As for the rest, it was again coal that guaranteed the highest levels of prosperity.[4]

The rapidly expanding traffic in every category, the growing pressures on existing facilities, in places approaching the limits of capacity, the high net incomes that for the most part were more than enough to pay interest charges, rentals, and generous dividends, public demand for improvements in terminals and equipment—all these factors combined in the early years of the new century to push the various railroad companies in the direction of planning a true union terminal at Cincinnati. The fact that such plans were not to bear fruit for nearly thirty years was partly a consequence of natural and man-made cataclysms wholly beyond the directors' control. The failure to act, or the impossibility of acting, as some saw it, in the great days of rail ascendancy was a serious misfortune for the orderly development of the city, one that had lasting undesirable effects. No industry was richer in the production of plans than the railroads of the United States, in part because of their quasi-public character under the aegis of private ownership, and in part because of the unplanned, frequently chaotic, and sometimes self-defeating ways in which cities and the transportation arteries they depended on had grown up. Cincinnati was no exception, and its own problems were intensified by the peculiarly tangled form of its rail system and by the extreme disparities in the financial status of its various constituents. The idea of a unification of station facilities goes back to the Front Street transfer line of 1864 and to the rather grandiose proposals for union freight and passenger terminals that appeared in the succeeding three years. Except for sporadic and fruitless plans for interconnecting belt lines that came and went in the last two decades of the century, however, no serious program of terminal construction was advanced until 1904.

The precarious thread that bound the original plans for the unification of terminals to those that began to multiply after 1900 was the series of proposals for local belt lines. The first came in 1883 with the incorporation of the Cincinnati Suburban Belt Railroad, the directors of which proposed to connect the Cincinnati Northern terminal on East Court Street with the Ohio River and the West End rail lines at the foot of Smith Street. At the same time the officers of the CN announced their intention of moving the company's station to Government Square on East Fifth Street, where the new Post Office and Federal Building was then under construction, and of extending lines to various suburbs.[5] The city's Board of Public Works, however, refused to authorize the construction of an elevated rail line over the canal, Eggleston Avenue, and East Fifth Street, so that the scheme died before it advanced beyond the stage of preliminary planning.

A more ambitious venture came in 1889, when the officers of the CNO&TP, the Little Miami, and the Ohio and Northwestern incorporated the Cincinnati Circle Road with $1,000,000 in capital stock. They proposed the construction of a belt line that was intended to encircle the city from Sedamsville at the western edge to Red Bank in the far East End, the latter being the junction point of the Little Miami and the Cincinnati, Richmond and Chicago. The circuit offered direct connections with all but the two Kentucky roads, the C&O and the L&N. The obvious defect in the plan, which also proved abortive, was that since it was impossible to build a railroad line in the circuit of hills that surround the city, the proposed line could only have duplicated already existing trackage. Except for the missing link necessary

143

to join the Richmond line with the Cincinnati, Washington and Baltimore in Norwood, the circuit was for all practical purposes already in existence. A similar project was launched in February 1896 by Melvil E. Ingalls and a local civil engineer, Robert L. Read, to build a railroad line along the Miami and Erie Canal from Cumminsville to West Fourteenth Street and a union freight depot at the downtown terminal, the whole construction estimated to cost $750,000. Both the trackage and the station were to be jointly owned by the participating rail companies, like the Belt Railway of Chicago. Another proposal for a circuit road came in 1904, when the Cincinnati Suburban Railroad was incorporated to build a line from Red Bank through Oakley, Norwood, Bond Hill, and Winton Place to a junction with the B&OSW at Cumminsville. A similar scheme was offered by Peter Eichels with the incorporation in December 1905 of a company that proposed an electrified belt line along an identical route. Two years later various entrepreneurs represented by John E. Bleekman reorganized the Suburban Belt as the Cincinnati Intersecting Railroad and offered a plan that differed from those of its predecessors only in the higher cost of a continuous double-track line. All these schemes died at the stage of incorporation largely because the extension of the Cincinnati, Portsmouth and Virginia line from Norwood to the Ivorydale yards of the Big Four and the CH&D, intersecting the B&OSW en route (in Bond Hill), very nearly answered the need that the belt lines were designed to satisfy.

Meanwhile, the directors of various railroad companies began to entertain far grander schemes aimed at giving Cincinnati genuine union terminals for both freight and passenger traffic. A great flurry of plans, projects, and announcements emerged from the professional journals and the local press at the turn of the century. In the fall of 1901 the directors of the Pennsylvania Company, controlling the PCC&StL Railroad through majority stock ownership, announced a preliminary plan for a new station at Cincinnati and even went so far as to state that working plans were to be prepared by the prestigious architectural firm of D. H. Burnham and Company, beginning in February 1902. The announcement, however, appears to have been the extent of the company's commitment. In November of the same year the trustees of the Cincinnati Southern Railway announced their own preliminary plans to build a new station in the vicinity of Western Avenue and Banks Street, and to issue terminal bonds in the amount of $500,000 in July 1903 to cover the cost of construction.

144

This modest sum suggests that the road intended only to build for its own accommodation, since the figure stands grossly at odds with the grandiose amounts of money proposed by the backers of a true union terminal. July came and went without further action, but by October much larger schemes began to be publicized. In that month the editors of *Railroad Gazette* reported that plans were "under consideration . . . to build a union station in Cincinnati," and in December they went so far as to say that preliminary drawings for a station to be located at Third and Walnut streets were in preparation at Burnham's office.[6] By mid-1904 the matter had progressed to the point where a union station company had been established to construct a terminal in Cincinnati "to be completed in three years."[7]

During the same period, however, three railroads began in 1903 to initiate what proved to be a far more productive kind of planning with respect to freight-handling facilities. At very nearly the same time the L&N Railroad began constructing a new freight station on West Water Street between Race and Elm, the C&O followed with a similar facility on West Third Street near John, and the CNO&TP, as operating company for the Cincinnati Southern, began building the largest of these structures close to the city core, on the three-block area bounded by Vine and Plum streets, east and west, and Front and Commerce, north and south (fig. 35). All three were opened to service by 1906. The last of the three was easily the best with respect to formal design, planning, and relation to surrounding streets. The two-story office building facing Vine Street was constructed of brick facing on reinforced concrete piers and steel roof trusses, the articulation of its exterior surfaces enhanced by a restrained classical detail. At the center stood the customary clock tower. The station proper was simply a gable roof 1,000 feet long surmounting the rows of columns and bay-wide doors that constituted the side walls. The designers were G. B. Nicholson and H. E. Warrington, successively chief engineer of the railroad company, and they provided a nice demonstration of how even so utilitarian an object as a merchandise-freight station can play a modest role in the enhancement of the civic order. One might question whether the sports stadium and parking lots that presently occupy this and the surrounding areas do as much.[8]

The Vine Street freight station seems to have been regarded by the officers of the CNO&TP as one element in a projected terminal complex, since the record indicates that the company

Fig. 35. Freight station, CNO&TP Railway, Front and Vine streets, 1905-6. *Railroad Gazette.*

was granted a permit in September 1904 to construct a passenger facility in the same general location. At the beginning of the summer, however, plans of a radically different character had already been launched, and there was no ground for the CNO&TP to continue an independent program, even though its municipally owned affiliate might have been the logical choice to implement it. On 30 June 1904 the Union Terminal Railroad Company was incorporated to construct a union station in Cincinnati together with approach and yard tracks, engine terminals, and subsidiary structures to accommodate the fourteen trunk-line railroads then serving the city. Detailed planning for this program was carried out largely in the following year. The proposed location was close to the one that had been recommended by Melvil Ingalls in 1896 for a union freight station: the passenger headhouse was to be constructed on the block bounded by South Canal and Court Street north and south, and by Race and Elm streets east and west. The reasons underlying the decision to build and the choice of location were intimately bound up with the history of Cincinnati railroads as we have traced it to this point. First was the need to unify the many scattered stations and the equally scattered administrative and ticket offices, and second, to place the new union facility in the core area of the city. Next was the elimination of congestion on main lines and approach tracks arising from high traffic density and the presence of freight and passenger trains, transfer movements, and light engines on the same tracks. This end was served by the plan to disentangle freight and passenger facilities, leaving the former on the lower alluvial terrace and placing the latter on the upper flood plain. Crucial to the city as well as the railroads was the placing of the station and the approach tracks out of reach of the annual floods of the Ohio River. Finally, there was a need to make a start on the monstrous task of separating street and railroad grades, a problem that was compounded by the difficulty of securing adequate drainage in flat areas traversed by street and railway embankments.[9]

The headhouse of the proposed union station was to be a seven-story building with the form of an open skylighted rectangle in plan, centered between track-platform areas extending eastward to Vine Street and westward to Plum (fig. 36). The ground-floor area of 84,000 square feet would have been devoted to the usual terminal spaces—waiting rooms, restaurants, ticket and telegraph offices, and service facilities, and the upper six floors, disposed around the open light court, were to be given over to

147

Fig. 36. Proposed union passenger terminal, West Court Street between Race and Elm, 1904-5. From the private collection of Gibson Yungblut; reproduced with permission.

railroad offices.[10] The track area was to encompass eleven tracks and five platforms within the 214 feet of its out-to-out width. The approach tracks were to lie in an open cut extending eastward from Walnut Street to a connection with the Pennsylvania and the CL&N at Broadway and Eggleston Avenue, and westward mostly along the north side of Ninth Street to Mound Street in the far West End, where the rest of the rail lines lay. The plan called for an approach 100 feet wide, sufficient for six tracks, for the cuts to be floored and walled in reinforced concrete, and for the intersecting streets to be carried over them on concrete girders. The coach yards, embracing a total of 6,000 lineal feet of track, were to be located east and west of the station, probably on East Court Street and in Mill Creek Valley, since it is inconceivable that the necessary area of land would be taken from the built-up street system of the central city. Although it was planned that express would be handled in a separate terminal, baggage and mail were to be worked in the station proper; and the necessary facilities were to include a system of pneumatic tubes connecting the station with the Central Post Office, newspaper headquarters, and office buildings in the core area to the south. It was a generous and well-planned complex, served by a number of contiguous streetcar lines and located at no more than a ten-minute walk from the focal point of the city center, but it included serious defects that made the whole plan abortive shortly after it was launched.[11]

The precise location chosen for the first union terminal project was dictated by a compromise between the ideal solution and the exigencies imposed by the surrounding urban fabric. The first consideration was to place the station as close as possible to the working heart of the city, the spine of which may be taken as Vine Street from Third to Sixth. This idea was undoubtedly influenced if not actually suggested by the decision to place the two New York stations in the central area of midtown Manhattan, and since their construction had been initiated in 1903, the plans were widely known to all who were concerned with railroad matters. Offsetting the first consideration in the case of Cincinnati, however, was the negative factor of wiping out a considerable area of prime downtown property in order to provide space for the terminal and its approaches. Location along the canal, on which operations had ceased in 1895, represented a compromise: the belief was that the rows of warehouses, shops, breweries, and small family manufactories that lined the waterway were expendable, and certainly in terms of monetary and urban cost they were more readily available than the substantial buildings at the edge of the inner core. But the destruction of urban fabric would nevertheless have been extensive, and the plan of six-track approaches lying east and west directly across the upper downtown area was indefensible in terms of money, land, and practical need. The trackage was wholly unjustified: for the 74 regularly scheduled daily trains entering and leaving the city on the east two would have been sufficient; for the 162 on the west three would have worked well enough and four would have provided a comfortable margin. The cost of constructing these depressed, concrete-lined rights of way with their associated overpasses was hardly realistic to railroads transporting little more than 20,000 passengers per day in and out of the city.

The railroad companies, as a consequence, quickly and decisively revealed their lack of enthusiasm. In 1905 those roads operating trains at Central Union Depot agreed jointly to build and to use a union passenger terminal located above any foreseeable high water at Fourth and John streets, one block north of the existing station.[12] The various railroads prepared preliminary plans in 1905-6, but the only step they took that might be regarded as a partial implementation of this program was the construction by the C&O of the Inter-Terminal Railroad viaduct. But nothing came of the rest of it: interurban railway competition, rising costs, floods that culminated in the disasters of 1913 combined once more to inhibit the easily discouraged railroad bureaucracies, and the city had no authority to act on its own, either to draw up a long-term urban plan or to enter into some kind of building and leasing agreement. There was a clear irony in all this: the city that pioneered in constructing the first municipally owned railway line in the face of formidable natural obstacles seemed powerless to improve the properties at its doorstep. The railroads themselves were content with piecemeal improvements, some of them, it is true, of great benefit to the general movement of goods and passengers through the metropolitan area. The CH&D in 1905-6 built a locomotive repair shop in Ivorydale that is historically noteworthy as embodying an early forerunner of the systems and critical-path methods in the construction process. In the following year the PCC&StL opened a suburban station at Torrence Road in the East End for East Walnut Hills passengers, some of whom could very nearly look down on the station roof. The greatest construction program of the time was again undertaken by the C&O. In the three years of 1909-12 the company completed the double-tracking of its entire main line from Cincinnati to Covington, Virginia, and from Richmond to Newport News, and opened its first classification yard in the Cincinnati area, at Silver Grove, Kentucky.[13] Such improvements as were made to Central Union Depot were mainly restricted to renovating or rebuilding the offices damaged in the fire of 21 October 1909.

The next step in the process of terminal unification was marked by an entirely different approach from those that had preceded it, one that appeared to have sprung more from high finance and a concern for financial return on the investment than from functional railroad planning. In the early months of 1910 the General Assembly of Ohio passed an enabling act authorizing the establishment of a union station company at Cincinnati, and in May of the same year a group of local and New York business executives, with little if any consultation among railroad officers, incorporated the Cincinnati Union Depot and Terminal Company to construct union freight and passenger stations within the city. The initial capital, to be raised by stock issue, was $1,000,000, although the total cost of constructing all the planned facilities was estimated at the time to be $25,000,000. The officers of the new company stood on the highest plateau of financial respectability: the president was Archibald S. White, president of the Columbia Gas and Electric Company; the vice-president and general manager was the New York financier John E. Bleekman; the secretary and treasurer was F. R. Williams, treasurer of the Cincinnati Trust Company; the directors were G. H. Worthington of Cleveland, and G. L. Seasongood, J. L. Hauck, and C. Bentley Matthews of Cincinnati. Used to command, the officers moved with dispatch. They sought and secured the authorization to build on a core-area site from the Cincinnati City Council in August 1910 and obtained final approval of a detailed ordinance from the council in January 1912. The contract for preliminary work on the passenger station was awarded to Winston and Company of Richmond, Virginia, in December 1912, by which date the estimated cost had risen to the fantastic total of $36,000,000 (about $470,000,000 at the 1975 building cost level). The chief provisions of the franchise were that the company was to raise its assets to $2,000,000 within twenty-one months and to complete construction within five years, or by the end of 1916.

This remarkable scheme embodied novelties that had no precedent in previous terminal design and were not to appear until the implementation of air-rights programs in New York following World War I. In the plan that was drawn up at the request of the promoters in 1910, the station was to serve as a terminal for all the steam railroads using the existing station facilities, all electric interurban lines, and a new belt line of somewhat ambiguous function and location. The central element in the whole complex was a combined station headhouse and office skyscraper of thirty-six stories, divided between a lower 14-story block and a twenty-two-story tower, the precise architectural relations being reminiscent of the Metropolitan Life Insurance Building in New York (fig. 37). The office building was to be located in the very heart of the city at the center of the station track area, which extended along the south side of Third Street from Broadway on the east to Elm Street on the west, a length of six blocks. The entrance to the building and presumably to the station opened on Vine Street between Third and Fourth, the main floor of the headhouse and the ground floor of the skyscraper lying on the same plane. The overall dimensions of this area in plan were 200 × 400 feet, the equivalent dimensions of the tower 90 × 100 feet, and the overall height of the whole structure 500 feet above the street grade. The track-platform area was immense, measuring 309 × 2,000 feet out-to-out, sufficient to embrace fifteen tracks and seven platforms, and elevated far enough above the grade of Third Street to place it out of the reach of all Ohio River floods (including the worst, which was destined to come in 1937). The intention was to operate the through track system as though it were two stub-end terminals placed back to back, with entries and departures on both the east and west ends. The only precedent for this novel and ingenious though sometimes troublesome arrangement was the original Union Station in Chicago (1879–80), and it was embodied in a much more sophisticated form in the masterful plan of its successor (1916–25).

The track-platform area stood a full two stories above the grade of Second Street, flanking it on the south, and the sub-track space was to be occupied by freight-handling facilities on the intermediate level and by a warehouse at the lowest. The freight station was to be connected to a belt line eight miles in length designed to carry 1,326 cars of interchange freight per day, nearly double the number of interline cars on Cincinnati rails at the time and equal to 74 percent of the total of 1,788 cars originating, terminating, or passing through the city in any one day. The approach system was divided into three parts: a four-track elevated line from the west for the Kentucky and the western lines; a simi-

Fig. 37. Proposed union passenger and freight terminal, with associated office building, Third and Vine streets, 1910. Reproduced with the permission of the Cincinnati Historical Society.

lar line probably of two tracks (number unspecified) from the east for the Pennsylvania Lines and the N&W; and most remarkable of all, a low-grade five-track line from the north for all interurban companies and the steam railroads serving Ohio and the Lake Erie cities. In the case of the northern approach two of the

153

five tracks were to be reserved for interurban cars. Its location was never determined, to my knowledge, and one cannot help but wonder whether the old Walnut Hills tunnel was to be resurrected once more. This immense system, astonishing in its magnitude, its daring, and its thoroughly controversial features, was designed to serve 20,000,000 passengers per year, or about 62,500 on an average weekday. The steam railroads carried about 24,000 passengers within the same period of time in 1910, and the interurbans probably close to the same number, for a total of about 40,000 passengers per day. The planners of the terminal were thus generously far-sighted in their estimates, but not quite so wildly optimistic as many other station-planners in the halcyon days of rail ascendancy.

The main floor of the station headhouse was actually the major part of the ground floor in the office block. The entrance arcade, reached from Vine Street and flanked by ticket offices, telephone and telegraph centers, stores, and shops, opened into the main waiting room, which lay under a vaulted and skylighted ceiling. The passenger concourse extended south from the waiting room, crossing the tracks at right angles to their axes at an elevation one full story above the track-platform area. The platforms themselves were to be protected by separate umbrella sheds, or platform canopies, as they were later called. If the station had been built, this arrangement of headhouse, tracks, and concourse would have represented the fourth example after Pennsylvania Station in New York, Union Station in Baltimore, and Union Station in Kansas City (opened respectively in 1910, 1911, and 1913) of the double-level plan in which separate stairways provide access from the concourse to the individual platforms, lying at or near right angles to the concourse axis. The office tower was designed to provide space for the administrative staffs of the railroads as well as extensive rental areas in the prestige class that Cincinnati so far lacked. The decorative work in the exterior sheathing of brick, stone, and terra cotta was to be executed in the style of the French Renaissance, the masonry curtain walls covering a steel frame. It would have been a very impressive addition to the urban milieu, bordering, indeed, on the sensational, and Bleekman in particular vigorously publicized the costly plan as offering great civic and financial benefits to the city and much needed advantages to the economies of the railroad companies. He rightly claimed that it was superior to all alternative plans for separate or unified facilities.

It is difficult to make a full critical assessment of the 1910 plan

154

without detailed knowledge of the provisions for coach yards, engine terminals, other subsidiary structures, and possible electrification of service. If we set aside the question, however, of how these were to be related to the terminal proper, we can make a partial judgment of the operating and urbanistic features. The only precedent for a near-waterfront station expressly designed as part of a grand civic composition was Daniel Burnham's proposal for a Cleveland Civic Center and associated rail terminal (1902). The plan indicated that it was entirely possible to locate a station within an easy walk of the waterfront while at the same time enhancing the aesthetic possibilities of the water setting and in no way preventing public access to the existing or potential recreational areas bordering the shore. The elevated track in the Cincinnati project offered special problems, but the station might nevertheless have been a first step to a great riverfront development. The planning of passenger spaces in the headhouse and of the track layout, and the close association of separate passenger and merchandise facilities represented the most advanced thinking of the time and suggest a sure hand. The track-platform level would have been elevated at last above floodwaters, but whether this would have been the case with coach yards and engine terminals cannot now be determined. One difficult problem that the planners did not face was the disposition of the track approaches with respect to the roadway approaches of the Broadway and the Suspension bridges, which would have respectively cut across the elevated east approach and the track-platform area. The location of the terminal in the very edge of the city core and its association with a high-quality office tower had everything to recommend them, and no serious argument could be advanced to the contrary. That location, however, virtually dictated the necessity for electrification if the surrounding riverfront area was to be opened to its maximum recreational and residential potentialities (compare, for example, the development of park space over and around the electrified freight line of the New York Central Railroad on the Manhattan West Side). The great arguments against the scheme were the grossly inflated size of the station areas and the exorbitant cost of the whole project. A through station with fifteen tracks and the standard platform length of around 800 feet could easily accommodate 450 trains per day and very likely an equal number of interurban cars. In a double-end station with 2,000-foot platforms the number of trains could have risen to 600 or more. The internal spaces could probably have accommodated 250,000 passengers per day (the designed capacity, for example, of North Western Station in Chicago, opened in 1911). The size lay far beyond Cincinnati's needs, and the cost equally beyond its resources.

But all these arguments quickly became academic at the time, although we will demonstrate later that the whole project contained valuable lessons for the future. The proposed office skyscraper was realized through the construction of the Union Central Life Insurance Company's tower in 1911–13 at the southwest corner of Fourth and Race streets. The architects were Cass Gilbert of New York, who also designed the celebrated Woolworth Building, which was erected in the same years, and Garber and Woodward of Cincinnati. In the case of the station, however, no earth ever seems to have been turned by the contractor who was chosen to initiate construction. As a matter of fact, the promoters appeared to be more concerned with the return on their investment than with civic improvement, but they claimed that the rail companies would have benefited financially through the payment of rentals for a single unified facility in place of the operating and amortization costs of separate stations, and that the directors of at least one road, the Pennsylvania, approved the plan. The second claim must have rested on a misunderstanding: none of the major carriers had approved the plan when it was announced in 1910, as the *Gazette*'s correspondent indicated. "An officer of the Pennsylvania says that that company has no connection with the new company and that no definite conclusions as to a union station have been reached by the interested railways; and an officer of the New York Central Lines makes a statement substantially to the same effect."[14] The rail executives thus delayed their decision until disasters natural and man-made completely stopped further consideration for more than a decade.

The sudden rise of electric interurban transit made deep and wholly unpredicted inroads into rail passenger traffic, so that even directors who had not lost enthusiasm for spending money on new stations in Cincinnati must have looked with loathing on the proposal to give their thorny competitors a comfortable berth alongside their own trains. Far more decisive events, however, came in the form of an old and implacable enemy in the Ohio valley. In the five days of 25–29 March 1913 steadily rising floodwaters in the Ohio River and its tributaries suddenly surged to record crests and struck at towns, highways, and rail lines with destructive fury. The railroads of the area suffered what was described as "the greatest disaster of their history."[15] The damage was worst in the

Great Miami valley and reached devastating proportions at Dayton, Ohio, where the lines of the CH&D, the Big Four, and the PCC&StL were cut to pieces by flooded tracks, washed-out embankments, and collapsed bridges. Near-similar destruction was wrought at Columbus, Middletown, and Cincinnati, where every track in the north-south area of Mill Creek Valley was under water. The C&O main line was either flooded by tributaries dammed at culverts or washed out for nearly two weeks, from 25 March to 6 April, and the portion of the Chicago line in the Great Miami flood plain was out of service until 9 April. A few freight and passenger trains of the Pennsylvania's affiliate managed to escape the city by being transferred to the Court Street Station, and the New York sleepers of the B&O, the Big Four, and the PCC&StL were handled by the CNO&TP from a temporary station on McLean Avenue via Knoxville and Bristol, Tennessee, over a route 1,142 miles in length. Full reconstruction was delayed and damage repeated or extended by flash floods that struck southern Ohio streams on 14–15 July 1913. When the final tallies were made, the costs in money alone were staggering: the total for all roads in Ohio and Indiana was $20,000,000, and for the individual roads serving Cincinnati it was nearly $8,000,000.[16]

The chief consequences of this sudden and extensive destruction of rail property were predictable, for the railroad lines located in vulnerable areas had suffered losses repeatedly and were to continue to do so until the federal government belatedly adopted flood control programs for the major waterway systems of the Ohio drainage area. The first result, and the one that most immediately affected the terminal program of Cincinnati, was that funds for continuing improvements and new construction in the two years following the floods had to be diverted to the reconstruction of damaged property and the replacement of ruined motive power and rolling stock. The weaker roads were forced into receivership or into the sale or lease of their property at unfavorable terms. Finally, the loss of traffic resulted in a decline of revenues and earnings that was compounded by the brief recession following the beginning of the European war in August 1914. These factors were reflected first in the sharp drop in operating income of the Cincinnati roads for the fiscal year ended 30 June 1914, when the operating ratios of all but one of the eight roads climbed to 70 percent or higher, and second in substantial losses of revenue between the fiscal years 1914 and 1915.[17] Yet the floods at the same time demonstrated the great recuperative power of the railroads, and

157

they were quickly prepared to meet the upsurge of traffic that the war eventually brought—prepared at least until the entry of the United States in 1917. As the *Gazette*'s correspondent wrote,

> The promptness with which the railways have met the emergency is best evidenced by the fact that in spite of the great damage done the main lines were in most cases reopened for service within a few days and nearly all tracks were reopened within two weeks. This has required the prompt assembling of thousands of men from a wide area, the gathering of hundreds of car loads of piling and other bridge timber, stone and other filling material, etc., and the collecting of many pile drivers, derricks, and other equipment and their crews. The mobilization of these forces, which were brought together hurriedly, without any warning or preparation, into a working organization, has called for a high degree of ability and efficiency. Nor is the experience of the past few weeks exceptional, for other emergencies have been dealt with as skilfully by the railways.[18]

Natural disasters in the Ohio valley and the first engagements of what was soon to become a worldwide conflict combined to put a stop to further planning of a union terminal in Cincinnati after ten years of discussion in newspapers, financial circles, and the municipal government, the issuance of booklets and manifestos, the incorporation of station companies, the raising of money, and the letting of at least one contract. Precisely what went on behind the public pronouncements has never been exactly determined, and by the time of the American entry into the war the earlier plans had been shelved and new projects extremely vague in outline were being launched by official parties. The whole matter was nicely summarized by an anonymous correspondent of the *Gazette*.

> Cincinnati has a union station project which seems to be enveloped in considerable mystery. Two forces are at work. On one side is the mayor, who claims that he has been working with prominent railway officers who have settled to their own satisfaction the point in the city where the station should be placed. On the other hand, the trustees of the Cincinnati Southern, the railroad owned by the city, have made plans which they have placed before the governor of Ohio, with a request for an enabling law to allow them to proceed. The trustees' plan has been in process of formation for several months. It calls for the expenditure of some twenty millions of dollars in the purchase of a large tract of land—about a half mile in length—to make room for connection with other lines running through the Mill Creek Valley. . . .
> In recent years the Cincinnati Southern trustees have spent millions in creating freight terminals that looked ambitiously to avoiding [the] narrow right of way [of the former Whitewater Canal]; but not one word has leaked out as to the possible location of the union station that the trustees propose. . . . It has been intimated that the passenger station of the trustees would be placed in close proximity to [the proposed interurban and rapid transit terminal (see the following two sections of this chapter)]. The governor is

158

understood to have favored their scheme, but he has suggested a referendum be taken by the people of the city on the issue of such a large bonded indebtedness. Several conferences have been held between the trustees and committees from powerful business organizations, and in most cases the verdict has been in favor of the plan.

The project of the mayor had its birth eight or nine years ago when Archibald White and his partner spent thousands in plans and specifications that were intended to solve both the electric and steam road problems of the city. The city council thought so well of these that a franchise was granted to the promoters, but they were unable to make progress and their franchise was finally abrogated. But the project never died. The daily press saw to it that rumors were kept afloat. About a year ago certain moves that were made by railway people indicated that conferences were being held between terminal engineers, superintendents and local officers, with a union station bearing; and three weeks ago the mayor left Cincinnati on a mysterious mission to New York City. On his return he announced that he had definite assurances that the railways concerned in the union station deal were in line and "Cincinnati could expect definite action in the near future."

One serious cloud on the whole fabric . . . is that the element of politics pervades the whole matter. The mayor is a Republican, with aspirations. On the board of the Cincinnati Southern are two men who have been prominent in democratic circles.[19]

Before the next act in this somewhat tedious drama could begin, however, war, labor conflicts, and postwar depression had to pass, and the lessons of wartime operating chaos had to be thoroughly understood.

Interurban and Rapid Transit Plans

Electric interurban transit is the prime curiosity in the transportation history of modern industrial economies: within thirty years it experienced an unparalleled expansion of mileage and traffic followed by an equally swift and nearly total collapse. The electric traction motor was first applied to street railway transportation in 1884, but it was 1895 before it could be operated with sufficient reliability and at sufficient power and speed to be used in standard rail service, in the lighter single-car intercity variety, or in urban rapid transit systems. The earliest interurban companies began the construction of lines in 1891, and by 1910 the network that spread over the area between the Great Lakes and the Ohio River was substantially in place. At the time of its greatest extension Ohio was first in interurban mileage, with 2,798 route miles; no town with a population of more than 10,000 was left without service, and many communities depended absolutely on the new form of transportation for intercity travel. The growth in traffic to its high point was simply astonishing, and not even the automobile produced such a concentrated increase in the number of riders. It is doubtful whether the interurban lines of Ohio carried more than 10,000,000 passengers in the first year of the new century; in less than twenty years this volume was to expand twenty-five times, for an annual revenue density of nearly 92,000 passengers per mile of line. Among the standard railroads only the big commutation carriers of Chicago and the cities of the eastern seaboard could show higher figures.[20] At the same time, precisely what gave the interurbans their value as rural carriers, uniting small towns and farms with the large urban centers, is what made them vulnerable to highway competition. Dependent on short-haul passenger traffic and local l.-c.-l. freight because few of the interurban lines could interchange carload lots with the standard railroads, they were quickly killed off by all the highway carriers combined, automobiles, buses, and trucks. It is questionable now whether this could in any important way be regarded as progress.

Of the Cincinnati interurban group the first company to be placed under construction was also the one to survive for the longest time and to pass through a corporate history most nearly corresponding to that of the standard railroads. In its final transformation its official title was Cincinnati and Lake Erie Railroad, but that name came only after a thirty-three-year history of vicissitudes, including the customary bankruptcies, mergers, leases, and acquisitions. The nucleus of the system was the Cincinnati and Miami Valley Traction Company, which began operations between Hamilton and Dayton in 1897. Not far behind it in age was the Cincinnati and Hamilton Electric Street Railway, which inaugurated service between an outlying station in College Hill and Hamilton in 1898. For twenty-five years before this date, however, the little College Hill Railroad and its successor, the Cincinnati-Northwestern, had been operating steam-powered trains first to College Hill and then to Mount Healthy, a few miles to the north. In 1901 this line was acquired and converted to an electric interurban by the Southern Ohio Traction Company, and in the following year the ambitious corporation bought the Hamilton-Dayton lines and organized the Cincinnati, Dayton and Toledo Traction Company to provide through standard-gauge service between the terminal cities of its title for the longest interurban run in the state. A series of mergers led to the establishment of the Ohio Electric Railway in 1907, but this grand system suffered damages of about $1,500,000 in the 1913 floods, which quickly forced it into bankruptcy and dismemberment. The southern lines, lying between Cincinnati and Dayton, passed through various changes to emerge

160

in 1926 as the Cincinnati, Hamilton and Dayton Railway, similar in name but wholly unrelated to the steam railroad that the B&O had acquired. Still other mergers produced the Cincinnati and Lake Erie Railroad in 1930, which offered service to Detroit as well as numerous intermediate cities in eighty-mile-an-hour parlor-observation cars placed in operation during the same year. In spite of the heroic efforts of Thomas Conway, an interurban financial expert and a professor of economics at the Ohio State University, time had run out for the electric line, and the C&LE died in 1939.

Competing in the same area as one of the Lake Erie's predecessors was the Ohio Traction Company, built up piecemeal in 1897-1901 to provide service to Hamilton via Wyoming and Glendale over tracks with a 5-foot 2 1/2-inch gauge adopted in order to use the lines of the Cincinnati Street Railway Company. A pattern of mergers and leases ended in the incorporation of the Cincinnati Interurban Company, which passed to the control of the local street railway in 1905. The new owner abandoned the Springdale-Hamilton interurban segment in 1925 and incorporated the remainder into the street railway system in 1926. The rest of its history is a chronicle of contracting streetcar lines and eventual replacement by buses. Considerably more lively in its history by virtue of its location and its mode of operation was the Cincinnati, Lawrenceburg and Aurora Electric Street Railroad, completed to its terminal cities as well as to Harrison, Indiana, in 1900. The standard-gauge line lay immediately adjacent to the Big Four's main line from Anderson's Ferry at what was then the west city limit to Lawrenceburg Junction, and adjacent to the B&OSW line from near the junction to Aurora, so that passengers traveled in terrifyingly close proximity to fast passenger trains and earth-shaking freights. The manual-block system of the CL&A was a model of either efficiency or madness, according to one's view of the operation: the signals were set by the motorman of the passing car, who flipped the controlling switch by hand usually with only a modest reduction of speed. The officers of the company introduced a far-sighted innovation when they inaugurated a coordinated rail-highway program for carrying l.-c.-l. shipments. In conjunction with the Cincinnati Motor Terminals Company, the originator of the idea, the interurban line began the practice in 1921 of placing freight in unit containers that were handled by rail between terminals and by truck between the trackside and the shipper or consignee, the transfer being made by electrically operated overhead cranes. Although the road had offered no previous freight service, the traffic grew rapidly, but it was insufficient to save the company from bankruptcy. Reorganization of the Aurora line in 1928 kept in a little life, but the inevitable abandonment came in 1930. The Cincinnati Street Railway Company bought the portion between the Anderson's Ferry terminal and Fernbank in 1940, converting it to the 5-foot 2 1/2-inch gauge, and operated streetcars on the new track until the age of buses.

On the east side of the city a later company followed a history somewhat like that of the College Hill lines. The Cincinnati, Georgetown and Portsmouth began existence as a narrow-gauge steam railroad in 1886 and was converted to standard-gauge electric operation in 1902, when the lines reached Georgetown, Batavia, and Cincinnati's Coney Island through the pleasant wooded scenes among the hills east of the Little Miami valley. Reorganized as the Cincinnati-Georgetown Railroad Company in 1928, it underwent progressive abandonment in 1933–36. Other eastern roads came into existence at about the same time. The Interurban Railway and Terminal Company sought to implement the most ambitious plans and in fact experienced very nearly the shortest life of the local companies. Beginning construction through subsidiaries of a system of broad-gauge lines (5 feet 2 1/2 inches) in 1900, it opened the first to New Richmond in 1902, the second to Bethel in June 1903, and the third to Lebanon in October of the same year.[21] In spite of the advantage of trackage rights over various lines of the Cincinnati Street Railway, the floods of 1913 proved disastrous: receivership came in 1914 to be followed by piecemeal abandonment in 1918 and 1922.

The Cincinnati, Milford and Loveland Traction Company passed through the usual receivership, but it fared a little better and was kept alive for a final decade of operation by the street railway company. It inaugurated service from the far eastern area of the city at Madisonville to Milford on the Little Miami River in 1903. Built to the 5-foot 2 1/2-inch gauge, the company took advantage of the opportunity for trackage rights over the streetcar lines to establish a downtown terminal at Fifth and Sycamore streets, but the hostile Cincinnati Street Railway charged so high a rental that the city line had to be abandoned in 1915. The loss of traffic led to a receivership two years later and to an early abandonment of the whole property in 1926. The street railway acquired the line in the same year and continued operations to Milford until 1936, when service was cut back to suburban Mariemont and finally terminated in 1942. By contrast the last of the Cincinnati interurban companies projected the grandest scheme and passed most quickly into oblivion. The Cincinnati and Columbus Traction Company opened its standard-gauge line from Norwood to Hillsboro in 1906 only to see most of it wiped out by the 1913 catastrophe. A long receivership ended with total abandonment in 1920.

The Cincinnati interurban system, as we have seen, began its role in local transportation at the very turn of the century; and in little more than thirty years all of it was gone, victim of the automobile-and-highway mania. At its maximum extent its seven constituent companies operated thirteen lines with an aggregate length of 343 miles. They carried somewhat more than 12,500,000 passengers in 1908, nearly 15,000,000 in the year before the record floods, and possibly double the latter total in the peak year of 1919. That the builders of interurban lines regarded Cincinnati as a major focal point, a goal to be sought and achieved in construction programs, is attested by the fact that a total of twenty-three companies either served the city directly or included its name in their always hopeful corporate titles.[22]

The distribution of traffic on the various interurban lines nicely reflected the fundamental economic and demographic facts of the Cincinnati hinterland and metropolitan area. The largest carriers (the Ohio Electric and the Ohio Traction companies) served the well-populated, highly industrialized, relatively high-income corridors connecting Cincinnati with Hamilton and Dayton. The CL&A, next in volume of traffic, served the long chain of flourishing communities that extended westward along the Ohio River to the terminal points of the company's main line. A similar though thinner succession of rural towns and suburbs in the Lebanon corridor guaranteed the somewhat smaller though still lively traffic load of the Interurban Railway and Terminal's Rapid Division. The other companies served the sparsely populated, low-income, generally failing rural area to the east of Cincinnati, where there was abundant scenery but little of anything else. The tides of commerce and travel moved north and northeast of the city, toward Toledo, Dayton, Columbus, and Cleveland, or westward and northwestward toward Saint Louis, Indianapolis, and Chicago. Between the Little Miami valley and those of the Scioto, Muskingum, and Hocking rivers to the east towns were few, and the thin, clay-bound soil was unsuited to intensive agriculture.

Though its life was short, a transportation system carrying some 15,000,000 passengers per annum was obviously more than useful; it was in its time absolutely essential. If the standard railroads of Ohio had been called upon to handle this traffic, which would have doubled their annual totals, they would either have been paralyzed by their burden or would have been compelled to expand drastically their Cincinnati facilities. The interurban companies made deep inroads into local rail traffic for the reason that they offered obvious advantages that the ponderous steam roads could not match. Single-car operation made possible a flexibility and frequency of service at regular intervals that one could easily recall without consulting a timetable: the cars ran hourly or half-hourly at least during the active daytime period and passed through communities with highly reliable fidelity to schedules, and they could be added or withdrawn as traffic rose or fell. They ran on the streets of towns, close to offices, stores, saloons, or homes, and they skirted the edges of farms where a shelter every few miles offered convenient rural transportation that the farmer had never known. Fares were so much lower than those on the steam railroads that many people rode the interurban cars who had never traveled by train. The average interurban fare in Ohio in 1907 was 1.7 cents per mile, the variation ranging from 0.91 cent minimum to 2.08 cents maximum, against 3.6 cents per mile on the railroad. The speed was at least equal to that of the accommodation train on the steam roads, the average for the Ohio interurbans in 1907 being 23.9 miles per hour and the range 16 to 28.7 miles per hour. The safety record was good, though somewhat inferior to that of the standard railroads chiefly because of the inadequate signaling and the hazards of head-on collisions on single-track lines. An immediately striking advantage offered by the interurban was cleanliness combined with summertime coolness, since the cars could be operated with closely spaced windows opened to the point of very breezy ventilation. The larger interurban lines, scheduling cars on through runs of more than a hundred miles, offered a full complement of parlor-observation and parlor-cafe units, and a few of them even operated sleeping and dining cars. One consequence of these numerous and very real virtues was the generation of a form of traffic that one always associated with the automobile: the interurban stimulated a new kind of personal travel for picnics, family outings, pure pleasure riding, and shopping tours in the nearest city.[23]

The interurban railway pattern of Cincinnati, however, suffered from a serious handicap that ultimately proved to be a cause of the decline in single-car ridership. Each company operated its own terminal, and all of them were scattered at varying distances on the periphery of the city (fig. 38). Lines with standard-gauge track were physically barred from using the street railway lines, and those with a conforming gauge were almost as effectively barred by the street railway company's high rentals for trackage rights, the charges calculated, of course, precisely to achieve this end. The radial streetcar lines and the outward-extending interurban lines formed two interdependent parts of a coordinate and hierarchical system, of which the steam railroads constituted the topmost level, but to prevent the interurban cars from operating in the city was to place a handicap on them that could only work to everyone's disadvantage. The municipal government was aware of this irrationality and took the first step in hopefully breaking the impasse by appointing a commission whose members engaged the electric railway and terminal planner Bion J. Arnold to draw up various unification programs with their associated cost estimates. His admirable report, offering five alternative plans, was submitted to the commission in October 1912.[24]

Arnold's solution to the problem of interurban terminal unification and the extension of the lines into the inner city was predicated on the belief that an adequate plan must also comprehend a rapid transit system for the city. The essence of the problem was to provide rapid transit rights of way for the interurban lines that would otherwise have to be built within the city limits to reach the proposed union interurban terminal in the core area. The question then was the location of these lines. In working out his detailed answer, Arnold showed a thorough grasp of both the demographic and the topographic facts of the city, for there was a mutual interdependence between the two. Beginning about 1900 as a consequence of the extension of streetcar lines, there had been a rapid growth of the urban neighborhoods and of the contiguous ring of suburbs in the areas lying to the north and east of the previously built up portions of the city. The provision of a rapid transit service offered a solution to the interurban problem, and the expanding areas where such service was most urgently needed dictated a belt line plan making a continuous circuit throughout the then peripheral areas of the city proper. At first sight the topography of Cincinnati seemed to offer nothing but obstacles to the realization of such a plan, especially if one were to compare it with such level interurban capitals, for example, as Columbus and Indianapolis. As a matter of fact, however, the topography provided natural corridors through which high-speed electric lines could be built and along

165

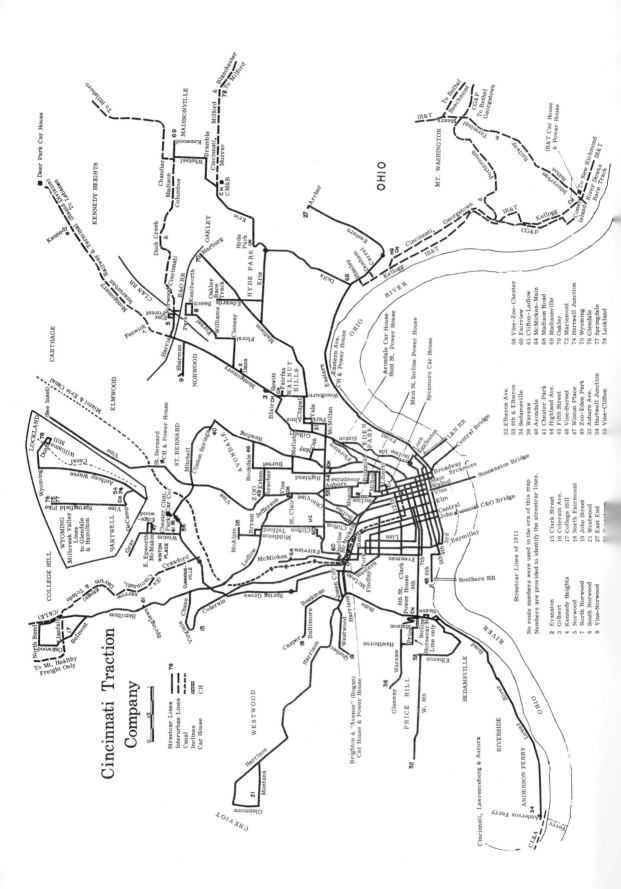

Cincinnati Traction Company

Streetcar Lines of 1911

No route numbers were used in the era of this map. Numbers are provided to identify the streetcar lines.

Streetcar Lines		78
Interurban Lines		
Canal		
Inclines		
Car House		CH

2 Evanston
3 Gilbert
4 Kennedy Heights
5 Norwood
7 North Norwood
8 South Norwood
9 Vine-Norwood

15 Clark Street
16 Colerain Ave.
17 College Hill
18 North Fairmount
19 John Street
21 Westwood
27 East End

32 Elberon Ave.
33 8th & Elberon
34 Sedamsville
36 Warsaw
40 Avondale
41 Chester Park
44 Highland Ave.
45 Fifth Street
46 Vine-Burnet
49 Zoo-Eden Park
53 Auburn Ave.
54 Hartwell Junction
55 Vine-Clifton

56 Vine-Zoo-Chester
60 Fairview
61 Clifton-Ludlow
64 McMicken-Main
68 Madison Road
69 Oakley
70 Oakley
72 Mariemont
74 Hartwell Junction
75 Wyoming
76 Glendale
77 Springdale
78 Lockland

which to a considerable extent the residential, commercial, and industrial belts of the city had been concentrated.

The broadest and most inviting of these corridors was Mill Creek Valley and the upper alluvial plain of the Ohio River, and it was here, as we have repeatedly observed, that the greatest working concentrations in the urban fabric existed. Moreover, an admirable access way into the central city was ready at hand: the Miami and Erie Canal had ceased operations in 1895, and the municipality had leased the bed from the state for an annual rental of $32,000; the proposal to use the bed for rail or rapid transit purposes had been made as early as 1911. It offered a level, nearly straight path through major manufacturing areas and the densely built West End into the upper edge of the city's core. At the same time it offered near connections with the Hamilton-Dayton and the abortive Indianapolis interurban lines, the latter having been planned to enter Mill Creek Valley over the tracks of the Cincinnati and Westwood Railroad. Toward the east and northeast of the city there were various ravines and valleys that offered low-grade passages, like Duck Creek Valley, for example, or at least manageable grades like Torrence Road, which provided the only way up or down the steep river face of East Walnut Hills. Finally, there was the broad belt of relatively level land (the Norwood trough) through which the B&O line passed and which was the site of a number of manufacturing and residential communities stretched out from Oakley on the east to Saint Bernard on the west. Thus the topographic features and the transportation needs together determined the belt form of the projected interurban-rapid transit line.

The basic plan that Arnold proposed was drawn up in considerable detail (fig. 39).[25] The focal point was the downtown subway loop under Canal, Plum, Fourth, and Sycamore streets (a square six blocks on a side) serving three core stations located at Seventh and Plum, Fourth and Vine, and Seventh and Sycamore streets. Coordinated with the group of passenger stations was a freight terminal extending under Canal Street east and west of Vine. Alternatives represented detailed variations on elements of this plan. From the northwest corner of the subway loop a double-track belt line was to extend in a great circuit through the canal

Opposite: Fig. 38. Map showing the Cincinnati street railway and interurban lines as they existed in 1911. Wagner and Wright, *Cincinnati Streetcars*; reproduced with permission.

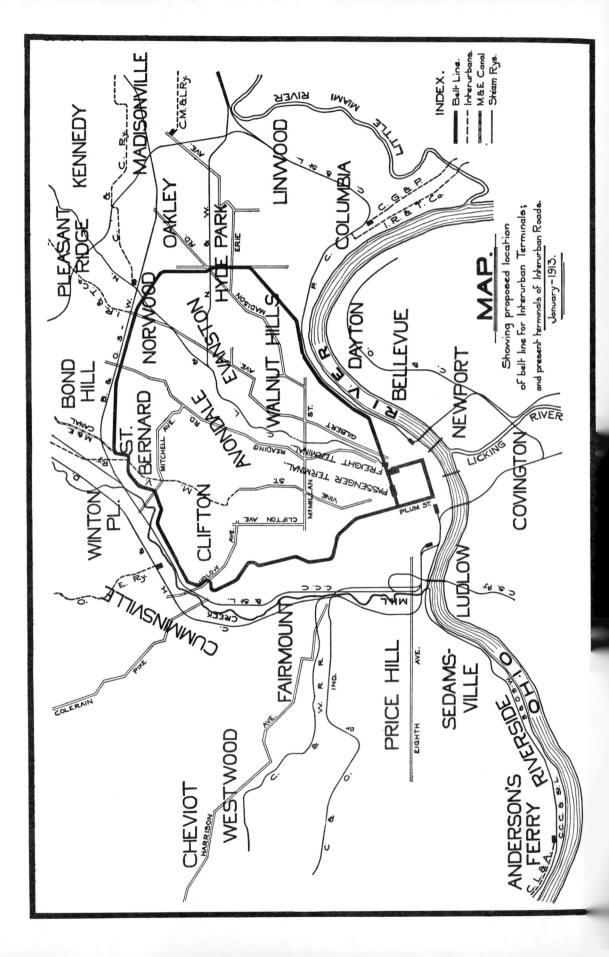

MAP.

Showing proposed location of belt line for Interurban Terminals; and present terminals of Interurban Roads.

January–1913.

INDEX.
Belt-Line.
Interurbans.
M & E Canal
Steam Rys.

Grand Schemes for the New Century

bed, Mill Creek Valley, and the Norwood trough to Saint Bernard and Norwood, along Duck Creek and various streets into Hyde Park and East Walnut Hills, down the Torrence Road ravine into the PCC&StL right of way, thence back along the canal bed to the downtown loop. Arnold proposed a third track at stations for rush-hour express trains, four tracks under Canal Street, automatic block signals, and a variety of cut-and-cover subway tunnels, open cuts, embankments, and bridges along the way. The whole system was to be entirely free of grade crossings. The belt line was to serve the dual purpose of providing circumferential transit service between the peripheral and core areas of the city and to offer the avenue for the operation of interurban cars from various junction points near their existing terminals to the stations on the downtown loop. This circuit pattern of connecting points was worked out with care and in detail by Arnold and his staff, so that arrangements were made for all the existing and projected interurban lines, although in one case the chosen route seems to have been the most costly of possible alternatives.[26]

Arnold estimated the cost of the entire program, including property, tracks, stations, tunnels, power plant, substations, electrical distribution system, and interest, but excluding rolling stock, as a modest $7,000,000 at the 1912 price level (the equivalent of about $95,000,000 at the 1975 building cost level). Yet the figure was discouraging to seven small companies whose aggregate revenues in 1912 were only $1,665,000, or less than one-quarter of the expected cost.[27] It was clear that the city would have to lend a hand, most likely through the issuance of revenue bonds to be redeemed by rentals for the use of the municipally built facilities. If this method of financing had been adopted, it would have marked the first time in the United States that a municipality constructed terminal space and metropolitan trackage to be leased to privately owned intercity railroad companies, although there was a local precedent in the building of the Cincinnati Southern Railway. But as far as the interurban roads were concerned, the issue was never to arise. As we have seen from the sketches of company histories, the floods that struck the Ohio River and its tributaries in the spring of 1913 were an unmitigated disaster for most of the interurban companies: precariously financed and with

Opposite: Fig. 39. Map showing the proposed belt line and terminals for the electric interurban railroads, 1913. Arnold, *Report on an Interurban Electric Railway Terminal System for the City of Cincinnati.*

169

thin profit margins, the staggering costs of repairing flood damage made any large investment or high rentals on the part of the affected lines impossible. Economic dislocations attendant upon the European war and the difficulty of carrying out a large-scale construction program under wartime exigencies delayed further consideration until the postwar years. The depression that came with the end of the war coincided with the beginning of the precipitous decline of interurban traffic, steep enough to force one company out of existence as early as 1920. Each year the idea of implementing the interurban plan receded further into the background.

The city, however, was prepared to act on its own, for the program presented in the Arnold plan seemed to offer so many valuable improvements in local and metropolitan transportation that it could not be allowed to fall into neglect. Mayor Henry T. Hunt, accordingly, appointed the Cincinnati Interurban Rapid Transit Commission to consider the question of municipal implementation of the Arnold proposals. The members of this commission included William Cooper Procter of the soap manufacturing family and Herman Schneider, the dean of the University of Cincinnati's engineering college who had established the cooperative work-study program for engineering and architectural students. This commission was charged with issuing a report in October 1915, following the passage by the Ohio General Assembly earlier in the same year of an act authorizing the creation of a permanent commission to build the rapid transit system. In March 1916 the Cincinnati City Council took the next step by passing an ordinance revising the franchise of the Cincinnati Street Railway Company to make possible the establishment of the Cincinnati Rapid Transit and Interurban Railway Company and to allow the operation of both the street railway and the transit line by the Cincinnati Traction Company.[28] In April the voters of the city approved a $6,000,000 bond issue to cover the cost of constructing the rapid transit trackage and appurtenant structures by a majority of six to one. It was a decisive expression of feeling, one that indicated unmistakably how much importance the citizens attached to improving a slow-moving hillside transportation system that held the interurban cars outside a distant ring like so many unwanted animals beyond the barnyard enclosure.

The program that was to be implemented was the same as the Arnold plan without the expensive subway loop in the core area. The city was to build the double-track belt line, originally

15.56 miles in length, together with stations and electrical installations, and the Cincinnati Rapid Transit and Interurban Railway was to provide the rolling stock and the electrical power and to operate the system. The separate interurban companies were granted trackage rights over the rapid transit line if they chose to exercize them, but the construction of physical connections with interurban tracks was left in what turned out to be a permanently unsettled state. Under the ordinance of March 1916 the city was given the authority to fix standards of service, schedules, type of rolling stock, and various operating techniques on both the rapid transit and the street railway lines.[29] The financial arrangements under which operations were to be conducted appeared to be beneficial both to the city and the corporate operators, but in truth they rested on a principle that was later to make public subsidization of transit systems a necessity. The gross revenues from the fares and rentals collected by the Cincinnati Traction Company for its rapid transit, surface, and interurban service within the city were to cover all operating expenses, the earnings tax owed to the city, depreciation charges, interest, and rentals—a requirement that was everywhere demonstrated to be physically impossible by 1930. The traction company in turn demanded a five percent return on the preferred stock of the controlling Ohio Traction Company. The city hoped to take the lion's share of what was left after all expenses and charges: this residue of net earnings was to be divided 55 percent to the municipality and 45 percent to the Cincinnati Traction Company; the city was finally granted the right to buy the entire property along with rolling stock and other operating elements for $26,238,950 plus the debt outstanding at the time of the purchase. Thus by 1917 every detail was properly attended to, and as soon as an armistice might put an end to the unsettled state of the world, the city, acting through the Cincinnati Rapid Transit Commission, was prepared to order working drawings and to let contracts.

The hoped-for new day did not dawn until 1920, but before the sun rose very far, all these brave plans proved to be no more than a prelude to the most expensive tragicomedy in municipal history. Yet the whole program showed much intelligent planning together with a concern for economy and with a penetrating, reasonably farsighted assessment of the city's character and potentiality. Arnold's interurban route had everything to recommend it, and the commission adopted it with changes only in the downtown terminals. The grand circuit of the rapid transit system involved minor changes in routing that extended the length to 16.45 miles, and the elaborate inner-city loop with its three stations was abandoned in favor of a single five-track terminal for interurban and rapid transit passengers and merchandise freight under the canal bed (later Central Parkway) at Race Street (fig. 40). This big terminal was to be supplemented by a smaller core station at Fountain Square (Fifth Street at Walnut), which would have marked the deepest penetration into the city. From Fifth Street the line was to lie in a subway as far north as Brighton, although the tunnels were in fact constructed about a mile beyond the proposed terminating point. The right of way for the rest of the circuit was a combination of grade-level construction where there were no intersecting streets, elevated street bridges and stations, and trestlework.[30] The economy of the circuit route, dictated as we have seen by original topographic conditions as well as by the later growth of the urban population and fabric, was nicely sum-

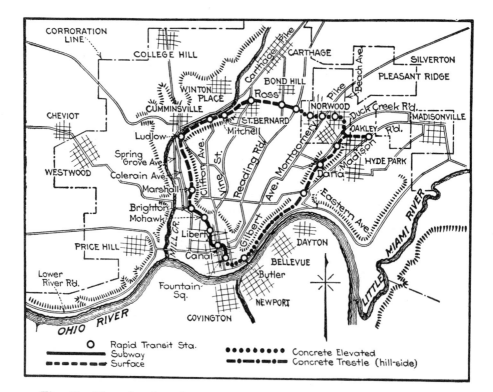

Fig. 40. Map showing the proposed rapid transit system, 1916. *Engineering News-Record*; reproduced with permission.

marized by the commission's assistant chief engineer. ". . . The conditions which seemed, upon superficial observation, to present unusual difficulties, in reality simplified the solution; for the right-of-way to be acquired is cheap, the streets to be crossed are few, there are fewer sewer and water pipes to be replaced . . . , and a private right-of-way insuring speedy and direct entrance for interurban and suburban cars is easily obtainable."[31]

Construction of the rapid transit system was inaugurated in 1920, following the drainage of the canal in its lower reaches; and by 1923 some eleven miles of subways, graded right of way, over-passes, and stations, extending roughly to the estern boundary of Norwood, had been completed, but the track work and electri-cal installations were to be delayed until the entire right of way was prepared. In the seven years since the passage of the bond issue, however, war and its economic aftermath brought about the worst inflation in prices and building costs since the first records were kept in 1854 (the price level almost exactly doubled between 1916 and 1923). It was estimated that a supplementary bond issue of no less than $5,000,000 would be required to complete the re-maining 5 1/2 line miles of construction and grading, but this could hardly have been regarded as sufficient to cover the costs of track and electrical work. If the second bond issue had ever been passed and adequate additional funds provided, the entire project might have been completed in working order by 1926. As matters turned out, this event was never to occur. A long entrenched polit-ical machine was driven from power and replaced by a city-man-ager system in 1924–26. The courts declared the street railway franchise illegal, the whole traction issue was thoroughly "unset-tled" (to use Assistant Engineer Raschig's polite understate-ment),[32] automobile traffic was expanding rapidly, and interurban traffic was falling at a rate likely to discourage any plans for ex-pansion and unification. Construction was never resumed after the temporary halt of 1923, and $6,000,000 worth of tunnels, graded right of way, stations, and other structures stood unused for forty years, until the properties were reclaimed by the city and mostly buried under Mill Creek Expressway, along with much of the area's beauty and useful working fabric.

As late as the spring and summer of 1927, however, the con-sulting engineer John A. Beeler of New York, at the request of the Rapid Transit Committee, prepared an elaborate report on intermodal coordination among the rapid transit, interurban, and street railway systems and submitted it to the committee with the recommendation that the transit line be completed to working order though at a somewhat reduced length. He was confident that the program would prove successful, in spite of the fact that his statisticians had correctly established the discouraging facts: street railway traffic in the seven years from 1919 to 1926 had declined from 118,000,000 to 91,000,000 passengers per annum, and automobile registration in the five years following 1921 had increased 126 percent. If the city could complete the project by 1930, he estimated that the rapid transit system would transport 37,400,000 passengers for the year, or 33.9 percent of the total carried by all forms of public transit, rail and bus. Although the planned loop had been abandoned in favor of an Oakley terminal and the projected income calculated as sufficient to pay all expenses, taxes, interest, and increment of principal with a deficit of only $246,111 out of revenues of $9,544,185, Beeler's admirable report failed to arouse official enthusiasm and thus proved to be the last gasp.

Yet in many respects the proposed belt line would have been a model of transit operation for its day and a valuable concept for future transportation planning. The double-track standard-gauge line would have been laid out on a nearly level gradient save in the eastern part of the city, where except for a short stretch of 3.5 percent grade (the Torrence Road declivity), the ruling grade would have been two percent. The original plan was to operate trains of four seventy-foot cars at forty-five miles per hour under the control of automatic color-light block signals, the power to be delivered to the 100-horsepower motors by means of a third rail. (The Beeler report proposed a much more flexible mode of operation, with trains of varying lengths and fifty-foot cars.) It was estimated that the maximum capacity under these operating arrangements, with trains despatched at sixty-nine-second intervals, would be 110,000 passengers per hour, or 55,000 passengers per hour per track. All structures were to be built exclusively of reinforced concrete. The subways were designed as parallel single-track cut-and-cover tubes of rectangular section with a clearance close enough to ensure ventilation through the piston action of trains but generous enough to allow the passage of standard railroad cars, since it was planned to provide rail switching service in the late night hours.[33] Long continuous sections of elevated track were to be carried on trestlework of spread-legged bents tied and braced in the transverse planes, and street overpasses were to be supported by simple long-span girders. All trackwork

174

was the standard form—100-pound rail on rock ballast and creosoted wood ties at grade and concrete-imbedded ties in subways and elevated structures. The close headway of the short, easily controlled trains guaranteed the extraordinarily high capacity even at the modest top speed of forty-five miles per hour.

While construction was proceeding in 1921, the Rapid Transit Commissioners were filled with an optimistic confidence; and in their appraisal of the future system they saw great benefits flowing to the metropolitan area at once and into the future, as Raschig's summary indicates.

> There is a great stretch of open land from Norwood to Saint Bernard through Bond Hill which has been almost encirclued by the city's growth northward and which will develop rapidly with proper transportation facilities. . . . The line runs through the heart of the business district and should have the effect of spreading this district from the southern part of the city where it is now very congested. This is especially true of Canal Street, where the combined interurban and loop station is located; this street, 150 feet wide and twelve blocks long, is to be made into a wide boulevard and should develop rapidly. . . . The ideal method of operation would be to combine the rapid transit system with the local street railway system. By throwing as much traffic to the loop as possible, the street-railway traffic would be relieved, especially on long hauls to the suburbs, which are at present very unprofitable. By throwing most of the traffic from the suburbs into the loop there would be a saving in cost of operation to the surface system but there would also be a great saving of time to the people using the loop. The surface system should act as a feeder to the loop wherever possible, and as the loop encircles the entire city it would provide contact at all important transfer points, so that a great many surface lines running through the congested parts of the city could be cut off at the loop.[34]

The most valuable potentialities of the proposed rapid transit belt, as the summary suggests, represented a rational and efficient exploitation of a fundamental characteristic of mass transportation in the years immediately following World War I. In the few cities large enough to support both rapid transit and railroad commutation lines as well as the commonplace street railway, the three forms of steel-rail transportation constitued a hierarchical system in which each type performed a service that it was best suited to provide—short-haul in-city transit by the streetcar, faster suburban inner-ring service by the rapid transit, and maximum-speed outer-suburban transport by the standard railroad. In the even fewer cities that were also interurban centers, the electric cars constituted a fourth level in the hierarchy.[35] For the most part, however, these various modes of transportation went their separate paths in wholly uncoordinated fashion, sometimes competing in useless and costly ways, usually leaving broad corridors

175

of space inadequately served by any form, and their officers regarding general transfer privileges or even transfer points with contempt. Only in Cincinnati was there the beginning of an attempt to form a genuinely coordinated system where each mode served the sphere in which it could operate most efficiently and economically, and where all were organized through transfer points and trackage rights into a unified system. What was needed to round it out, of course, was a union railroad terminal. The other advantage of the Cincinnati program was the provision of a transit belt or circuit line uniting a great number of peripheral suburbs and providing an essential supplement to the fundamentally radial system of the street railway and standard railroad lines. It was a remarkably farsighted idea, full of promise for the future, and we will return to it again. If the plan was never realized, its central concepts have nevertheless survived to offer useful lessons for the future.

Traffic and Trains in the Extravagant Decade

General Operations

The railroad prelude to the halcyon days of the twenties was a long period of man-made troubles that culminated in a physical and financial breakdown of the national rail system, and the troubles afflicted Cincinnati as severely as they did any of the major eastern terminals. The crisis that led to government control of the railroads arose from an enormous expansion of traffic combined with financial, technological, and operational problems of which some originated long before the war and others came with wartime difficulties. The sudden upsurge of traffic was the immediate factor: the volume of freight carried by the roads serving Cincinnati rose nearly 40 percent between 1915 and 1918, and the number of passengers increased by almost one-quarter.[36] Over the years from 1900 to the beginning of the war the general price level rose 35 percent, railroad wages rose 50 percent, and rail taxes more than tripled, whereas the gross revenues of the industry as a whole doubled while the average freight rate per ton-mile remained fixed. One school of economic historians holds that following the Hepburn Act of 1906 the Interstate Commerce Commission failed to grant the increases in freight rates and passenger fares that would have guaranteed a return on the railroad investment sufficient to attract the capital necessary to modernize the plant and equipment to the point where the roads could cope with the rising traffic. But the main underlying cause of the failure to handle the new tonnage arose from an unbalanced technological development of which the remoter causes were beyond the railroad or ICC control. The onset of the war intensified every problem: the great bulk of wartime freight moved to the eastern ports, where inadequate yard, terminal, unloading, and lighter facilities coupled with the effectiveness of the German submarine campaign resulted in paralysis; the inability to unload cars and keep them moving on the line magnified an already severe freight-car shortage, amounting to 158,000 cars in 1917. The inevitable consequence was that the government somewhat belatedly but at one stroke established a national transportation policy by placing the railroads under federal control on 26 December 1917.

All these difficulties were compounded by problems that had always existed but had grown more acute with the upsurge of traffic that accompanied the recovery from the depression of 1893. Foremost, perhaps, were the increasingly exasperating frustrations attendant upon moving freight cars through yards, to and from terminals, and into and away from industrial spurs, team tracks, and shippers' sidings. The spotting, classification, loading, and unloading of rolling stock presented problems that simply defied solution, as many of them do to this day. Adding to these burdens were other factors arising from the irrational distribution of terminals and lines, the unnecessary duplication of facilities marked by numerous crossings and junctions, and the inefficient use of labor following the featherbedding practices that grew up in the wake of the perfectly valid legislation embodied in the Adamson Act of 1916. Underlying these factors was the difficulty of acquiring urban land at the locations and in the quantity necessary to conduct rail operations at maximum efficiency, either because of financial exigencies or outmoded land-use arrangements. The need for government control demonstrated the great fundamental cause of all the problems, namely, the absence of a national railroad system and a national transportation policy. The success of governmental operation is attested by the number of valuable benefits that came during the hegemony of the United States Railroad Administration in 1917-20: the standardization of motive power; the eradication of the freight-car shortage by the spring of 1918; the addition of 100,000 new freight cars and 1,930 locomotives to the stock of rolling equipment. The great lesson in these years of upheaval can be put in a sentence: technological progress in the design of motive power, rolling stock, and signaling gave the roads an immense reserve capacity that was frustrated by primitive economic, legal, and municipal institutions.

The brief postwar depression of 1920-21, coupled with a continuing inflation in prices, did still further damage to the rail fabric; and by the time the government relinquished control of the roads in 1920, the accumulated backlog of unfulfilled needs had reached the level of more than $6,000,000,000, of which about $70,000,000 represented a necessary investment at Cincinnati.[37] The city was one of the first three railroad centers with respect to freight traffic in the United States, but it enjoyed this eminent position because of the peculiar fact that the tonnage passing *through* the city stood out of all proportion to that originating or terminating *within* the city. In other words, interchange traffic overwhelmed terminal traffic. In the first full year following the end of the war, the railroads serving the city carried almost 35,000 tons of originating and terminating freight and 200,000 tons of interchange freight each day, for a ratio of nearly six to one. The movement of this cargo required the operation of 213 separate freight trains per day within the city's switching district. The number of daily passengers is a matter of calculation, but it was undoubtedly close to 30,000 using the terminal and suburban stations, and they were carried in 274 weekday trains.[38] This represents a high density of traffic of every description, and the multiplicity of terminals, bridges, junctions, crossings, and sharp curves, combined with annual floods that frequently covered the trackage along the Ohio River and in the lower Mill Creek Valley, led to such congestion, delays, inconvenience, and expense as to render the city in periods of peak traffic an intricate bottleneck rather than the gateway to the South. William G. McAdoo, director-general of the United States Railroad Administration, singled the city out for less than favorable comments during testimony before the Senate Committee on Interstate Commerce on 3 January 1919.

> It is estimated that there ought to be spent in the near future about $45,000,000 in the rehabilitation of Cincinnati terminals so as to make them equal to modern public needs, with probably $25,000,000 additional for passenger terminals. . . . Virtually the whole expenditure has to be made in the common public interest and without the interest of any one railroad company paramount as to any particular item. If this matter is left to be worked out by the separate railroad companies without any controlling public authority to shape up the whole situation for the benefit of the general public, there is no reason to believe that it ever will be successfully worked out. Certainly the railroad companies have had many years in which to work out the problem and they have never done so. If the problem is not adequately solved the result will be that a great burden of delay and inconvenience,

uncertainty and cost will continue to rest upon the people of the United States simply because a thing which ought obviously to be done at Cincinnati in the public interest is not done and it will not be done because the power of government which ought to be exercised to promote the public interest is allowed to remain dormant and subordinate to the separate interests and to the disagreements of various privately managed railroad companies.[39]

McAdoo was one of the few figures on the top level of the federal administration to propose a public authority as the directing and controlling voice in the construction of railroad facilities designed to serve the public in the urban milieu. His primary theme was the confusion and costliness of the Cincinnati rail pattern, yet this tangled web was during the coming decade to carry reasonably expeditiously an ever increasing volume of freight and Pullman traffic beyond even the high levels generated by the wartime demands. The peak year for the total of all classes of passenger traffic was 1920, when the railroads serving Cincinnati carried nearly 85,000,000 passengers, representing an increase of 112.5 percent over the previous twenty years (Appendix C, table 5). In spite of the postwar depression, this total marked an increase over 1919 for most roads, and even over the wartime year of 1918 in a few cases. The traffic growth over the years 1918-20 required an increase of about 10 percent in the number of schedules and a considerably greater expansion in the number of cars, especially Pullmans, for which the demand continued to grow throughout the decade, while coach traffic steadily declined. The Cincinnati passenger stations accommodated an average of about 275 trains per day in 1919, according to the *Railway Age* survey; but the number listed in the public timetables was 232, indicating that the scheduled total had to be increased by about 15 percent to arrive at a just estimate of the actual total. Central Union Depot continued to handle the majority, or 53 percent, of the total in 1919. In the following year the number of listed trains had grown to 252 per weekday, for a probable total of about 290, if we base the count on the *Railway Age* figure for the previous year. Of these the union station provided space for well over half, 144 listed trains and a likely daily total of 160.[40]

The capacity of this aging station to accommodate a high traffic density in the peak hours of the morning seems astonishing to an age that has seen all public services deteriorate, and it is probably to be attributed to the *esprit de corps* of railway employees as much as to the sheer number of them. In 1919-20, between the hours of 7:00 and 9:00 A.M., thirty-six trains arrived and departed each weekday, and of these sixteen were concentrated in the half-hour of 8:00 to 8:30. Through sleeping-car runs had risen to a total of 116 by 1920, which required anywhere from one to twelve cars per run to handle the traffic, the high figure being characteristic of wintertime Florida trains and Christmas holiday travel to and from New York on the New York Central and the Pennsylvania lines. The distribution of sleeping-car runs by road indicated that the union depot again had the lion's share, with seventy-four Pullman routes, or 64 percent of the total. Most of the balance were housed in the Pennsylvania Station (thirty-six), leaving the remaining six to the Baymiller. What was specially characteristic of Cincinnati—characteristic, indeed, to a unique degree—was the great number of sleeping cars transferred from one road to another, a consequence of the city's position as a gateway to the South and the Pocahontas-Tidewater region. There were eighteen such transfer runs in 1919-20, ordinarily requiring the movement of forty to fifty cars per day from one train to another. This switching traffic, again falling most heavily on the union station, placed even greater burdens on the stub-end terminals with hand-thrown switches. The average speed of the premier trains had advanced to thirty-five miles per hour by 1920, with the Pennsylvania and the New York Central lines locked in a mortal competition that compelled them to operate the fastest and most luxurious Pullman trains. The tempo had slowed somewhat, however, from the lively days at the turn of the century because the Interstate Commerce Commission had required both the major Pullman carriers to extend the fast time for the New York-Chicago run from eighteen to twenty hours, with a corresponding lengthening of schedules for the Saint Louis and Cincinnati trains.[41] If Central Union and the PCC&StL stations seemed overcrowded in the early morning hours, their overall traffic density for the day was respectively only a little above and a little below the average density for metropolitan terminals at the time, and very much below the density of the busiest stations. In 1921 the union depot accommodated 158 weekday trains on eight tracks, for an average of 19.8 trains per track per day, substantially above the average of 13.3 trains for representative large terminals but well below the maximum of 33.1 trains at Broad Street Station in Philadelphia, a record that was never challenged until the opening of the Philadelphia Thirtieth Street Station in 1934.[42]

The railroad plant of metropolitan Cincinnati had been completed with respect to track, right of way, and structures in 1904, and it was to retain the basic form until the tremendous and final construction program that was initiated in 1928. There were minor corporate changes around the time of World War I that did little more than alter the relations between certain trunk lines and the older, smaller Cincinnati companies. A long receivership of the Cincinnati, Hamilton and Dayton Railroad, which prevented its wholehearted acceptance into the B&O fold, culminated in a new and short-lived rail corporation in 1913. The long Hamilton-Indianapolis-Springfield, Illinois, branch of the CH&D was detached from the parent company and reorganized as the Cincinnati, Indianapolis and Western Railroad, which survived as a separate company until 1927, when it was acquired by the B&O, ten years after the larger road finally merged the Hamilton line into its own system. In the same year (1917) the Southern Railway acquired control of the CNO&TP but did not alter the rental agreement between the smaller company and the municipally owned Cincinnati Southern. In 1921 the prosperous PCC&StL Railway lost what independence it still possessed when it was leased to, and progressively merged with, the Pennsylvania. The arrangement was to be repeated on an equal scale nine years later, when the Big Four entered into the same relation with the New York Central Railroad.[43]

The one large structure in the Cincinnati area that could not survive the heavy wartime traffic was the Ohio River bridge of the Cincinnati Southern and its operating affiliate, the CNO&TP. Much of the original bridge had been replaced over a period of years up to 1911, and although it was decided within a few years that a renewal of the river crossing was an essential next step, the war held up construction for more than four years. The War Department issued the permit to undertake the work in 1916, and the celebrated structural engineer Ralph Modjeski completed the plans in the following year; but construction was not initiated until the spring of 1921, so that completion was put off until April 1922 (fig. 41). The bridge remains unique among Cincinnati truss spans: except for the lift span at the Ludlow end, carried by subdivided Pratt trusses, the structure consists of Warren trusses continuous over three spans. The level profile of the top chord does not reflect the bending-moment distribution, as it does in the similar Ohio River structures of the C&O Railway; instead, a uniform truss depth of seventy feet was held throughout the length of the bridge. The pivot pier of the old swing span was abandoned for the new bridge, but the remaining piers were retained, raised, and encased

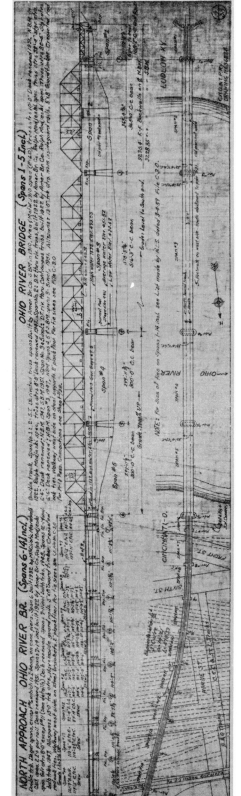
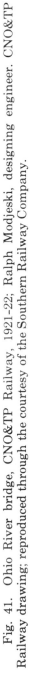

Fig. 41. Ohio River bridge, CNO&TP Railway, 1921–22; Ralph Modjeski, designing engineer. CNO&TP Railway drawing; reproduced through the courtesy of the Southern Railway Company.

in reinforced concrete to take the double-track line and the heavier loading of the 1920 trains. The entire Cincinnati approach was replaced by a steel plate-girder viaduct the construction of which was complicated by the necessity to build over the extremely busy forty-five yard tracks that lay in an unbroken file from Sixth Street to the CNO&TP loop tracks near Eighth Street. The trusses of the river crossing were erected by the novel device of building them around the existing trusses, so that the structure could be kept in service for all but short intervals between heavy traffic flows.[44]

The least conspicuous form of railroad technology to the layman, but the one that may yield the greatest improvements in the efficiency and safety of operations, is signaling. By the time the United States entered the war, the railroads serving Cincinnati had placed nearly all of the main lines radiating from the city under block-signal control, although the major portion of the mileage was still the manual type rather than the more economical and more reliable automatic form. The one holdout was the L&N, with only 14 percent of its passenger-line mileage under block signals at the beginning of 1917. The company drastically expanded this proportion during the year, however, by placing the northern 351 miles of its Atlanta line under automatic block in one continuous installation. This large investment was actually only part of an extensive reconstruction program involving yard improvements and expansions and the double tracking of the entire Kentucky Division main line, extending from Cincinnati to Corbin, Kentucky, a distance of 187 miles. The cause of these generous expenditures was most gratifying to the railroad. The lines serving the eastern Kentucky coalfields, centered respectively at the towns of Harlan and Hazard, experienced an astronomical increase in coal traffic in the period around and immediately after World War I: in the years between 1913 and 1927 the total tonnage expanded more than 6 1/2 times, from 87,500 to 577,000 cars per annum.[45] These unexciting and even tedious data constitute a prime example of how an immense increase in rail traffic, amounting to nearly 25,000,000 tons in fourteen years, could be expeditiously handled with an almost negligible quantitative increase in the volume of physical plant. This expansion consisted almost entirely of the addition of a second track to Corbin, which added a fourteen-foot ribbon of rail property through the breadth of central Kentucky, for a total increase in property area of about 320 acres.

The unique innovation in block-signal operation and one that was prophetic of the new developments that were to come in the

183

1930s was the technique that was later to be known as reverse-direction signaling. Beginning in 1899 on an experimental basis, the operating staff of the Big Four adopted the practice on double track of moving fast trains around slow by allowing the former to cross over to the left-hand track and to run against the normal current of traffic (that is, in the reverse direction for the track in question) for a sufficient distance to complete the passing movement and return to the right-hand track. (All railroads in the United States and Canada except the Chicago and North Western ordinarily follow the right-hand practice.) By 1923 the technique had been established as a standard operating procedure in all double-track territory, which would include the lines extending from Cincinnati to Greensburg, Indiana (62.8 miles), and to Springfield, Ohio (79.3 miles). The signaling system in effect on these lines at the time was the manual-block variety with upper-quadrant semaphores. In order for the new practice to work safely and at maximum efficiency, crossover tracks had to be spaced at intervals of about five miles, an interlocking tower located at each crossover point, and indications given by two masts of home signals, one for the right-hand and one for the left-hand track. The authorization to move from one track to the other was given both by train order and signal indication. The greatest reduction in train delays and hence in train-hours per day occurred in those territories with the highest traffic density combined with the maximum diversity of traffic, and the railroad company found that the resulting saving in most cases more than offset the cost of additional interlockers and towermen.

The segment of the Big Four system on which these conditions existed in the most concentrated form was the main line of what was then the Chicago Division between Cincinnati and Greensburg, where by the mid-twenties traffic in the Cincinnati zone had risen to twenty-two passenger and forty-four freight trains per day. Traffic congestion was a consequence not only of sheer density along with the mixture of through and local traffic, but also of the nineteen-mile Tanner's Creek grade above Lawrenceburg Junction, where a heavy through freight train moving upgrade would act like the stopper in a bottle's neck. It was on the Greensburg line, accordingly, that the company took the decisive step of substituting automatic color-light block signals for the older manually controlled semaphores in the fall of 1926. The next step of merging the separate interlocking towers into a single installation and the abolition of train orders in favor of signal indications alone would have resulted in centralized traffic control, but the Big Four allowed the honor of inaugurating this valuable technique to fall to the Missouri Pacific Railway in 1927. Under the need for economies compelled by depression and postwar inflation, the new method of traffic control spread rapidly during the thirties and the fifties so that it became universal on single-track lines with a sufficient number of trains to justify a signaling system. The automatic block signals installed by the Big Four marked the beginning of a twenty-year program of the progressive replacement of semaphores by light signals on the main lines serving Cincinnati. For the most part these were varieties of color-light signals, which were first used in 1907, but the Pennsylvania and the B&O adopted special forms of their own. The former preferred the costly position-light signals, having made the original installation at Philadelphia in 1915; and the latter chose a combination of the two types known as color-position lights, first used on an experimental length of track between Deshler and Hamler, Ohio, in February 1925. The N&W later followed the Pennsylvania in also electing the position-light form, which was installed on the Cincinnati branch in 1926. With the light signals came the general adoption of automatic block on main lines, but the installations of centralized traffic control waited for the end of another world war.[46]

Locomotives

The traffic carried by the Cincinnati group of railroads in the decade following the end of federal control underwent complex changes difficult to characterize without extended analysis. The total number of passengers traveling on the Cincinnati roads declined by an ominous 41.2 percent between 1920 and 1928, from nearly 85,000,000 in the earlier year to 50,000,000 in the latter. The flourishing street railway system and the interurban lines continued to take away suburban traffic that might otherwise have gone by rail, but the inroads made by the wholly unpredicted expansion of the automobile into local intercity travel were devastating. The appearance and rapid spread of intercity buses during the decade brought another form of highway competition that ate still further into passenger earnings. Timetables of 1920 showed multiple local schedules on every branch as well as on every main line; by 1929 branch-line locals were either disappearing or had been reduced to one train in each direction, and these were operated mainly to carry mail. The depression of the thirties, with terrifying swiftness, killed off nearly all the remainder. Yet the extravagant decade seemed at the time to be the heyday of rail travel: the 1928 issues of the *Official Railway Guide* were the most voluminous in its sixty years of publication; announcements of the chief Pullman trains were filled with the promise of luxurious adventure, on which one could drink the illegal Prohibition liquor (if one could drink it at all) safe from the police, in surroundings of almost sybaritic comfort. The passenger train and the locomotive were still popular symbols of power and speed and national fulfillment; they were only beginning to be eclipsed by the automobile, and were as yet unaffected by the airplane. The reason was that while local business fell at an accelerating rate, commercial and holiday travel in sleeping and parlor cars continued to grow; so that the greatest size of the Pullman fleet came in 1930, when the company operated 9,890 units. The small number of sleeping cars owned and operated by individual railroad companies (notably the Milwaukee Road and the Soo Line) brought the total to more than 10,000. Since such traffic looked like the source of passenger prosperity to the railroad officers, they understandably poured money into luxury Pullman equipment, high-speed service, and costly stations.

More than offsetting the decline in passenger revenues during the twenties was a continuing increase in freight tonnage, though the rate of expansion fell far below the spectacular growth of the years between 1900 and 1920. The chief reason for this slowing-down in the rate of traffic increase was the growing competition of waterways and motor trucks, the latter eventually reaching the point where they took nearly all the merchandise and less-than-carload tonnage. In the eight years preceding 1928 the freight traffic of the Cincinnati roads climbed only 17.1 percent beyond the 1920 level, but the individual roads experienced such extreme differences in traffic growth that the underlying pattern of change was too complex for general characterization. In the period of 1920–28 the B&O Railroad gained tonnage at an overall rate equal to little more than one-tenth of the average for the seven roads, in part because of the diversion of traffic destined for the Chicago area and the Lake Erie ports to other, newly completed lines. Two of the big coal-carriers, on the other hand, the N&W and the L&N, saw their traffic increase by nearly a third over the 1920 level, while the C&O experienced an unparalleled 61 percent jump, first, because of the demand for Pocahontas coal, and second, because traffic previously diverted to connecting roads at Cincinnati could now be carried to Toledo and Detroit over a combination of the company's newly opened Columbus line and those of its greatly improved affiliates, the Hocking Valley and the Pere Marquette (respectively merged with the larger company in 1930 and 1947). The other roads, with a substantial tonnage of manufactured products and perishable commodities that was vulnerable to truck competition, enjoyed only modest increases, ranging from 9.6 percent for the Pennsylvania to 16.4 percent for the Big Four.

The significance of these changes in traffic for the development of motive power rested on two factors: the emphasis in both freight and passenger service was on speed and weight of trains to meet inter-railroad and highway competition, to reduce costs, and to increase efficiency by combining trains as the local traffic declined. The mechanical problem was to design increasingly powerful locomotives with the capacity to develop high horsepower at a sustained rate over long periods of time. The light, fast passenger and the slow-moving freight engines of the pre–World War era were no longer adequate for main line service. The last of the older forms of power to be manufactured for use on Cincinnati lines was a group of Pennsylvania Railroad Ten-wheelers (4-6-0 type) that came from the company's shops at Altoona in 1923. They were undoubtedly the most powerful engines of their wheel arrangement ever built in the United States, their tractive force of 41,330 pounds placing them in the class of many of the heavier Pacific types. They were used in the Cincinnati region mostly for the Michigan trains, but they were increasingly confined to the territory north of Grand Rapids, where light rail and train-order operations kept speeds at the modest level suitable for lake-and-woodland vacation service.[47] But a substantially enlarged Pacific type (4-6-2) was essential, and it was the Pennsylvania Lines that created the prototype of the new and heavier form. The first of the celebrated Class K-4 Pacifics emerged from the Altoona shops in 1914, and before manufacture ceased in 1928 the railroad company had produced 350 of them and the Baldwin Locomotive Works another 75. Combining unusual power (44,400 pounds tractive force) with the big eighty-inch driving wheels necessary for high-speed service, they constituted very nearly the universal motive power for the road's immense and diversified passenger traffic. There were so many of them spread out through a system-wide pool that when wartime demands greatly increased the length of trains and eastern electrification had released steam power, the company adopted the practice of using two engines on every train of 1,000 tons or more and lengthening locomotive runs to compensate for the reduction in the number of available units.[48]

The L&N Railroad began a program of motive power acquisition in 1920 that not only substantially increased the power of existing types but ultimately gave the company the greatest diversity of passenger locomotives among the lines terminating at Cincinnati. This double aim arose in part from increased traffic requirements and in part from the fact that the road's long main lines to Atlanta and New Orleans traversed regions of great topographical diversity. The first step came when the company's shops produced the Pacific type locomotive of Class K-4B, which was comparatively light but at the same time a transitional work to the much heavier engines that were to become the rule in the latter half of the decade. The Brooks Locomotive Works manufactured the L&N's own version of the heavy Pacific in 1924, the Class K-5, which marked a 28 percent increase in tractive force over its predecessor.[49] The Southern Railway and its numerous controlled lines followed the new program in the same year, when the American Locomotive Company's plant at Schenectady turned out the striking Class Ps-4 Pacifics. These were the most powerful engines of their type at the time they were built, with a tractive force of 47,500 pounds, and they were a visual sensation among locomotives by virtue of their balanced proportions and their green and gold-striped livery. The conventional olive-green rolling stock seemed almost drab by comparison. Two years later the C&O followed suit with an equally powerful locomotive, the Class F-19 Pacific, which was the end product of a steady evolution in the direction of constantly increasing weight and tractive effort. The C&O engines, manufactured at the Richmond Works of the American Locomotive Company, were the strangest looking machines on the Cincinnati lines because of the company practice of placing air compressors and feedwater heater on the front of the smokebox to keep the fat boilers and their appurtenances within clearance limits.[50] These heavy locomotives were seldom used at Cincinnati until the inauguration of the train designated the *George Washington* in 1932, since the company found that the lighter Pacifics and the Atlantics were adequate for the level lines along the Ohio and Kanawha rivers.

The Big Four and the B&O, each through its own special requirements, carried the Pacific-type locomotive to the highest stage of its development in the United States. The New York Central Railroad, acting as parent and drafter of motive power specifications for its numerous affiliates, had brought the 4-6-2 form through a virtually orthogenetic evolution as one class followed another from 1903 to 1923. As the already immense volume of passenger traffic grew steadily, as trains lengthened, and as the schedules of numerous multisection Pullman flyers grew more exacting, the road was compelled to develop engines not only marked by increasing tractive effort but more importantly by the capacity to deliver power at sustained high speeds over long runs. A major step in the realization of this aim came in 1925, when the American Locomotive Company manufactured a high-horsepower experimental Pacific locomotive arbitrarily designated as Number 5000. The engine became the basis of the Big Four's impressive Class K-5 4-6-2s of 1926, which were designed essentially for speed and horsepower, but which were equipped with a booster engine on the trailing truck that could add 9,700 pounds to the tractive force. In this way additional short-term starting power was available to set heavy trains in motion (booster engines were automatically cut out at very low speeds, about ten miles per hour). The B&O's new Pacifics were more sober in appearance and character, and were thus less spectacular than the Big Four classics. Manufactured by the Baldwin Locomotive Works in 1927, designated Class P-7, and named after presidents of the United States, they represented the ultimate design for this type of locomotive among the Cincinnati roads. Unusually high boiler pressure gave the engines a starting tractive force of 50,000 pounds, the highest up to the time of manufacture for the 4-6-2 wheel arrangement.[51]

The 4-8-2 locomotive had established itself in mountain railroading following its introduction on the C&O in 1911, but it was to lead to one of the anomalies of motive power evolution in the years following World War I. The New York Central and its family were made up for the most part of relatively level lines, as the parent company regularly proclaimed to the world. The only mountain grades were on the Berkshire crossing of the Boston and Albany, on the lightly traveled Adirondack Division, and to a lesser degree on the coal-carrying lines of the Pennsylvania and the Ohio Central divisions. Yet the New York Central began to order 4-8-2 locomotives in 1916, originally for freight service, and before the company turned to other forms of freight power twenty-eight years later, it had acquired a total of 600 engines of this type. Since the road's water-level image prevented it from acknowledging the existence of mountains, or of motive power suitable to operations among them, the vast fleet of Class L locomotives was designated the Mohawk type. In repeated orders to the American Locomotive Company the weight, boiler pressure, speed, horsepower, and tractive effort were steadily increased: a typical machine of the mid-twenties was Class L-2a (1926), with a tractive force for the main engine of 60,000 pounds, which could be increased another 12,700 pounds by means of the booster engine. In spite of the limitations on steam-generating capacity imposed by the relatively small firebox on a two-wheel trailing truck, the Mohawk classes of 1940–44 (L-3 and L-4) were expressly designed as dual-service engines to be used in either fast freight or heavy passenger service.[52] The New York Central Lines retained what seemed by 1930 to be an obsolete form for high-speed service because the road needed an engine that could handle long freight trains of merchandise and perishable commodities on exacting schedules and at the same time heavy passenger trains (sixteen to nineteen cars) at eighty miles per hour. This necessary combination of high starting tractive force with reasonably high speed was obviously best satisfied by the 4-8-2 arrangement.

The only other roads to operate 4-8-2 locomotives at Cincinnati were the CNO&TP and the L&N. The former acquired two groups of such engines in 1917 and 1919 from the Baldwin Locomotive Works, but they were so modest in weight and tractive effort as to be little more powerful than the big Pacifics of the late twenties. On the formidable Erlanger Hill directly across the river from Cincinnati, they had to be supplemented with helper engines on all trains of fourteen cars or more. The L&N was expressly searching for a passenger locomotive capable of handling heavy trains over the grades extending throughout the irregular topography of central Kentucky and Tennessee. Baldwin 4-8-2s of Class L, delivered in 1926 and 1930, filled the prescription so nicely that they saw daily service on all the long passenger trains between Cincinnati and Nashville.[53]

The Norfolk and Western Railway was the stepchild of Cincinnati railroads as far as its motive power was concerned. It was a latecomer to the local scene, and whereas the other roads either operate through the city or have established end-to-end main line connections, the N&W west of Portsmouth is a single-track branch. Through the acquisition of the Cincinnati Connecting Belt Railroad in 1901 the larger road gained a direct connection with the CH&D and the Big Four at the Ivorydale yards in Elmwood, but the location and form of that connection precluded the possiblity of operating heavy freight trains through the yards. The bulk of the N&W's immense coal tonnage moves either to the eastern seaboard at Norfolk or to the Lake Erie ports over the main line via Columbus and connecting roads north thereof, so there is little left for the Cincinnati end. The light and slow-moving passenger trains were comfortably handled by modest locomotives of the Pacific type built by company forces in 1910-14. These began to be superseded about 1930 by 4-8-2 engines built in 1919 and 1923, but it was not until the war years of the forties that the heavier power entirely displaced the aged 4-6-2s.[54]

The final innovation in steam locomotive design to appear among the Cincinnati railroads represented the last step in the motive power revolution of the mid-twenties. The New York Central's mechanical engineers had conducted a never-ending search for a locomotive that would keep heavy Pullman trains moving on the most exacting schedules over runs extending the length of entire main lines, with portions up to 171 miles (Buffalo to Collinwood, Ohio) to be covered without stops at sustained high speed. They found it at last in the 4-6-4 or Hudson type, introduced in 1927 as a wholly novel form designed by the engineering staff of the American Locomotive Company from the specifications prepared by Paul W. Kiefer, the railroad's chief engineer of motive power and rolling stock. It was the most celebrated, most photographed, most powerful per pound of weight, and most expensive locomotive so far built, and it worked so well on the New York Central Lines that the parent company ordered a total of 275 machines from the American plant over the decade of 1927-37 (fig. 42). The Hudson (Class J) appeared on the Big Four in 1929, at first restricted to the premier all-Pullman trains such as the *Ohio State Limited* among the Cincinnati flyers, but used throughout the system by the time the merger was physically completed in 1936. The secret of its success, of course, was the four-wheel trailing truck that allowed a 20.2 percent increase in the grate area of the firebox over the Class K-5 Pacific, with a comparable increase in the capacity to generate steam. Another advantage arising from the same feature was the large booster engine that pushed the starting tractive force to the level reached by 4-8-2 locomotives. The mechanical stoker, superheater, power reverse gear, automatic stop, speed recorder, and feedwater heater made it the last word in all respects. Its appearance was distinctive, if not rather peculiar: the enlarged boiler, the close clearance restrictions, and the optimum weight distribution required that the feedwater heater be partly buried in the smokebox and the compound air compressors be located on the pilot deck behind steel shields. The visual consequence was a compact and ponderous silhouette that suggested power rather than speed.[55]

Grand Schemes for the New Century

The evolution of freight power on the Cincinnati roads produced nothing so marvelous as the Hudson, or even its most recent predecessors among the Pacifics. The Consolidation type (2-8-0) began to give way to the Mikado (2-8-2) in the early years of the century, and the later forms that came in the 20s were derived in great measure from the standard 2-8-2 adopted by the United States Railroad Administration in 1918. They were heavier, more powerful, and more efficient than their predecessors, but their innovative features lay in mechanical details such as power-driven stokers, power reverse gears, and feedwater heaters. The New York Central and the American Locomotive Company brought the type to its highest stage in 1923 for the constituent Michigan Central Railroad and put its successors to work on the Big Four in the following year, but that was destined to be the end of its evolution.[56]

There were two exceptions to the dominance of the 2-8-0s and the 2-8-2s among the freight trains of the Cincinnati roads. One was the most powerful freight locomotive to appear on the local scene, the 2-10-2 or Santa Fe type that the B&O acquired in sizable numbers over the years from 1914 to 1926. The company used them on the Toledo Division, the former CH&D main line, to move heavy coal trains up the long grade extending north out of Mill Creek Valley through Wyoming and Glendale. The other was a curiosity that most railroads regarded with scorn. The 4-8-0, variously called the Twelve-wheel and the Mastodon type, was confined to the N&W, which was said to have operated at one time two-thirds of all such engines in the United States, although the company's entire fleet was built in 1910-11. The B&O engines were behemoths, the last forms weighing more than 200 tons and delivering 84,300 pounds of tractive effort. The N&W oddities, on the other hand, were limited to 52,457 pounds at the drawbar. The company retained them, apparently, because the twelve wheels held the rails well on the uneven and tortuous track of the coal-mining country.[57]

The majority of Cincinnati rail lines carried either a traffic of intermediate density that could be comfortably accommodated

Opposite: Fig. 42. CCC&StL Railway train at Central Union Depot, 1931. A massive pier of the C&O bridge approach stands beside the track. The train is probably the *Ohio State Limited*, outbound for New York, since it was the only train at the time for which the New York Central Lines Class J (4-6-4 type) locomotive was regularly used. Reproduced with the permission of the Cincinnati Historical Society.

on single track outside the area of local concentrations, or they carried a homogeneous traffic on a relatively level right of way. This was most obviously the case with the C&O, which skirted a succession of river banks from Cincinnati to the mountains of West Virginia, and which operated chiefly heavy coal trains and a few passenger trains that rarely exceeded a speed of sixty miles per hour. Most of the roads, as a consequence, did not have to face special operating difficulties in any very acute form. The conspicuous exceptions to these general circumstances were the L&N and the Big Four, although they fell into this category for radically different reasons. The long main lines of the Louisville company traverse a great variety of topography, ranging from rugged hills and mountain spurs to Gulf Coast marshlands where the track is as level as the water surface and no more than a few feet above it. The lines of the Big Four, on the other hand, lie in country largely free of grades and sharp curves, but they carried from the beginning the greatest diversity as well as the greatest density of traffic. Both roads required a diversified motive power, one to deal with the varied configurations of the land, and the other to haul expeditiously every kind of train in large numbers. Throughout the 1920s the Big Four regularly used Atlantic, Ten-wheel, three classes of Pacific, and Hudson type locomotives to move passenger trains that ranged from three-car locals to twelve-car Pullman flyers and even longer mail and express trains. The Pennsylvania Lines faced something of the same problem on a lesser scale, so that Atlantics and a single weight of Pacifics served the road's needs. The L&N, on the other hand, used four classes of engines to haul a single premier train, the *Pan-American*, over the long run from Cincinnati to New Orleans.[58] The company provided a model example of the efficient and rational utilization of motive power, with each class of locomotive being operated under conditions of topography and train weight for which it was best suited. The irregular hill, ridge, and valley topography extends from Cincinnati to Montgomery, Alabama, with the heaviest grades and the sharpest and most numerous curves in the 114 miles en route to Louisville, where speed restrictions were forty-five, fifty, and fifty-five miles per hour. Along the Gulf Coast, at the other extreme, the track lies on trestles over open water or over marshes where one cannot distinguish the land from the sea. The heaviest power, 4-8-2 of Class L-1, was used between Cincinnati and Nashville, and the lightest, Pacifics of Class K-2A, between Mobile and New Orleans. Pacifics of intermediate weight protected the intermediate portions of the run, where train weights were lighter and topography less demanding than they were north of Louisville.[59]

The combined locomotive pool at Cincinnati probably remained constant throughout the twenties in spite of the steady drop in passenger traffic and an attendant though lesser decline in the number of trains. With the emphasis on Pullman travel the roads had to be prepared for the operation of numerous extra sections of scheduled runs during the periods of peak movement, such as the Florida winter season, the Christmas holidays, and the summer vacation months. In 1928, when the working plans for the long-delayed union terminal were being prepared, the Cincinnati roads operated a total of 197 weekday passenger trains listed in the public timetables, and a full total of 224 per day, including special runs, mail and express trains, and extra sections of regularly scheduled trains. The union depot traffic continued to account for nearly two-thirds of the total, while the once lively Baymiller Street Station was falling into permanent eclipse.[60] The number of sleeping and parlor car runs originating at, or passing through, Cincinnati steadily increased throughout the decade, most rapidly in the case of the wintertime Florida trains. The average number of sleeping cars regularly scheduled and listed in 1928 was 289 per day, of which slightly more than one-quarter were operated by the Big Four alone. The number of transfer routes had risen to 38, which required the connecting movements of a minimum of 66 and a probable maximum of 110 cars every day of the week. This high total, undoubtedly the highest for any terminal area in the national rail system, became a major element in rail operations at Cincinnati and was a decisive factor in the planning for the new union terminal.[61] Another determinant, which was intensified in its effect by the large number of transfer sleepers, was the extreme concentration of morning arrivals: there was an average at Central Union Depot alone of thirty-four between seven and nine o'clock, and a total of fifty-two for all stations, or one train every 2.3 minutes. The problems posed by these two factors were compounded by the constantly growing length, speed, and servicing costs of the long-distance sleeping car trains. They were becoming a burden with which the forces of limited station, engine terminal, and coach yard facilities found it increasingly difficult to cope.[62]

If the railroads had made any serious efforts to meet the highway competition for short-run daytime traffic, the terminal situation at Cincinnati might have approached paralysis by 1928; but there was only one attempt, and that a very belated one, to revive the falling day-coach travel. In April 1929 the Big Four inaugurated a new all-coach train on the run between Cincinnati, Toledo, and Detroit, the first of its kind outside the local and accommodation runs. The train consisted of coaches with individual reclining seats, a dining car, and a full-length observation-lounge car, all the equipment completely rebuilt from standard rolling stock at the company's Beech Grove Shops. The decorative scheme represented a marked improvement over dreary day-coach interiors, and the external livery of buff and tan was a welcome change from the tiresome Pullman green. The schedule of the train, however, hardly suggested a new age of rail speed: the distance of 267 miles was covered in six hours, for an average speed of 44.5 miles per hour. Rather oddly named the *Motor Queen*, after the Motor City and the Queen City, the elegant train failed to generate the traffic that the Big Four's officers expected, and they withdrew it in December 1929, eight months after its maiden run. Unsuccessful though it was regarded, it proved to be the beginning of a great improvement in day-coach service that culminated in the establishment in 1939 of the once celebrated all-coach trains between New York and Chicago, the *Pacemaker* of the New York Central and the *Trail Blazer* of the Pennsylvania. The new day came, however, only because of economic depression and a drastically lower schedule of fares.

1. The following tables provide a comparison of the growth of the two types of rail traffic with that of the national population:

POPULATION OF THE UNITED STATES

Year	Population	Percent of Increase (1900 = 100)
1900	75,994,575	100.00
1910	91,972,226	121.02
1920	105,710,620	139.10

RAILROAD PASSENGER TRAFFIC

Year	Number of Passengers	Percent of Increase (1900 = 100)
1900	576,865,000	100.00
1910	971,683,000	168.44
1920	1,269,913,000	220.14

Grand Schemes for the New Century

RAILROAD FREIGHT TRAFFIC

Year	Tons of Freight	Percent of Increase (1900 = 100)
1900	593,971,000	100.00
1910	1,026,492,000	172.81
1920	1,362,999,000	229.47

SOURCES: United States Census; *Poor's Manual of the Railroads of the United States.*

2. The following .tables give the total traffic of the Class I Cincinnati railroads at five-year intervals from 1900 to 1920, with data for 1918 included to indicate wartime peaks (CC&L omitted; rate of increase over 1900 exaggerated because of inclusion of N&W in 1905 and subsequent years):

PASSENGER TRAFFIC OF CINCINNATI RAILROADS

Year	Number of Passengers	Percent of Increase (1900 = 100)
1900	36,416,116	100.00
1905	51,081,099	140.27
1910	65,997,427	181.23
1915	67,694,742	185.89
1918	83,444,264	229.16
1920	85,135,018 [a]	233.78

FREIGHT TRAFFIC OF CINCINNATI RAILROADS

Year	Tons of Freight	Percent of Increase (1900 = 100)
1900	93,529,872	100.00
1905	148,846,371	159.14
1910	218,214,097	233.31
1915	232,623,708	248.72
1918	321,646,880	343.90
1920	328,261,388 [a]	350.97

SOURCE: *Poor's Manual.*

[a] Traffic for the PCC&StL Railroad is estimated for 1920 because data are included in totals for Pennsylvania Railroad, lessee.

3. The increase in freight traffic for the two companies is given in the following table:

LOUISVILLE AND NASHVILLE

Year	Tons of Freight	Percent of Increase (1900 = 100)
1900	15,839,470	100.00
1920	47,098,325	296.80
1928	61,241,738	386.60

CHESAPEAKE AND Ohio

Year	Tons of Freight	Percent of Increase (1900 = 100)
1900	9,746,840	100.00
1920	40,838,116	418.90
1930	72,764,685	746.30

SOURCE: *Poor's Manual.*

The peak years indicated in the above tables are the peaks for the period of rail dominance prior to the depression of 1930. Traffic on the L&N and the C&O reached new records following World War II (see Appendix C, tables 5 and 6).

4. Revenues, expenses, net operating incomes, and operating ratios of the Class I Cincinnati railroads for the fiscal year ended 30 June 1910 are given in the table on page 199.

5. The CN's rather fatuous program was a forerunner of the interurban plan of 1912 and the rapid transit plan of 1916, but it is doubtful whether the later planners were aware of this fact (see pp. 159-76).

6. "Cincinnati, Ohio," *Railroad Gazette* 35:41 (9 October 1903), p. 729, and 35:52 (25 December 1903), p. 929.

7. "Cincinnati, Ohio," under "Railroad Structures," ibid., 37:6 (22 July 1904), p. 41.

8. The overall dimensions of the CNO&TP freight station were 130 × 1,142 feet 6 inches, in area of plan the largest building in the city center. The station was followed by the construction in 1908-9 of a viaduct extending from Eighth Street and McLean Avenue to Front Street near Plum. Because of the alignment at a sharp angle to the ruling street pattern, some of the street crossings required truss bridges so extremely skewed that the two parallel trusses were displaced more than the length of a panel. Such bridges, with the top and bottom frames in the form of a parallelogram, are subject to high torsional forces. The viaduct added still another artery to the fantastic tangle of depressed, grade-level, and elevated rail lines and city streets that once characterized Cincinnati's lower West End.

9. The city engineers had realized by 1900 that the elevation of railroad lines would have interfered so drastically with local drainage that the only alternative was to build long street viaducts in the areas of most extensive trackage. The first of these was Harrison Avenue Viaduct over Mill Creek Valley, planned in 1901 and opened in 1908.

10. I have not been able to discover the architect who designed the proposed union station, but the open rectangular plan with surrounding offices suggests a Chicago hand, and he may very well have been one of Burnham's staff.

11. Planning of the 1904 terminal rested on a survey of traffic at the six Cincinnati stations conducted in the winter of 1904-5, with the following results:

NUMBER OF TRAINS OPERATED PER DAY
(By Station)

Station	Arrivals	Departures	Total
Central Union	57	57	114
Pennsylvania Lines	24	24	48
Baymiller Street	24	24	48
Court Street	7	7	14
Fourth Street	5	5	10
Eighth Street (CC&L)	1	1	2
Total	118	118	236

NUMBER OF PASSENGER-TRAIN CARS
ASSEMBLED PER DAY
(By Station)

Station	No. of Cars
Central Union	672
Pennsylvania Lines	208
Baymiller Street	194
Court Street	33
Fourth Street	46
Eighth Street (CC&L)	6
Total	1,159

The announced plans of the 1904 station project offered no details on sig-

Railroad	Freight Revenue	Passenger Revenue	Total Revenue	Total Expenses	Net Operating Income	Operating Ratio
B&O	$68,228,441	$14,110,841	$87,068,976	$59,989,470	$27,079,506	68.9%
C&O	24,901,199	5,002,205	31,237,169	18,936,699	12,300,470	60.6
CC&L	1,152,245	300,519	1,542,519	1,442,241	100,278	93.5
CH&D	6,757,319	1,682,031	9,446,524	7,587,296	1,859,228	80.3
CNO&TP	7,082,859	1,536,939	9,079,471	5,530,873	3,548,598	60.9
CCC&StL	19,276,750	7,475,514	29,330,985	21,234,065	8,096,920	72.4
L&N	38,421,779	10,796,997	52,433,381	34,985,578	17,447,803	66.7
N&W	30,037,796	3,924,890	35,063,870	21,046,760	14,017,110	60.0
PCC&StL	27,702,416	7,601,046	39,589,164	27,778,107	11,811,057	70.2
Total/Average	223,560,804	52,430,982	294,792,059	198,531,089	96,260,970	67.3

SOURCE: *Railroad Gazette.*

naling or engine terminal facilities. My estimate of the required approach track-age rests on the assumption that the new terminal would have been equipped with automatic signals and an electro-pneumatic interlocking.

12. The participating companies at the time were the B&OSW, C&O, CNO&TP, CCC&StL, and L&N.

13. The C&O operates alternate single-track main lines between Covington, Virginia, and Richmond, Virginia. It is thus the only railroad serving Cincinnati that operates in effect a continuous double-track line between the city and any other terminal point.

14. Reported in "Cincinnati, Ohio," under "Railroad Structures," *Railway Age Gazette* 48:21 (27 May 1910), p. 1327.

15. "Damage by Flood to Railroads," ibid., 54:14 (4 April 1913), p. 806.

16. The cost of damage per road as of June 1913 was as follows:

B&O (including CH&D)	$3,000,000
CCC&StL	2,500,000
PCC&StL	1,640,000
N&W	526,500
C&O	300,000
Total	$7,966,500

SOURCE: ibid.

(Translated into building costs of the 1975 level, this total would come close to at least $105,000,000.) The CNO&TP sustained only minor damage, and figures for the L&N were not reported, although its line in the Licking valley was vulnerable.

17. The following tables indicate the decline in net income in the year ended 30 June 1914 and the general loss of traffic between 1914 and 1915:

DECLINE IN NET INCOME

Railroad	Total Operating Revenues	Total Operating Expenses	Net Operating Income	Operating Ratio
B&O	$ 97,411,441	$ 72,054,892	$25,356,549	76.0
C&O	36,690,021	25,653,937	11,036,084	69.9
CH&D	10,084,217	9,737,841	346,376	96.6
CNO&TP	10,872,690	7,706,720	3,165,970	70.9
CCC&StL	36,027,653	31,872,040	4,155,613	88.5
L&N	59,682,778	44,782,708	14,900,070	75.0
N&W	44,470,619	29,935,842	14,534,777	67.3
PCC&StL	42,096,662	33,201,786	8,894,876	78.2
Total/Average	$337,336,081	$254,945,766	$82,390,315	75.6

TRAFFIC LOSS

Railroad	Operating Revenues 1914	Operating Revenues 1915	Percent Change
B&O	$ 99,085,091	$ 91,815,797	-7.3
C&O	37,459,864	39,464,037	5.4
CH&D	10,084,217	9,725,972	-3.6
CNO&TP	10,962,100	9,422,252	-14.0
CCC&StL	36,405,577	35,824,106	-1.6
L&N	59,906,467	51,606,015	-13.9
N&W	44,650,310	42,987,044	-3.7
PCC&StL	42,117,598	38,412,030	-8.8
Total/Average	$340,671,184	$319,257,253	-6.3

SOURCE: *Railway Age Gazette*. (I cannot account for the small discrepancies between these two tables.)

Grand Schemes for the New Century

18. "The Lessons of the Recent Floods," *Railway Age Gazette* 54:16 (18 April 1913), p. 886.

19. "Proposed Union Station in Cincinnati," *Railway Age Gazette* 62:8 (23 February 1917), pp. 327-28.

20. The revenue passengers carried per year by Ohio interurban companies, 1907-33, is given in the following table:

Year	Number of Passengers
1907	74,090,750
1908	97,076,387
1909	154,251,425
1910	157,851,752
1911	168,998,448
1912	188,159,788
1913	180,995,437
1914	193,273,618
1915	181,563,665
1916	190,987,015
1917	211,123,417
1918	234,285,911
1919	256,963,473
1920	234,885,075
1921	245,330,709
1922	226,294,810
1923	196,616,679
1924	210,125,773
1925	193,134,819
1926	179,418,298
1927	166,106,891
1928	156,075,916
1929	126,755,878
1930	110,940,104
1931	84,872,813
1932	56,192,527
1933	39,544,202

From George W. Hilton and John F. Due, *The Electric Interurban Railways in America* (Stanford, Calif.: Stanford University Press). Source: *Annual Reports* of the Railroad Commission of Ohio, 1912; *Annual Report* of the Public Service Commission of Ohio, 1912; *Annual Reports* of the Public Utilities Commission of Ohio, 1913-33. Reprinted with the permission of the Stanford University Press.

Before the end of the decade of the thirties the Ohio system was gone, and so were most of the others.

21. The subsidiaries of the Interurban Railway and Terminal Company were the Cincinnati and Eastern Electric Railway (New Richmond line), the Suburban Traction Company (Bethel line), and the Rapid Railway (Lebanon line). The three were merged in 1902.

22. Reliable figures compiled over the years on the traffic of the Cincinnati interurban companies range from scarce to nonexistent. The table for the years 1908-12 on page 202 provides some idea of the magnitude and expansion of their operations in the days of their ascendancy.

Since the expansion of Cincinnati-based traffic began earlier than that of the state as a whole and reached the high level more rapidly, it is difficult to calculate the traffic of the Cincinnati interurban lines by extrapolation from the state totals. In the peak year of 1919 the local roads carried about 25,000,000 passengers, the actual number lying between 20 and 31 million, depending on whether one takes 1912 or 1908 as the base year. By 1929 this number had fallen back to the level of twenty years earlier, about 13,000,000, and by 1933 the fast shrinking total was no more than 5,000,000 passengers for the year.

201

NUMBER OF PASSENGERS CARRIED BY CINCINNATI INTERURBAN COMPANIES

Company	1908	1909	1910	1911	1912
Cincinnati and Columbus Traction	537,529	503,680	555,429	586,596	608,470
Cincinnati, Lawrenceburg and Aurora	1,385,150	1,368,357	1,431,404	1,467,506	1,519,873
Cincinnati, Georgetown and Portsmouth	790,244	878,237	905,034	830,633	1,021,551
Cincinnati, Milford and Blanchester	527,345	725,956	692,365	709,838	811,300
Interurban Railway and Terminal					
Cincinnati and Eastern Division	332,111	294,722	301,528	360,357	356,791
Rapid Division	1,089,989	1,155,941	1,215,956	1,200,247	1,320,019
Suburban Traction Division	578,635	521,361	527,666	597,826	553,199
Total (IR&T)	(2,000,725)	(1,972,024)	(2,045,150)	(2,158,430)	(2,230,009)
Ohio Electric	3,544,772	3,255,672	3,632,739	4,340,529	4,342,215
Ohio Traction	3,859,254	3,896,292	4,060,602	4,280,301	4,413,460
Total	12,645,029	12,600,218	13,322,723	14,373,833	14,946,878

SOURCE: Arnold, *Report on an Interurban . . . System.*

Grand Schemes for the New Century

23. A considerable proportion of the interurban-company advertising in the years of ascendancy was aimed at women, who were invited to ride the cars for shopping trips to a neighboring city and who were assured that even light-colored dresses would remain clean and nicely pressed throughout the round trip. The interurban car offered a more informal, less intimidating surrounding than the train, and there is good reason to believe that the electric cars constituted at least one factor in the new mobility of women that came with the twentieth century.

24. Bion J. Arnold has so far escaped the attention of historians outside the area of electrical technology, but he was an important figure in the evolution of electric railroad transportation and urban transit in the United States. A graduate of Cornell University in electrical engineering (1888), he served in the engineering department of the Iowa Iron Works and the General Electric Company before establishing an independent consulting engineer's office in 1893. Having gained national attention for his design of the Intramural Railway at the World's Columbian Exposition (1893), he was invited to act as consultant or planner for a great number of street railway, transit, rail terminal, and main-line railroad electrification projects. He was a member of the Electric Traction Committee of the Erie Railroad (1900-1904), consulting engineer to the municipal government of Chicago for the street railway plan of 1902, author of the basic plan for the electrification of Grand Central Terminal in New York (1902-3), consulting engineer to the Wisconsin State Railway Commission (1905-7), chief engineer for the planning and reconstruction of the Chicago street railway system (1907), consulting engineer for the electrification of the Saint Clair Tunnel of the Grand Trunk Western Railroad (1907-8), consulting engineer at various times on street railway, rapid transit, and railroad terminal plans for Toronto, Pittsburgh, Cleveland, Cincinnati, Chicago, San Francisco, and Los Angeles. He died in 1942 at the age of 81 years. He was one of the foremost authorities on railroad terminal electrification during the period in which many of the leading projects were carried out (1903-33).

25. The map of the Arnold plan contains one error and two omissions: the north-south rail line toward the east side of Mill Creek Valley is incorrectly designated CCC&StL and should be B&OSW; the C&O's Fourth Street Station and the N&W's transfer line between Idlewild and Elmwood are not shown.

26. The junction points between the belt and the interurban lines, taken in clockwise order, are given in the following outline:

Ohio Electric: Mill Creek Valley near Spring Grove Cemetery, at the foot of the north slope of Clifton hill.

Ohio Traction: Saint Bernard near Vine Street.

Interurban Railway and Terminal Rapid Division: Montgomery Road crossing in Norwood.

Cincinnati and Columbus Traction: CL&N crossing in Norwood.

Cincinnati, Milford and Loveland: by extension westward along the B&OSW right of way through Oakley to the B&OSW-CL&N crossing in Norwood.

Cincinnati, Georgetown and Portsmouth: by extension westward along the PCC&StL right of way to the Eastern Avenue crossing.

Interurban Railway and Terminal Cincinnati and Eastern and Suburban divisions: by trackage rights over the CG&P.

Cincinnati, Lawrenceburg, and Aurora: by extension eastward at Cleves over the far western hills to a connection with the Cincinnati and Westwood at Westwood, thence over the proposed Queen City viaduct to the West End; or the alternative, by extension eastward by Muddy Creek ravine in the western hills to a connection with the Cincinnati and Westwood. (Either of these routes would have been extremely costly because of steep grades, narrow, tortuous rights of way, and extensive cutting and filling in the rugged topography of the high hills that extend in an unbroken range westward to the Great Maimi valley.)

Cincinnati and Indianapolis Traction (proposed): connection with Cincinnati and Westwood in Westwood. (Only a small part of this line was ever placed under construction.)

27. The revenues of the Cincinnati companies in the year ended 30 June 1912 indicate their modest resources and the extent to which they relied on passenger traffic:

Company	Passenger Revenues	Freight Revenues	Total Revenues
Cincinnati and Columbus Traction	$ 96,446	$ 14,424	$ 110,870
Cincinnati, Lawrenceburg and Aurora	137,054	. . . . . .	137,054
Cincinnati, Georgetown and Portsmouth	130,016	51,210	181,226
Interurban Railway and Terminal			
Cincinnati and Eastern Div.	49,650	14,823	64,473
Rapid Div.	129,779	20,831	150,610
Suburban Div.	65,524	37,363	102,887
Ohio Electric	447,713	73,499	521,212
Ohio Traction	280,492	. . . . . .	280,492
Total	$1,425,881	$238,843	$1,664,724

SOURCE: Arnold, op. cit.

The relatively high proportion of freight to total revenues in the case of the CG&P and the two eastern lines of the Interurban Railway and Terminal may be attributed to the scarcity of railroad mileage in the areas they served.

28. Financial developments involving the street railway company in recent years underlay these complex relations. The Cincinnati Street Railway Company was organized as a unified system in 1896, with a uniform city-wide fare of five cents. The enabling legislation passed by the General Assembly in the same year allowed the unification of the previously separate companies, fixed the fare, and granted a 50-year operating franchise, renewable at the end of the first 20 years and at 15-year intervals thereafter. In 1901 the street railway company was leased to a holding company known as the Cincinnati Traction Company, which was controlled in turn by the Ohio Traction Company, a relationship that explains the adoption of the 5-foot 2 1/2-inch gauge on the part of the operating interurban company.

29. The precedents for this combination of municipal construction and ownership with operation by a private corporation were, first, the Cincinnati Southern Railway and, second, the Interborough Rapid Transit in New York City, which was built by the municipality through a private contractor (1900–1904) and leased for operation to a private corporation.

30. The main segments of the route were the following: north from Fountain Square in Walnut Street; west under the canal bed through the Race Street station to Plum; northbound by subway to Brighton under the canal bed; north and east on the canal bed to Saint Bernard; through Bond Hill and the Norwood trough to Norwood and Duck Creek Valley; through Duck Creek Valley and Hyde Park to the ravine occupied by Torrence Road; along the PCC&StL right of way and under East Fifth Street to Fountain Square (construction everywhere beyond Brighton was to be at or above grade level). The detailed planning was done by the office of the chief engineer, Cincinnati Rapid Transit Commission.

Grand Schemes for the New Century

31. Frank L. Raschig, "Cincinnati Builds Belt-Line Rapid-Transit Railway," *Engineering News-Record* 87:7 (18 August 1921), p. 265.

32. Ibid., p. 267.

33. The actual clearance was 13 feet in width × 14 feet 9 inches in height above the top of rail. The only other rapid transit company to provide freight service was the Chicago Rapid Transit, which moved freight cars from a connection with the Milwaukee Railroad at Wilson Avenue in Chicago to an Evanston terminal (this service was abandoned in 1973). The rail connections at Cincinnati would have been established by connections with standard-gauge interurban lines.

34. Raschig, op. cit., pp. 265, 267. The boulevard designed to take the place of old Canal Street was eventually built along the canal bed and over the subway tunnels as far out as Ludlow Avenue on the near North Side. Designated Central Parkway, it was opened for its entire length in 1927.

35. The only cities of the United States with both rapid transit and rail commutation service are Boston, New York, Philadelphia, Chicago, and San Francisco; and among these only Boston, Philadelphia, and Chicago were also served by electric interurban lines, of which one still survives in Chicago (1975), namely, the Chicago, South Shore and South Bend Railroad. Major interurban capitals such as Columbus and Indianapolis had no rail suburban service since they had no need for it.

36. The comparative traffic of the Cincinnati lines for 1915 and 1918 is given in the following table:

Year	Tons of Freight	Number of Passengers
1915	232,623,708	67,694,742
1918	321,646,880	83,444,264
Increase	38.3%	23.3%

37. The staff of *Railway Age* estimated the various needs for motive power, rolling stock, and property improvement at the end of 1919 as follows: 6,000 miles of new line; 10,850 miles of automatic block signals; 13,177 new locomotives; 15,000 miles of multiple main tracks; 30,000 miles of side and yard tracks; 24,500 new passenger-train cars; 712,400 new freight cars; total investment $6,010,000,000 ("Six Billion Dollars for Capital Expenditures," *Railway Age* 68:1 [2 January 1920], pp. 9–11).

38. The average daily volume of freight and passenger traffic at Cincinnati in 1919, broken down by type and direction, is given in the following table:

Freight terminating	
Industrial sidings	12,243 tons
Freight houses	5,910
Total	18,153
Freight originating	
Industrial sidings	11,946 tons
Freight houses	4,480
Total	16,426
Total originating and terminating	34,579
Freight interchanged	
Inbound	102,600 tons[a]
Outbound	97,400
Total	200,000
Total freight in and out	234,579
Number of freight trains	
Inbound	106
Outbound	107
Total	213

Number of Passenger Trains	
Inbound	134
Outbound	140
Total	274
Total all trains	487
Estimated number of passengers	30,000

SOURCE: Morris, "Cincinnati as a Railroad Center," *Railway Age* 68 (1920): 586.

[a] The difference of 5,200 tons between the inbound and outbound figures is accounted for by the freight that arrives and leaves in the same cars carried by identical railroads, which would be the case only for the B&O and the C&O, the only companies that operate through the city.

39. Quoted in "McAdoo's Testimony before Senate Committee," *Railway Age* 66:2 (10 January 1919), p. 127.

40. The average number of daily trains by station and railroad for 1920 is given in the following table:

Central Union Depot		
CCC&StL	66	
B&O	38	
CNO&TP	19	
L&N	10	
C&O	7	
Cincinnati Northern[a]	4	
Total		144
Total plus 15 percent		165
Pennsylvania Lines Station		
PCC&StL	33	
L&N	12	
N&W	4	
Total		49
Total plus 15 percent		57
Baymiller Street Station		
B&O	28	
Cincinnati, Indianapolis & Western	8	
Total		36
Total plus 15 percent		41
Court Street Station		
CL&N	8	
N&W	4	
Total		12
Total plus 15 percent		14
Fourth Street Station		
C&O	5	
L&N	2	
Total		7
Total plus 15 percent		8
Eighth Street Station[b]		
B&O	3	
CNO&TP	1[c]	
Total		4
Total all stations		252
Total plus 15 percent		289

[a] Cincinnati Northern trains operated by trackage rights over the Big Four between Cincinnati and Franklin, Ohio.

[b] The Cincinnati Transfer station.

[c] This single train was either a work train for crews or the Royal Palm, operated as a through train to and from Chicago via the Big Four. It was probably more convenient to make the transfer movements for the sleepers from one road to another at the junction at least in one direction. If this is the case, I have discovered no reason why the Eighth Street transfer was not made in both directions, as it was in the case of the premier B&O train (later *National Limited*) between Saint Louis and Jersey City.

Grand Schemes for the New Century

41. Times and average speeds of representative premier trains in 1920 are given in the following table.

Railroad	Train	Destination	Time (Hrs. - Min.)		Distance (Miles)	Average Speed (MPH)
B&O	Nos. 1 and 2	Saint Louis-Jersey City	32	45	1,116.8	34.1
C&O	Nos. 2 and 3	Washington	18	55	598.1	31.6
CNO&TP	Crescent City Special	New Orleans	26	30	835.7	31.6
CCC&StL	N.Y.-New England Special	New York	22	30	883.4	39.3
CCC&StL	Queen City Special	Chicago	8	05	303.3	37.5
L&N	Southland	Atlanta	13	50	489.0	35.4
N&W	Nos. 15 and 16	Norfolk	22	45	683.7	30.0
Pennsylvania	Metropolitan Express	New York	19	05	751.1	39.4
Avg. speed						34.85

42. Total traffic and traffic density for representative U.S. and Canadian stations in 1921 are given in the following table:

Station	Type	Year Opened	Number of Tracks	Number Trains Per Day	Number Trains Peak Hour	Number Trains Per Track Per Day
Boston, South Station	Stub	1899	28	660	87	23.6
Buffalo, Lehigh Valley	Stub	1917	9	18	4	2.0
Chicago, North Western	Stub	1911	16	314	50	19.7
Chicago, Grand Central	Stub	1890	6	44	7	7.3
Cincinnati, Central Union	Stub	1883	8	158	32	19.8
Cincinnati, PCC&StL	Stub	1881	6	54	12	9.0
Denver, Union	Through	1914	10	94	13	9.4
Detroit, Michigan Central	Through	1914	11	90	12	8.2
Hoboken, Lackawanna	Stub	1906	14	227	34	16.2
Indianapolis, Union	Through	1920[a]	12	186	18	15.5
Jacksonville, Union	Stub & Through	1919	21	102	15	4.9
Jersey City, Central of New Jersey	Stub	1914[b]	18	272	36	15.1
Jersey City, Erie	Stub	1888	12	376	49	31.3
Kansas City, Union	Through	1913	16	223	33	13.9
Memphis, Union	Through	1912	10	64	12	6.4
Montreal, Windsor	Stub	1888	11	84	20	7.6
New York, Grand Central	Stub & Loop	1913	66	400	49	6.1
New York, Pennsylvania	Through	1910	21	525	55	25.0
Ottawa, Union	Stub & Through	1912	8	70	12	8.8
Philadelphia, Broad Street	Stub	1893	16	529	70	33.1
Richmond, Union	Through[c]	1919	10	48	8	4.8
Saint Louis, Union	Stub	1894	32	269	48	8.4
Washington, Union	Stub & Through	1907	26	280	20	10.8
Average number trains per track per day, all stations						13.3

SOURCES: Droege, *Passenger Terminals and Trains*; Meeks, *The Railroad Station*; *Railway Age*.

[a] The original union station at Indianapolis was completed in 1886, but the track-platform area was totally rebuilt and much expanded in 1919-20.

[b] The original Central Railroad of New Jersey station at Jersey City was opened in 1888, but the track-platform area was rebuilt in 1913-14.

[c] The track system of Richmond Union Station actually lies on an immense loop, but for all practical purposes the operation is that of a through station. The plan of the station is unique in this respect.

43. The legal merger of two corporations may be accomplished in a matter of hours once the financial basis has been laid, but the physical union of two big rail systems may require years. It was 1930, for example, before the unification of shop facilities and the reclassification, renumbering, and renaming of rolling stock and motive power were completed in the case of the PCC&StL, and 1936 before the Big Four disappeared as a separate entity.

44. The total length of the river crossing in the 1922 bridge is 1,481 feet 3 inches between bearings, divided as follows: lift span, 365 feet; continuous-span lengths, one at 516 feet 3 inches and two at 300 feet; truss depth, 70 feet. The unit loading factor (based on two 2-8-0 locomotives followed by cars with a maximum gross weight of 115,000 pounds) was 3,400 pounds per lineal foot, as compared with the 1,820 pounds per foot for the 1877 structure. The construction of the bridge was accompanied by an extensive program of replacement and renovation of CNO&TP stations, interlocking towers, and viaducts in the Cincinnati area (the last chiefly the bridges on the branch serving the Vine Street freight station).

45. The increase of L&N coal traffic on the Cumberland Valley Division (Harlan region) was 326 percent, from 82,670 loaded cars in 1913 to 352,748 in 1927; on the Eastern Kentucky Division the increase was an unparalleled 4,592 percent, from 4,792 cars to 224,868 over the same years; the totals were thus 560 percent, or from 87,462 to 577,016 cars.

46. Even the most elaborate light signals are more efficient, more reliable, and less expensive than the movable semaphore blades with their electric motors. In color-light signals the standard block indications of stop, approach, and clear are given by lights respectively of red, yellow, and green color. The position-light signal, on the other hand, gives the indication by means of rows of three yellow lights (the color chosen for maximum visibility) which duplicate the positions of the upper-quadrant semaphore, namely, horizontal for stop, diagonal for approach, and vertical for clear. Since the individual row has to contain at least three lights in the event that one burns out, the three simple block indications require seven lights. The signal engineers of the B&O, determined to find a foolproof system, combined the two forms in such a way that a pair of red lights stands in the horizontal row, yellow in the diagonal, and green in the vertical. Many years of experience under all conditions demonstrated that the simple color light is the least expensive and at least the equal of the other two in legibility.

Further improvements to the properties of the N&W and the Big Four coincided with the installation of new signaling systems. Over the years 1923-26 the Norfolk line rebuilt its Cincinnati branch to the level suitable for heavy freight and passenger trains: bridges were either strengthened or reconstructed; the light rail was replaced by a heavier form (100 pounds per yard in weight); new treated ties and new stone and slag ballast took the place of untreated wood on a thin gravel bed. The maximum traffic on the line at the time came to 18 trains per day, divided between 8 passenger and 10 freight trains. The Big Four greatly extended its freight-handling facilities at Cincinnati with the construction of Riverside Yard and its associated engine terminal in 1926-28. By carving out the flank of a hill along the Ohio River about a mile west of Mill Creek, the company made room for a classification yard with a capacity of 2,315 cars. Its operating function was to classify freight from the western lines for delivery to connections and to make up trains for western terminals. When Cincinnati adopted eastern standard time in 1927, the transition point to the central time zone for the railroad was the interlocking tower that controlled the switches and signals for the western lead tracks of this yard.

47. Physical data for the Pennsylvania locomotives (designated Class G-5s) were as follows: diameter of driving wheels, 68 inches; cylinder dimensions,

24 × 28 inches; weight of engine, 237,000 pounds; boiler pressure, 205 pounds per square inch; tractive force, 41,330 pounds. (For illustrations see Staufer, *Pennsy Power*, pp. 117-23.)

48. Physical data for the Pennsylvania 4-6-2 locomotives of 1927 were the following: diameter of driving wheels, 80 inches; cylinder dimensions, 27 × 28 inches; weight of engine, 310,500 pounds; boiler pressure, 205 pounds per square inch; tractive force, 44,400 pounds. (For illustrations see ibid., p. 163; Bruce, *The Steam Locomotive in America*, fig. 32.)

49. Physical data for the L&N Class K-4B Pacifics were the following: diameter of driving wheels, 69 inches; cylinder dimensions, 22 × 28 inches; weight of engine, 233,000 pounds; boiler pressure, 200 pounds per square inch; tractive force, 33,400 pounds. For the Class K-5: diameter of driving wheels, 73 inches; cylinder dimensions, 25 × 28 inches; weight of engine, 284,000 pounds; boiler pressure, 210 pounds per square inch; tractive force, 42,735 pounds. (For illustrations of both engines see Prince, *Louisville and Nashville Steam Locomotives*, pp. 116-17, 120.)

50. Physical data for the Southern Class Ps-4 Pacific: diameter of driving wheels, 73 inches; cylinder dimensions, 27 × 28 inches; weight of engine, 304,000 pounds; boiler pressure, 200 pounds per square inch; tractive force, 47,500 pounds. (For illustrations see Prince, *Southern Railway System Steam Locomotives and Boats*, pp. 118-21.)

Data for the C&O Class F19 Pacific: diameter of driving wheels, 74 inches; cylinder dimensions, 27 × 28 inches; weight of engine, 331,500 pounds; boiler pressure, 200 pounds per square inch; tractive force, 46,900 pounds; maximum cylinder horsepower, 2,624. (For illustrations see Shuster et al., *C&O Power*, pp. 237-38, 247-49.)

51. Physical data for the Big Four Class K-5 Pacific were the following: diameter of driving wheels, 79 inches; cylinder dimensions, 25 × 28 inches; weight of engine, 302,000 pounds; boiler pressure, 205 pounds per square inch; tractive force of main engine, 38,850 pounds, of booster engine, 9,700 pounds, for a total of 48,550 pounds. (For illustrations see Staufer, *Steam Power of the New York Central System*, pp. 61, 63, 70.) The experimental engine of the American Locomotive Company was acquired by the Big Four as Class K-5 locomotive Number 6525, or later, New York Central System Number 4925, following the merger of 1930.

Physical data for the B. and O. Class P-7 Pacific were the following: diameter of driving wheels, 80 inches; cylinder dimensions, 27 × 28 inches; weight of engine, 326,000 pounds; boiler pressure, 230 pounds per square inch; tractive force, 50,000 pounds. These locomotives survived in active service for 31 years, the last retired in 1958 with the conversion to diesel-electric power. (For illustrations see Sagle, *B & O Power*, p. 241.) The only Pacifics to exceed the B. and O. Class P-7 in power were those manufactured in 1930 for the Chicago, Saint Paul, Minneapolis and Omaha Railroad. They represented the high point in sheer drawbar power, with 51,300 pounds starting tractive force.

52. Physical data for the Class L-2a Mohawk were the following: diameter of driving wheels, 69 inches; cylinder dimensions, 27 × 30 inches; weight of engine, 364,000 pounds; boiler pressure, 225 pounds per square inch; tractive force of main engine, 60,000 pounds, of booster engine, 12,700 pounds, for a total of 72,700 pounds. The tractive force of the L-3 and L-4 classes was raised only 100 pounds, but maximum horsepower and speed were considerably increased. (For illustrations see Staufer, *Steam Power of the New York Central System*, pp. 128-30.)

53. Physical data for the CNO&TP 4-8-2 of 1917 were the following: diameter of driving wheels, 69 inches; cylinder dimensions, 27 × 28 inches; boiler

pressure (maximum), 200 pounds per square inch; weight of engine, 314,800 pounds; tractive force (maximum) 50,300 pounds, raised to 53,900 pounds for the 1919 engines. (For illustrations see Prince, *Southern Railway System*, p. 125.)

For the L&N Class L 4-8-2: diameter of driving wheels, 70 inches; cylinder dimensions, 27 × 30 inches; boiler pressure, 200 pounds per square inch; weight of engine, 334,240 pounds; tractive force, 53,900 pounds. (For illustrations, see Prince, *Louisville and Nashville*, p. 126.)

54. Physical data for the N&W Class E-2 Pacific (1914) were the following: diameter of driving wheels, 70 inches; cylinder dimensions, 22 1/2 × 28 inches; boiler pressure, 200 pounds per square inch; weight of engine, 247,000 pounds; tractive force, 34,425 pounds. (For illustrations, see Rosenberg and Archer, *Norfolk and Western Steam*, pp. 17-20.)

55. Physical data for the New York Central Class J-ld 4-6-4 were the following: diameter of driving wheels, 79 inches; cylinder dimensions, 25 × 28 inches; boiler pressure, 225 pounds per square inch; grate area, 81.5 square feet; weight of engine, 353,000 pounds; tractive force of main engine, 42,300 pounds, of booster engine 10,900 pounds, for a total of 53,200 pounds. (For illustrations see Staufer, *Steam Power of the New York Central System*, pp. 86-125.)

56. Physical data for the Big Four Class H-10b 2-8-2 were the following: diameter of driving wheels, 63 inches; cylinder dimensions, 28 × 30 inches; boiler pressure, 200 pounds per square inch; weight of engine, 334,500 pounds; tractive force, 74,700 pounds, the highest for this type of locomotive on any road. (For illustrations of the various Mikado types see the following: B&O, 1910-22, Sagle, *B & O Power*, pp. 124-51; C&O, 1911-24, Shuster et al., *C & O Power*, pp. 58-85; New York Central Lines, 1912-25, Staufer, *Steam Power of the New York Central System*, pp. 27-45).

57. Physical data for the B&O Class S-1a 2-10-2 (1926) were the following: diameter of driving wheels, 64 inches; cylinder dimensions, 30 × 32 inches; boiler pressure, 220 pounds per square inch; weight of engine, 436,510 pounds; tractive force, 84,300 pounds. (For illustrations see Sagle, *B & O Power*, pp. 152-67.)

For the N&W Class M-2 4-8-0 (1911): diameter of driving wheels, 56 inches; cylinder dimensions, 24 × 30 inches; boiler pressure, 200 pounds per square inch; weight of engine, 262,000 pounds; tractive force, 52,457 pounds. (For illustrations see Rosenberg and Archer, *Norfolk and Western Steam*, pp. 14-16.)

58. The L&N engine classes were as follows: Pacific Class K-2A (1909)—engine weight, 201,500 pounds; tractive force, 30,900 pounds; Pacific Class K-4B (1920)—engine weight, 233,000 pounds; tractive force, 33,400 pounds; Pacific Class K-5 (1923)—engine weight, 277,000 pounds; tractive force, 40,700 pounds; Mountain Class L-1 (1926)—engine weight, 334,240 pounds; tractive force, 53,900 pounds. The beauties in the L&N stable were the engines of Class K-2A: high-wheeled, slim, elegantly proportioned, their pure utilitarian form carried a potent suggestion of speed and controlled power. (For illustration of all these engines see Prince, *Louisville and Nashville*, pp. 110-25.)

59. The utilization of motive power on the L&N provides so clear an illustration of passenger train operation in the late twenties that the movement of the all-Pullman *Pan-American* (nos. 99 and 100) deserves to be presented in quantitative detail (see table, page 211). Operations on the shorter run to Atlanta were simpler, but revealed something of the same techniques of motive power utilization (see table on page 211; the schedule is that of one of the Florida trains, the *Flamingo*, southbound [no. 17], in 1929). The line on the Cincinnati-Atlanta run is a continuous succession of grades and curves except for the relatively level tangent stretches along the Licking River. The minimum consist of the *Flamingo* was ordinarily nine cars, but this grew to twelve and frequently many more during the Florida winter season.

LOG OF THE "PAN-AMERICAN," SOUTHBOUND, 1929

Stations	Distance (Miles)	Ruling Grade (Percent)	Class of Locomotive	Number of Cars	Weight (Tons)	Running Time (Hrs. - Min.)	Average Speed (MPH)	Number of Stops
Cincinnati-Louisville	113.7	1.56	L-1	8	600	3 20	34.2	2 reg. 2 flag
Louisville-Bowling Green	113.6	1.50	L-1	9	675	2 34	44.2	None
Bowling Green-Nashville	72.9	1.20	L-1	8	600	1 40	43.7	None
Nashville-Decatur	120.9	0.95	K-4B	8	600	2 40	45.3	None
Decatur-Birmingham	84.5	1.30	K-4B	8	600	2 05	40.5	None
Birmingham-Montgomery	97.7	0.90	K-5	8	600	2 09	45.4	None
Montgomery-Flomaton	118.8	0.95	K-5	8	600	2 55	40.7	None
Flomaton-Mobile	59.6	0.78	K-5	7	525	1 42	35.1	None
Mobile-New Orleans	139.7	0.42	K-2A	6	450	3 49	36.6	7

Over-all distance, Cincinnati to New Orleans; 921.4 miles; time southbound (no. 99): 23 hrs., 45 min.; over-all average speed: 38.8 miles per hour; number of regular stops, southbound: 18; time allowed for changing locomotives or altering consist, each stop: 7 mins.; consist variation, minimum: 6-9 cars

SOURCE: *Baldwin Locomotives.*

LOG OF THE "FLAMINGO," SOUTHBOUND, 1929

Stations	Distance (Miles)	Ruling Grade (Percent)	Class of Locomotive	Number of Cars	Weight (Tons)	Running Time (Hrs. - Min.)	Average Speed (MPH)	Number of Stops
Cincinnati-Corbin	186.9	1.35	K-5	9	675	5 15	35.6	3 reg.
Corbin-Etowah	165.0	1.00	K-4	9	675	4 23	37.7	1
Etowah-Atlanta	136.5	1.00	K-4	9	675	3 25	39.9	2 sig.

Over-all distance, Cincinnati to Atlanta: 488.4 miles; time southbound: 13 hrs., 45 min.; over-all average speed: 35.5 miles per hour.

SOURCE: *Baldwin Locomotives.*

The problem of the most efficient form of motive power utilization gave rise to questions that were never satisfactorily answered in the days of steam locomotives. As we have seen, most roads preferred a variety of power to deal with a diversity of conditions, whereas the New York Central's mechanical engineers sought a superpower form that could haul any train on the road at high speeds and over long runs. But the perplexing question was, At what speed and with what weight of train did the engine operate at maximum efficiency? If a Class L 4-8-2 could handle 120 cars on any required schedule, was it operating more efficiently when it pulled no more than 80, or was it throwing away reserve power in the unnecessary combustion of fuel? If a Hudson could pull a 16-car train at an average speed of 55 miles per hour up to 930 miles, was it wasting its power when it pulled a ten-car train at the customary 40-miles-per-hour average on the Cincinnati-Chicago run? The question was never resolved, and a satisfactory solution was not to appear until the advent of the diesel-electric locomotive made it possible to operate any required number of relatively small power units under a single control. The problem does not exist under electric operation because the engine draws only so much power, measured in kilowatts, as it needs to move the train at any given speed.

60. The survey of passenger traffic conducted for the planning of Cincinnati Union Terminal in 1928 indicated that the actual number of trains was nearly 15 percent higher than the number of scheduled runs listed in the public timetables. The number of such runs per weekday, by station and railroad, is given in the following table:

Central Union Depot		
CCC&StL	54	
B&O	41	
CNO&TP	16	
L&N	8	
C&O	7	
Total		126
Total plus 15 percent		145
Pennsylvania Station		
Pennsylvania	24	
L&N	14	
Total		38
Total plus 15 percent		44
Fourth Street Station		
C&O	9	
L&N	2	
Total		11
Total plus 15 percent		12
Court Street Station		
N&W	6[a]	
Pennsylvania	4	
Total		10
Total plus 15 percent		11
Baymiller Street Station		
B&O	8	
Total		8
Total plus 15 percent		9
Eighth Street-Cincinnati Transfer		
B&O (*National Limited*)	2	
B&O (locals)	2	
Total		4
Total plus 15 percent		5
Total all stations		197
Total plus 15 percent		224

[a] Before the end of the year the N&W had added one train in each direction and transferred six of the total to the Pennsylvania Station.

Grand Schemes for the New Century

61. The distribution of daily sleeping car runs among the various Cincinnati roads in the summer of 1928 was as follows:

CCC&StL	73
L&N	52
B&O	50
Pennsylvania	48
CNO&TP	40
C&O	20
N&W	6
Total	289

Four trains passing through, or originating and terminating at, Cincinnati were operated with Pullman cars only: B&O, *National Limited* (Saint Louis–Jersey City); Big Four, *Hudson River Limited*, later *Ohio State Limited* (Cincinnati–New York and Boston); L&N, *Pan-American* (Cincinnati–New Orleans); Pennsylvania, *Cincinnati Limited* (Cincinnati–New York).

62. The increase in average speeds of representative through trains is shown by the following table, based on schedules for December 1929:

Railroad	Train	Destination	Time (Hrs. - Min.)		Distance (Miles)	Average Speed (MPH)
B&O	*National Limited*	Saint Louis–Jersey City	27	45	1,109.1	40.0
C&O	*Fast Flying Virginian*	Washington	17	10	598.1	34.8
CNO&TP	*Queen and Crescent Limited*	New Orleans	23	30	835.7	35.6
CCC&StL	*Ohio State Limited*	New York	18	15	883.4	48.4
CCC&StL	*Sycamore*	Chicago	7	45	303.3	39.1
L&N	*Georgian*	Atlanta	12	35	488.0	38.8
N&W	*Pocahontas*	Norfolk	19	50	683.7	34.5
Pennsylvania	*Cincinnati Limited*	New York	17	05	751.1	44.0
Avg. speed						39.4

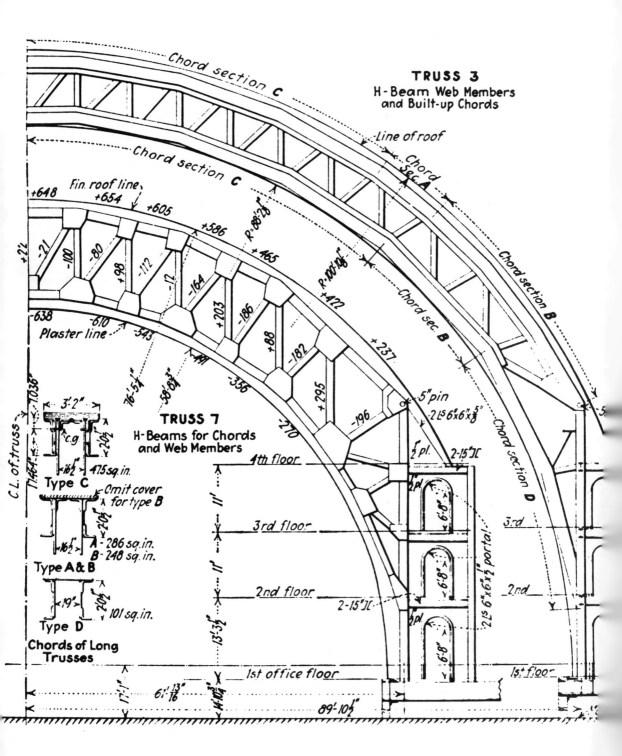

TRUSS 3
H-Beam Web Members
and Built-up Chords

Line of roof

Chord section C

Chord section C

Chord sec. A

Chord section B

Chord sec. B

Chord section D

Fin. roof line
+648   +654   +605
+586
+465
+422
+237

-21 -100 -80 -98 -112 -12 -164 -186 +203 +88 -182 +295 -196

R-88'-2⅝"
R-100'-10⅜"

-638   -610   -543   -356   -270

Plaster line

76'-5¼"   58'-6⅜"   491

C.L. of truss

T-1.035"
7.464"

3'-2"

c.g.
20½"
16½"   475 sq. in.
Type C

Omit cover
for type B
20½"
16½"   A-286 sq. in.
B-248 sq. in.
Type A & B

19"   20½"   101 sq. in.
Type D

Chords of Long
Trusses

TRUSS 7
H-Beams for Chords
and Web Members

4th floor

3rd floor

2nd floor

1st office floor

11'

11'

13'-3½"

17'-1"

61'-13/16"

14'-0½"

89'-10½"

5"pin
2 L⁵ 6"x6"x⅝"

⅝ pl.   2-15"⏊C

⅝pl.

6'-8"

3rd

⅝pl.

6'-8"

2-15"⏊C   2nd

⅝pl.

6'-8"

2 L⁵ 6"x6"x⅝" portal

1st floor

5

Cincinnati Union Terminal

Organization, Planning, and Design

As we learned in the previous chapter, the idea of unified railroad
terminal facilities in Cincinnati appeared to have reached a perfect
impasse about the time the United States entered World War I.
Within a few years, however, the individuals, organizations, programs, and theories directly or indirectly having to do with the
city's terminal problem had reached such a number that though the
impasse showed signs of breaking, it appeared to be yielding more
to confusion than to progress. Wartime exigencies again were a
major factor in reestablishing continuity with earlier plans. At the
request of the United States Railroad Administration late in 1918,
the directors of the Cincinnati companies prepared a comprehensive plan for the improvement of freight and passenger terminals,
the construction of a belt line, the establishment of a union freight
station on the site of the Central Union Depot, and the building of
a union passenger terminal on an unspecified site. The trustees of
the Cincinnati Southern Railway, being the officers of a municipal
corporation, made the greatest effort to bring this rather vague
plan to realization. In 1919 they secured from the city government
the authority to issue $20,000,000 worth of revenue bonds, subject
to approval in a popular referendum, to meet the cost of constructing a union passenger terminal, the interest charges to be met and
the principal to be retired by means of revenues derived from ren-

Facing page: detail from figure 49.

tals to be paid by the users (the forerunner of the later method of municipal financing of airport construction). The problem underlying the local chaos and frustration was most clearly understood by Ward Baldwin, the chief engineer of the Cincinnati Southern. The immediate obstacle lay in the strictly parochial approach, manifested in the "uncorrelated haphazard arrangements that immediate necessities have . . . compelled the several transportation companies to provide for the single purpose of meeting their individual emergency demands. The futility of these efforts has been due mainly to two causes, the lack of sufficient money, and the non-existence of a bureau such as the City Planning Commission we now have, vested with authority and charged with the duty of preparing a harmonious plan for the city to grow up to in respect to transportation as well as all other civic needs."[1]

By 1920 the municipal and financial establishment had come to see the obvious fact, namely, that the passenger as well as the freight stations were inconvenient in their multiplicity and immediate environments, dirty, worn, in one case jerry-built (Court Street), and in another its equivalent in deteriorating fabric (Fourth Street). The chief need was to find the man who could bring the railroads together in drawing up a comprehensive program and in pooling the resources necessary to implement it. The first step in a hopeful new direction was the appointment in 1921 of George Dent Crabbs, the president of the Philip Carey Manufacturing Company, to the initial position of a liason official charged with persuading the railroad officers to build a union passenger terminal as part of a comprehensive urban plan. But in spite of all the proposals that had come and gone in the previous twenty years, many of the essential difficulties remained to thwart any ready action. In the first place, earlier works that might serve as precedents were rare: genuine union stations centrally located and designed for the use of all lines serving the city were by long odds the exception rather than the rule in the English-speaking lands. The only major cities in Great Britain with unified facilities were Aberdeen and Newcastle, and in the United States, where private interest rather than public need has always determined how resources are used, the only union terminals in major rail centers by the end of World War I were those of Washington, Jacksonville, Indianapolis, Saint Louis, Dallas, Kansas City, and Denver; and among these only the stations at Indianapolis and Saint Louis were erected before the turn of the century. Moreover, the unification of facilities in huge rail ganglia like Saint Louis and Kansas City was possible only through the simultaneous construction of extensive belt, transfer, and terminal trackage undertaken by terminal railroad companies specifically organized for the purpose.

The situation at Cincinnati was not one that would yield to quick solutions and ready plans. Beyond the construction of the necessary buildings the whole project involved many changes in the urban fabric and the railroad system of the city: first was the selection of a site of nearly three hundred acres to provide space for station tracks, approaches, coach yard, engine terminal, steam-generating plant, and other subsidiary structures, and the assembly of a multitude of land parcels to put together this acreage; second, the rerouting of four railroads (C&O, L&N, N&W, and Pennsylvania) and varying extensions to the tracks of the remaining three (B&O, Big Four, and CNO&TP) to reach the new terminal; third, changes in the street pattern in the vicinity of the station, including the vacation of certain streets and the building of new access drives; fourth, the abandonment of the five existing passenger stations; and finally, the coordination of the rail terminal complex with a new post office. It was obviously going to be an expensive venture, and the directors of the various companies showed a marked tendency to drag their feet until 1923. The railroad economy presented a mixed picture, promising in some places, troublesome and even threatening in others. The revenue traffic density of the Cincinnati roads was substantially higher than the average for the industry as a whole, and there was a reserve capacity that was steadily enlarged through innovations in signaling and improvements in motive power. In 1923, for the first time in their history, the railroads of the nation handled more than 1,000,000 loaded freight cars per week for a total of nineteen weeks scattered throughout the year. Freight tonnage of the Cincinnati lines was increasing irregularly during the twenties at an average rate of 2 percent per year. Passenger traffic, on the other hand, was dropping at an average rate of 5 percent per year, and the rate of decrease was accelerating through the decade. The total revenues of the seven companies in 1923 generally showed increases over previous years, but operating expenses revealed even greater increases, so that operating ratios were discouragingly high, the average being 77.41 percent for all seven and the specific figures for two companies being above 80 percent.[2] George D. Crabbs was used to speaking to men on the highest financial plateau, but it required all his persuasive eloquence to win the agreement that marked the decisive step.

The Cincinnati Railroad Development Company was incorporated in the summer of 1923 with a capital of $250,000, a sum that clearly indicated that its establishment was only the preliminary phase of the long procedure. The next step was the incorporation of the Cincinnati Union Terminal Company with a capital of $20,000,000, regarded at the time as sufficient to cover the costs of building a terminal complex "in the lower section of the city," the facilities of which were to be leased to the seven roads serving Cincinnati.[3] This sum was to be raised by means of stock and bond issues distributed according to the following plan: preferred stock issue in the amount of $3,000,000 to be subscribed by the Railroad Development Company; common stock in the amount of $3,500,000 to be divided equally among the seven tenants; the remainder of the funds to be raised by the sale of bonds guaranteed by the tenant roads. It was the traditional method of financing the construction of large terminals, but in the case of the Cincinnati project the initial capital proved to be less than half the actual cost of construction.

The establishment of the Cincinnati Union Terminal Company, quickly followed by the preliminary financial arrangements and the initial preparations for final planning and construction, rested on the lessons learned from thirty years of progress (1890–1920) in the design of large metropolitan terminals, lessons that made it possible to lay down general principles applicable to any combination of roads in any urban milieu.[4] The first and most useful of such principles from an operating standpoint was the segregation of traffic by type of service (through, suburban, or mail and express), by destination or general direction thereof, and by railroad. There had been steady improvement in the track and platform layout in a variety of ways—the lengthening of all platforms; the extra lengthening of particular platforms to accommodate certain trains that regularly ran well beyond the average length; the adoption of switches, frogs, and turnouts of the smallest possible angle, allowing easier, faster, and more comfortable movements over the terminal trackage; the adoption of the through-type station, or of combinations of stub and through or stub and loop wherever the exigencies of land use and rail location permitted the choice; the use of double-level plans, again where the local situation made it possible; and finally, and perhaps most important, placing the design of the track-platform layout on a comprehensive investigation by graphic methods of all factors affecting its form.[5] Engineers had come to recognize chiefly through experience with the

Cincinnati Union Terminal

Boston and Philadelphia terminals, with their immense volume of suburban traffic, that the advantages of the most spacious track layout could be realized only by means of an adequate approach system. Maximum operating capacity in large metropolitan stations required at least four and preferably six approach tracks, double ladder tracks to allow two parallel and simultaneous movements across the approach, an electropneumatic interlocking system, automatic overhead signals on the approach, and dwarf signals for the throat and station tracks. Platform width was constantly increased, in a few cases to twenty-two feet, not only to accommodate the rapidly increasing number of passengers but the equally increasing volume of baggage, express, and mail, the last suddenly and drastically expanded with the introduction of parcel-post service in 1913. The island platform, elevated to the level of the car floor, was clearly the best form in safety and convenience of the passenger if not always for the employees, but although it was standard in England and on the Continent, the expensive type was confined in the United States to the electrified terminals of New York (until the completion of the electrified suburban lines of the Illinois Central at Chicago in 1926).

Throughout the nineteenth century railroad terminals with rare exceptions were located where space was available, land-use patterns permitted rail operations, and land values were such that the capital-hungry railroads could afford the acreage. Growing traffic, however, coincided with a growing awareness of the architectural and urbanistic importance attaching to the proper planning, design, and location of the station facilities. In the formal design of the headhouse the architect sought to emphasize both the gateway motif and the sense of municipal pride and authority, or even national pride, as in the case of Washington Union Station. The revival of Roman and Renaissance classicism at the turn of the century gave the architect the formal means to an adequate symbolic expression, and it was probably the stations of Washington and New York that revealed the fullest exploitation of these means. Location and site planning came increasingly to rest on concern with the convenience of the passenger both as traveler and entrant into the urban milieu, although it was seldom that the ideal of maximum personal comfort was realized. For terminals accommodating a large number of suburban passengers (as in Boston, New York, Philadelphia, and Chicago) the chosen site lay as close to the city as numerous economic and urbanistic determinants allowed. For those stations with a predominantly through traffic the proximity of hotels and urban services became the prime considerations, although again it was only the electrified systems of New York that allowed a full realization of this aim. From both the standpoint of the railroad companies and the city, the ideal terminal site was one free of any restrictions and unlikely to suffer any unwanted change from future urban development, but once more it was only in New York that the railroads themselves virtually guaranteed this freedom.

If designers agreed that the ultimate aims of internal planning were the convenience of the passenger and the maximum efficiency of train and station operation, they soon learned that the realization of these aims in practical terminal design involved widely ramifying complexities. A large railroad station is in fact a megastructure, or indeed, a microcity, that embraces a great multiplicity of elements divided between those introduced for the comfort and convenience of the passenger on one hand and those essential to the movement of trains and the servicing of cars on the other (for example, providing steam lines and electrical conduits to maintain heat and power in parked cars). The internal facilities of the well-designed metropolitan terminal of 1910 included waiting rooms, ticket offices, baggage-checking counters, baggage rooms, toilets, drugstore, newsstand, restaurant and bar, lunch counter, special rooms for invalids, aged immigrants, and women with small children or infants, telephone and telegraph centers, information center, first-aid room, stairs, elevators, concourses, street entrances and exits, special entrances and exits for subways, elevated lines, and streetcar lines, entrance and exit drives for automobiles and taxis, in addition to the offices of the terminal company, the stationmaster, and his staff. The ideal arrangement—and there were nearly as many solutions as there were stations—was to place entrance, waiting room, ticket offices, baggage-checking counter, passenger concourse, train concourse, train gates, and platforms in as close to a linear series as possible, but the dimensions of the site as well as its size and double-level plans usually prevented a complete realization of the ideal. Service facilities were most conveniently grouped in a ring around the main waiting room. In some stations planning seemed needlessly complex, as in the Pennsylvania Station in New York, for example, whereas in others, such as Grand Central in New York and Union Station in Washington, in spite of their great size and complexity, the plan came astonishingly close to the linear arrangement. The overall problem of design and its most general guiding principle could be put in very simple terms: to bring great numbers of people (100,000 to 1,000,000 per day) from the street past the ticket offices and certain service facilities to the trains; or to bring a train (measuring 10 1/2 × 16 × 150 to 1,000 feet in maximum overall dimensions) into a close juxtaposition with people. The area necessary to encompass headhouse, station tracks, and platforms ranged from thirteen acres for North Western Station in Chicago to seventy-eight for the two-track level Grand Central Terminal in New York.[6]

The headhouse, for all its details, is only one part of the terminal complex; and when the numerous subsidiary structures and utilities were added to the station proper, the megastructural or microurbanistic character of the whole work reached a level of size and intricacy that has had no parallel in any other kind of building or interconnected group of buildings. Since passenger trains from the early years of rail history have carried mail and express as well as people, the appropriate terminal buildings and the facilities for handling such cargo grew to the point where by World War I they were together larger than the headhouse itself. The location of a combined mail terminal and central post office directly above the approach tracks of the station appeared first shortly after the construction program for Pennsylvania Station in New York (1903–10), and the practice of handling mail on belt conveyors below platforms came with North Western Station in Chicago (1906–11). Except for railroads carrying so large a volume of mail and express as to necessitate the operation of special mail and express trains to terminals wholly separate from the passenger station (the New York Central Railroad was the prime example), such facilities were generally located at the sides of approach tracks close enough to the track-platform area to allow the handling of cargo to the appropriate terminal by means of trucks or belt conveyors. Working mail and express from the same trains and on the same platforms as those used by passengers is an obvious nuisance and even a danger, and the problem was not finally solved until separate mail, express, and baggage platforms were introduced at the new Union Station in Chicago (1916–25), a masterpiece of railroad, architectural, and urbanistic planning now grotesquely disfigured by irresponsible reconstruction of the concourse area. An earlier solution was the practice of reverse entry into the track-platform area, as at Saint Louis Union Station (1892–94), so that passengers would not have to walk past the so-called head-end cars when leaving the train. The delays and expense involved in turning trains on wye tracks, however, discouraged the spread of this mode of operation, which was adopted at only one other station, the Union Terminal at New Orleans (1952–54).

A plaguing and costly element in the construction of large terminal stations was the coach yard and the engine terminal, with their associated repair, servicing, storage, dormitory, and communications facilities. If it were a matter of perfectly unencumbered choice, which it never was, the chief engineer of a terminal project would have located coach yards on both sides of the approach tracks as close to the station as the space necessary for turnouts and yard leads would allow in order to minimize the time and expense of empty movements. The facts of the urban economy, however, seldom offered him this choice: the great area of land required, the high cost of urban property, and the many competing uses for land in the immediate area of the station meant that the yard usually had to be laid out at a distance of a mile or more from the terminal. The union stations at Washington, Jacksonville, Chicago, and Kansas City came closest to realizing the ideal principle, but the exorbitant cost of land on Manhattan Island forced the New York Central to locate the Grand Central coach yard above 138th Street in the Bronx, more than four miles from the terminal, and the Pennsylvania to place its immense yard (the largest in the world) on the other side of the East River, at Sunnyside in Queens. The most extreme case was that of the Nickel Plate Road (New York, Chicago and Saint Louis Railroad) at Chicago: the directors could see no point to investing money in expensive downtown land for the company's modest passenger traffic, so they chose a site ten miles from La Salle Street Station (1902–3). Engine terminals in the days of steam were always characterized by the ubiquitous roundhouse and turntable, along with fuel and water facilities, repair space, storage for repair parts, and special lead tracks. Coach yards and engine terminals were nearly always laid out with loop or wye tracks to turn motive power and rolling stock, the loop being preferable because it obviated the necessity for reverse movements.

Buildings, tracks, yards, and enginehouses had to be supplemented by a host of special utilities that filled the interstices left among the larger structures. A steam-generating plant was necessary to heat stations and subsidiary buildings and to heat trains during their idle time on station tracks before boarding by passengers. An electrical substation with switches, transformers, and sometimes generators was required to provide power at suitable voltages for signals, interlocking controls, lights, clocks, special communication facilities, and eventually the air-conditioning equipment in parked cars. All these compelled the installation of miles of electrical conduits, steam lines, air lines, water pipes, ducts, and cables, and a vast multitude of valves, switches, and special fixtures. In the great terminals of Boston, New York, Philadelphia, Washington, Pittsburgh, Chicago, and Kansas City, this enormous and intricate web was bound together in a unified engineering-architectural design that carried the modern building art to its highest formal, functional, and urbanistic levels. And as a consequence these stations played a major role in lifting the whole domain of American civic architecture to the high point it came to occupy in the two decades of 1910–30.

By the time the Cincinnati Union Terminal Company was founded, the architect Alfred Fellheimer was moving toward the commanding position as an authority on the design of large stations, and it was on this basis that the firm of Fellheimer and Wagner was to win the commission for the terminal group. As early as 1923 he had formulated his own principles of station design, which were presented at length in an article published in *Railway Age.* The specific practical and urbanistic ends to be sought in siting and preliminary planning embodied permanently valuable concepts and are worth quoting in full. They were prescriptive in character and indicated the criteria under which the construction program was to be undertaken and the aims that ought to be realized.

    1. The improvement at the proposed site is desirable from the viewpoints of construction and operating costs and has advantages equal or superior in these respects to the results that can be secured at any other available location.

    2. Suitable development can be made in stages to meet the expected normal growth in the services involved for a sufficient term of years to justify the project.

    3. The proposed improvement is desirable from the viewpoint of the municipality and in harmony with its plans for development.

    4. The advantages offered to the public are sufficient to justify such concessions as may be required from the municipality.

    5. The project in its entirety presents a sufficiently favorable economic aspect, free from insurmountable prior obligations to insure its complete, rational financing.

    6. The by-products of the development such as the overhead or air rights can be utilized in a practical and profitable way so as to absorb, or at least substantially reduce, the carrying charges of the improvement.

    7. The project as planned is so sound and free from imposing burden-

some conditions upon the railroad, that controlling or governing bodies will readily approve same.

8. The cost of the station facilities per car unit and their operation will not be excessive in comparison with that of other sites. . . .

9. The improvement is of such a type that adequate enhancement of land values within the terminal area will necessarily follow.[7]

The remainder of Fellheimer's principles had for the most part to do with utilization and economic criteria of site selection and internal planning. The overall plan of the facility, unless it is in a new location relatively free of existing encumbrances, ought to fit the established patterns of land use, street arrangement, and railroad trackage, so that construction of the new work could proceed without interfering with the operations of the existing structure, with a minimum of conflict between the old and the new, and with a minimum of disturbance to the urban environment. As for the plan of the station proper, he recommended the principle that ought to guide all civic design, namely, the maintenance of a balance between public convenience, economy of construction, and minimization of operating costs. This end is most likely to be served if the architect follows as closely as possible certain other fundamental concepts of planning—maximum simplicity of station design and civic setting to avoid, or at least to minimize, disharmony, disorder, and confusion between terminal functions and the surrounding urban activities; coordination of the station design with the city plan, where it exists, and with the foreseeable developments of surrounding streets and spaces; predicting future rail needs as far as possible to provide adequate capacity for the present and space for the future expansion of the headhouse, the station approach, throat, coach yard, and engine terminal.

Internal planning of the headhouse had to rest on the initial choice of station type, whether stub-end or through, and Fellheimer examined their relative merits before taking up the questions of traffic circulation and the distribution of facilities. The through type, as we have seen in the foregoing pages, is obviously the more efficient for the operation of trains, though not necessarily so for the movements of passengers. Through types obviate the need for reverse movements of rail equipment except for engines running light, and thus minimize interference between loaded and empty trains, with a consequent sharp reduction in the number of tracks required for parked and moving equipment. (The leading example is Pennsylvania Station in New York, which has accommodated as many as 750 trains per day on sixteen through and five stub-end tracks.) For the convenience of the passenger, however, the stub-end type is usually superior to the through: tracks, platforms, and all headhouse facilities can be placed on a single level; vertical travel from the concourse to the track level can be eliminated; circulation may be more rapid and less confusing because there is only one set of gates, and facilities may be arranged more nearly in a unidirectional pattern; for the terminal company construction, maintenance, and operation are likely to be more economical than in the case of the alternative.

The criteria of detailed internal planning were shaped by the choice of headhouse, which Fellheimer divided into waiting room and concourse types. In the former the waiting room constitutes the central space, and all other elements are grouped around it and are subsidiary to it (Washington Union Station, for example); whereas in the latter the concourse is central and other elements are subsidiary to it (Grand Central in New York is the leading example). Most stations, however, are composite in these respects, and any attempt to classify them is a hair-splitting artificiality. The criteria having to do with circulatory plans were shaped by initial choices as to type, but Fellheimer formulated them in terms of general applicability. The ideal overall aim, as we have noted previously, was to provide for a continuous movement in one direction from entrance to train with a minimum of obstacles or interfering lines of traffic, and to minimize disturbances to the traffic flow on city streets and walks around the station. To achieve these ends, Fellheimer recommended four means that must be embodied in the working plans—separation of through and suburban traffic (Grand Central again affords the best example), adequate space for vehicular entrance and exit drives, disposition of certain entrances and exits to make direct connections with streetcar and rapid transit lines, and the location of entrances and exits according to natural lines of movement rather than the demands of formal composition.

In the planning of headhouse facilities Fellheimer reworked the general conclusions drawn from the experience of the previous thirty years into terms of practical detail. Following the order of train gate to street (the path of the exiting passenger), he dealt first with the train concourse and recommended that it be spacious, heated, well lighted, and separated from the track-platform area by a weathertight screen wall. Train gates he thought were best distributed along only one side of the concourse in order to minimize confusion, but this practice can be followed only in stub-end stations. By giving the waiting room a central location, all service facilities can be placed immediately adjacent to it on all four sides and hence made directly accessible from the waiting area. The chief problem in locating the waiting room proved to be ultimately insoluble—that is, to locate and plan the waiting area in such a way as to place it in easy relation to the entrances and to the concourses without at the same time making it a thoroughfare. The only valid formula for the location of ticket offices, baggage-checking counter, and other service facilities was so general that it provided little guidance to an architect: such elements should be placed along the lines of movement from street to train concourse without forming obstacles along the way. The chief violators of this criterion, it must be admitted, were the drugstore and newsstand concessionaires, whose enclosures may be outside the architect's control. The final principle for the design of the headhouse constituted the fundamental doctrine of all good architecture created for practical use: the formal treatment of building elevations ought to express the purpose of the building, clearly distinguish entrances and exits (that is, indicate how the building is to be used), and place the emphasis on mass and surface for aesthetic effect rather than on detail. Fellheimer was silent on the question of the expressive or symbolic role of the station, but his numerous executed designs indicate that he was well aware of how these ends can be achieved.

Fellheimer's proposals for the design of the track-platform layout and the track system itself summarized the lessons that had already been codified from earlier progress. His only new principles were that baggage elevators be located at the ends of platforms, that the whole layout be designed with a view to ease of future rearrangement, and that ramps be used rather than stairways for vertical circulation. In the case of the tracks themselves he recommended clearances and other provisions for future electrification and for air-rights construction, including the necessary protection of the columns of future overhead buildings, and the placing of the entire track area on a straight-line axis to avoid the nuisance of curves, which obstruct a clear view of the train length, fixed signals, and trainmen's signals. On the question of determining station capacity, he recognized that this is bound up with the traffic capacity of the approach, the throat, and the signaling system as well as that of the terminal tracks. The answer to the question of the number of station tracks must rest on an analysis of previous traffic, projections from trends in traffic, and on the design and operating practices of other stations, the last of which he did not regard as a particularly useful guide, although there is no reason why this should be the case if proper attention is paid to errors of design as well as to intelligent solutions to the problems that everywhere arise. The whole essay remains a prize example of architectural theory relating to public building in the modern city, a valuable though forgotten source document on the design practice of our time.[8]

The concern with the relation between urban planning and civic amelioration that accompanied the rise of the Progressive movement led to a consideration of the place of the railroad terminal in the city, which probably received its earliest practical formulation in Daniel Burnham's Washington Plan (1902) and its pioneer theoretical discussion in Charles Mulford Robinson's *Modern Civic Art* (1903). By the time Alfred Fellheimer was formulating his own principles of station design, a similar theory of the relation of the terminal to urban planning was being presented at the Twelfth National Conference on City Planning, convened at Cincinnati on 19-22 April 1920. The papers given at the appropriate session of the conference were published in *Railway Age* before the end of the same month. The discussions turned on two issues that proved to be complex enough to defy the ready formulation of principles applicable to all situations—the relative merits of union versus multiple terminal facilities and the location of such facilities with respect to the urban core. William J. Wilgus, the original author of the plan for Grand Central Terminal and its associated program of air-rights construction, argued that a rail terminal is not literally a terminating boundary to the passenger but rather a locus of transition from the train to the vehicles on the city streets. Before the invention and spread of the electric street railway and rapid transit it was most desirable that the station be placed close to the city core as a matter of physical necessity, although what was advantageous to the passenger and what the railroad company could afford were often two different matters. The factors determining location, however, changed radically with the advent of mass transit and motor vehicles, with the rapid expansion of metropolitan areas and populations, and the associated increase in land costs.

The benefits conferred by the inner-core location of the terminal and by the unification of all terminal facilities were obvious enough to the passengers and the citizens. To locate it at the heart of the central business district guaranteed maximum interaccessibility of station, hotels, office buildings, the institutions of finance and government, the major shopping district, the centers of entertainment, and sometimes of the intellectual life and the arts. The decade of the twenties was little concerned with the conservation of energy and material resources, in spite of the valuable pioneer efforts of Gifford Pinchot and President Theodore Roosevelt, but the wasted motion of people and goods arising from the wide separation of transportation from other urban elements was something everyone could at least see and is now something that can no longer be tolerated. Beyond the questions of convenience and utility there are also intangible factors of a psychological and semiotic character. The heavily used terminal is a center of intense urban life in itself and in its interaction with the multitude of activities that go on in the urban core, and as a consequence it is more than a place having to do only with practical matters; it is also a key visual and symbolic element in the individual's sense and emotional experience of the city. Yet central location offers disadvantages, especially in the United States, where essential public services like the railroad have been supported exclusively by private investment. From the standpoint of the railroad company the most immediate drawbacks to central location were the exorbitant cost of land and the high, ever increasing taxes resulting as much from a grossly inequitable distribution of the tax burden as well as from inflation. Perhaps equally decisive from the municipal view is the removal of large areas of land from productive urban use. This loss can be overcome by intensive air-rights development, of which the foremost examples are the Chicago Union and the New York stations. If because of land cost and the problems attendant upon the interference with urban traffic and normal land use the terminal must be located outside the central business district, then the only plausible answer to the question of accessibility is the construction of special rapid transit and surface arteries to connect the station with the core.

All these arguments were much refined by participants in the Cincinnati conference and by theorists who continued the discussion in subsequent years. Among the Cincinnati group Charles H. Cheney and J. P. Newell were vigorous proponents of the concepts of terminal unification and the close correlation of terminal design with city planning. They advanced six principles on which to base the realization of these aims. The first two they regarded as fundamental—namely, the unified control preferably under municipal ownership of terminal facilities and of all rail lines serving them within the local switching district. The long-established examples involving traditional private ownership are the Indianapolis Union Railway and the Terminal Railroad Association of Saint Louis, but municipal ownership of rail properties did not come until the completion of New Orleans Union Terminal in 1954. The authors believed on good ground that unified operation and control under municipal authority is essential to business enterprise, public activity related to rail usage, proper circulation, and the full development of urban life. Their remaining four principles spelled out these broad concepts in greater detail. The first was a correlative of the previous two: unification ought to include the elimination of duplicate facilities, which are wasteful in themselves and costly in money to both the railroad companies and the public, inconvenient and confusing to the public, and costly to the city in unnecessary consumption of land. The other principles embraced the following: the coordination of rail and water terminal facilities in port cities; provision for the rapid circulation of traffic, with minimal conflicts among different forms of transportation, by means of broad arterial streets, vehicular drives, and protected accessways for pedestrians; and the landscaping of terminal drives and plazas and of the area bordering rail facilities by means of cooperation between municipal park boards and terminal authorities.

The whole body of theory on terminal location as it stood in the mid-twenties was conveniently summarized by C. F. Loweth in the issue of *Railway Age* for 5 June 1926.[9] All factors affecting the location of a major terminal station, he thought, rest on certain economic and utilitarian determinants of both a positive and a negative character having to do with the mutual influence between urban growth and the expansion of rail traffic: first, the precise causal relations existing among industrial, population, and traffic growth; second, the potential stimulus to overall economic development in the metropolitan area through the expansion of rail traffic; and finally, the potentially inhibiting effect of railroad operations on the proper development of contiguous areas. The immediate factors influencing terminal location, Loweth believed, all have to do with circulation—the realization of the maximum efficiency of circulation with a minimum of congestion; the avoidance of conflicts among civic, business, and transportation interests; stimulation of a desirable growth rate of the urban fabric; and minimizing or screening the noise, dirt, and danger of railroad operations. All city plans, following the influential Chicago Plan of 1909, called for union railroad stations, but this was not a concept that could be taken in all cases as an axiom of civic design.

In certain cities exigencies of space, topography, land use, or sheer volume of traffic made unification impractical or unfeasible (Boston, New York, Philadelphia, and Chicago are the prime examples). In still others it might be undesirable through the high cost of rearranging lines or because of the inhibitions imposed on the beneficial development of contiguous properties, especially those bordering coach yards and engine terminals. The chief value of terminal unification for the passenger *per se* lay in the ease of making connections, but if the number of transfer passengers is a small proportion of the total, it is difficult to defend the high cost of unified facilities solely for their benefit. The question of what constitutes a convenient location for all passengers, through, transfer, and suburban, is endlessly debatable; but it is obvious that the minimization of movement over the secondary branches of the "access tree" (streets, sidewalks, and internal spaces) is a fundamental criterion of location and site-planning in every case.[10]

Further questions arose over the issue of locating a unified station in the core area, even when it can be shown that such a site is generally advantageous. The presence of extensive transportation facilities can readily obstruct normal growth and desirable land-use patterns over a wide area precisely in those places where the most intensive and diversified activities would normally occur. On the other hand, if the opportunities for air-rights construction exist, exactly the opposite may occur: obstruction to full development may give way to multiple forms of intensive development of a kind not available on ordinary core land because of the absence of a full-grown access tree, from rail tunnels and subways to the tops of neighboring elevator shafts. Although union stations have long characterized urban rail patterns in Europe, they were not a logical product of railroad development in England and the United States, so that the planners' enthusiasm for them after 1910 was something of a novelty; and few such stations, as we have seen, existed before 1920. The ultimate aim of organic rail-urban planning is not necessarily to bring everything together but to establish a close integration with numerous points of access and transfer among railroad, rapid transit, street railway, vehicular, and pedestrian modes of travel. In later years, of course, the planners would be compelled to add the aerial forms of travel.

Daniel Burnham and Edward Bennett, in their Chicago Plan of 1909, were the first planners to consider the question of locating and unifying freight-handling facilities, and Loweth considered the matter in some detail. In cities where a high proportion of rail freight moved through the metropolitan area from one carrier to another, as is most emphatically the case with Cincinnati, he recommended that yard and other facilities for the handling of through freight be separated from those established for shipments originating and terminating in the city. The implementation of this principle had to rest on the availability of land, and in urban areas marked by rugged topography such available space might be in short supply, as is again the case with Cincinnati. The question of belt lines within the city Loweth examined critically and at length. Their presence had always been taken as axiomatic, but he showed that under certain conditions there are more advantageous solutions to the problem of transferring freight from one line to another. Under the simple alternative of direct interchange of shipments between trunk lines versus transfer by means of belt lines, the latter is obviously preferable, but interchange by means of bridge and by-pass lines located at varying distances outside the metropolitan area and exclusively designed to handle such traffic offers much superior advantages. Belt lines, which do not originate traffic but require highly developed signaling systems and extensive areas of urban land for yard and main tracks, were particularly expensive to build because of the numerous interchange points with their wye tracks, elaborate signals, and multiple interlockings as well as track and yard space. Although transfer tracks offer an obvious urbanistic advantage through the abandonment of superfluous inner-city facilities, they also require a multiplication of engine terminals and yard tracks, increasing the likelihood of delays at connections, and resulting in divided responsibility between trunk and belt lines through duplicated or jointly owned facilities. The problem of building bridge lines over north-south routes in the Cincinnati region, however, has always been complicated if not rendered insoluble by rugged topography and the great barrier of the Ohio River.

When the New York architectural firm of Alfred Fellheimer and Stewart Wagner was awarded the commission for the design of Cincinnati Union Terminal in the late spring of 1928, all these theories were well known to architects who had become leading specialists in the design of railroad stations and who had contributed substantially to the body of doctrine. The new concepts were in good part to be embodied in the location and planning of the sprawling terminal complex, but whether their implementation represented the best solutions in all cases is questionable. Discussion of a union station had dragged on for thirty years; it was high time to end the arguments and begin the job, and 1927 seemed a propitious year to launch into what was to be the city's largest single building project. Cincinnati had in 1925 adopted its own Comprehensive Plan, the work of George B. Ford and Ernest P. Goodrich, established a City Planning Commission with something more than mere advisory authority, and outlined an extensive program of public works of which a union terminal with its associated streets and drives were key elements. Although the railroads serving the city had suffered a marked decline in passenger traffic since 1920, the total volume was great enough to warrant a substantial investment either in the drastic improvement or the replacement of existing facilities. The crucial factor in making the old system work was the inordinate number of sleeping cars transferred from one train to another, which had reached a level in the mid-twenties where the tightly disposed facilities of the union and the Pennsylvania stations seriously hampered switching operations.[11] If the financial position of the various companies gave some ground for their chronic complaints, it was nevertheless sound enough and had improved somewhat over the year when the Cincinnati Terminal Development Company was established (1923). Passenger revenues in the five years of 1923 through 1927 had declined $35,000,000, but this was partly offset by an increase in freight revenues and a decline of expenses, which together produced a $69,000,000 increase in net operating income and a drop of nearly three percentage points in the average operating ratio.[12]

The establishment of the union terminal company and the construction of the station group coincided with a building boom in Cincinnati that was concentrated in the immediate area of Fountain Square, the chief nexus of the core area, extending along Fifth Street between Vine and Walnut. The first step was the construction in 1927 of the Albee Theater, located on the south side of the square and quickly seen following its opening to be the finest theater in the city in size and luxury of appointments. Designed by Thomas Lamb of New York for both motion-picture and stage performances in alternate succession, its facade above the marquee is a magnificent Palladian window in which the glass is pulled back from the wall plane to the rear end of a short tunnel vault. The theater marked the beginning of a city-center renaissance. In the next year an extensive building group was placed under construction at the west end of the square, to be completed in 1930. These handsome works in the Art Deco manner include the Carew Tower, the former Netherland Plaza Hotel, and the former Mabley and Carew Company's department store, all erected from the plans of the Chicago architect Walter W. Ahlschlager. The tower is a particularly colorful example of its style, with vertically accented curtain walls of tawny brick terminating in a gold-leaf trim at the top that immediately made it a prominent landmark visible from every hilltop ringing the basin area. Matching the Carew Tower group in size and cost is the new Ohio River bridge of the C&O Railway, but this impressive structure is properly to be considered a part of the union terminal program. Before the depression of 1930 put a stop to such ambitious works, the board of education placed the new building of Walnut Hills High School under construction on a superb site overlooking the wooded park land bordering Bloody Run and Victory Parkway. The architects of its sober classicism were the local firm of Garber and Woodward.[13] This building renaissance indicated not simply that Cincinnati was sharing in the extravagant life of the 1920s, but also that it was creating a new image of itself as a modern, progressive, expansive city willing to spend at the going rate. Nothing but the best in union railroad stations would do in such a climate, and nothing but the best in modern design would be appropriate.

The legal, financial, and organizational machinery necessary to implement these brave plans was quickly put together and set in motion once the decision to act committed all who were concerned. The Cincinnati Railroad Terminal Development Company entered into an agreement with the seven participating roads on 14 July 1927 to construct a union station and to organize an owning and operating corporation to be called the Cincinnati Union Terminal Company. The city council passed the necessary ordinances for vacation of streets, sharing of costs in street rearrangements, alterations to water and sewage lines, and the building of the terminal and its subsidiary structures. The new company appointed Henry M. Waite as chief engineer of construction and drew up a preliminary estimate of the total cost of constructing buildings, yards, approach tracks, and service facilities, the figure coming to $75,000,000, which fortunately proved to be grossly exaggerated.[14] The engineering staff began its comprehensive survey on 1 November 1927, planned to initiate construction on 1 May 1928, and to complete it by 1932. The immense operation proved more formidable than anyone expected, however, and the contractor was unable to start work until August 1929.[15] The terminal company applied to the Interstate Commerce Commission in January 1928 for the authority to construct a union passenger station in Cincinnati, the work to include 5.79 miles of double-track approaches and yard leads, and 13.55 miles of single track, distributed among approaches, yards, and terminal areas. The cost of construction was to be met chiefly by a $25,000,000 bond issue of which the interest and principal were to be guaranteed by the seven participating companies. The balance of the cost was borne through the issuance of preferred and common stock in the total amount of $6,500,000.[16] The ICC approved the terminal program in March 1928, and the directors awarded the commission for architectural design to Fellheimer and Wagner in June of the same year. The senior partners of this large and busy office placed the responsibility for the design of the terminal in the hands of a relatively young and not widely known architect, Roland Anthony Wank, whose role in the development of architecture and urban planning in the United States was considerably more important than his modest reputation would suggest.[17] The contract for the construction of the huge project was awarded early in 1929 to James C. Stewart and Company.

The formal treatment of the main terminal building developed by Wank and the Fellheimer staff was changed drastically and much improved during the course of design as the result of discussions with an architectural consultant outside the commissioned firm. Wank's original plan was a mixture of the new style that has come to be known as art deco, with its strong vertical patterns of inflectional lines, and of Renaissance forms marked chiefly by full-centered arches over the concourse windows. The train concourse and the waiting areas were combined in a single enclosure, and the furnishings for waiting passengers included the conventional seats of wood arranged in parallel rows. In 1930, while the fill for the terminal and approach tracks was being placed but prior to the building of any superstructure, the directors of the terminal company persuaded Fellheimer and Wagner to invite the Philadelphia architect Paul Philippe Cret to act as a consultant.[18] It was Cret who appears to have suggested at least in broad outline and preliminary form the unique decorative features of the terminal headhouse—the smooth planes and simple masses, the multiple prismatic and fluted moldings in parallel and concentric lines, the aluminum trim, and above all the rich, warm palette of yellows, tans, oranges, browns, and woody tones. The result was a brilliant display of color that proved to be less expensive per square foot of usable area than the classical intricacy it replaced. As Chief Engineer Henry M. Waite put it, "We tried to build something new, fresh and joyous. At first we planned a classical design with its pillars, cornices, pilasters and pedestals. It would have been cold and costly. . . . We decided that the Terminal, which leads into all parts of the world, should be as bright and gay as the flowers and birds of the open country. And when we tried the bright colors the effect was joyous and stimulating."[19] The changes proposed by Cret were embodied in working drawings dated 1 June 1931.

Construction and Operation

The most refractory problem associated with planning the terminal prior to the detailed work of design and construction was the question of locating the complex to provide maximum accessibility to passengers on the one hand and to the railroads on the other, the two generally coming together from opposite directions and along radically different routes. The solution proved to be Waite's most trying task, since railroads are notoriously unwilling to give up what they have, or to make any alterations and additions to it. The criteria for determining the site of the Cincinnati project were exactly those that we have considered in the previous section, but their realization posed peculiar difficulties arising from local topography, the existing rail pattern, and the cycle of floods in the Ohio valley. The principles underlying the choice of site were familiar and well tested: first, proximity to the core area of the city for easy access to hotels, office buildings, other places suitable for business transactions, shopping and entertainment facilities; second, easy access to public transportation and the urban circulatory system; third, a sufficient area for the numerous parts of the vast terminal complex, the area so located as to minimize interference with, or disturbance to, existing urban functions; and fourth, access to existing rail lines so as to minimize new construction. The final principle, one particularly applicable to Cincinnati, was the placing of the terminal and approach trackage out of reach of any predictable Ohio River flood.

The principles together contained inherent contradictions, and to reconcile them seemed to present insuperable difficulties. The first two obviously called for a site close to Fountain Square, which is still the flourishing heart within the heart of Cincinnati, and immediately adjacent to the chief ganglion of its public transit system. The third was easy to decide on if one disregarded the first two, since any part of Mill Creek Valley north of Eighth Street and east of the existing yards of the B&O and the CNO&TP would have answered perfectly, but not without some demolition of buildings along the margin between the workaday world and the rail jungle. The fourth would also seem to imply a Mill Creek site, but the railroad map of the city reveals serious obstacles to accessibility for the eastern lines (C&O, L&N, N&W, and Pennsylvania; see fig. 43). Over all the choices loomed the threat of flood: it precluded any riverfront site at grade level below the elevation of Third Street; it compelled a location far enough north of the riverbank to reach the 510-foot contour, and it made unavoidable either an enormous filling operation or the building of an extensive elevated structure. The chosen site lay on the east side of Mill Creek Valley somewhat west of Freeman Avenue, at the end of Laurel Street roughly on the line of Thirteenth, further from the core than any previous station but most satisfactory to the railroads that had to construct the connecting tracks (fig. 44).

Taking the passenger-carrying railroad lines in clockwise order, we might logically begin with the CNO&TP, since the terminal was virtually made to order for easy access by that company. Its bridge stood only slightly to the west of the longitudinal axis of the terminal track layout, and the north approach to the bridge ended less than half a mile from the south approach. (The bridges and their approaches are all in place carrying an extremely heavy traffic, but the terminal track system is gone.) Only a short connecting track to join the bridge approach to the south terminal approach had to be built, partly on a viaduct with the grade ascending sharply toward the bridge in order to compensate for the twenty-six-foot difference between the track elevation of the terminal and the bridge deck (fig. 44). The B&O and the Big Four lines from the west were joined to the south terminal approach by means of a sharply curved, steep-graded viaduct that passes under the CNO&TP bridge and over the east end of Eighth Street Viaduct to provide the intermediate element in a spectacular three-level work of bridge engineering (fig. 44). All the lines that have always descended through Mill Creek Valley (C&O Chicago Division, B&O, and Big Four by trackage rights over the second) were tied to the north approach of the terminal by connecting tracks of varying lengths (fig. 45). The chief problem in designing this web of interconnecting lines was that of bringing the Pennsylvania Railroad's three lines (to Xenia, Richmond, and Lebanon) into the West End of the city. The straightforward solution of

Opposite: Fig. 43. Map showing the railroad lines and passenger stations of Cincinnati, 1910-33. *Railway Age*; reproduced with permission.

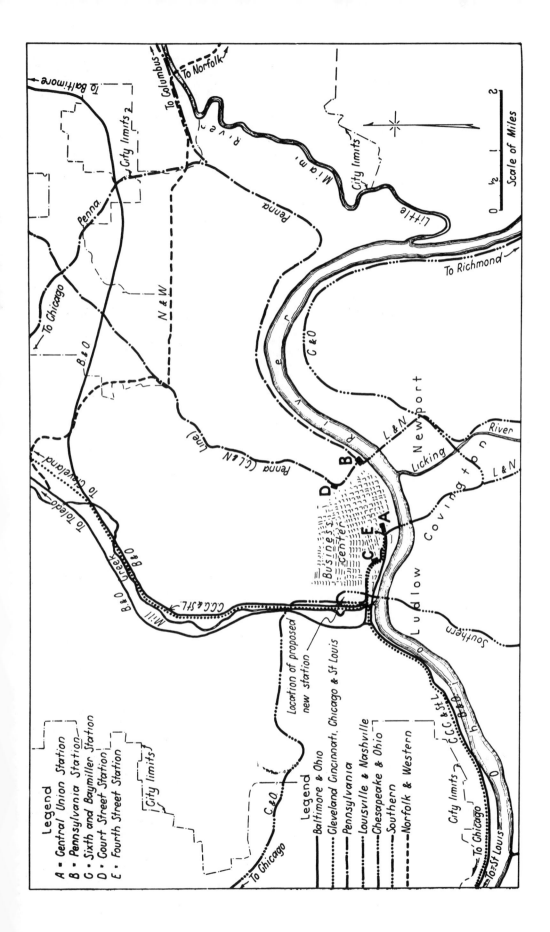

Legend
A = Central Union Station
B = Pennsylvania Station
C = Sixth and Baymiller Station
D = Court Street Station
E = Fourth Street Station

Legend
━━━ Baltimore & Ohio
•••••• Cleveland Cincinnati, Chicago & St Louis
━━━ Pennsylvania
━━━ Louisville & Nashville
━━━ Chesapeake & Ohio
•••••• Southern
━━━ Norfolk & Western

Scale of Miles
0 ¼ ½ 1 2

To Baltimore
City limits 2
To Columbus
To Norfolk
Penna.
Miami
River
N & W
Penna. (C.&N. line)
Little
Miami
River
To Richmond
C & O
City limits
To Chicago
B & O
To Toledo
To Cleveland
B & O
Mill Creek
B & O
C.C.C. & St.L.
Business Center
Location of proposed new station
L & N
Newport
Licking River
Covington
L & N
Ludlow
Southern
C.C.C. & St.L.
B & O
City limits 2
To Chicago
C & O
To Chicago
To St Louis
City limits

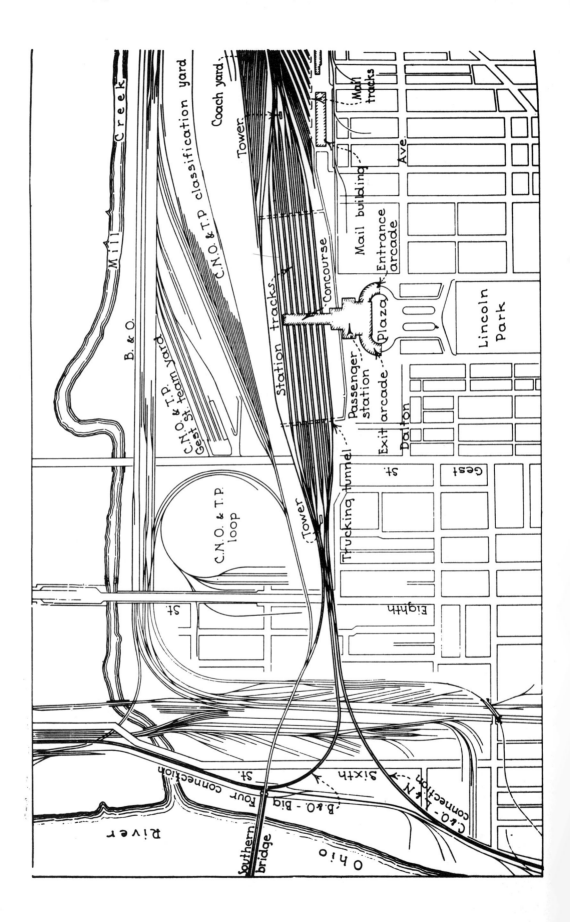

Cincinnati Union Terminal

building a viaduct to connect the East End station tracks of the Pennsylvania with the C&O bridge was rejected because of cost and floods, and the least expensive solution of operating by trackage rights over the B&O from Loveland, Ohio, where the two roads intersect, was rejected for reasons that still appear to be a mystery. This left the Pennsylvania Railroad only one alternative, namely, to build a series of sharply curving connecting tracks in Linwood (far East End) and Norwood to join in succession its Cincinnati and Chicago divisions with the B&O. In this way the Pennsylvania reduced to a minimum its operation by trackage rights over the B&O, but only at the high cost of building connections in the irregular topography east of Norwood, where numerous curves greatly restricted the speed of trains. Since the Lebanon Branch (former CL&N Railroad) had always crossed the B&O in central Norwood, trains could be operated by trackage rights over the latter without the necessity of building a new line.[20] Since the Norfolk and Western had for some years operated its trains by trackage rights over the Pennsylvania from Clare in the Little Miami valley, its trains followed the new Pennsylvania-B&O route into the union terminal.

The most expensive single work of construction as well as the most impressive example of structural engineering in the system of connecting lines was the extension of the C&O Railway's Interterminal Viaduct to the south approach tracks. This work was carried on as part of the replacement of the company's Ohio River bridge (1928–29) and consequently forms the proper starting point for the construction history of the union terminal (fig. 27). The original bridge, constructed in 1886–88, had become a bottleneck that posed the serious threat of breaking down entirely. Since the L&N operated the trains of its Atlanta line over the tracks of the Chesapeake company from KC Junction in Covington to the Mill Creek yards in Cincinnati, the total volume of traffic on the bridge had reached at least two hundred train and engine movements per day, which included thirty-four passenger trains and a considerable though varying number of 10,000-ton coal trains. An examination of the span conducted in 1916 revealed that it was carrying locomotives 55 percent heavier and train loads 100

Opposite: Fig. 44. Cincinnati Union Terminal, Lincoln Parkway at Dalton Avenue, 1929–33; Fellheimer and Wagner, architects; Henry M. Waite, chief engineer. Plan of track-platform area, south approaches, and mail terminal. *Railway Age*; reproduced with permission.

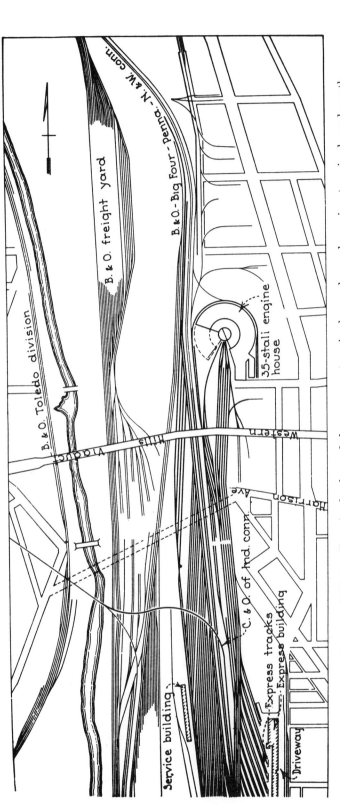

Fig. 45. Cincinnati Union Terminal, plan of the express terminal, coach yard, engine terminal, and north approaches. *Railway Age*; reproduced with permission.

percent greater than those for which it had been designed. By drastically restricting the weight of engines and the speed of trains, the road kept the bridge in service until 1928, when it initiated Cincinnati's greatest single program of construction outside the terminal group itself. The project was carried out under the direction of C. W. Johns, the chief engineer of the C&O, and the design of the double-track bridge structure and its approaches was the work of the J. E. Greiner Company. The river crossing is composed of a pair of subdivided Warren trusses continuous over four supports, with an overall length for the three spans of 1,575 feet, of which the channel crossing is 675 feet and the side spans 450 feet each. These dimensions and a maximum truss depth of 106 feet make the superstructure the second-largest continuous-truss span ever built, the largest being the same company's Ohio River bridge at Sciotoville, Ohio (1914–17). The concrete piers of the Cincinnati span rest on a bed of limestone strata that is under high compression induced by a fifty-foot overlay of sand and gravel and hence of good bearing capacity. The entire bridge project includes one and a half miles of approach viaducts, divided between the Kentucky approach (1,600 feet) and the extension of the Inter-terminal Viaduct in Cincinnati to the south approach of the union terminal (6,200 feet), and a new six-track station in Covington. The immense structure made the C&O line through Covington and Cincinnati a continuously elevated track system for a length of 9,375 feet.[21] It remains the most heavily traveled length of track in the Cincinnati switching district with respect to the number of daily trains, although the CNO&TP bridge usually carries a greater number of cars because of heavy transfer traffic.

The building of the C&O bridge formed a prelude to the construction of the terminal complex, and by the time the earlier work was completed in the fall of 1929, the emplacement of the fill for the terminal trackage had begun. The filling operation raised the immediate area of the terminal track layout from 12 to 20 feet above the existing grade level, so that the base of the rail would stand at an average of 513 feet above sea level, hopefully above any possible Ohio River flood and in fact 4 feet above that of the record reached in January 1937. The fill required the placing of 5,663,000 cubic yards of earth and rock over most of the 287 acres covered by the terminal trackage, its approaches, coach yard, and enginehouse. The site of the station building was largely occupied by the classification yard and local freight house of the CNO&TP Railway, both of which were moved westward on a slightly raised grade level near the central area of Mill Creek Valley. The area covered by the terminal headhouse and its numerous tracks and subsidary structures extended north and south from the station building, centered on the line of Thirteenth Street, in a strip measuring roughly 1,600 × 10,000 feet on its periphery. The passenger terminal stood near the south end of this area, about one and a half miles from the central point of the core area at Fifth and Vine streets.[22] With the fill largely in place by mid-1930, the construction of the many buildings of which the terminal complex was composed could begin. It was completed four years and nearly $41,000,000 later, in March 1933, about two weeks ahead of the scheduled opening date to move the Cincinnati passenger trains for the first time out of the grip of another Ohio River flood. In addition to the terminal proper the entire operating group included mail and express terminals, coach yard, engine terminal, associated storage buildings, and a steam-generating plant, which were strung out in a linear series northward to the line of McMillan Street (2500 north in the city's block-numbering system). Outside the working structures but properly to be included in the whole project are the broad landscaped plaza on which the station building faced and Western Hills Viaduct, both constructed by the municipal government (figs. 44, 45, 46, 47, 52).[23] Baggage, mail, and express were moved from the station platforms to their respective terminals and handling facilities through tunnels under the track-platform layout.

The terminal building was planned as a through station of the so-called two-level type in which the concourse floor was fixed at an elevation of twenty-one feet above the finished grade level of the fill, providing the standard underclearance over tracks of seventeen feet. The through form was adopted to allow entry from both directions and to accommodate those trains of the B&O Railroad that operated through the city en route between Saint Louis and Jersey City and between Detroit and Louisville. The overall aim of internal planning was to arrange spaces and facilities in such a way as to minimize interference between streams of incoming and outgoing passengers, to eliminate conflicting movements among streetcars, buses, taxis, and private automobiles, between pedestrians and vehicles, and between baggage trucks and pas-

Opposite: Fig. 46. Cincinnati Union Terminal, main elevation. Photograph by F. T. Kihlstedt; reproduced with permission.

Fig. 47. Cincinnati Union Terminal, view of the dome over the West End. Photograph by F. T. Kihlstedt; reproduced with permission.

sengers. These ends were realized mainly through generous plat-form and floor areas, spacious entrance drives, the location of park-ing spaces below grade level, and the separation of the access ways for different kinds of vehicles within the body of the station building. The capacity of the headhouse and the fourteen station tracks was calculated to be 216 trains per day, but in truth this figure is no more than half the number of trains that could have been accommodated in the big terminal. The track-platform layout was admirably designed for the movement of passengers and bag-gage vehicles and the expeditious handling of transfer cars, which, as we have seen, posed a serious problem at Cincinnati. The plat-forms measured 28 feet in width outside the areas covered by the enclosures for ramps and stairways and 1,600 feet in length, suffi-cient to provide adjacent platform space for seventeen Pullman cars and a typical road locomotive. Supplementing the platform tracks were two passing tracks at the east side of the station group and eight lengths of transfer tracks located in tandem pairs be-tween four pairs of platform tracks in the west half of the platform area, with switches between the two kinds of tracks at both ends of each transfer track. This unique feature made it possible to trans-fer sleeping cars from an incoming to an outgoing train without moving the latter out of the station area, as would ordinarily be the case in a station with a conventional track system. It also made it possible to park two different trains of relatively short length on the same station track.[24]

The elevation of the floor for the train concourse was fixed primarily by the grade level of the track system, but it also served to place the main mass of the headhouse far enough above the surrounding streets to give the half-dome great visual prominence and to locate parking facilities and one north-south street (Dalton) under the sloping plaza (figs. 46, 47). The remaining space be-neath the rotunda and train concourse floors was planned for bag-gage facilities, truck delivery drives, and three concentric semi-circular drives respectively reserved for buses, taxis, and streetcars (the last of which were never installed). The most conspicuous feature of the building, and all that survives of it today (1975), is the great half-dome that rises to a clear interior height of 106 feet (the dome and the enclosures for the semicircular drives ap-pear most clearly in figure 48). The semicircular rotunda covered by the half-dome served as an entrance lobby, a concourse for the movement of passengers to and from the train gates, waiting facilities, and street vehicles, and as space for the usual service

245

elements of large stations—ticket offices, telephone and telegraph center, restaurant, shops, a theater, and the access corridor to the office floors that flank the dome. The shape, the multiple functions, the presence of a theater, and the powerful sweep of lofty internal space made the magnificent rotunda unique in railroad terminals throughout the world. The low-ceilinged midway that joined the entrance concourse to the train concourse was flanked by baggage-checking facilities, toilets, a small waiting room for women, offices, and a private dining room.

The train concourse, extending westward over the tracks and platforms, was architecturally pedestrian on the exterior but second only to the dome in color and spatial magnificence. Measuring 78 × 415 feet in clear floor area and covered by a slightly vaulted ceiling with a clear interior height of 36 feet 8 1/2 inches at the crown, the train concourse served not only the usual function of an avenue to the train gates on the north and south sides, but also as a waiting room, which actually consisted of circles of leather-covered upholstered chairs located on either side of the track gates. Like the rotunda, the train concourse was thus open and devoted to a mixture of functions that gave the terminal its lively air. The provision of both ramps and stairways connecting the concourse floor with the platforms, and of two gates for each platform located on opposite sides of the concourse, made possible a nearly complete separation of incoming and outgoing streams of passengers. Another unique feature of the terminal headhouse was the interlocking tower, which was not a separate structure, as is usually the case, but a rearward extension of the office block behind the dome (fig. 51). The two-story enclosure contained electrical instruments on the first floor and the electropneumatic interlocking machine and illuminated track diagram on the second. Distinguished by ribbon windows on three sides to provide a view of the whole track area, jutting from the main mass of the building high above the concourse roof, the "tower" looked like the bridge of a ship, an appearance not far removed from its function.[25]

The formal treatment of the terminal that emerged from the consultation between Wank and Cret was clearly in the art deco mode, which was most obvious in the pronounced vertical emphasis of window bands, the buttresses in the semicircular facade of the

Opposite: Fig. 48. Cincinnati Union Terminal, plaza, headhouse, and track-platform area. *Cincinnati Enquirer*; reproduced with permission.

dome, in the wall panels, in the tight patterns of moldings and flutings that provided accents to the smooth planar surfaces, in the graphics, and in the linear, flat, severely geometrized ornament. The overall design nicely combined the expression of function in the main divisions of the enclosure with the gateway motif that appears most strongly in the huge semicircular arch that constitutes the central vertical section of the dome. The exterior materials were thoroughly traditional—limestone for the facade and the outer walls of the entrance drives, light buff brick everywhere else, and terra cotta for the original dome covering, but this was replaced by aluminum sheathing in 1945. The structural system was everywhere steel framing carrying the masonry curtain walls and the reinforced concrete floor and roof slabs. Nothing on the exterior, however, prepared one for the stunning exhibition of color, texture, and mural art on the interior, features that constituted a major step in an architectural revolution that was most fully developed at the Century of Progress Exposition in Chicago (1933-34).[26]

Only color photographs, of which too few survive, can do justice to this vivid yet harmonious palette, but a simple catalogue of materials and their distribution may suggest something of its richness. The domed ceiling of the rotunda concourse and certain wall areas were finished in yellow and orange plaster with a trim of Red Verona, Tennessee Fleuri, and Virginia Black marbles, and the lower wall areas over the service facilities were covered with highly colored mosaic murals created by the German-born artist Winold Reiss and executed by the Ravenna Mosaic Company.[27] The sidewalls of the train concourse were devoted almost entirely to Reiss's murals, which in this case depicted aspects of the leading industries of Cincinnati, and the end wall was covered with a world map and clock dials showing the hour differences in various time zones. Elsewhere on the walls there was a trim of Red Verona and various domestic gray and black marbles; the low vault of the ceiling was again done in orange and yellow plaster, and the floor was finished in red and tan terrazzo. Wood veneer finishes with aluminum trim characterized the lounges and offices: zebra wood, walnut, and holly in the men's lounge were arranged in abstract designs derived from railroad locomotives, cars, and signals; panels of zebra and madrone wood covered the women's lounge; and gum, harewood, and holly were used in the offices along with cork flooring. In the restaurant the walls were finished in zebra, birch, red and black marbles, and the floors in terrazzo;

in the theater walls of Tennessee Fleuri, black, and white marbles stood in subdued contrast to a mulberry carpet; the interiors of the ticket offices were finished in Hauteville marble and terrazzo, and the private dining room entirely in Rookwood tile. The designers and executors of this magnificence created at one stroke a new architectural world, and when we consider the color poverty of the architecture that came after World War II, we are forced to conclude that the whole brilliant movement largely died with the Century of Progress Exposition in 1934.[28]

The structural systems embodied in the various parts of the union terminal formed appropriate though less innovative technological counterparts to the imaginative architectural design. The great semi-dome, adopted to give the facade and the entrance concourse a monumental gateway motif, required for its support the most extensive departures from conventional steel framing. The enclosure actually consists of two structuro-geometric forms, which can be seen from the aerial view of the entire building: the main part is a true bisected hemisphere, the largest semi-dome ever constructed for a permanent building, and the smaller is a semicircular cylindrical vault that extends forward from the dome to the plane of the facade (fig. 48). The roof and ceiling are supported by a novel system of arched trusses of diminishing radius rather than the conventional frame of radial trusses, which was technically feasible but was rejected for a number of complex reasons (fig. 49). Perhaps the most decisive of these factors was that the continuous semicircular tension ring and the chords necessary to absorb the arch thrust at the springing would have led to an unmanageably awkward problem because of the rectangular extensions on the flanks of the dome for the ticket and company offices on the north side and the restaurant on the south. The situation at the upper ends of the arched trusses would have posed still other difficulties: the compressive thrusts of the radial half-arches would have been concentrated at the crown of the inner vault arch, which would have formed a full semicircle, and hence subjected it to severe bending in the vertical plane, a problem that would have been intensified by the indeterminate factors arising from the thirty-five-foot height of the springing points above the ground, which precluded the use of skewbacks and anchorages. An additional complicating element was that the geometric perimeter of the concourse could not be made to conform to the semicircular distribution or radial symmetry of anchor and abutment columns. Finally, the broad opening between the rotunda and

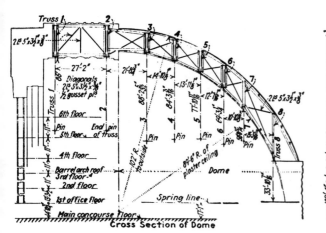

Cross Section of Dome

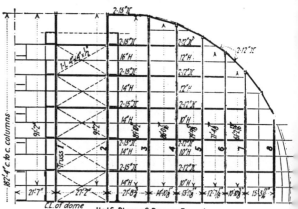

Half Plan of Dome Framing

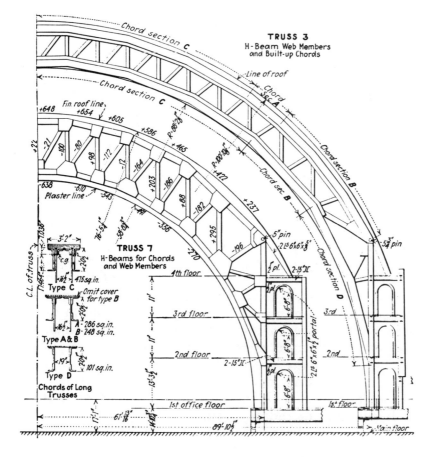

TRUSS 3
H-Beam Web Members
and Built-up Chords

TRUSS 7
H-Beams for Chords
and Web Members

Type C

Type A & B

Type D

Chords of Long
Trusses

the train concourse made it virtually inadmissible to bring the radial arches down to abutment columns between the outer limits of this passage. Thus a complex of factors dictated the use of parallel trusses diminishing in radius from front to back. Of the eight trusses two support the vault and the remaining six support the dome, their out-to-out span contracting from 209 feet for the first two to 67 feet 8 inches for the eighth. The ends of the trusses are built into the conventional column-and-girder frames of the four-story enclosures flanking the dome, the frames thus acting to absorb the thrust of the dome arches as well as to support floors, roof, and walls.[29] The successive trusses are joined by roof purlins, ceiling beams, and double-diagonal bracing set in the panels defined by the other three types of members. All connecting and bracing elements lie in parallel planes extending at right angles to the planes of the trusses.

The concourse frame was a sober work of traditional form compared with the dome framing. Because the axes of the headhouse were oriented in accordance with the city street pattern in the immediate area, and the direction of the track-platform axis was fixed by surrounding rail yards and approach lines, the transverse axis of the concourse does not exactly coincide with its longitudinal equivalent in the track system but lies at an angle of almost five degrees to it.[30] The overall length of the concourse was 414 feet 8 inches center to center of columns and its maximum interior width (at the plane of the train gates) was 82 feet (fig. 50). The gable roof and the ceiling vault were carried on a series of transverse trusses with a gabled top chord and an arched bottom chord the curve of which conformed to the profile of the much-flattened ceiling vault. Since the web of the truss was riveted through its depth to the supporting columns, the truss and two columns together constituted a rigid frame, although it was given a traditional form compared with the more advanced design of the similar structural systems supporting the platform canopies and the terminal tracks over one of the local streets. The maximum clear height of the concourse vault was 36 feet 8 1/2 inches, sufficient to give it a generous volume that avoided the depressing tomb-like effect of low-ceilinged enclosures. A more difficult problem than the roof support was that of carrying the broad floor over the track-

Opposite: Fig. 49. Cincinnati Union Terminal, dome framing. *Engineering News-Record*; reproduced with permission.

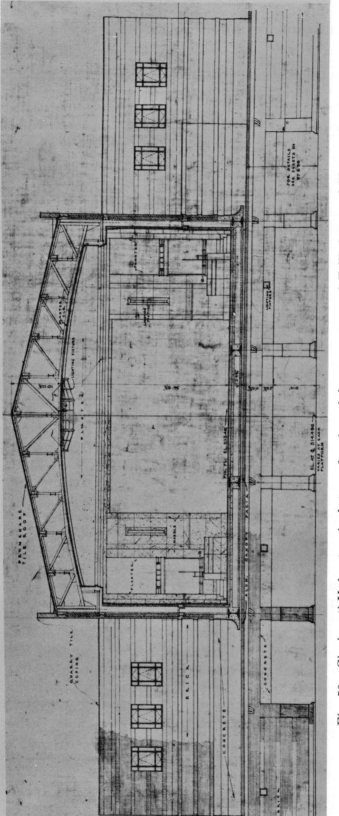

Fig. 50. Cincinnati Union terminal, truss framing of the concourse roof; Fellheimer and Wagner drawing. From the private collection of Gibson Yungblut; reproduced with permission.

platform area with a minimum of obstruction to the spaces underneath it. The solution was a grid-like framework composed of four series of longitudinal girders sustaining transverse beams and spanning between massive transverse trusses carried on paired posts set along either side of the platform center line.[31]

The most advanced forms of structural technology at the Cincinnati terminal were not embodied in the fabric enclosing its monumental spaces but rather in such utilitarian elements as the platform canopies and the underpasses for secondary streets. The adoption of the separate platform shelter in place of the all-covering train shed at the turn of the century led to the replacement of once spectacular railroad structures with the most commonplace forms of roof framing, but in the Cincinnati station these were treated with a certain measure of engineering imagination. The aim in the design of the platform canopy was to use spans of considerably greater length than customary in order, first, to reduce the number of pile foundations in the newly placed fill, and second, to fix the length of the clear span to correspond to that of the standard passenger car between end walls, or eighty feet. To insure maximum rigidity in a narrow framework supported on a single row of columns and to avoid excessive depth of the main girder, the designers adopted a primary roof structure in which the central girder was continuous for three spans, or 240 feet, and was connected to the roof columns in such a way as to form a three-span rigid frame (fig. 51). Since in such a frame there may be no bending moment at the foot of the leg, the downward-tapering columns were designed so as to be attached to the footing below the platform surface by means of hinged bearings. The full roof frame consisted, in addition to the main girder, of a pair of transverse brackets at each column and double-diagonal bracing between the central element and the edge beams to resist bending and torsional forces arising from wind and snow loads. With a high proportion of the roof loads falling on the bracing and with the presence of a counter-moment resulting from uplifting forces on the anchor ends of the cantilevered brackets, the engineers were able to hold the long main girders to a depth of only three feet for an eighty-foot span.

The most remarkable structural work among the subsidiary elements of the terminal group is in great part so thoroughly hidden and in its visible details so commonplace that few have paid any attention to it. The problem that led to the most innovative feature of the vast complex was that of carrying the tracks and the light wells of the south station layout and three yard leads to the CNO&TP Railway over an intermediate east-west thoroughfare known as Gest Street. The resulting "bridge" actually consists of two parallel concrete-lined box tunnels extending 328 feet from portal to portal, of which the openings are unequal in width, the one on the north having a clear interior span of twenty-one feet, and the one on the south twenty-six feet six inches, the latter adopted to include a sidewalk as well as a vehicular roadway. An intricate complex of loadings—heavy live loads of locomotives and cars generating high shearing forces; impact loads; horizontal traction forces arising from the acceleration of trains (especially high in the case of yard locomotives switching cars); dead load of structure, fill, and trackage; horizontal earth pressure; thermal expansion and contraction; settlement of foundations—added to the asymmetrical section, and the skewed alignment (accompanied by torsional forces) dictated the novel choice of a rigid-frame structure in reinforced concrete. It was the first of its kind to be designed for railroad loadings, and the first in which the monolithic construction made the parallel vaults in effect a single structure continuous over two spans along the transverse direction and hence highly indeterminate. Even the construction of the Gest Street underpass was a complicated procedure because of the presence of a broad concrete mat underlying the footings of an earlier bridge and of a stone masonry interceptor sewer with a twelve-foot interior diameter.[32]

As far as the citizens were concerned, the most prominent and very likely the most welcome feature of the terminal project other than the station building itself is Western Hills Viaduct, which was constructed in its original form in 1930–32 along with the laying-down of trackage and the building of subsidiary terminal facilities in its immediate area (fig. 52).[33] Extending as a double-deck concrete bridge from Central Parkway on the east to Harrison Avenue at Beekman Street on the west, with an original overall length along the upper deck of 3,500 feet, the once impressive structure was built to serve a number of needs that the city finally had to face when the expanding trackage of the terminal put an end to further delays. The immediate necessity was that of replacing the old Harrison Avenue Viaduct with a more capacious struc-

Fig. 52. Western Hills Viaduct, 1930-32. Cincinnati Union Terminal Company and Cincinnati Department of Public Works engineering staffs, engineers. Reproduced through the courtesy of the Cincinnati City Planning Commission.

ture at an elevation sufficient to clear the trains on the new terminal fill, which rose close to the iron deck frame of the Harrison span. More deeply rooted needs of an urbanistic character, however, underlay these practical exigencies. The great belt of railroad trackage in Mill Creek Valley, poor internal drainage, and floods coming almost on an annual basis had isolated the Western Hills from the central and eastern areas of the city, and the few streets that were carried over or under the jungle were inadequate to maintain communication across this broad gap. The extension of McMillan Street down the west face of Clifton and Fairview hills (1923), which made possible through streetcar service across the mid-portion of the valley, underscored the need to unite the two chains of hills, but it was the planning of the terminal track system that compelled the city to act. The double-deck form of the viaduct was required to meet this diversity of needs: the long upper deck joining Central Parkway and Harrison Avenue was reserved exclusively for passenger vehicles, and the shorter lower level was designed primarily to carry streetcars and commercial vehicles from Spring Grove Avenue to the western end of the viaduct at Harrison. The $3,500,000 cost was shared among the municipal government, the terminal company, and the B&O Railroad, the owner of nearly all the rail property in the middle section of the valley. Western Hills Viaduct consists for the most part of double-deck column-and-girder spans, but this long linear series is interrupted by two handsome arch spans, the longer over Spring Grove Avenue near the east end, and the smaller over Mill Creek toward the west.[34]

The mechanical and electrical equipment of the union terminal with one exception embodied practices that had been developed during the great period of rail terminal construction, roughly the first quarter of the twentieth century. The operation of a large metropolitan station requires immense quantities of steam not only for heating the numerous buildings, with their extensive open interiors, but also for heating parked cars, cleaning locomotives, and heating water for minor cleaning chores. Steam for the Cincinnati complex was generated in a separate plant located immediately north of the engine terminal about one and a half miles from the station headhouse. The steam was piped to various buildings, where the smaller interior spaces were heated by steam radiators and the larger by passing air drawn from the outside over heating units from which fans circulated it through ceiling grills. In the warm-weather seasons the same process was followed without heating the air. Illumination in the station building was divided among indirect lighting in the main concourse or rotunda (then something of an art deco novelty) and direct and semidirect in the long train concourse. A teletype system connected the train announcement board with the stationmaster's office, the interlocking tower, and the train platforms. The electrical outlets at the platforms served not only to provide power for car illumination but for air-conditioning as well, the latter having been introduced while the terminal was under construction. The interlocking system was the electropneumatic type, and all signals were the color-light variety divided between the dwarf type within the station track area (between throat tracks) and the overhead form on gantries along the approach tracks. All water for whatever purpose, from drinking to filling locomotive tenders, was drawn from the city water supply, and that which supplied the decorative fountains and the cascade in the plaza was continuously recirculated. Chilled brine for the refrigerators in the restaurant and the cooling devices in the theater rounded out the complex of utilitarian elements necessary to render this microcity inhabitable, comfortable, and workable.[35]

Reality and Potentiality

A straightforward assessment of Cincinnati Union Terminal in its day-to-day functioning, in its potential capacity, and in its urban role is impossible because of a number of factors complex and unpredictable in their consequences—the extreme economic and social dislocations of a worldwide character that marked the thirties and forties, changes in modes of transportation in the United States, the changing economy of Cincinnati, and the relocation of American manufacturing centers into previously unindustrialized areas, with attendant drastic shifts in the relative traffic volumes of the Cincinnati railroads. Perhaps the logical starting point in our evaluation is the actual performance of the terminal during the short period prior to its final decline. The depression that followed the stock market crash of October 1929 was accompanied by an extensive paralysis of the basic manufacturing and transportation industries of the United States. The full effects were not felt immediately, and 1930 remained a relatively lively year for the railroads. By 1933, however, rail traffic had dropped so disastrously that the chief operating questions among company officers were how long maintenance could be deferred and where to find storage space for idle locomotives and cars. The freight tonnage handled by the seven railroads serving Cincinnati dropped 40 percent in the five years from 1928 to 1933 (the actual decline was somewhat offset by the C&O's acquisition of the Hocking Valley Railroad in 1930), while the total number of passengers fell by a little more than half in the same period of time. The fortunes of the individual carriers, however, varied in the extreme. The two largest passenger carriers, the New York Central System and the Pennsylvania, fared rather well compared with the smaller lines: the first managed to retain a little better than half of its predepression passenger traffic, and the second lost slightly more than half. At the other extremes the passenger volume of the B&O and the L&N dropped by a little more than two-thirds of the 1928 totals, while the C&O and the N&W both lost a staggering 70 percent. These figures provide one quantitative index to the fact that the depression was a total catastrophe for the Appalachian states, where outright starvation and the diseases of dietary deficiency became commonplace phenomena.

The loss of passenger business was soon reflected in the curtailment of schedules. When the new terminal was opened for service in March 1933, the number of scheduled trains listed in the public timetables had fallen to 134 per day and the total number of trains operated to 142, as against 224 in 1928. By the end of the following year the curtailments had been even greater, as the cumbersome machinery of abandonment reacted to the continuing depression of traffic: the listed daily trains fell to 122, and the maximum number operated to 134.[36] The kind of service most vulnerable to the economic stagnation was the local or accommodation train, which had already suffered drastically from streetcar and motor vehicle competition, and in the early years of the depression all of those that had served the smaller communities of the Cincinnati area from the beginnings of their respective railroads fell one by one. The L&N began the process by dropping its central Kentucky local trains in June 1930, and the Pennsylvania ended it by abandoning service to Lebanon and Morrow in September 1934. And with the accommodation trains went the older terminals and the minor stations that had once sheltered them: the Eighth Street transfer station inherited by the B&O from the CH&D, Baymiller Street, and Fourth Street were closed before the union terminal was completed, and the rest followed when the new station was opened to service.[37] In the year following its opening it is doubtful whether the grand spaces of the new terminal accommodated as many as 10,000 passengers per day, but the number was to increase slowly and irregularly until wartime preparations in 1940 finally ended the persistent depression.

The economic difficulties of the thirties brought a number of changes in the character of passenger service, although schedules, motive power, and the operation of trains continued according to the techniques and practices that had been established in the previous decade. Many new procedures were adopted to reduce the costs of maintaining rolling stock and motive power, but these were of the housekeeping, penny-pinching variety that involved no technological changes. Far more welcome to the passenger was the radical upgrading of day-coach accommodations and service, which was accomplished at Cincinnati by the roads that had suffered the greatest losses of passenger traffic, most notably the B&O and the C&O, with the L&N not far behind. The first two companies began in 1931 to operate coaches with individual reclining seats and with greatly enlarged lavatory and toilet facilities.[38] The C&O even went so far as to take a half-step toward transforming the coach into a parlor car: the individual movable seats were restricted to a single row along one side of the aisle, thus reducing the total occupancy of the car to forty-five passengers. Of greatest importance for the comfort of the passenger was the introduction of air-conditioned cars in 1931. Once again the B&O led the way: on 24 May 1931 it placed in service the first completely air-conditioned train, the *Columbian*, on the Washington–Jersey City run, the event falling 101 years to the day after the road sold the first ticket for the transportation of a railroad passenger in the United States. The first Cincinnati train to be reequipped with air-conditioned cars and the first train in the country to carry air-conditioned sleeping cars was the B&O's *National Limited*, which first offered the new service on 20 April 1932. Four days later the C&O followed in the same path when it inaugurated an entirely new train, the *George Washington*, on the Cincinnati-Washington run.

The general decline in prices and income during the thirties and the serious threat from the low-tariff competition of trucks and motor buses finally compelled the railroads to reduce freight rates and passenger fares and to introduce an equitable differential between coach and sleeping-car charges. The standard fare of 3.6 cents per mile for all classes of service that was the rule in the twenties was reduced by stages to a low point of 1.5 cents per mile in day coaches by 1934. A similar reduction in dining-car prices eventually reached an all-time minimum of seventy-five cents for a full and well-prepared dinner on the B&O. The extra fares that the Big Four, L&N, and Pennsylvania had added like a tax for travel in their all-Pullman flyers were abolished, and the restriction of certain trains to sleeping cars only was ended in favor of the usual mixture of day coaches, parlor cars, and sleepers. The average speed of the premier through trains was steadily increased throughout the depression, and in the case of the major carriers, the New York Central System and the Pennsylvania, the premier trains were advanced to average speeds in the fifty-mile-per-hour category before wartime exigencies put a stop to further reductions of schedules. The high point, and indeed the prewar end point, of these extensive improvements in passenger service came when the New York Central, in April 1941, inaugurated a new coach train on a new schedule between Cincinnati and Chicago. The *James Whitcomb Riley*, as it was called, marked a net addition to the Chicago schedules, and it was operated at the highest average speed of any train in the Cincinnati family. It thus proved a decisive factor in raising the general average of all premier trains to very nearly forty-five miles per hour in the spring of 1941.[39]

The average number of trains operated to and from the union terminal throughout the depression and the wartime years was 128 per weekday, and even the addition of numerous special trains and extra sections during World War II left the total substantially below the maximum of 160 daily trains accommodated in the old union depot. The new facility could thus hardly be regarded as taxed, and given the volume of traffic comfortably handled at the busiest metropolitan stations in the United States, there is no question that the Cincinnati terminal could have accommodated 420 trains per day, or nearly double the number for which it was theoretically designed. As a matter of fact, the rejected 1881 plan for Central Union Depot, if the station had later been equipped with an electropneumatic interlocking system and a three-track approach, could have accommodated at a squeeze all the Cincinnati schedules in the period of rail ascendancy. A great many features embodied in the design of the union terminal and having to do with the movement of trains underlay this great reserve capacity and its associated efficiency of operation. The chief factors were the generous interior spaces in the headhouse and all subsidiary buildings, the fourteen station tracks, the existence of transfer tracks (an innovation in the planning of permanent stations, as we have seen), and the 1,600-foot platforms with a width of 28 feet (long enough for seventeen cars and a locomotive). Among subsidiary facilities the decisive features were the unified coach yard and engine terminal, used by all roads except the CNO&TP, a loop track circling the enginehouse for turning trains, the drastic expansion of mail and express terminals, and their separation from the passenger station. The electropneumatic interlocking system and the automatic light signals formed a *sine qua non* for safe and efficient operation, and they served at last to bring the terminal facilities of Cincinnati up to date.

A factor as important as all the rest in terminal capacity, however, is the system of approach tracks, and at Cincinnati it was a peculiarly complicated one. This intricate pattern of incurving and interweaving lines formed as a whole an approach of maximum extent, since it originally consisted of a total of nine tracks divided among five separate routes, but an extremely unbalanced distribution of train movements tended to offset some of the advantages conferred by sheer space.[40] The 134 daily trains that were regularly scheduled in 1933 were distributed among the various approach lines in such a way that the three converging on the south throat of the terminal carried fifty-two trains, and the single north approach, serving four railroads, carried eighty-two, but two of these were operated over the single track of the C&O's Chicago Division and hence occupied only a very short length of the north approach. This double-track line, however, served through part of its length as the access route to the engine terminal and coach yard leads, and since these facilities were used by all roads except the CNO&TP, the two tracks carried all empty trains and light engines as well as scheduled trains, for a total of 332 movements per day. If the terminal had ever been used to its estimated maximum capacity of 420 trains per day, the total number of movements over the lower end of the north approach would have risen to about 840, which would have necessitated separate lead tracks extending over the whole distance from the terminal to the enginehouse. As a consequence of this imbalance, we can see how the spatial distribution of the utilities at Cincinnati tended to offset some of the advantages of a through station.[41] The great virtue of the extensive track and platform layout of the new terminal, and one for which it was specifically designed, was its capacity to accommodate the extreme concentration of early-morning arrivals and departures. A total of 34 scheduled trains entered and left the station between 7:00 and 9:00 A.M. in 1933-34, which resulted in 116 train and engine movements on the north approach during a two-hour period.

Cincinnati Union Terminal

Cincinnati Union Terminal was used to its full capacity with respect to the number of daily passengers only during the war years of 1942–45, but it never accommodated more than half the number of trains at its ultimate capacity and seldom more than a third. The upturn in railroad passenger traffic began in 1934, but the climb was so slow and irregular and highway competition so effective that the total number of passengers carried in 1940 was less than 5 percent above the depression-bottom total of 1933. World War II suddenly changed the transportation pattern of the United States in an extreme and wholly unpredictable way. In the volume of freight and the number of passengers the railroads found themselves in the position they enjoyed through the early twenties, and the great total of passenger-miles by 1944 more than doubled the similar figure for 1920. For the Cincinnati roads the freight tonnage more than doubled (123 percent) in the eleven years from 1933 to 1944, and the number of passengers increased more than two and one-half times (170 percent) in the same period. The combination of troop movements, heavy commercial travel, and the shipments of military hardware with the imposition of gasoline rationing quickly pushed the railroads once again to the front rank as common carriers. The pattern of wartime travel, however, was radically different from what it had been during World War I and the expansive days of the 1920s. Indeed, if it had not been different, the railroads would never have been able to handle the flood. The vanished local traffic never reappeared, and as a consequence there was no increase in the number of regularly scheduled trains between depression stagnation and the wartime peak. The total number of passengers and hence the number of passengers per train doubled between 1940 and 1944, while the average journey increased four times in the same period, which accounts for the spectacular and record-breaking total of 95.5 billion passenger-miles in 1944. The Cincinnati roads operated 123 regularly scheduled trains per day in 1944, but the actual total was very likely 20 percent higher at times of special troop movements, or about 145 per day.[42]

The actual number of passengers using the union terminal is difficult to estimate with accuracy. If the increase is calculated on the basis of the total of all passengers carried in the United States, then the number at Cincinnati was about 22,800 per day in 1944; but if it is based on the number of through passengers only, which is justified by the fact that all suburban and accommodation service had been abandoned at Cincinnati by the mid-thirties, the

263

number was probably at least 34,000 per day. If the latter is a reasonable estimate, 1944 was a record year for Cincinnati as well as for the nation as a whole. The ability of the railroads to produce 737 billion ton-miles of freight and 95.5 billion passenger-miles in a single year—far above all previous totals—was predicated on several factors of which some, ironically enough, were born of the depression itself. New high-horsepower steam locomotives were entirely a development of the 1920s, but the installation of light signals in place of semaphores, the extension of lines operated under centralized traffic control, the expansion and multiplication of classification yards equipped with remote-controlled car-retarders, the merger of numerous small divisions into a few large operating entities (a reduction from nine to three on the Big Four, for example), and simplified administrative organizations, though in some cases initiated in the twenties, arose mainly from experiments in operating economies compelled by the depression of the thirties. The overriding consequence was that the paralyzed yards and terminals of 1917 were avoided, and the immense wartime traffic was handled efficiently and for the most part expeditiously, although there were many occasions when day-coach passengers had good grounds for complaint.

Even more drastic changes in the volume and pattern of rail traffic occurred after the war, and they led to a melancholy end at Cincinnati. From the high point of 1944 passenger traffic dropped steadily and at an accelerating rate until so little was left that only a rescue operation by the federal government preserved railroad passenger service. The National Railroad Passenger Corporation, established by an act of Congress, pared the few schedules existing at the time in half and began to operate the remaining trains in May 1971 under the public-relations name of Amtrak. The few trains still serving Cincinnati were canceled except for one in each direction that ran over the long-established through route from Chicago to Washington, Richmond, and Newport News originally on the lines of the Big Four and the C&O. Designated numbers 50 and 51, named the *James Whitcomb Riley* eastbound and the *George Washington* westbound, the trains continued to use the union terminal for nearly two years. The route through the terminal complex was a strange makeshift: since both the Big Four connection from the west and the C&O from the east entered the south approach, it was impossible to maintain a unidirectional movement through the city, and the only alternative was to run the train on the loop track around the former engine terminal.

Cincinnati Union Terminal

That proved to be a prelude to more curious ironies. The deterioration of the former Big Four line forced Amtrak in 1973 to operate the trains on a circuitous route over Pennsylvania lines via Logansport, Indianapolis, Richmond, Indiana, and Hamilton, Ohio, on which no single continuous run had ever been made before. The equally severe deterioration of these lines, however, compelled the new corporation in the following year to operate the trains over the C&O Railway for the entire distance from Chicago to Newport News and Washington, thus reviving a service that had disappeared in 1917.

Before these changes of route, however, time had run out on the union terminal. Declared a National Historic Landmark in November 1972, the headhouse had already been acquired by the Southern Railway, which had merged the CNO&TP as part of its Western Division, and was demolished by its new owner up to the passage between the rotunda and the train concourse. Winold Reiss's now celebrated murals were transferred to the new Greater Cincinnati Airport in 1973. Amtrak had built a little way station in the summer of 1972 on River Road almost under the deck of the Sixth Street Viaduct. The two trains passing through the city followed a route in 1973 made up of segments of Big Four, B&O, and C&O lines that had not carried passenger trains since the terminal opened in March 1933. The condition of the track strongly suggested the fact.[43] Perhaps the chief irony and certainly a matter of considerable historical interest is that the Amtrak trains, in using the old union depot approach, were following the line laid down on the bed of the Whitewater Canal by the Cincinnati and Indiana Railroad in 1863. Half the union terminal headhouse is gone, but the deep roots of the railroad in the technology of the nineteenth century are attested by the presence of the original limestone masonry of the canal throughout much of the east retaining wall along the S-curve that the waterway followed in its passage to the West Pearl Street basin. The oldest portions of this masonry very likely date from no later than 1848, although there is evidence of minor repair work other than the concrete abutment walls of later bridges. Other archaeological remains are still visible at the site of the union depot (1975): the limestone masonry, varying from local freestone to carefully dressed massive blocks, is intact in the retaining wall along the south side of Third Street; the red brick office building of the original Big Four (CIStL&C) and the similar steam-generating plant still stand; various cast-iron column bases, wrought iron anchor bolts, lengths of partly buried rail, odds and ends of wall at the carriage rotunda, the blast plates on the soffit of the Smith Street overpass, and the iron-girder bridge itself are all surviving fragments of a once busy and crowded scene. Similar lengths of platform, a little gravel ballast, massive ashlar masonry in the low retaining wall along Eastern Avenue form other indestructible remnants of the Pennsylvania Station. Since the Penn Central Railroad continues to interchange freight with the L&N and to serve the industries along Eggleston Avenue, the two connecting tracks respectively on the north and south sides of the former station trackage lie intact and in modest though regular usage.

The presence of these fragmentary elements of the past together with the destruction of half the terminal headhouse to make way for a greatly expanded freight yard provides a clear index to the profound changes that occurred in the movement of freight through the Cincinnati gateway after World War II. The railroads serving the industrialized areas of the Great Lakes region, the Northeast, and New England, roads that had once carried the lion's share of the tonnage and the passengers, saw their traffic shrink by 1975 to little more than half the wartime peak of 1944. The trend continued, and the predictable results for the New York Central and the Pennsylvania were underused facilities, deteriorating track and equipment, dwindling resources, eventual bankruptcy, and the threat of liquidation.[44] The B&O, with lines in both the Pocahontas and the Great Lakes regions, managed in the long run to improve its position over the levels of the twenties, but it never regained its high wartime volume. The C&O, on the other hand, which eventually came to penetrate extensively into the Great Lakes region by virtue of the acquisition of the Pere Marquette Railway in 1947, more than held its own and by the beginning of the 1970s was carrying a tonnage about 16 percent above that of 1944. Trends in the case of the coal-carrying N&W appeared to point in the same direction, but the numerous mergers that more than doubled its size in 1964 now make an exact comparison impossible. It is the experience of the southern carriers, however, that reveals how drastically the tides of industrial production have shifted in the postwar period. On the L&N tonnage increased 67 percent between the wartime peak of 1944 and 1975 and the total expansion of freight traffic in the half-century of 1920-75 came to 2 1/2 times the volume of the earlier year. The continuing demand for coal was a major factor, but the products of manufacture accounted for a growing proportion of the total freight moved. For the CNO&TP the expansion was astounding, the envy of all other rail officials: World War II marked the beginning of the industrial migration to the South, so that the 77 percent growth in tonnage between 1944 and 1975, falling on top of a doubling of tonnage in the four years preceding the wartime peak, meant that the 1975 traffic amounted to nearly 4 times the 1920 total.

The CNO&TP, now the main stem of the Southern Railway System's Western Division, was a pioneer in the installation of automatic block signals and is now in all technological and operating aspects a prime example of the existing and potential capacity of a railroad in the latter half of the twentieth century. The line consists essentially of a single main track supplemented by numerous lengths of double and passing tracks, with an overall length of 337 miles from the north end of the Gest Street yard in Cincinnati to Central Street at the south end of Chattanooga Yard. The train movements are governed exclusively by signal indication, and all non-block signals and all switches are operated under centralized traffic control, for which the operator and his single machine are located at Somerset, Kentucky. Written train orders, rights of trains by class, superiority of train by direction, distinctions between scheduled and extra trains, and other elements of traditional railroad practice have been abolished except in cases of emergency or temporary speed restrictions, when written orders may be issued to train crews. All trains are assigned numbers and operated as separate, individual units governed by signal indications and the standard rules applying to the movement of trains. All main track is composed of welded rail on rock ballast, with few grades above 1 percent except for the average of 1.25 percent on Erlanger Hill, rising from the south bank of the Ohio River at Cincinnati, and with a few curves above four degrees—in short, a first-class engineering work in the rolling and in some places rugged topography of Kentucky and Tennessee. Three classification yards lie respectively at the strategic junction and connection points, Cincinnati, Danville, and Chattanooga.

To maintain the flow of traffic, the aggregate length of double track and of combinations of main and passing track totals nearly half the mileage between the terminal cities, and all tracks are everywhere operated in both directions, as opposed to the right-hand rule that was once nearly universal on American railroads. The government of train movements requires a total of nearly five hundred separate signals over the entire length of line, a separate signal unit being defined as a mast with one or more groups, or heads, as they are called, of color-light signals of the searchlight type.[45] All these features together clearly represent a costly investment, but they have guaranteed the efficient, expeditious, and economical operation of trains that had reached an average of thirty-five per day passing through Danville Yard in the summer of 1972. The total was high enough and expanding steadily enough to lead various operating officials to consider the necessity of returning the entire line to the continuous double track that once characterized it. But the grand lesson of the whole performance ought to be perfectly obvious: with the technological means available in the post-World War II period—signaling, communications, diesel-electric motive power, yard facilities, and track—together with the highest standards of operating procedures, the railroad system that converges on Cincinnati could comfortably move twice the traffic it carried in 1970, with enormous advantages for the region and the nation in the lowered consumption of energy, space, money, and clean air.[46] The restoration of the crippled lines of the Penn Central, used far below their capacity, would appear to offer the greatest benefits to their regional economy, but this would require a new and more enlightened national transportation policy.

It is against the new pattern of the movement of freight by rail that we ought to make a final assessment of the functional and urbanistic character of the expensive union terminal (its replacement value about $300,000,000 at the 1975 building-cost level). The domed headhouse has always been recognized as an architectural masterpiece of the art deco movement, one not only possessed of an intrinsic excellence of form and plan, but also of a unique quality in the history of terminal design. It was the first metropolitan station in the modern style, and all the more impressive in comparison with those that came after it—the coldly classical monumentalism of Thirtieth Street Station in Philadelphia (opened in 1934), the conventional adaptation of Mediterranean styles to rail terminal requirements at Los Angeles (1939), the vacuities of the union stations at Toledo (1950) and New Orleans (1954). Beside these the Cincinnati terminal was a paragon of distinction in the building and decorative arts. Unfortunately for American architecture its influence was small, if it existed at all. As a highly specialized building coming nearly at the end of construction for works of its type, it could offer little guidance beyond its formal principles for other kinds of structures. Its role in the evolution of modern architecture bordered on the tragic:

the depression blasted the promise of the new forms that managed to survive only through the Century of Progress Exposition and a few schools and post offices erected by the Public Works Administration. When building was resumed again in 1950, the concepts of a little handful of European architects swept everything before them. Cincinnati Union Terminal appears to have embodied ideas that no one had either the wit or the courage to follow.

With respect to the functional planning of the whole terminal complex, it is difficult to raise any serious criticism if we confine ourselves first to the internal character of the group. The ideal arrangement of station building and appurtenant structures is to locate them as compactly as possible, but this is seldom realizable in practice. The various elements at Cincinnati were strung out in a linear series, and if the nearly two miles from the south throat to the engine terminal seemed excessive for the Cincinnati scale, it was less than the comparable distances for other metropolitan stations. (This criticism is a little ironic in view of the destruction of urban fabric and urban scale carried out with reckless defiance of all civic values in the building of expressways.) Internal spaces within the headhouse were generous to a fault, and though wartime exigencies brought unlooked-for crowds, there is no evidence that the terminal facilities were ever taxed to their ultimate capacity. Indeed, the one charge that can be leveled against its design is that the total area of the headhouse and its track system bore no logical relation to the transportation requirements of Cincinnati. This was not only overwhelmingly true of the greatly reduced number of schedules that followed the abandonment of local service and the other curtailments of the depression; it was true of any year in the period of rail ascendancy. If William W. Boyington's 1881 design for the union depot had been adopted, and if the resulting station had later been equipped with an electropneumatic interlocking system, automatic signals, a three-track approach, and the necessary enlargement of coach and engine facilities, there is no question that it could have served Cincinnati's needs at the peak of rail traffic, when schedules exceeded 300 daily trains in the years immediately before and during World War I. Union Terminal, as we have seen, could have accommodated double the maximum number of trains for which it was presumably designed.

But a far more serious criticism can be made about its location, which was bound up with historical realities and unrealized potentialities of the city. If there is no question that the terminal complex was grossly oversized for Cincinnati's requirements, there is equally little question that the site was chosen for the convenience of the railroads rather than that of the passengers. The arguments of the railroad officers were that the terminal company needed 300 acres, that so extensive an area existed nowhere else, and that other locations, where it might conceivably be made available, involved prohibitive expenses in the construction of connecting tracks. Given the great area of land involved and the problem of raising terminal trackage above all likely Ohio River floods, the arguments had a certain plausibility. When the decision was made in favor of the Laurel Street site, the terminal company demolished the surrounding buildings; and the city, with grants from the federal Public Works Administration and Public Housing Authority, cleared the existing slums, widened and landscaped the approach streets into Lincoln Parkway and the terminal plaza, and built a public housing group to replace the dwellings that had been demolished. The whole program offered welcome open space and a handsome addition to the urban fabric, and even the public housing was a little above the dreary standard; but since the terminal stood two miles from the core area, neither it nor the related civic developments could play any role in the day-to-day life of the city or in the natural flow of its traffic. The great headhouse stood at the west end of an axis of which the old Gothic Music Hall formed the east end, but that axis and its monumental terminators formed an isolated and hence meaningless appendage to the circulation system of the core. Moreover, neither the terminal nor the Music Hall could play any continuing role in what Kevin Lynch has called the "imageability" of the city. For all the inherent architectural power in these two contrasting buildings, they could not act as visual anchor points in the way that the old station buildings did. They were pulled so far away from the central business district that they could not function as public landmarks, giving organization, boundary, and coherence to the mass of office buildings, hotels, stores, theaters, and special services within that district. These simply organize themselves, so to speak, around the open spaces of Fountain Square and Government Square, of which the latter is an empty bore used as a bus turn-around.

The remote location of the terminal, in an area of small industrial enterprises of marginal or even derelict character, was the chief factor in the failure of its meeting rooms, special dining rooms, and theater to generate any continuing life of their own, or to enrich and expand the existing life of the core area. Backed against the sea of railroad yards in Mill Creek Valley and facing the deteriorating fabric of the West End, for the renewal of which the city had no plans at the time nor in the foreseeable future, the magnificent building provided no enhancement of land values and hence offered no one an incentive to build in the immediate area. Both these ends were among the cardinal principles in Alfred Fellheimer's theory of terminal location, and one can only assume that he was unable to present them as convincing arguments to the railroad officers. And the same discouragements applied to the possibility of air-rights developments. The absence of any incentive to build in the terminal area meant that there were no financial interests concerned with such a development, and the elevation of the track-platform area above the local street grade and the Mill Creek rail lines effectively killed the likelihood of such construction even if there had been some urbanistic and economic value attached to it. All these characteristics militated against any continuing use of the terminal spaces after the building had died as an active railroad entity. Thus the great civic and financial developments associated with the New York stations, Cleveland Union Terminal (now reduced to a rapid transit nexus), and the union stations of Chicago, Toronto, and Washington were made permanently unavailable at Cincinnati.

Planners and concerned citizens may argue that these questions are entirely academic since the terminal ceased to exist as a going concern, but in truth they involve enduring civic issues that transcend the endlessly shifting complex of immediately practical concerns. In 1910 various financial interests, as we have seen, proposed a union station at Third and Vine streets in Cincinnati, along with a skyscraper office building adjoining the station headhouse. That the business community of the city had need for such a skyscraper is indicated by the presence of the Union Central Building, which was placed under construction close to the proposed site in the following year. It is questionable whether the possibilities of this location were ever seriously explored in their full spatial, structural, economic, and urbanistic terms. Obvious factors militated against such a choice: the whole track-platform area would have had to be elevated on a steel-frame bridge raised to the level of Third Street; elevated and inclined approach tracks would have had to be constructed from both directions to connect existing eastern and western lines; the approaches to the Broadway and the Suspension bridges would have had to be recon-

271

structed to disentangle them from the station approaches; and new, much-expanded coach and engine facilities would have been required on both the east and west sides, near where they had always been located. But these problems were readily susceptible of technological solutions, which would have been no more complex and expensive than those required for the union terminal as it was built.

The advantages, on the other hand, stood out of all proportion to the costs and difficulties. A modest station of ten through tracks, comfortably adequate for Cincinnati's needs, could have become a working element of the urban core, and its associated office spaces could have formed a civic anchor point in both the visual and the economic senses. Public facilities and the track-platform area would have offered maximum accessibility to both passengers and trains, since the street pattern of the core lay immediately adjacent to the site on the north, and the riverfront belt line provided the nucleus of an approach-track system to the east and west. The station would have offered a generous invitation to air-rights construction, and the whole group of structures could have formed simultaneously the gateway to the city and the foreground to a potential riverfront development. The New York stations and the Chicago Plan of 1909 offered abundant evidence that rail terminals properly planned and located provide enormous possibilities for civic enhancement, so that, far from blocking or preempting new developments, they were capable of generating powerful stimuli to the most prestigious kinds of building. The question of protection from floods along the Cincinnati waterfront could not be taken seriously as the railroad officers posed it. The trackage at the union terminal was raised above the flood of 1937, but the access lines used by four of the seven tenants were under water for varying lengths within the city, which would have been exactly the case with a riverfront station and its supporting facilities. And however slow-moving and myopic the Corps of Engineers, the Mississippi disaster of 1927 had at last opened their eyes; and by the 1930s, under the direction of General Lytle Brown, they were moving toward a reliable flood-control program for the Ohio valley. But the planners of public works in Cincinnati, like good red-blooded civic officials everywhere in America, elected to throw away a substantial part of their birthright for an expressway and a sports stadium. They left virtually all the railroad trackage intact, removed from the possibility of beneficial urban uses an area of land equal in its extent, did incalculable damage to natural beauties and to the urban fabric through the destruction of park land and the uprooting of residential communities, and spent great sums of money to provide arteries, interchanges, bridges, and parking spaces for the most costly, inefficient, and destructive form of transportation. It is a curious irony that a station plan of 1910 and a rapid transit plan of 1916 offer once again the starting point for productive thinking about the rebuilding of the modern industrial city for human uses.

1. Ward Baldwin, quoted in "Relation of Railroad Terminals to City Plan," *Railway Age* 68:18 (30 April 1920), p. 1287.

2. Freight revenues, passenger revenues, total revenues, total expenses, operating incomes, and operating ratios of Cincinnati railroads for the year 1923 are given in the table on page 275.

3. News items, *Railway Age* 75:4 (28 July 1923), p. 180; 75:5 (4 August 1923), p. 196.

4. The largest and in all respects the most noteworthy metropolitan terminals completed in this period, with dates of completion, are the following:

Broad Street, Philadelphia, 1893 (stub)
South Station, Boston, 1899 (stub)
Pennsylvania, Pittsburgh, 1901 (stub and through)
Union, Washington, 1907 (stub and through)
Pennsylvania, New York, 1910 (through)
North Western, Chicago, 1911 (stub)
Grand Central, New York, 1913 (stub and loop)
Union, Kansas City, 1913 (through)
Union, Dallas, 1916 (through)
Union, Jacksonville, 1919 (stub and through)

5. Chief of the factors relating to track-platform design were the following: type of layout (stub or through); volume and type of traffic, whether through with heavy sleeping-car traffic, local, suburban, mail, or express; nature and capacity of approach, throat, signaling, and interlocking system; time available to park trains for loading and unloading; and methods of working baggage, mail, and express. It was obvious that a through station was the leading type for efficiency and economy of operation, but it must be constructed as a double-level facility so that passengers need not and preferably cannot cross the tracks. The two levels also allowed a depressed or elevated approach. In a stub station with the standard forward entry baggage, mail, and express cars cannot be detached for working, and the road engine cannot be moved to the engine terminal for servicing, until the passenger cars have been removed from the station area, and all loaded train movements must be preceded or followed by empty movements in the reverse direction. Loop tracks make it possible to avoid some of these difficulties, but they are less satisfactory than the through variety.

The average traffic density for major metropolitan terminals in the United States and Canada for 1915 is given in the following table:

	Through	Suburban
Passengers per track per day	1,141	4,933
Trains per track per day	15.4	29.4
Passengers per train	84	169
Time departing train parked at platform, minutes	27	14

Time arriving train parked at platform, minutes   16   8
SOURCE: T. L. Busfield, in *Railway Age*

6. A set of standard dimensions for a headhouse cannot be determined because of the great number of variables that differ with each installation. Unit dimensions for the track-platform area, however, can be established within precise limits. For narrow sites platform widths may be reduced to 12 feet, but in stations with a large volume of passenger, mail, and express traffic, it is necessary to raise this figure to at least 22 feet to provide adequate clearance for mail and baggage trucks, train shed columns, and passengers. The standard side clearance measured from the center line of track was fixed at 7 feet shortly after the turn of the century; in narrow sites this has been reduced to as little as 6 feet, although the various railway engineering associations recommend a minimum of 6 feet 6 inches. In the case of elevated island platforms, which must be built out close to the edge of the car so that a passenger cannot put a foot in the narrow slot between car and platform, the clearance must be reduced to 5 feet 3 inches. If we assume construction with standard low-level platforms, the minimum and maximum dimensions of track area would be as follows: 5 platforms at 12 feet, 60 feet; 10 tracks at 6-foot clearance on each side, 120 feet, for a total width of 180 feet; 5 platforms at 22 feet, 110 feet; 10 tracks at 7-foot side clearance, 140 feet, for a total of 250 feet; length variable, generally 650 to 900 feet for most stations.

7. Alfred Fellheimer, "Principles of Terminal Station Design," *Railway Age* 75:3 (21 July 1923), p. 109.

8. The foregoing paragraphs represent a condensation of Fellheimer, ibid., pp. 110–11. He was the author of other articles on the same subject; see Bibliography for chapter 5.

9. See Bibliography for chapter 5 for complete entry.

10. The term *access tree* was coined by the staff of the Regional Plan Association of New York; see, for example, Regional Plan Association, *Urban Design Manhattan* (New York: Viking Press, 1969). The enormous range of secondary travel within the metropolitan area is one of the most pernicious defects of air travel.

11. A brief résumé of Cincinnati passenger traffic in 1927–28 is given in the following table:

Number of daily trains	224
Number of daily passenger cars	1,356
Number of daily passengers, maximum	20,000
Number of transfer sleeping cars, minimum	66
Number of transfer sleeping cars, maximum	110

SOURCES: *Railway Age; Official Railway Guide*

12. Freight revenues, passenger revenues, total revenues, total operating expenses, operating incomes, and operating ratios of Cincinnati railroads for the year 1927 are given in the table on page 275.

13. Walnut Hills High School is nationally famous as a public school with a six-year continuous program and a special entrance requirement both of which are aimed strictly at college preparatory work.

14. Henry M. Waite belonged to the new breed of professional engineers who had arisen with the Progressive movement. He had entered municipal affairs and served for some years as the city manager of Dayton, Ohio. He conceived the Cincinnati appointment as an extension of his career of public service.

1923

Railroad	Freight Revenue	Passenger Revenue	Total Revenue	Total Expenses	Net Operating Income	Operating Ratio
B&O	$ 208,587,996	$ 30,752,791	$ 255,594,435	$ 199,323,961	$ 56,270,474	78.0%
C&O	85,202,379	11,650,942	101,975,798	78,889,781	23,086,017	77.4
CNO&TP	17,407,412	4,520,807	23,049,393	16,522,285	6,527,108	71.7
CCC&StL	69,395,847	17,891,955	94,941,444	72,114,741	22,826,703	76.0
L&N	101,680,240	26,001,967	136,375,673	109,865,090	26,510,583	80.6
N&W	81,320,794	10,194,497	95,494,687	72,632,799	22,870,888	76.1
Pennsylvania	502,698,606	155,516,003	721,397,408	590,518,030	130,879,378	81.9
Total/Avg.	$1,066,293,274	$265,528,962	$1,428,828,838	$1,139,857,687	$288,971,151	77.4%

SOURCE: *Railway Age*

1927

Railroad	Freight Revenue	Passenger Revenue	Total Revenue	Total Expenses	Net Operating Income	Operating Ratio
B&O	$ 203,567,887	$ 26,286,707	$ 246,078,510	$ 186,168,521	$ 59,909,989	75.7%
C&O	119,581,503	8,571,444	133,431,722	89,984,785	43,446,937	67.4
CNO&TP	16,974,395	3,621,032	21,811,757	15,560,226	6,251,531	71.3
CCC&StL	67,979,881	15,570,227	91,185,737	70,322,699	20,863,038	77.1
L&N	116,384,472	20,026,869	144,605,117	112,857,834	31,747,283	78.0
N&W	99,992,235	6,893,708	110,948,200	69,696,125	41,252,075	62.8
Pennsylvania	461,612,156	140,810,692	664,851,023	510,668,662	154,182,361	76.8
Total/Avg.	$1,086,092,529	$221,780,679	$1,412,912,066	$1,055,258,852	$357,653,214	74.5%

SOURCE: *Railway Age*

15. An additional agreement between the terminal company and the Hamilton County Commissioners, entered into in October 1927, required the company to pay one-third of the cost (estimated at $300,000) for the construction of a new Eighth Street Viaduct, necessitated by the three rail viaducts that were to converge on the south approach of the terminal.

16. The stock issue was divided as follows: common stock, $3,500,000, to be bought in equal shares by the seven owner-tenants; preferred stock, $3,000,000, to be subscribed by various financial interests in Cincinnati.

17. Wank was born in Budapest in 1898 and immigrated to the United States in 1924, following architectural and engineering study at Budapest, Brünn (now Brno, Czechoslovakia), and the Ecole des Beaux Arts in Paris. He was awarded the Gold Medal of the American Institute of Architects for the Grand Street Apartments in New York and again for the Cincinnati terminal, which is easily his greatest achievement though perhaps overshadowed in its ultimate sociohistorical importance by his work for the Tennessee Valley Authority. Wank held the office of chief architect during the initial phase of hydroelectric construction (1933–44) and thus provided the most extensive implementation of the concept of total design in modern architecture. He designed the buildings and prepared the site plans for Green Hills, Ohio, one of the greenbelt towns of the Farm Security Administration, and served as architectural consultant to the Rural Electrification Administration in 1935–36. After leaving TVA, he spent nearly two years in the office of Albert Kahn in Detroit (1944–45), then founded his own partnership in New York (Wank, Adams, and Slavin), which he maintained until his death in 1970.

Other major figures responsible for the design and early operation of the terminal were the following: Engineering Department, Fellheimer and Wagner, structural engineers; George P. Stowitts, engineer of construction; Pusey Jones, engineer of design; D. A. McGavren, designing engineer; H. A. Worcester, vice-president, CCC&StL Railway, president of the terminal company.

18. The precise events leading to this decision are not clear, but the person who seems to have been primarily responsible for the suggestion was Edgar Tyler, a member of the C. U. T. engineering staff and a designer of various auxiliary structures who had studied architecture under Cret at the University of Pennsylvania. Cret was not unknown in Cincinnati: he had prepared architectural plans for the University of Cincinnati in 1909 and 1923 and had acted as consultant in the preparation of plans for the Cincinnati suburb of Mariemont in 1927. (These facts were brought to light by graduate students in the Department of Art History at the University of Cincinnati in connection with an exhibit of drawings and photographs of the terminal and its decorative details presented at the university in 1972–73 [see note 19, *infra*.])

19. Originally quoted in the *Cincinnati Times-Star*, 31 March 1933; requoted in *Art Deco and the Cincinnati Union Terminal* (Cincinnati: University of Cincinnati Department of Art History, 1973), p. 14.

20. Enlisting the cooperation of the Pennsylvania Railroad required the full persuasive powers of George Dent Crabbs and Henry M. Waite partly because of the cost of new construction and also because of a traditional unwillingness on the part of the Pennsylvania directors to enter into any cooperative arrangement with other railroads. The conspicuous exception of Chicago Union Station existed only because the presence of two Pennsylvania subsidiaries as parties to the agreement gave the company a controlling voice.

The map of Cincinnati rail lines (fig. 43) does not show the Pennsylvania-B&O connecting tracks, but their location can be readily fixed in the immediate area of the Norwood crossings and at the junction point of the Pennsylvania's Cincinnati and Chicago divisions.

Cincinnati Union Terminal

21. The Interterminal extension lies on a descending grade westward to bring the track down through the 28-foot difference in elevation between the base of rail on the bridge and the equivalent level of the terminal track layout. The elevation of the bridge underclearance (that is, the soffit of the bottom chord) is 535.34 feet above sea level, sufficient to place it a little more than 26 feet above the water surface during the record flood of January 1937. The extension of the Interterminal Viaduct to the south approach of the union terminal is actually a branch that diverges from the original bridge at a point near Baymiller Street and extends in a westerly direction over West Second Street, crosses the old union depot approach at the third of four arterial levels in the area (that is, old depot approach and surrounding tracks, original street system, C&O viaducts, and expressway), then curves sharply into the north-south alignment of the terminal approach. The C&O trackage in the West End thus falls into three roughly parallel lines from north to south, the Interterminal Viaduct, its union terminal extension, and the old bridge approach that descends to the original track level of the area. Together with the various elevated approach and connecting tracks of the B&O, Big Four, and CNO&TP in the West End, the C&O lines form part of what is probably the most intricate system of multilevel railroad bridges in the United States.

22. The source of the fill material for the terminal group was an unattractive, steep-sided hill at the west edge of Mill Creek Valley known as Bald Knob. It consisted of the mixture of bedded clay, shale, and limestone that is characteristic of the whole Cincinnati area. The fill was brought to maximum compaction in a much shorter time than that of natural settlement by the technique of forcing high-pressure jets of water into the mass of earth and broken rock.

23. The subsidiary structures of the terminal group were themselves complex entities embracing the following appurtenances:

Express terminal, including headhouse for handling cargo, offices, tracks, elevated platforms, warehouse, and cold storage space for perishable commodities.

Mail terminal, including headhouse for handling mail, platforms, tracks, office space, truck facilities, and belt conveyors.

Coach yard, including in addition to storage and service tracks, yard service buildings, dining car commissaries, Pullman service and storage facilities, shops, and an electrical substation.

Engine terminal, including a 20-stall engine house (with reserve space for 15 more), shops, storehouse, turntable, storage tracks, and coal and water facilities.

Steam-generating plant, equipped with three 1,000-horsepower boilers.

Various minor buildings and facilities for yard service employees.

The interlocking tower was incorporated into the terminal building.

24. The transfer tracks with their interconnecting switches were located between tracks number 6 and 7, 8 and 9, 10 and 11, and 12 and 13. The origin of the idea of intermediate tracks appears to have been the temporary railroad terminal built for the World's Columbian Exposition in Chicago (1893), but it is doubtful whether this detail was widely remembered among station planners. The advantage offered by internal transfer tracks may be better understood with some explanation of the standard practice in making up trains. On all trains carrying the usual assortment of passenger-train cars the traditional order from front to back has been mail, express, and baggage cars, coaches, dining and lounge cars, sleeping cars, and observation-lounge car (if present). There were several reasons for this arrangement: to separate cars worked en route from passenger-carrying cars; to place the dining car midway in the length of the train; to place the sleeping cars at a maximum distance from the noisy locomo-

277

tive; and to avoid the necessity for coach passengers to walk through sleeping cars (this laudable practice has been repeatedly violated in recent years). Since incoming and outgoing trains would be facing in opposite directions in a stub-end station, the outgoing train had to be moved out of the station beyond the nearest switches in the approach tracks in order to attach sleeping cars to the rear end. If the transfer cars included coaches as well, the whole operation was obviously more complicated, since the train frequently had to be separated into two parts. All that was necessary at Cincinnati was to park the outgoing train with breaks at the places where additional mid-train cars might be located.

25. Signals on the approach tracks were overhead, and those within the terminal area were the dwarf form. The overhead signals were the three-light color-light type in which the lights were arranged in a vertical row, and the dwarf signals were divided between the three-light and two-light varieties.

26. Paul Cret was one of the five architects who composed the board of architects for the Century of Progress Exposition. Since design work on the fair had begun in 1929, it is clear that Cret had moved away from the neoclassicism of his earlier work before the end of the extravagant decade.

27. The Reiss murals were important enough in the recent history of the visual arts to deserve more extended comment. The artist was born in Germany in 1886, immigrated to New York in 1913, and founded an art school in the city shortly after he settled there. He was appointed professor of mural art at the City College of New York in 1933 and held the post until his death in 1953. He was much influenced by the flat, strongly colored, highly geometrized art of American Indians, whose work he knew only through studying exhibits at the American Museum of Natural History in New York. There were three steps in Reiss's preparation of the designs from which the actual work was executed: first, he assembled photographs of civic spaces and industrial activities in Cincinnati, of terminal construction, city officials, and officers of the terminal company, along with drawings made by himself of generalized scenes and figures; second, he drew preliminary sketches in simplified form on ordinary drawing paper; finally, he prepared maquettes at one-third of the size of the cartoons, and drawings of the final cartoons at one-third of their full size. The execution of the murals themselves was carried out by the Ravenna Mosaic Company in the following steps: photographing of cartoons; preparation of full-size working drawings, done as though seen from behind; cutting of tracings into two-foot squares; manufacturing of mosaic tessarae from 8,000 separate colors; emplacement as full mosaic, ground as well as figures, or as mosaic figures in a ground of pigmented stucco. The various human figures and objects range from strongly representational to abstract. The mural work of linoleum and wood veneers in the men's and women's lounges was done by the French-born painter Pierre Bourdelle. (The details on the execution of the mural art at the Cincinnati terminal were assembled by graduate students in art history at the University of Cincinnati, working under the direction of Professor Gabriel P. Weisberg, at the time chairman of the art history department.)

28. The number of special features at the station indicated the extent to which such buildings had become microcities as well as megastructures of still unparalleled size. The Cincinnati terminal included, in addition to the standard working parts and service facilities, a restaurant, cafeteria, lunchroom, tearoom, public and private dining rooms, two soda fountains, theater, toy shop, bookstore, bootblack, drugstore, men's and women's clothing stores, bakery, newsstand, barbershop, beauty parlor, first-aid station, invalids' waiting room, and a refrigerator plant. The presence of a theater and private dining rooms (which could also serve as conference rooms) reveals that the terminal was intended to be a kind of civic center, generating a life of its own, like the motels that sur-

round the airports, but its location and the changing state of rail traffic militated against this role.

29. The size of these massive arched trusses may be further gauged from the 380-ton weight of the largest. The web members of the trusses follow the Pratt arrangement, and both the polygonal chords and web members of the two smallest trusses are composed of H-section elements. The chords of the remaining trusses, however, are built up of angles and plates into a hollow box of U-section. Since the top chord of the truss takes the compressive load, that is, since it is subject to true arch action, each end of the chord is fixed to the side framing by means of a pin to allow rotation following bending and elongation under load. The radial compressive thrust of the dome roof is absorbed in the two outer, or vault, trusses, which results in a maximum allowable lateral deflection in either of 3 7/8 inches. The roof structure is a concrete shell five inches thick reinforced by wire mesh and originally covered with tile but later recovered with aluminum sheathing. The loading factors were 25 pounds per square foot for wind, 25 pounds for the dead load of the tile, and 50 pounds for that of the concrete. The tile was replaced by aluminum in 1945 because of repeated fractures of the bronze hooks that helped support the tiles on the outer concrete surface.

30. The precise angle between the axes of the concourse and the track-platform area is 85° 2' 10".

31. The maximum depth of the roof truss in the train concourse was 9 feet 6 inches (at the ends) and the minimum 6 feet (at the center line). In the floor frame both the girders and the beams were built-up I-section members, and the trusses were the Warren type with a uniform depth of 8 feet 6 inches. The posts were set 7 feet 6 inches center to center. Deep brackets were cantilevered about nine feet on either side of the posts along the long axis of the concourse to reduce the clear span of the girders.

32. The Gest Street underpass was treated as a monolithic ballast-deck bridge of two spans for which only a cross section would indicate the form of a rigid-frame structure, as the accompanying sketch reveals.

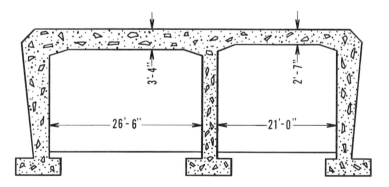

33. The viaduct bisected the area of the terminal utilities, such as the coach yard, engine terminal, coaling and water facilities, generating plant, and appurtenances. The tracks in this area have been taken up, the buildings either demolished or converted to other uses, and the viaduct considerably altered and extended at its eastern end to provide an interchange with Mill Creek Expressway.

34. Both arches are parabolic, the one over Spring Grove Avenue having a span of 120 feet and the other (actually segmental) a span of 109 feet. The shorter span of the Mill Creek arch and the need to carry it through a rise of 62 feet to

receive the girders of the top deck dictated the unusual ogival or Gothic profile of the ribs.

35. The quantitative summary of the construction and the operation of Cincinnati Union Terminal provides a clear picture of its magnitude:

Construction

Dates of construction	4 August 1929–31 March 1933
Total cost, including land and readjustment of rail facilities	$41,000,000
Total area, all facilities	287 acres
Fill, volume	5,663,065 cubic yards
Buildings, number	22
Rail, aggregate length	94 miles
Concrete in structure, volume	224,534 cubic yards
Concrete in pavement, volume	100,500 cubic yards
Bricks, number	8,250,000
Steel in buildings and bridges, weight	45,421 tons
Contracts, number	300

Operation

Water consumption per year	550,000,000 gallons
Steam-generating capacity per hour	225,000 pounds
Electrical consumption per year	8,500,000 kwh
Capacity, trains per day	216*
Capacity, passengers per day	17,000*
Trains per day, date of opening	142

SOURCE: *Cincinnati Union Terminal, A Pictorial History.*

* Both these figures are grossly underestimated.

36. The number of regularly scheduled weekday trains operated by the Cincinnati railroads in 1933–34 is given in the following table:

	Number of Trains, March 1933	Number of Trains, December 1934
B&O	38	32
CCC&StL	32	28
Pennsylvania	22	18
L&N	20	20
C&O	8	10
CNO&TP	8	8
N&W	6	6
Total	134	122
Number operated	142	134

37. The schedule of abandonment of local or accommodation service at Cincinnati is given in the following table:

L&N, central Kentucky	June 1930
B&O, Oakley	April 1931
CCC&StL, Aurora, Ind.	May 1931
B&O, Hamilton, Ohio	September 1932
CCC&StL, Franklin, Ohio	April 1933
CCC&StL, Whitewater line, Ind.	April 1933
B&O, Loveland, Ohio	September 1934

Pennsylvania, Lebanon, Ohio   September 1934
Pennsylvania, Morrow, Ohio   September 1934
C&O, Hammond, Ind.   October 1949 [a]

    [a] The Chicago train of the C&O was terminated at Hammond, Ind., in September 1932; it survived until the postwar years on local mail revenue.

Abandonment of local stations at Cincinnati came in the following years:

Eighth Street transfer   April 1931
Baymiller Street   September 1932
Fourth Street   September 1932
Central Union   March 1933
Court Street   March 1933
Pennsylvania   March 1933

    The original Plum Street Depot (1865) survived as the Plum Street Warehouse of the Big Four until the construction of the Mill Creek Expressway in 1961, as did the fragments of the CH&D freight-handling facilities at Fifth and Baymiller streets.

    38. The reclining-seat coach (or chair car, as it was known on the western roads) was not a depression-born innovation. The first such cars were introduced by the Chicago and Alton Railroad in 1905 for the *Alton Limited*, the company's premier Chicago-Saint Louis train.

    39. Running times and average speeds for representative premier trains for 1940-41 are given in the following table:

Railroad	Train	Destination	Time (Hrs. - Min.)		Distance (Miles)	Average Speed (MPH)
B&O	*National Limited*	Saint Louis–Jersey City	24	22	1,110.8	45.6
C&O	*George Washington*	Washington	14	19	599.0	41.8
CNO&TP	*Royal Palm*	Jacksonville	22	14	840.4	37.8
CCC&StL	*James Whitcomb Riley*	Chicago	5	30	302.5	55.0
CCC&StL	*Ohio State Limited*	New York	16	10	881.0	54.5
L&N	*Southland*	Atlanta	11	35	489.0	42.2
L&N	*Pan-American*	New Orleans	23	30	922.0	39.2
N&W	*Pocahontas*	Norfolk	18	15	676.6	37.1
Pennsylvania	*Cincinnati Limited*	New York	14	55	755.1	50.6
Avg. speed						44.9

    40. The approach system at Cincinnati was in fact the most generous ever designed, but the number of tracks was dictated more by local topography and the geographical distribution of rail lines than by a conscious effort to provide plenty of space for the movement of trains. The most extensive concentrated approach line of any American terminal was that of Broad Street Station, Philadelphia, which included nine tracks, and it was the decisive feature in enabling this station to accommodate the maximum traffic density of any facility in the United States (well over 500 trains per day throughout its pre-depression history).

281

41. The precise distribution of tracks and daily trains in the terminal approach system for 1933 was as follows:

Line	Number of Tracks	Number of Movements
C&O, Chicago Division	1	2 train
CNO&TP	2	8 train
		8 reverse
		8 light engine
B&O-CCC&StL West	2[a]	18 train
C&O Viaduct[b]	2[a]	26 train
North Approach[c]	2	80 train
		126 reverse
		126 light engine
Total movements		402[d]

[a] The two tracks in both these approachs were later reduced to one.

[b] The trains of the L&N were operated by trackage rights over the C&O viaducts.

[c] The eastern and the Detroit trains of the B&O and the Big Four and all trains of the N&W and the Pennsylvania used the north approach.

[d] The foregoing figures and the total are based on the numbers of regular scheduled trains only. The actual number of trains operated was about 5 percent higher during the depression and as much as 20 percent higher during the peak wartime traffic. The maximum number of train and engine movements on the terminal track system was thus about 480 from time to time throughout 1944.

42. The distribution of scheduled trains by railroad in the summer of 1944 was as follows:

CCC&StL	31
B&O	26
L&N	20
Pennsylvania	16
C&O	14
CNO&TP	10
N&W	6
Total	123
Total plus 20 percent	147

A high proportion of the special trains operated during the wartime years were troop trains moving men to ports, military camps, and airfields. Since few of these originated or terminated at Cincinnati, and since nearly all of them were operated through the city on routes that by-passed the terminal, they had very little effect on the station traffic.

43. The precise route in 1973, with the eastbound trains as an example, was as follows (I am using the traditional railroad names to identify the lines precisely): from the PCC&StL to the CCC&StL via a connecting track at the crossing of the two lines between Sharonville and Lockland, Ohio, two suburban towns north of the city; CCC&StL to Ivorydale Junction; B&O through Winton Place to Cincinnati Transfer and over various freight tracks to new station; CCC&StL over the old union depot approach to the foot of the original Ohio approach of the C&O bridge; upgrade to the bridge and the C&O main line across the river and through Covington. Since the station lies west of the junction points at Cincinnati Transfer, the trains had to make reverse movements both east and west. The Amtrak trains were shifted to the C&O Chicago Division in the late summer of 1974 to end intolerable delays.

44. The decline in the combined freight tonnage of the New York Central System and the Pennsylvania Railroad between 1944 and 1970 was exactly 40 percent. (See Appendix C, table 6, for trends in freight traffic of the Cincinnati roads since 1920.)

45. The CNO&TP line is made up of 145.8 miles, or 43.26 percent, of double track and 191.2 miles, or 56.74 percent, of single track. There are 263 overhead

signals located on gantry bridges or cantilevered brackets and 208 wayside signals for a total of 471. The signals give indications for diverging into or out of a parallel track, passing or second main track, whatever the case, as well as the standard block, home, and distance indications. Signals are supplemented by radio communication among trainmen and trainmen and operators.

Danville, Kentucky, is the junction point of the CNO&TP line proper, between Cincinnati and Chattanooga, and the original Southern Railway line extending westward through Louisville to Saint Louis. The Ohio River bridge of the CNO&TP carries so high a level of connection traffic that it is the busiest single interchange line in the Cincinnati terminal area, with an average volume of 3,800 cars per day through 1973. (Source of quantitative data: Track Profile, Western Division, CNO&TP line, Southern Railway System.)

46. A single additional example may suffice: the single-track Chicago Division of the C&O Railway, which is also operated by centralized traffic control, carried 6 trains per day in the summer of 1974, but the total was 18 in 1949 and as high as 28 during periods of exceptional traffic flow. Two main tracks under double-direction operation can easily handle 100 trains per day.

Appendix A

Specifications for Bridges and Trestle-works, Cincinnati Southern Railway, 1875

Bridges will be constructed either in *iron, wood,* or a *combination* of both.

Iron and wood trestle-works will be built in accordance with the standard plans on file in the engineer's office.

Contractors must submit with their proposal a strain sheet of each span, and plans showing the form and size of each typical member of the bridge or trestle-work.

The strain sheet must show, for each member of the truss, the total strain sustained, and the dimensions and area of cross section; also the dead weight assumed in the calculation, and the resulting weight of the truss, which must not be less than the dead weight assumed.

Through bridges must not be less than fourteen (14) feet in width in the clear, and eighteen feet six inches (18 1/2) in height in the clear, measuring from the top of the rail.[1]

ROLLING LOAD.—All parts of the bridge and trestle-works must be proportioned to sustain the passage of the following rolling load, at a speed of not less than thirty miles per hour, viz.: two locomotives coupled, each weighing thirty-six tons on drivers in a space of twelve feet; total weight of each engine and tender loaded, sixty-six tons in a space of fifty feet, and followed by loaded cars weighing twenty tons each in a space of twenty-two feet. Weight of locomotive and tender to be distributed according to the appended diagram (see drawing below).[2] An addition of twenty-five per cent, will be made to the strains produced by the rolling load (considered as static) in the calculation of floor beams, stringers, trestle posts, suspension-rods, counter-rods, middle-ties and posts, and all other parts which are liable to be thrown suddenly under strain by the passage of a rapidly moving load. A similar addition of fifty per cent, will be made to the strain on suspension links, and riveted connections of stringers with floor beams and floor beams with trusses.

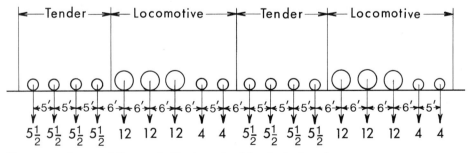

(Lowermost row of figures indicates wheel loads in tons.)

WIND PRESSURE.—Strains due to the wind will be calculated for a pressure of wind equal to thirty (30) pounds per square foot on all members of each truss, and on a train surface averaging ten (10) square feet to the lineal foot of track.

DIMENSIONS OF PARTS

TENSILE MEMBERS.—The iron work shall be so proportioned that the weight of the structure including the floor, with forty-four (44) pounds per lineal foot added for rails, spikes and joints, together with the above specified rolling load, shall in no part cause a tensile strain of more than ten thousand pounds per square inch of sectional area, nor a shearing strain of more than seven thousand five hundred pounds to the square inch.

COMPRESSIVE MEMBERS.—The strain in compression will be reduced with the ratio of diameter to length of post, according to the following formula, with a factor of safety of one-fifth; length of column not to exceed forty eight diameters:

	Phoenix Post	Square Post closed on all sides, or open and latticed on two opposite sides	H-Post	Trough Post latticed on open sides
Flat Ends	$R = \dfrac{45,000}{1 + \dfrac{l^2}{36,000r^2}}$	$R = \dfrac{38,600}{1 + \dfrac{l^2}{36,000r^2}}$	$R = \dfrac{36,500}{1 + \dfrac{l^2}{36,000r^2}}$	Same as square post. Radius of gyration computed from an axis passing through the centre of gravity of the section.
Pin Ends	$R = \dfrac{45,000}{1 + \dfrac{l^2}{18,000r^2}}$	$R = \dfrac{38,600}{1 + \dfrac{l^2}{18,000r^2}}$	$R = \dfrac{36,500}{1 + \dfrac{l^2}{18,000r^2}}$	

R = Ultimate resistance of column per square inch.

l = Length of column in inches.

r = Least radius of gyration of cross-section of column.[3]

Should columns of other shapes of cross section be used, columns for testing shall be furnished by the contractor, and a sufficient number of tests be made under the direction of the engineer, to determine the value of the constants in the formula. The thickness of metal in the columns must not be less than 1/25 of the width of plate between supports, nor less than 1/4 inch when both faces are accessible for painting, and 5/16 inch when one face only is accessible. In all members subject to transverse strains, the maximum compression must not exceed 8,000 pounds per square inch.

In I-beams the compression per square inch in the compressed flanges must not exceed

Appendix A

$$1/5 \left[\frac{40{,}000}{1 + \dfrac{l^2}{5{,}000 b^2}} \right],$$

where l = length of beam in inches, and b = breadth in inches of the compressed flange. The shearing strain per square inch in web of I-beams must not exceed

$$1/5 \left[\frac{40{,}000}{1 + \dfrac{d^2}{3{,}000 t^2}} \right],$$

in which d = distance in inches between flanges or stiffeners, measured on a line inclined at 45°, and t = thickness of web in inches.

CONNECTIONS AND ATTACHMENTS of all members with each other must be so proportioned, that the strain per square inch on any part thereof shall not exceed the foregoing specified limits of strain per square inch. In cases of doubtful distribution of strain, the connection will be tested by the contractor, under the direction of the engineer, to the rupture of the members connected.

Tensile strains will not be allowed in a transverse direction to the fibres of the iron. Shearing strain will not be allowed in a direction parallel to the fibres of the iron.

PINS AND RIVETS.—The shearing strain on pins and rivets must not be more than 7,500 pounds per square inch; the strain on extreme fibres caused by bending must not exceed 15,000 pounds per square inch; and the mean pressure on semi-intrados of pin and rivet holes must not be more than 10,000 pounds. The area of rivets shall not be less than the sectional area of the joined pieces. In compressive members, the distance from center to center of rivets must not exceed sixteen times the thickness of plates, and the sectional area of rivets in one segment, in the distance of two diameters from the end, must be not less than the sectional area of the segment.

EYE BARS.—The eye must not be less in strength than the body of the bar, and the area of the section through center of eye perpendicularly to the direction of the bar must not be less than given in the following table:

Ratio $\dfrac{\text{Diameter of Pin}}{\text{Diameter of Bar}}$	Ratio $\dfrac{\text{Area of Eye through Centre}}{\text{Area of Bar}}$	
	For hydraulic forged weld-less Bars	For hammer forged welded Bars
Less than 1.00	1.50	1.40
1.00	1.50	1.50
1.25	1.60	1.60
1.50	1.80	1.67
1.75	2.00	1.71
2.00	2.30	1.75

For wind strains an increase of 50 percent will be allowed on all the foregoing specified limits of strain per square inch.

BED PLATES AND FRICTION ROLLERS.—The size of the bed plates must be such that the pressure per square inch on the masonry does not exceed 25,000 pounds, and the friction rollers must be so proportioned that the pressure per lineal inch of roller does not exceed $\sqrt{540,000 \times d}$, in which "d" represents the diameter of the rollers in inches.

QUALITY OF IRON

Iron used under tensile strain shall be tough, ductile, of uniform quality, and capable of sustaining not less than fifty thousand pounds per square inch of sectional area without fracture, and twenty-five thousand pounds per square inch of area, without taking a permanent set. The reduction of area at breaking point shall average twenty-five per cent.; elongation fifteen per cent., when cold it must bend without sign of fracture from ninety to one hundred and eighty degrees.

Iron used under compressive strain must be tough, fibrous, of uniform quality, and capable of sustaining twenty-five thousand pounds per square inch of area without taking a permanent set.

The engineer will have the privilege at any time to select any of the bars manufactured for the bridge, cut from the same specimen bars one and one-half inches in diameter and twelve inches long, and submit them to the foregoing tests. Should the bars thus tested fail to stand the tests, this will be considered sufficient evidence that the iron used does not comply with the requirements of the specifications.

All bars subject to tensile strain shall be tested by the contractor, under the direction of the engineer, to twenty thousand pounds per square inch of sectional area, without permanent set. While under the test strains, should any bar extend more or less than it should do according to coefficients of extension previously determined from experimental tests of sample bars of the grade of iron to be used, all such bars shall be rejected, for this or any other imperfection. A variation of 1/1000 of an inch per foot each way for a strain of twenty thousand pounds per square inch of area will be allowed. One-half only of this variation will be allowed in bars working together as one member of the truss. Bars subject to shearing strain shall be of the best quality of iron, and subject to such tests as the engineer may desire. Rivets must be of the best quality of double refined iron.

Every bid must be accompanied by six specimen bars one and one-half inches in diameter and twelve inches long, stamped with the name of the bidder, and to be of the quality of iron that is intended to be used. All iron used must be equal in strength and all other qualities to the specimen bars.

Castings must be made of good tough cast iron; the metal must not be less than three-quarters of an inch in thickness, unless otherwise specified, and must be subjected to the following tests: A bar of iron five feet long, one inch square, four feet six inches between supports, shall bear without breaking a weight of five hundred and fifty pounds suspended at the center. The engineer may at any time require such specimen bars to be cast from the same metal as that used in the structure. Castings must be smooth, free from air holes, cinders and other imperfections. No castings will be permitted except in the minor details.

Appendix A

WORKMANSHIP

All workmanship must be first class. All abutting joints must be planed or turned in a plane perpendicular to the line of strain. One sixty-fourth of an inch will be the maximum error allowed in eye-bars, and not more than one-hundredth of the diameter of the pin or hole. Pin holes must be bored—not punched—on a true perpendicular to the line of strain. Pins must be turned true to size and straight. Must fit closely and must be turned down to a smaller diameter at the ends for the threads. They must be driven in with a "pilot nut" to save the threads. There must be a washer under each nut. No discrepancy in the length of pins through the bearing parts will be allowed.

In riveted work all joints shall be square and truly dressed. Rivet holes shall be spaced accurately and directly opposite each other. Rivets must be of the best quality of iron, and must completely fill the holes.

The rivets must be uniformly heated when used.

Ends of bars having threads upon them must be enlarged beyond the diameter of the bar, enough to make the bar full size at the bottom of the thread.

Washers and nuts must have a uniform bearing.

All tests of material will be made by the contractor under the direction of the engineer, without charge. N---- cents per pound will be paid for the material destroyed in experimental tests ordered made by the engineer.

An expert inspector appointed by the engineer will inspect the material, supervise the work whilst in progress at the shop and all the tests to be made. All parts of the structure must be inspected and stamped by him before shipment. The timber and framing of all structures must be in accordance with the specifications for wooden bridges and trestle-works.

The camber, measured on the center line of bottom chord for wooden bridges, and on the center line of pins in bottom chord for iron bridges, must not be less than one six-hundredth of the span for wood, and one twelve-hundredth of the span for iron trusses. The camber line must not deviate from an arc of a circle more than 1/4 inch at any place, and the ties must be sized down on top of the stringers that the rails may have a full bearing on each, and that the camber line of the track may be a true arc of a circle. The camber in the track must be one-half of the camber in the truss in wooden bridges.

All bars working together as parts of one member of the truss must have equal tension.

Counter rods, lateral and vertical wind bracing, and all other members requring adjustment must be provided with adjusting screws and nuts easily accessible with a wrench.

PAINT

All iron before leaving the shop must be soaked in boiled linseed oil. All planed or turned surfaces must be coated with white lead mixed with tallow. All inaccessible surfaces must be painted beforehand with two coats of red lead or other metallic paint approved on sample by the engineer. After erection, the entire structure, including the galvanized iron on wooden stringers, must be painted with two coats of the same paint.

WOODEN BRIDGES AND TRESTLE-WORKS

Will be built in accordance with the general plans on file in the engineer's office.

The timber shall be of white or long-leaf yellow pine or white oak, sawed true and out of wind, full size, free from wind shakes, large or loose knots, decayed wood, worm holes, sap, or any defect that will impair its strength or durability. No sap angle will be allowed. All timbers must be inspected by the engineer and none used without his approval.

Cross ties must be of long-leaf yellow pine or white oak, not less than five inches by eight inches after being sized down for the rail, and placed one foot from center to center. Every tie must be fastened to the stringer at both ends.

Guard timbers, five inches by eight inches, must be placed about one foot outside the rails, must be closely notched one inch on each side and bolted to the ties every four feet. (See diagram below.)

Angle irons, three (3) inches by three (3) inches by three-eights (3/8) of an inch, must be spiked to the guard timber every eighteen inches alternately on the top and side. The spike holes must be counter-sunk to receive the heads of the spikes.

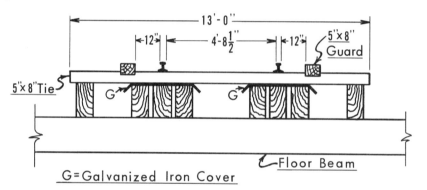

The adjoining diagram (above) shows the section of floor on all structures where wood stringers are used and details not given on plan, the opening between floor beams not exceeding fifteen feet.

When the opening is increased or diminished, the stringers must be proportioned accordingly. The stringers must be securely bolted to the floor beams and covered with No. 15 galvanized iron, thirty inches in width for the entire length.

All bridges must be completed ready for the rails.

All framing must be done to a close fit and in a thorough and workmanlike manner. No open joints or filling shims will be allowed.

All surfaces where wood touches wood must be thoroughly painted before being put together, with hot coal tar properly thickened with lime.

Angle-blocks, tubes, splicing keys, washers, parting blocks, brace shoes and bridge seats for wooden bridges are to be made of cast iron.

High hexagonal nuts dressed on both ends perpendicularly to the line of the rods must be used for truss-roads. No round headed bolts will be allowed. The use of more than one washer under the nut to make up for deficiency in length of thread will not be allowed.

Appendix A

All bolts must be provided with washers under head and nut.

All nuts must be checked.

GENERAL CONDITIONS APPLICABLE TO BRIDGE
AND TRESTLE-WORK

All bridges and trestle-works must be sufficiently anchored in the masonry to resist displacement by the wind.

Contractors must furnish and put in place wall-plates, ties, guard rails, and angle irons over piers and abutments of all structures and the aprons at each end of the structure, so as to connect the roadway of the structure with the ballasted track. No extra allowance will be made for the same.

Holes in the masonry for fastenings, anchorage of bridges and trestle-works must be drilled, and the fastening and anchor bolts put in by the contractor without extra charge.

On bridges and trestle-works on curves, the outside rail will be elevated one-half inch for every degree of curvature unless otherwise specified.

The contractor shall take all risks from floods and casualties of every description, and must furnish all materials and labor incidental to or in any way connected with the manufacture, transportation, erection and maintenance of the structures, which must be kept at all times in thorough repair and adjustment until the final acceptance of the entire work under contract.

A copy of every approved drawing will be sent without charge by the contractor to the engineer, for file in his office, not more than ten days after its approval.

MEASUREMENT

Truss bridges and trestle-works for which masonry is built will be paid for, so much for each structure complete.

Wooden trestle-works for which no masonry foundation has been prepared, and the superstructure of open drains, will be paid for by the thousand feet B. M. of the neat amount of the timber left for use in the trestle-work after framing and trimming off.

The price must cover the iron and all other materials used.

When piles are used in trestle-works, they will be paid for at so much per lineal foot, counting only the actual number of feet of piles left for use in the structure.

RIVER NAVIGATION

When rivers are navigable they must at all times during the construction and erection of the bridge be kept free for navigation.

All coffer-dams, staging, and other obstructions must be removed by the contractor, when directed by the engineer, leaving the river entirely unobstructed, except the actual space occupied by the masonry.

TESTS

Before the final estimate is paid, a thorough test of the structure will be made by the engineer, by loading each span with such rolling load or its nearest equivalent obtainable, at such rate of speed as described under the head of rolling load, and also by causing the load to remain on the span for the space of one hour or more. Each span must not deflect under such a train more than one nine-hundredth

291

of its length if made of wood, and one eighteen-hundredth of its length if made of iron.[4] And each span must return to its original camber when the load is removed.

The word "Engineer" shall mean the Consulting and Principal Engineer, unless otherwise expressed.

1. The figure of 14 feet given as the minimum clearance in width of a through-truss bridge is the standard clearance for a single-track rail line, equivalent to seven feet on either side of the center line of tracks.

2. Although the live-load factors were based on the weight of 4-6-0 locomotives, the available evidence indicates that the Cincinnati Southern and the CNO&TP used 4-4-0 locomotives exclusively until 1884. The heavier engine was probably chosen in anticipation of its future use.

3. The *radius of gyration* is the radius of a hypothetical cylindrical surface whose axis is identical with the axis of the body in question and whose radius is such that if the entire mass of the body were concentrated at that surface, the rotational energy and the moment of inertia of the body would remain the same. The *area moment of inertia* (which would apply in this case) is the sum of the products of all differentials of cross-sectional area of the body multiplied by the squares of their distances from the centroidal axis of the body. Both concepts represent mathematical measures of the strength and the internal rigidity of a structural shape.

4. If this deflection-length ratio applied to long-span truss bridges, the allowable deflection of the channel span of the Ohio River bridge would be $(515 \times 12)/1800$, or 3.43 inches.

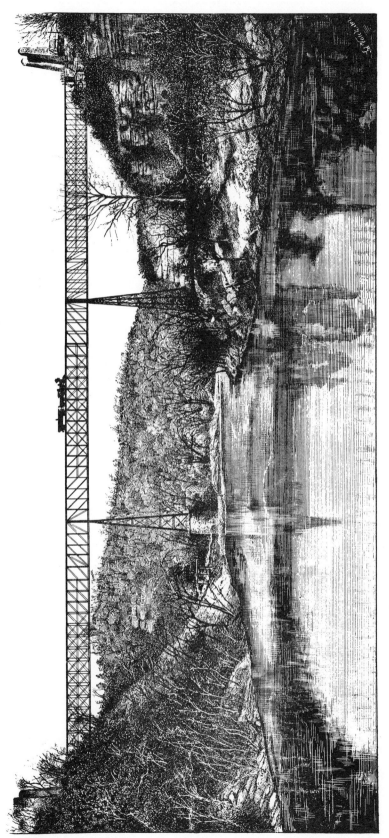

Fig. 53. Kentucky River bridge, CS Railway, Dixville, Kentucky, 1876–77; C. Shaler Smith and L. F. G. Bouscaren, engineers. *Railroad Gazette.*

Appendix B

The Cincinnati Southern Bridge at Dixville, Kentucky: Summary of Quantitative Data

ENGINEERS: C. Shaler Smith and Louis F. G. Bouscaren
CONTRACTOR: Baltimore Bridge Company

GENERAL DIMENSIONS

Length between abutments	1,138.00 ft.
Depth of truss	37.50 ft.
Width out to out of trusses	18.00 ft.
Height of rail above low water	275.00 ft.
Height of rail above base of pier	286.10 ft.
Weight of iron in spans	2,855,379 lbs.
Weight of iron in bents	798,901 lbs.
Modulus of elasticity of iron	$20.4\text{-}28.2 \times 10^6$ lbs.
Volume of masonry	12,635 cu. yds.
Maximum flood rise in river	57 ft.

MAJOR DIVISIONS AND THEIR LENGTHS

Middle span	375.00 ft.
Cantilever spans, each	75.00 ft.
End spans beyond free ends of cantiliver, each	300.00 ft.
Overall length of truss spans	1,125.00 ft.

LOADING FACTORS, DEAD

Weight of truss per panel, middle span	24,000 lbs.
Weight of truss per panel, cantilever span	26,000 lbs.
Weight per lineal foot, middle span[1]	3,840 lbs.
Weight per lineal foot, cantilever and end span	4,100 lbs.

LOADING FACTORS LIVE (based on load test, 20 April 1877)

Load per lineal foot, end span[2]	2,073 lbs.
Load per lineal foot, middle span	1,977 lbs.
Wind load	31.5 lbs. per sq. ft.

DEFLECTIONS UNDER TEST LOAD

I. Both end spans loaded, middle span unloaded

Maximum deflection, end span	1.518 in.
Maximum deflection, cantilever span	1.944 in.
Maximum depression of pier bent	0.372 in.
Maximum upward deflection, middle span	2.832 in.

II. Middle spans loaded, ends unloaded

Maximum deflection, middle span	3.498 in.
Maximum upward deflection, cantilever span	1.580 in.

III. Horizontal deflection under quick-braking[3]

Longitudinal motion of lower chord at hinge	1.500 in.

ALLOWABLE WORKING STRESSES

I. Trusses	
Compression	8,000 lbs. per sq. in.
Tension	10,000 lbs. per sq. in.
II. Bents	
Compression (maximum allowable)[4]	10,000 lbs. per sq. in.
Tension	10,000 lbs. per sq. in.
III. Top and bottom frames	
Tension (maximum allowable in diagonals)	12,500 lbs. per sq. in.
Compression (maximum allowable in floor beams)[5]	7,000 lbs. per sq. in.

RANGE OF FORCES IN FRAMING MEMBERS

I.   Cantilever truss, negative moment

        Tension in top chord: 0 (free-end panel) to 505,900 pounds (fixed-end panel, adjacent to bent)

        Compression in bottom chord: 278,100 pounds (free-end panel) to 855,000 pounds (fixed-end panel)

        Tension in diagonals: 207,200 pounds (free-end panel) to 335,000 pounds (two center panels)

        Compression in posts: 357,596 pounds (free end at hinge) to 709,500 pounds (directly over bent, and calculated from force in topmost post in bent)

II.   Middle span truss, negative moment

        Tension in top chord: 224,500 pounds (panel adjacent to center line) to 682,800 pounds (end panel, adjacent to bent)

        Compression in bottom chord: 242,300 pounds (panel adjacent to center line) to 855,100 pounds (end panel, adjacent to bent)

        Tension in diagonals: 52,000 pounds (two center panels among the eight with double diagonals) to 288,800 pounds (two-panel diagonal adjacent to bent)

III.   Middle span truss, positive moment

        Compression in top chord: 0 (end panel) to 610,900 pounds (two panels on either side of center line)

        Tension in bottom chord: 0 (first three end panels) to 595,400 pounds (panel adjacent to center line)

IV.   End span truss (simple truss; positive moment only)

        Compression in top chord: 240,846 pounds (end panel) to 665,849 pounds (two panels on either side of center line)

        Tension in bottom chord: 0 (end panel) to 652,236 pounds (panels adjacent to center line)

        Tension in diagonals: 18,691 pounds (two-panel diagonal adjacent to center line toward abutment end) to 219,815 pounds (two-panel diagonal at hinged end)

V.   Cantilever top frame (stresses in top and bottom frames depend on wind direction)

        Diagonals: 93,700 pounds (free-end panel) to 136,900 pounds (fixed-end panel)

        Transverse beams: 66,700 pounds (free end) to 205,000 pounds (fixed end)

Appendix B

VI.   Cantilever bottom frame
      Diagonals: 42,200 pounds (free-end panel) to 57,100 pounds (fixed-end panel)
      Transverse beams: 28,300 pounds (free end) to 278,400 pounds (fixed end)
VII. Middle span top frame
      Diagonals: 7,200 pounds (panel adjacent to center line) to 136,900 pounds (end panel)
      Transverse beams: 10,300 pounds (center) to 205,100 pounds (end)
VIII. Middle span bottom frame
      Diagonals: 2,500 pounds (panel adjacent to center line) to 47,100 pounds (end panel)
      Transverse beams: 3,300 pounds (center) to 278,400 pounds (end)
IX.   End span top frame
      Diagonals: 7,200 pounds (6th and 7th panels from hinge) to 136,900 pounds (abutment panel)
      Transverse beams: 10,300 pounds (7th beam from hinge) to 102,550 pounds (abutment end)
X.   End span bottom frame
      Diagonals: 2,500 pounds (panels adjacent to center line) to 37,200 pounds (end panels)
      Transverse beams: 3,300 pounds (center) to 28,300 pounds (ends)
XI.   Bent, side or transverse elevation
      Compression in post: 756,100 pounds (top panel) to 954,400 pounds
      Tension or compression in diagonals: 34,200 pounds (bottom panel) to 72,400 pounds (top panel)
      Tension or compression in horizontal members: 33,800 pounds (3rd from bottom) to 138,000 pounds (top)
XII. Diagonals in transverse planes between trusses (extending between adjacent panel points): 458,600 pounds maximum (above bent)

SOURCES: Cincinnati Southern Railway drawings and strain diagrams; "The Kentucky River Bridge," *Railroad Gazette*, vol. 9 (19 January, 7 September, 14 September, 21 September 1877), pp. 29, 403, 413, 423, 428-29.

1.   Unit weight is based on the weight of both trusses and of top and bottom frames.

2.   The load test was performed by means of four locomotives and loaded cars weighing 40,000 pounds gross in a 22-foot length. Unit live load equals the total weight of locomotives and cars on the end or middle span divided by the length of the span. The test train was placed successively on the end span, cantilever, and middle span.

3.   In this test a train consisting of a locomotive and 24 loaded cars moving at 26 miles per hour was brought to a stop within 104 feet by reversing the engine and simultaneously applying brakes on every car.

4.   The allowable compressive stress in the transverse horizontal members of the bent was reduced to 2,000 pounds per square inch apparently to resist buckling.

5.   The allowable compressive stress in unsupported floor beams was reduced to 3,500 pounds per square inch again to resist buckling.

297

Appendix C

TABLE 1

POPULATION GROWTH OF CINCINNATI

Year	Population of City	Percent Increase	Population of SMA	Percent Increase
1810	2,540	.....	....	....
1820	9,642	279.6	....	....
1830	24,831	157.5	....	....
1840	46,338	86.6	....	....
1850	115,435	149.1	....	....
1860	161,044	39.5	....	....
1870	216,239	34.3	....	....
1880	255,139	18.0	....	....
1890	296,908	16.4	....	....
1900	325,902	9.8	....	....
1910	363,591	11.6	....	....
1920	401,247	10.4	....	....
1930	451,160	12.4	....	....
1940	455,610	1.0	....	....
1950	503,998	10.6	904,402	....
1960	502,550	- 0.3	1,071,642	18.5
1970	452,524	- 10.0	1,384,851	29.2

SOURCE: United States Census.

TABLE 2

STEAM RAILROADS SERVING CINCINNATI

B&O[1] — Baltimore and Ohio (incorporated 1827; merged with C&O 1960)

B&OSW — Baltimore and Ohio Southwestern (incorporated 1889 to control and operate CW&B and O&M railroads)

C&O — Chesapeake and Ohio (incorporated 1867; merged with B&O 1960)

CC&L — Chicago, Cincinnati and Louisville (incorporated 1904; acquired by C&O 1910)

Cincinnati and Baltimore (incorporated 1868 to connect Marietta and Cincinnati with lines in the Cincinnati terminal area)

Cincinnati and Columbia Street Railroad (incorporated 1863; acquired by Cincinnati Street Railway Company 1891, 1896)

C&E — Cincinnati and Eastern (incorporated 1881; reorganized as Ohio and Northwestern 1887)

Cincinnati and Hamilton (incorporated 1846; reincorporated as CH&D 1847)

C&I — Cincinnati and Indiana (incorporated 1861; leased to IC&L 1866)

C&R — Cincinnati and Richmond (incorporated 1881; merged with PCC&StL 1890)

Cincinnati and Springfield (incorporated 1870; leased to Cleveland, Columbus, Cincinnati and Indianapolis 1871)

Cincinnati and Westwood (incorporated 1874; abandoned 1926)

Cincinnati Connecting Belt (incorporated 1899; merged with Cincinnati, Portsmouth and Virginia 1901)

CG&P — Cincinnati, Georgetown and Portsmouth (incorporated 1873 as Cincinnati and Portsmouth; reorganized as electric interurban line 1902)

CH&D — Cincinnati, Hamilton and Dayton (incorporated 1847; acquired by B&O 1909)

CI&W — Cincinnati, Indianapolis and Western (detached from CH&D 1913; merged with B&O 1927)

CIStL&C — Cincinnati, Indianapolis, Saint Louis and Chicago (incorporated 1866; merged with various Ohio and Indiana lines to form CCC&StL 1889)

CL&N — Cincinnati, Lebanon and Northern (incorporated 1885; controlled by Pennsylvania 1896)

CNO&TP — Cincinnati, New Orleans and Texas Pacific (incorporated 1880 as lessee of CS; controlled by Southern 1917)

Cincinnati Northern (first company of that name incorporated 1880 and reorganized as CL&N 1885; second company incorporated 1894 and merged with CCC&StL 1938)

C-NW   Cincinnati-Northwestern (incorporated 1883; acquired by Southern Ohio Traction Company 1901)

Cincinnati, Portsmouth and Virginia (incorporated 1891; acquired by N&W 1901)

CS   Cincinnati Southern (incorporated 1869; leased to CNO&TP 1881)

Cincinnati Street Connecting (incorporated 1864 as Little Miami belt line)

CW&B   Cincinnati, Washington and Baltimore (incorporated 1882; reorganized as B&OSW 1889)

CCC&StL   Cleveland, Cincinnati, Chicago and Saint Louis (incorporated 1889; progressive control by NYC and Hudson River and New York Central 1889 et seq.; commonly known as Big Four)

CCC&I   Cleveland, Columbus, Cincinnati and Indianapolis (incorporated 1868; merged into CCC&StL 1889)

College Hill (incorporated 1874; reorganized as C-NW 1883)

Dayton and Cincinnati (incorporated 1852; reorganized as Cincinnati Railway Tunnel Company 1877; acquired by CL&N 1902)

Dayton Short Line (see Dayton and Cincinnati)

IC&L   Indianapolis, Cincinnati and Lafayette (incorporated 1861; merged with CIStL&C 1866)

KC   Kentucky Central (incorporated 1849; acquired by L&N 1890)

LM   Little Miami (incorporated 1836; leased to PC&StL 1869)

L&N   Louisville and Nashville (incorporated 1850)

LC&L   Louisville, Cincinnati and Lexington (incorporated 1831; acquired by L&N 1881)

M&C   Marietta and Cincinnati (incorporated 1845; reorganized as CW&B 1882)

NYC   New York Central (incorporated 1853; merged with Pennsylvania 1968)

N&W   Norfolk and Western (incorporated 1881)

O&M   Ohio and Mississippi (incorporated 1848; acquired by B&OSW 1893)

Ohio and Northwestern (incorporated 1887; reorganized as Cincinnati, Portsmouth and Virginia 1891)

PC   Penn Central (incorporated 1968 as merger of NYC and Pennsylvania)

Pennsylvania (incorporated 1846; merged with NYC 1968)

PC&StL   Pittsburgh, Cincinnati and Saint Louis (incorporated 1868; controlled by Pennsylvania 1869; merged with PCC&StL 1890)

PCC&StL   Pittsburgh, Cincinnati, Chicago and Saint Louis (incorporated 1890; progressive control by Pennsylvania 1890 et seq.)

SR   Southern Railway (incorporated 1894)

[1] Initials are given only for companies whose names were abbreviated to such in ordinary usage.

TABLE 3

ELECTRIC INTERURBAN RAILROADS SERVING CINCINNATI

Cincinnati and Columbus Traction Company (opened for service 1906; abandoned 1920)

Cincinnati and Dayton Traction Company (incorporated 1918 as reorganization of Ohio Electric Railway)

Cincinnati and Eastern Electric Railway (opened for service 1902; subsidiary of Interurban Railway and Terminal Company)

Cincinnati and Hamilton Electric Street Railway (opened for service 1898; merged with Ohio Electric Railway 1907)

Cincinnati and Hamilton Traction Company (opened for service 1901; leased to Cincinnati Interurban Company 1902)

Cincinnati and Lake Erie (incorporated 1930 as consolidation of Cincinnati, Hamilton and Dayton, Columbus and Eastern, and Lima-Toledo railroads; abandoned 1937–39)

Cincinnati, Georgetown and Portsmouth (opened for service as interurban 1902; abandoned 1933–36)

Cincinnati, Hamilton and Dayton (incorporated 1926 as reorganization of Cincinnati and Dayton Traction Company)

Cincinnati Interurban Company (lessee of Cincinnati and Hamilton Traction Company 1902; controlled by Ohio Traction Company 1905)

Appendix C

Cincinnati, Lawrenceburg and Aurora Electric Street Railroad Company (opened for service 1900; abandoned 1930)

Cincinnati, Milford and Blanchester Traction Company (opened for service 1906; abandoned 1926)

Cincinnati, Milford and Loveland Traction Company (opened for service 1903; reorganized as Cincinnati, Milford and Blanchester 1906)

Interurban Railway and Terminal Company (opened for service 1902; abandoned 1918–22)

Ohio Electric Railway Company (incorporated 1907 as successor to Cincinnati and Hamilton Electric Street Railway Company)

Ohio Traction Company (incorporated 1905 as successor to Cincinnati Interurban Company; abandoned 1925)

Rapid Railway Company (opened for service 1903; subsidiary of Interurban Railway and Terminal Company)

Southern Ohio Traction Company (incorporated 1901 as successor to Cincinnati-Northwestern [steam railroad]; merged with Ohio Electric Railway Company 1907)

Suburban Traction Company (opened for service 1903; subsidiary of Interurban Railway and Terminal Company)

TABLE 4

NUMBER OF PASSENGERS CARRIED PER YEAR BY CLASS I RAILROADS AND
NUMBER OF PASSENGERS PER DAY USING CINCINNATI TERMINALS

Year	Through Passengers Carried Per Year	Total Passengers Carried Per Year	Passengers at Cincinnati Per Day	Passengers at Cincinnati Per Day
1882	. . . .	289,031,000	7,314[1]	. . . .
1885	. . . .	351,428,000	10,000	. . . .
1890	. . . .	492,431,000	12,400	. . . .
1895	. . . .	507,421,000	13,200	. . . .
1900	. . . .	553,008,000	14,000	. . . .
1905	. . . .	711,498,000	18,000	. . . .
1910	. . . .	939,909,000	23,800	. . . .
1915	. . . .	957,683,000	24,200	. . . .
1920	. . . .	1,239,181,000	31,400	. . . .
1925	438,961,000	888,267,296	22,000	25,300[2]
1928[3]	347,376,000	790,597,447	20,000	20,000
1930	264,134,000	703,598,121	18,300	15,200
1933[4]	160,617,954	432,979,887	10,950	9,200
1935	186,321,044	445,872,300	11,300	10,700
1940	224,625,828	452,920,914	11,400	13,000
1944[5]	595,299,428	910,295,129	22,800	34,300
1945	571,225,032	891,127,614	22,700	32,900
1950	209,094,275	486,194,222	12,300	12,000
1955	183,618,130	431,998,922	10,900	10,500
1960	122,669,236	325,871,625	8,300	7,000
1965	c95,000,000	298,691,000	7,600	5,500
1970	c80,000,000	283,923,000	7,200	4,600

SOURCE: Interstate Commerce Commission and *Poor's Manual*.

[1] A figure for the number of passengers per day using Cincinnati terminals exists, to my knowledge, only for the year 1928. The figures in column four were calculated by extrapolation, with the figure for 1928 as the base, and varied according to the increase or decrease in the total number of passengers carried per year. Such an extreme use of extrapolation will hardly yield reliable figures, but it provides a plausible basis for making a rough estimate of the year-by-year change in passenger traffic at the Cincinnati stations.

[2] The figures in column five were again based on the figure for 1928 and varied according to the annual increase or decrease in number of through passengers.

[3] Preparation of plans for Cincinnati Union Terminal was begun in 1928, which is also the base year for calculating the number of daily passengers at Cincinnati terminals.

[4] The Union Terminal was opened in 1933, which was also the economic low point of the depression of the 1930s.

[5] The greatest volume of wartime traffic and the highest total of passenger-miles in the history of American railroads came in the year 1944. If the figures in column five represent a reasonable estimate, 1944 was probably also the year in which the greatest number of passengers traveled to, from, or through Cincinnati.

TABLE 5

PASSENGERS AND FREIGHT CARRIED BY
CINCINNATI RAILROAD COMPANIES, 1885–1975

Year	Number of Passengers	Tons of Freight
1. Baltimore and Ohio		
1890	2,560,693	3,513,325*
1895	2,450,453	3,678,036*
1900	11,665,862	31,895,143
1905	15,518,372	47,285,183
1910	21,107,120	62,797,745
1915	20,581,992	64,375,595
1918	23,605,199	94,152,556
1920	25,354,343	101,924,520
1925	14,745,684	104,637,773
1928	10,257,996	103,714,942
1930	7,143,358	91,907,620
1933	3,102,656	61,079,224
1935	3,442,031	65,945,938
1940	4,162,557	86,048,712
1944	14,303,937	147,314,981
1945	13,705,733	137,455,955
1950	4,133,533	115,766,122
1955	3,635,661	115,289,980
1960	2,631,432	99,545,134
1965	1,781,720	113,181,000
1970	960,727	115,817,000
1975		98,258,432

* B&OSW; B&O includes B&OSW after 1895 and CH&D after 1915.

Year	Number of Passengers	Tons of Freight
2. Chesapeake and Ohio		
1890	1,470,642	3,760,577
1895	1,813,379	5,671,200
1900	2,536,529	9,746,840
1905	3,438,030	13,304,791
1910	4,969,612	22,892,229
1915	6,487,803	30,048,454
1918	8,524,755	40,236,735
1920	8,767,811	40,838,116
1925	5,811,872	63,996,306
1928	3,931,443	65,935,659
1930	2,618,112	72,764,685
1933	978,835	58,151,220
1935	1,096,861	62,199,566
1940	1,589,400	74,811,378
1944	6,759,501	102,470,145
1945	6,433,150	96,848,375
1950	1,375,020	114,357,822
1955	1,261,849	121,712,784
1960	876,659	101,382,765
1965	749,410	118,340,000
1970	178,557	119,395,000
1975		99,514,716

Year	Number of Passengers	Tons of Freight
3. Cincinnati, Hamilton and Dayton		
1885	2,141,635	2,753,999
1890	3,094,867	3,689,314
1895	3,477,343	4,732,790
1900	2,964,898	5,888,242
1905	3,712,073	7,085,560
1910	3,195,963	9,988,050
1915	2,425,291	11,684,201

Year	Number of Passengers	Tons of Freight
4. Cincinnati, New Orleans and Texas Pacific		
1885	587,175	979,421
1890	813,852	1,923,306

(continued)

Year	Number of Passengers	Tons of Freight
1895	667,025	1,934,268
1900	881,296	3,192,020
1905	1,200,860	4,026,287
1910	1,394,439	5,062,538
1915	1,318,582	4,742,748
1918	1,671,029	5,711,395
1920	1,762,132	6,695,999
1925	1,161,160	7,726,655
1928	802,831	7,738,693
1930	527,628	6,756,468
1933	249,838	4,383,191
1935	318,442	5,089,513
1940	352,784	7,680,708
1944	1,519,375	15,039,343
1945	1,094,617	13,282,028
1950	341,313	12,828,009
1955	273,226	15,376,678
1960	137,831	13,047,178
1965	93,687	16,020,000*
1970	8,578	23,192,000
1975		26,773,594

* Estimated.

5. *Cleveland, Cincinnati, Chicago and Saint Louis*

Year	Number of Passengers	Tons of Freight
1890	3,500,881	6,591,610
1895	5,243,814	8,625,073
1900	5,792,421	11,006,304
1905	5,989,534	14,510,234
1910	7,680,336	22,929,632
1915	7,766,352	26,114,345
1918	9,479,864	39,215,867
1920	9,142,525	38,518,685
1925	4,656,340	45,387,869
1928	3,595,203	44,820,712

6. *Louisville and Nashville*

Year	Number of Passengers	Tons of Freight
1885	4,328,383	9,099,684
1890	5,193,630	16,695,477
1895	5,095,574	10,630,749
1900	6,282,042	15,839,470
1905	9,518,705	21,041,000
1910	11,030,027	30,155,217
1915	11,849,957	27,731,561
1918	17,086,598	44,789,609
1920	17,482,098	47,098,325
1925	10,381,039	58,076,917
1928	7,418,093	61,241,738
1930	4,556,815	51,735,263
1933	2,505,823	30,942,091
1935	4,028,974	35,830,970
1940	3,140,586	49,429,151
1944	12,440,022	73,374,452
1945	10,074,128	70,235,764
1950	2,624,955	68,283,021
1955	1,263,021	61,068,625
1960	1,066,129	73,678,902
1965	731,221	93,524,302
1970	122,640	109,321,000
1975		122,338,175

7. *New York Central**

Year	Number of Passengers	Tons of Freight
1930	72,951,015	150,046,279
1933	45,018,512	91,248,346
1935	44,381,459	104,482,468

(continued)

Year	Number of Passengers	Tons of Freight
1940	47,531,722	136,549,195
1944	81,554,513	196,186,843
1945	78,877,809	180,822,800
1950	46,627,062	165,834,716
1955	43,432,503	161,070,694
1960	30,451,557	133,361,424
1965	24,790,153	142,649,000

* New York Central includes CCC&StL.

8. Norfolk and Western*

1905	3,530,962	15,852,323
1910	4,930,108	25,412,529
1915	6,417,720	32,767,701
1918	7,855,937	46,801,920
1920	7,376,109	40,685,743
1925	4,538,851	50,266,557
1928	2,882,888	54,053,476
1930	1,791,416	50,626,522
1933	850,777	35,428,081
1935	1,431,040	39,345,242
1940	1,159,154	56,061,773
1944	5,168,580	71,523,960
1945	4,612,549	66,577,745
1950	923,494	63,051,400
1955	644,703	70,409,617
1960	415,945	78,929,724
1965	863,222	166,632,047
1970	385,526	164,052,081
1975		143,225,807

* After 1960 Norfolk and Western includes New York, Chicago and Saint Louis (Nickel Plate Road), Pittsburgh and West Virginia, and Wabash.

9. Pennsylvania*

1920	164,766,666	196,046,777
1925	128,701,385	228,889,365
1928	118,120,504	214,887,139
1930	99,019,359	191,315,758
1933	52,890,369	114,009,463
1935	56,739,729	129,941,499
1940	64,243,942	174,303,212
1944	163,587,080	275,768,347
1945	158,836,131	256,143,042
1950	75,191,753	207,102,828
1955	63,147,597	201,431,316
1960	46,271,208	161,314,785
1965	43,832,963	177,251,000

* Pennsylvania includes PCC&StL.

10. Penn Central

1970	86,922,466	281,724,000
1975		239,153,624

11. Pittsburgh, Cincinnati, Chicago and Saint Louis

1892	6,407,515	11,357,213
1895	5,881,636	11,648,499
1900	6,293,068	15,961,835
1905	8,172,563	25,740,993
1910	11,689,822	38,976,157
1915	10,847,045	35,159,103
1918	15,220,882	50,738,798

SOURCES: *Moody's Manual of Investments: Railroads* and *Poor's Manual of the Railroads of the United States, Street Railways, and Traction Companies.*

TABLE 6

TRENDS IN FREIGHT TONNAGE OF
CINCINNATI RAILROADS, 1920–1975

Year	Tons of Freight (millions)	Percent of Change (1920 = 100)
1. Baltimore and Ohio		
1920	101.92	100.0
1930	91.91	90.2
1940	86.05	84.4
1944	147.31	144.5
1950	115.77	113.5
1960	99.55	97.6
1970	115.82	113.6
1975	98.26	96.4
2. Chesapeake and Ohio		
1920	40.84	100.0
1930[1]	72.76	178.2
1940	74.81	183.2
1944	102.47	250.9
1950[2]	114.36	280.0
1960	101.38	248.2
1970	119.40	292.4
1975	99.51	243.7
3. Cincinnati, New Orleans and Texas Pacific		
1920	6.70	100.0
1930	6.76	100.9
1940	7.68	114.6
1944	15.04	224.4
1950	12.83	191.5
1960	13.05	194.8
1970	23.19	346.1
1975	26.77	400.0
4. Louisville and Nashville		
1920	47.10	100.0
1930[3]	51.74	109.9
1940	49.43	104.9
1944	73.37	155.8
1950	68.28	145.0
1960[4]	73.68	156.4
1970	109.32	232.1
1975	122.34	260.0
5. New York Central System		
1930	150.05	100.0
1940	136.55	91.0
1944	196.19	130.7
1950	165.83	110.5
1960[5]	133.36	88.9
6. Pennsylvania		
1930	191.32	100.0
1940	174.30	91.1
1944	275.77	144.1
1950	207.10	108.2
1960	161.31	84.3
7. New York Central-Pennsylvania Combined		
1930	341.37	100.0
1940	310.85	91.1
1944	471.96	138.2
1950	372.93	109.2
1960	294.67	86.3
1970	281.72	82.5
1975[6]	239.15	70.1

(continued)

Year	Tons of Freight (millions)	Percent of Change (1920 = 100)
	8. Norfolk and Western	
1920	40.69	100.0
1930	50.63	124.4
1940	56.06	137.8
1944	71.52	175.8
1950	63.05	155.0
1960	78.93	194.0
1970[7]		

SOURCES: *Moody's Manual* and *Poor's Manual*.

[1] C&O acquired and merged Hocking Valley Railroad in 1930.

[2] C&O acquired and merged Pere Marquette Railway in 1947.

[3] L&N acquired and merged Louisville, Henderson and St. Louis Railroad in 1929.

[4] L&N acquired and merged Nashville, Chattanooga and St. Louis Railway in 1957.

[5] New York Central and Pennsylvania merged in 1968.

[6] Figures for 1970 and 1975 include New York, New Haven and Hartford Railroad (part of Penn Central group).

[7] N&W acquired and merged New York, Chicago and Saint Louis (Nickel Plate Road), Pittsburgh and West Virginia, and Wabash railroads in 1964.

Bibliography

General Works

Berg, Walter G. *Buildings and Structures of American Railroads.* New York: John Wiley and Sons, 1893.

Bruce, Alfred W. *The Steam Locomotive in America: Its Development in the Twentieth Century.* New York: W. W. Norton and Company, 1952.

Busfield, T. L. "The Design of Large Passenger Terminals." *Railway Age Gazette* 60:18 (5 May 1916), pp. 989-93.

Caster, Kenneth E., et al. *Elementary Guide to the Fossils and Strata of the Ordovician in the Vicinity of Cincinnati, Ohio.* Cincinnati: Cincinnati Museum of Natural History, 1955.

Cist, Charles. *Sketches and Statistics of Cincinnati in 1859.* Cincinnati: [Charles Cist?], 1859.

City of Cincinnati and Its Resources, The. Cincinnati: Cincinnati Times-Star Company, 1891.

Condit, Carl W. *American Building Art: The Nineteenth Century.* New York: Oxford University Press, 1960.

Condit, Carl W. *American Building Art: The Twentieth Century.* New York: Oxford University Press, 1961.

Droege, John. *Passenger Terminals and Trains.* New York: McGraw-Hill Book Company, 1916.

Dubin, Arthur D. *Some Classic Trains.* Milwaukee: Kalmbach Publishing Company, 1964.

Dubin, Arthur D. *More Classic Trains.* Milwaukee: Kalmbach Publishing Company, 1974.

Engelhardt, George W. *Cincinnati, The Queen City.* Cincinnati: George W. Engelhardt Company, 1901.

Ford, Henry A., and Kate B. Ford. *History of Cincinnati, Ohio, with Illustrations and Biographical Sketches.* Cleveland: L. A. Williams and Company, 1881.

Goss, Charles F. *Cincinnati, The Queen City, 1788-1912.* Chicago and Cincinnati: S. J. Clarke Publishing Company, 1912.

Greve, Charles T. *Centennial History of Cincinnati and Representative Citizens.* Chicago: Biographical Publishing Company, 1904.

Interstate Commerce Commission. *Annual Report on the Statistics of Railways of the United States.* Washington: Government Printing Office, 1889 et seq.

Kenny, D. J. *Illustrated Cincinnati.* Cincinnati: Robert Clarke and Company, 1875.

Leonard, Lewis A. *Greater Cincinnati and Its People.* New York, Chicago, and Cincinnati: Lewis Historical Publishing Company, 1927.

Martin, A. *Enterprise Denied: Origins of the Decline of American Railroads.* New York: Columbia University Press, 1971.

Meeks, Carroll L. V. *The Railroad Station: An Architectural History.* New Haven, Conn.: Yale University Press, 1956.

Official Guide of the Railway and Steam Navigation Lines in the United States, Mexico, and Canada. New York: National Railway Publication Company, 1868 et seq.

Poor's Manual of the Railroads of the United States, Street Railways and Traction Companies. New York: Poor's Railroad Manual Company, 1869 et seq.

Railroads in This Century: A Summary of the Facts and Figures with Charts. Washington: Association of American Railroads, 1944.

Railroad Transportation: A Statistical Record, 1921-1963. Washington: Association of American Railroads, 1965.

Stover, John F. *American Railroads.* Chicago: University of Chicago Press, 1961.

United States Department of Commerce. *Historical Statistics of the United States.* Washington: Government Printing Office, 1960.

United States Department of the Interior, United States Geological Survey. *West Cincinnati Quadrangle* and *East Cincinnati Quadrangle.* Washington: United States Geological Survey, 1914.

United States Federal Writers Project, Ohio. *They Built a City: 150 Years of Industrial Cincinnati.* Cincinnati: Cincinnati Post Company, 1938.

United States Works Progress Administration, Ohio Writers Program. *Cincinnati: A Guide to the Queen City and Its Neighbors.* Cincinnati: City of Cincinnati, 1943.

White, John H., Jr. *American Locomotives: An Engineering History, 1830-1880.* Baltimore: Johns Hopkins University Press, 1968.

Chapter I. The Pioneer Roads and Their Stations

Anderson, J. A. "The First Interlocking Plant in America." *Railroad Age Gazette* 45:17 (25 September 1908), pp. 992-93.

Bibliography

"Annual Report and Results of the Little Miami Railroad." *Railroad Record* 48:1 (26 January 1854), pp. 754-55.

"Arrival and Departure of Trains." *Railroad Record*, vols. 1-20 (1853-73), passim.

"Atlantic & Great Western Railway." *Railway Age* 3:37 (12 September 1878), pp. 457-58.

Burgess, George H., and Miles C. Kennedy. *Centennial History of the Pennsylvania Railroad, 1846-1946*. Philadelphia: Pennsylvania Railroad Company, 1949.

"Central Avenue Warehouse" and "C. C. C. & St. L. Ry. Co. Warehouse." Cincinnati: Cleveland, Cincinnati, Chicago and Saint Louis Railway Company, Office of Chief Engineer, Plan No. 23547, File No. 506-13 (undated).

"Central Railroad Depot." *Railroad Record* 14 (10 January 1867): 553-54.

"Central Union Depot: Meeting of Council Committee and Railroad Representatives." *Railroad Record* 20 (12 December 1872): 337-38.

"Cincinnati and Dayton Railroad." *American Railroad Journal* 25:835 (17 April 1852), p. 244.

"Cincinnati and Hamilton Railroad, and Improvements in Ohio." *American Railroad Journal* 20:563 (3 April 1847), p. 218; 20:564 (10 April 1847), p. 237; 20:566 (24 April 1847), p. 265.

"Cincinnati and Indianapolis Short Line Railroad." *American Railroad Journal* 26:902 (30 July 1853), p. 494.

"Cincinnati and St. Louis Railroad." *American Railroad Journal* 20:572 (5 June 1847), pp. 357-58.

"Cincinnati, Hamilton and Dayton Railroad." *American Railroad Journal* 22:708 (17 November 1849), p. 724; 24:812 (8 November 1851), p. 711.

"Cincinnati, Hamilton and Dayton Railroad, Third Annual Report. . . . " *American Railroad Journal* 26:893 (28 May 1858), pp. 340-41.

"Cincinnati, Hamilton and Dayton R. R." *Railroad Record* 8 (3 May 1860): 124; 11 (30 April 1863): 136-38; 13 (18 May 1865): 155.

"Connection between the Railroads." *Railroad Record* 11 (31 December 1863): 533-34.

"Dayton Short Line Road and Tunnel." *Railroad Record* 1:1 (3 March 1853), p. 3.

Fisher, Charles E. "The Cincinnati, Hamilton and Dayton R. R." *Railway and Locomotive Historical Society Bulletin*, no. 96 (May 1957), pp. 80-82.

"Grand Central Depot for Passenger Traffic." *Railroad Record* 20 (28 November 1872): 321-22.

Hungerford, Edward. *The Story of the Baltimore and Ohio Railroad, 1827-1927*. New York: G. P. Putnam's Sons, 1928.

"Indianapolis and Cincinnati R. R." *Railroad Record* 10 (11 December 1862): 493-94.

"Little Miami Passenger Depot." *Cincinnati Daily Enquirer*, 27 August 1854, p. 3.

"Little Miami Railroad Report for 1847." *American Railroad Journal* 21:614 (25 March 1848), pp. 198-202.

Lord, Henry C. "The Cincinnati, Indianapolis, St. Louis & Chicago." *Railway Age* 8:31 (2 August 1883), p. 464; 8:32 (9 August 1883), p. 482; 8:33 (16 August

1883), p. 500; 8:34 (23 August 1883), p. 518; 8:35 (30 August 1883), pp. 538-39; 8:36 (6 September 1883), p. 554; 8:38 (20 September 1883), p. 591.

Lord, Henry C. "History of the Marietta and Cincinnati." *Railway Age* 8:30 (26 July 1883), pp. 448-49.

Lord, Henry C. "History of the Ohio and Mississippi Road. . . . " *Railway Age*, 8:28 (12 July 1883), p. 413; 29 (19 July 1883), p. 431.

Mansfield, E. D. "The Deer Creek Project—Shall We Have a General Depot?" *Railroad Record* 20 (17 October 1872): 273.

Map of Cincinnati, Newport, and Covington. Cincinnati: E. Mendenhall, 1855.

"Monument to the Lexington and Ohio." *Railway Age Gazette* 60:19 (12 May 1916), p. 1047.

"Moseley's Tubular Bridge." *Railroad Record* 3:7 (12 April 1855), p. 103.

"Moseley's Tubular Wrought Iron Bridge." *Railroad Record* 3:20 (12 July 1855), p. 315; 3:28 (6 September 1855), p. 438; 3:45 (3 January 1856), p. 714; 4:12 (15 May 1856), p. 178; 5:5 (26 March 1857), p. 80.

"New I. and C. Railroad Depot, The" *Railroad Record* 13 (14 December 1865): 518.

"Ohio and Mississippi Railroad." *American Railroad Journal* 22:675 (24 March 1849), p. 178.

Ohio State Railroad Guide, Illustrated, The. Cincinnati to Erie, via Columbus and Cleveland. Columbus: Ohio State Journal Company, 1854.

Pixton, John. *The Marietta and Cincinnati Railroad, 1845-1883: A Case Study in American Railroad Economics.* Pennsylvania State University Studies, No. 17. University Park: Pennsylvania State University, 1966.

"Project of a Great Union Railroad Depot in Cincinnati." *Railroad Record* 14 (10 January 1867): 551-52.

"Railroad Connections—Through Cincinnati." *Railroad Record* 15 (26 September 1867): 369-70.

"Railroad from Cincinnati to St. Louis." *American Railroad Journal* 20:588 (25 September 1847), p. 611.

"Railroad Interest at Cincinnati, The." *Railroad Record* 15 (4 July 1867): 225-26.

"Railroads of Cincinnati—Central Union Depot." *Railroad Record* 15 (15 August 1867): 298-99.

"Rebuilding of Plum St. Warehouse." Cincinnati: Cleveland, Cincinnati, Chicago and Saint Louis Railway Company, Office of District Engineer, Plan No. 31492, File No. 1853-92, 28 October 1944.

Schmid, R. C. "The Cleveland, Columbus, Cincinnati & Indianapolis Railroad." *Railway and Locomotive Historical Society Bulletin*, no. 16 (May 1928), pp. 23-33.

Shoemaker, R. M. "The Little Miami Railroad." *American Railroad Journal and Mechanics Magazine*, n.s., 1:10 (15 November 1838), pp. 303-4.

"Tunnel and Its Railroads, The." *Railroad Record* 7:30 (15 September 1859), pp. 349-50.

"Tunnel Railroad, The." *Railroad Record* 20 (3 October 1872): 258.

White, John H., Jr. *Cincinnati Locomotive Builders, 1845-1868.* Washington: Smithsonian Institution, Museum of History and Technology, 1965.

Bibliography

Chapter II. Links with the South

Bridwell, H. L. "Enlarging the Covington & Cincinnati Suspension Bridge." *Railroad Gazette* 29:38 (17 September 1897), pp. 644-45.

Butler, Tod Jordan. "The Cincinnati Southern Railway: A City's Response to Relative Commercial Decline." Ph.D. dissertation, Ohio State University, 1971.

"Cincinnati and Newport Bridge, The." *Railroad Record* 16 (17 December 1868): 503; 18 (29 December 1870): 364.

"Cincinnati Southern." *Railroad Gazette* 27 (14 June 1895): 397-98.

"Cincinnati Southern." *Railroad Gazette* 35:28 (17 July 1903), p. 520.

"Cincinnati Southern." *Railway World* 7:37 (10 September 1881), pp. 880-81.

"Erection of the Newport and Cincinnati Bridge." *Engineering Record* 38:8 (23 July 1898), pp. 158-60; 38:9 (30 July 1898), p. 182.

Hollander, J. H. *The Cincinnati Southern Railway: A Study in Municipal Activity.* Baltimore: Johns Hopkins University Press, 1894.

Klein, Maury. *The History of the Louisville and Nashville Railroad.* New York: Macmillan Company, 1972.

Lord, Henry C. "How a City Built a Railway. . . . " *Railway Age* 8:25 (21 June 1883), p. 356; 8:27 (5 July 1883), p. 395.

"New Bridge, The." *Railroad Record* 20 (21 March 1872): 34.

"Newport and Cincinnati Bridge, The." *Engineering Record* 37:21 (23 April 1898), pp. 448-49.

"Newport and Cincinnati Bridge, The." *Railroad Gazette* 27 (2 August 1895): 510.

"Newport and Cincinnati Bridge Company." *Railroad Record* 15 (13 February 1868): 613-14.

Wagner, Richard M., and Roy J. Wright. *Cincinnati Streetcars.* Cincinnati: Wagner Car Company, 1968-71.

White, John H., Jr. "The Cincinnati Inclined Plane Railway Company: The Mt. Auburn Incline and the Lookout House." *Cincinnati Historical Society Bulletin* 27:1 (Spring 1969), pp. 6-23.

White, John H., Jr. "Historical Notes: Incline Plane Railways in Cincinnati, Ohio." *Bulletin of the Historical and Philosophical Society of Ohio* 19:2 (April 1961), pp. 163-64.

White, John H., Jr. "The Mt. Adams and Eden Park Inclined Railway, 'The Kerper Road.' " *Bulletin of the Historical and Philosophical Society of Ohio* 17:4 (October 1959), pp. 243-76.

Chapter III. The Terminal Pattern of Half a Century

"Aggregate Length of Lines . . . on Which the Block System Is in Use, January 1, 1908." *Railroad Gazette* 44:16 (17 April 1908), pp. 544-45.

Alexander, Edwin P. *The Pennsylvania Railroad: A Pictorial History.* New York: W. W. Norton and Company, 1947.

Anderson, J. A. "The First Block Signal System in America." *Railroad Age Gazette* 46:10 (5 March 1909), pp. 457-59.

"Attractive Suburban Station on the Pennsylvania Lines, An." *Railroad Gazette* 42:22 (31 May 1907), pp. 733-34.

"Automatic Block Signals on the Cincinnati, New Orleans & Texas Pacific." *Railroad Gazette* 29:46 (12 November 1897), p. 795.

"Automatic Signals on the Cincinnati, New Orleans & Texas Pacific." *Railroad Gazette* 34:5 (31 January 1902), pp. 70-71.

Block Signals on the Railroads of the United States." *Railroad Gazette* 42:9 (1 March 1907), pp. 280-81.

"Bridge over the Ohio River, Cincinnati, Ohio." Huntington: Chesapeake and Ohio Railway, Office of Chief Engineer, Drawing no. C-227-1, August 1926, revised December 1927.

"Central Ave. Freight Station at Cincinnati, O.; C. C. C. & St. L. Ry." *Engineering News* 46:1 (4 July 1901), p. 16.

"4th Avenue Passenger Station, Cincinnati, Ohio." Huntington: Chesapeake and Ohio Railway, Engineer of Buildings, undated and unnumbered drawings.

"Cincinnati," under "Railroad Construction." *Railroad Gazette* 28 (21 February 1896): 137.

"Cincinnati & Louisville," under "Railroad Construction." *Railroad Gazette* 34:48 (28 November 1902), p. 917; 35:7 (20 February 1903), p. 124.

"Cincinnati & Westwood." *Railroad Gazette* 23 (26 June 1891): 458.

"Cincinnati Belt Lines." *Railroad Gazette* 43:4 (26 July 1907), p. 572.

Cincinnati Chamber of Commerce. *Terminal Facilities*. Cincinnati: Robert Clarke and Company, 1885.

"Cincinnati Circle Road." *Railway Age* 14:9 (1 March 1889), p. 148; 14:10 (8 March 1889), p. 161.

"Cincinnati Dispatch . . . , " in "Miscellaneous Notes." *Railway Age* 8:4 (25 January 1883), p. 53.

"Cincinnati, Hamilton & Dayton Railroad." *Railroad Gazette* 14 (old series):9 (28 May 1870), p. 193.

"Cincinnati, Indianapolis, St. Louis and Chicago." *Railroad Gazette* 15 (13 April 1883): 239.

"Cincinnati, Indianapolis, St. Louis & Chicago . . . Report." *Railway Age* 8:3 (18 January 1883), p. 38.

"Cincinnati, Lebanon & Northern," under "General Railroad News." *Railroad Gazette* 26 (16 March 1894): 203.

"Cincinnati, Lebanon & Northern," under "Railroad Construction." *Railroad Gazette* 26 (21 September 1894): 656.

"Cincinnati Northern." *Railway Age* 8:31 (2 August 1883), p. 470; 8:36 (6 September 1883), p. 560.

"Cincinnati, Ohio," under "Other Structures." *Railroad Gazette* 34:8 (21 February 1902), p. 135; 34:48 (28 November 1902), p. 916; 35:41 (9 October 1903), p. 729; 35:52 (25 December 1903), p. 929; 37:6 (22 July 1904), p. 41; 37:14 (16 September 1904), p. 94; 37:15 (23 September 1904), p. 102.

"Cincinnati, Ohio," under "Railroad Structures." *Railroad Age Gazette* 47:18 (29 October 1909), p. 832.

Bibliography

"Cincinnati, Ohio," under "Railway Structures." *Railway Age Gazette* 48:20 (20 May 1910), p. 1285; 48:21 (27 May 1910), p. 1327; 49:10 (2 September 1910), p. 442; 49:25 (16 December 1910), p. 1167; 51:23 (8 December 1911), p. 1190; 52:1 (5 January 1912), p. 37.

"Cincinnati, Richmond & Chicago." *Railroad Gazette* 22 (14 February 1890): 119.

"Cincinnati Suburban Belt." *Railway Age* 8:28 (12 July 1883), p. 418.

"Cincinnati Union Depot." *Railroad Gazette* 13 (8 July 1881): 379; 14 (16 June 1882): 367.

"Cincinnati Union Depot, The." *Railway Review* 21:40 (1 October 1881), p. 543.

[C. C. C. & St. L. block-signal system], under "Notes." *Railroad Gazette* 30:36 (9 September 1898), p. 653.

"Cleveland, Columbus, Cincinnati & Indianapolis." *Railway Age* 8:12 (22 March 1883), p. 168.

Collins, Thomas. *The Cincinnati, Lebanon & Northern Railway: Memories of the Old C. L. & N. Railway, "The Highland Route," 1882-1932.* Cincinnati: Thomas Collins, 1970(?).

"Covington and Cincinnati Suspension Bridge, The." *Engineering Record* 38:15 (10 September 1898), pp. 314-16; 38:26 (26 November 1898), pp. 554-55.

"Dayton & Cincinnati Terminal," under "Railroad Construction." *Railroad Gazette* 26 (8 June 1894): 413.

"Diagram Showing the Movement of All Trains Run over the Cincinnati Division of the Chesapeake & Ohio Railway on July 19, 1897." *Railroad Gazette* 29:48 (26 November 1897), facing p. 834.

"Flood Prevention in Ditch/Track Location in Vicinity of C[incinnati] U[nion] D[epot]." Cincinnati: Cleveland, Cincinnati, Chicago and Saint Louis Railway Company, Office of Chief Engineer, Chicago Division Plan no. 21965, File no. 515-11, 1 February 1924.

"Fourth Street Extension of the Chesapeake and Ohio at Cincinnati, The." *Railway Review* 30:12 (22 March 1890), pp. 162-63.

"Great Pullman Strike at Cincinnati, The." *Railroad Gazette* 26 (14 September 1894): 637.

"Hanna Locomotive Stoker, The." *Railway Age Gazette* 51:2 (14 July 1911), pp. 85-90.

Hilton, George W. "The Chicago, Cincinnati and Louisville Railroad." *Railway and Locomotive Historical Society Bulletin*, No. 114 (April 1966), pp. 6-14.

Interstate Commerce Commission, Bureau of Valuation. Valuation Record: C. & O. Ry., Cincinnati, O., Valuation Section 42, Station 11 + 0, 16 October 1919, pp. 9-12.

Johnson, Arthur H. "A Historical Sketch of Railroad Signaling." *Railroad Gazette* 26 (17 August, 7 September, 5 October 1894): 560-61, 614-15, 684-85, 689.

"Key Map/The Cleveland, Cincinnati, Chicago & St. Louis Ry. Co." Cincinnati: Cleveland, Cincinnati, Chicago and Saint Louis Railway Company, Office of Valuation Engineer, 30 June 1915; revised 5 May 1935, 1 July 1938, 31 December 1941.

"Length of Railways Worked by the Block System, January 1, 1909." *Railroad Age Gazette* 45:30 (25 December 1908), pp. 1638–39.

"Melville E. Ingalls." *Railway Age Gazette* 57:3 (17 July 1914), p. 100.

"Miles of Railroad Worked by the Block System, January 1, 1904." *Railroad Gazette* 36:4 (22 January 1904), p. 63.

"Mozier Three-Position Semaphore, The." *Railroad Gazette* 27 (5 April 1895): 218–19.

"Municipal Notes at Cincinnati." *Engineering News* 46:2 (11 July 1901), pp. 22–23.

"New C. H. & D. Freight-House at Cincinnati, The." *Railroad Gazette* 26 (20 April 1894): 283.

"Notes of Travel [C. H. & D . . . transfer station]." *Railway Age* 14:11 (15 March 1889), p. 173.

"Ohio River Bridge and North Approach Ohio River Bridge." Atlanta: Southern Railway System, Chief Engineer, Bridges, C. N. O. & T. P. Ry. Drawing No. 36828, 7 April 1959, revised 20 February 1962.

"Organization and Construction Methods Used on the Ivorydale Shops of the C. H. & D." *Railroad Gazette* 41:12 (21 September 1906), pp. 242–44.

"Pittsburgh, Cincinnati & St. Louis Report." *Railway Age* 8:24 (14 June 1883), p. 350.

"Pittsburgh, Cincinnati and St. Louis Railway Company." *Railway World* 8:17 (29 April 1882), pp. 396–97.

"Pittsburgh, Cincinnati, Chicago & St. Louis." *Railroad Gazette* 22 (28 February 1890): 151.

"Pittsburgh, Cincinnati, Chicago & St. Louis," under "General Railroad News." *Railroad Gazette* 27 (4 October and 15 November 1895): 664, 748.

"Plan to Accompany Agreement Showing Tracks/Storr's & Eighth St./to/C. U. D. Co.'s Connection, Cincinnati, Ohio." Cincinnati: Cleveland, Cincinnati, Chicago and Saint Louis Railway Company, Office of Chief Engineer, Plan No. 7553, File No. 502-37, 11 (?) November 1914.

Prince, Richard E. *Louisville and Nashville Steam Locomotives.* Green River, Wyoming: Richard E. Prince, 1968.

Prince, Richard E. *Southern Railway System Steam Locomotives and Boats.* Green River, Wyoming: Richard E. Prince, 1970.

"Proposed Semaphore, A." *Railroad Gazette* 39:10 (8 September 1905), p. 223.

"Railways Worked by the Block Signal System, January 1, 1910." *Railway Age Gazette* 48:22 (3 June 1910), pp. 1340–41.

Rehor, John A. *The Nickel Plate Story.* Milwaukee: Kalmbach Publishing Company, 1965.

"Report of the Reconstruction of the Ohio River Bridge of the Cincinnati, New Orleans and Texas Pacific Railway." Atlanta: Southern Railway System, Office of Chief Engineer, Bridges, undated typescript.

Rosenberg, Ron, and Archer, Eric H. *Norfolk and Western Steam.* New York: Quadrant Press, 1973.

Sagle, Lawrence W. *B & O Power: Steam, Diesel and Electric Power of the Baltimore and Ohio Railroad, 1829–1964.* Carrollton, Ohio: Alvin F. Staufer, 1964.

Bibliography

Shuster, Philip, Eugene L. Huddleston, and Alvin Staufer *C & O Power: Steam and Diesel Locomotives of the Chesapeake and Ohio Railway, 1900-1965.* Carrollton, Ohio: Alvin F. Staufer, 1965.

Staufer, Alvin F. *New York Central's Early Power, 1831 to 1916.* Carrollton, Ohio: Alvin F. Staufer, 1967.

Staufer, Alvin F. *Steam Power of the New York Central System. Modern Power, 1915-1955.* Carrollton, Ohio: Alvin F. Staufer, 1961.

Staufer, Alvin F., Charles Bertrom Pennypacker, and Martin Flattley. *Pennsy Power, Pennsy Power II.* Carrollton, Ohio: Alvin F. Staufer, 1962, 1968.

"Toledo, Cincinnati & St. Louis." *Railway Age* 8:5 (1 February 1883), p. 66.

Turner, Charles W. *Chessie's Road.* Richmond: Garrett and Massie, 1956.

"Union Depot at Cincinnati." *Railroad Gazette* 5:8 (22 February 1873), p. 79.

"Union Electric Semaphore Signal, The." *Railroad Gazette* 29:49 (3 December 1897), pp. 854-55.

Warner, Paul T. "The Locomotives of the Louisville and Nashville Railroad." *Baldwin Locomotives* 8:2 (October 1929), pp. 39-64; 3 (January 1930), pp. 3-22.

Warner, Paul T. "Motive Power Development, Pennsylvania Railroad System." *Baldwin Locomotives* 2:4 (April 1924), pp. 3-26; 3:1 (July 1924), pp. 33-57; 2 (October 1924), pp. 3-29.

White, John H., Jr. "By Steam Car to Mt. Lookout: The Columbia and Cincinnati Street Railroad." *Bulletin of the Cincinnati Historical Society* 25:2 (April 1967), pp. 93-107.

White, John H., Jr. "The Cincinnati and Westwood Railroad." *Bulletin of the Historical and Philosophical Society of Ohio* 15:2 (April 1957), pp. 131-40.

White, John H., Jr. "The College Hill Railroad." *Bulletin of the Historical and Philosophical Society of Ohio* 18:4 (October 1960), pp. 227-39.

Chapter IV. Grand Schemes for the New Century

Arnold, Bion J. *Report on an Interurban Electric Railway Terminal System for the City of Cincinnati.* Cincinnati: Cincinnati Interurban Rapid Transit Commission, 1912.

"Automatic Signals Reduce Operating Costs on Double Track." *Railway Age* 84:22 (2 June 1928), pp. 1291-92.

"Big Four Completes New Terminal at Cincinnati." *Railway Age* 85:16 (20 October 1928), pp. 749-55.

"Cincinnati as a Railroad Center." *Railway Age* 68:8 (20 February 1920), p. 586.

"Cincinnati, Indianapolis & Louisville," under "Railway Construction." *Railway Age Gazette* 56:15 (10 April 1914), p. 855.

"Cincinnati, Ohio," under "Railway Structures." *Railway Age Gazette* 53:16 (18 October 1912), p. 725; 25 (27 December 1912), p. 1236.

"Cincinnati Railroad Terminal Development Company." *Railway Age* 75:4 (28 July 1923), p. 180; 5 (4 August 1923), p. 196.

"Cincinnati's Rapid Transit Ordinance." *Electric Railway Journal* 49:14 (7 April 1917), pp. 633-37.

Cohan, J. "Canal Converted to a Parkway." *Contractors and Engineers Monthly* 16:5 (May 1928), pp. 314–17.

"Color-Position-Light Signals/Baltimore & Ohio." *Railway Age* 78:8 (21 February 1925), pp. 456–57.

"Container System Creates Freight Service." *Railway Age* 72:8 (25 February 1922), pp. 475–76.

"Co-ordination Essential for Rapid Transit in Cincinnati." *Electric Railway Journal* 70:13 (24 September 1927), pp. 542–47; 14 (1 October 1927), pp. 592–98.

"Damage by Floods to Railroads." *Railway Age Gazette* 54:14 (4 April 1913), pp. 806–08; 15 (11 April 1913), pp. 852–53; 16 (18 April 1913), pp. 903–04; 17 (25 April 1913), p. 967 [title varies].

"Disastrous Floods in the Central West." *Railway Age Gazette* 54:13 (28 March 1913), p. 767.

"Double-Track Spans Placed on Single-Track Piers." *Railway Age* 72:21 (27 May 1922), pp. 1215–20.

"Flood Damages." *Railway Age Gazette* 55:1 (4 July 1913), p. 26.

"Floods in Central Ohio . . . " under "General News." *Railway Age Gazette* 55:3 (18 July 1913), p. 118.

Ford, G. B. "The Cincinnati City Plan is Now Law." *Proceedings of the American Society of Civil Engineers* 52:8 (October, 1926), pp. 1636–39.

"Handling 560 per cent Increase in Traffic in 14 Years." *Railway Age* 85:7 (18 August 1928), pp. 295–99.

Hilton, George W., and John F. Due. *The Electric Interurban Railways in America*. Stanford, California: Stanford University Press, 1960.

Kellenberger, K. E. "Operating Trains Against Current Reduces Delays." *Railway Age* 75:1 (7 July 1923), pp. 9–13.

"Lessons of the Recent Floods, The." *Railway Age Gazette* 54:16 (18 April 1913), pp. 886–87.

Middleton, William D. *The Interurban Era*. Milwaukee: Kalmbach Publishing Company, 1961.

Morris, Ray. "Electric Railway Competition." *Railroad Gazette* 43:15 (11 October 1907), pp. 425–28.

Munyan, E. A. "Cincinnati Subway Construction Presents Difficult Problems." *Gas-Age Record* 59:26 (25 June 1927), pp. 919, 934.

"New Cincinnati Freight Terminal of the C., N. O. & T. P., The." *Railroad Gazette* 42:3 (18 January 1907), p. 76.

"New Freight Terminal at Cincinnati, of the Cincinnati, New Orleans and Texas Pacific." *Railroad Gazette* 39:13 (29 September 1905), pp. 293–96.

"Proposed Union Station in Cincinnati." *Railway Age Gazette* 62:8 (23 February 1917), pp. 327–28.

"Rapid Transit Practical for Cincinnati." *Electric Railway Journal* 70:12 (17 September 1927), pp. 534–35.

Raschig, Frank L. "Cincinnati Builds Belt-Line Rapid Transit Railway." *Engineering News-Record* 87:7 (18 August 1921), pp. 264–67.

Raschig, Frank L. "Cincinnati's Subway." *Engineering World* 18:1 (January 1921), pp. 15–18.

Bibliography

"Running Time Reduced 1 Hour 44 Minutes on Single-Track Division." *Railway Age* 85:5 (4 August 1928), pp. 213–16.

Union Terminal Railroad Co./Maps Plans and Profiles. Cincinnati: Union Terminal Railroad Company, 1905.

"University of Cincinnati Co-operative Course in Railway Engineering." *Railway Age Gazette* 55:7 (15 August 1913), pp. 296–98.

Wagner, Richard M., and Roy J. Wright. *Cincinnati Streetcars.* Cincinnati: Wagner Car Company, 1968–71.

Chapter V. Cincinnati Union Terminal

American Society of Planning Officials. *Rail Lines and Terminals in Urban Planning* (Planning Advisory Service Information Report No. 82). Chicago: American Society of Planning Officials, 1956.

Art Deco and the Cincinnati Union Terminal. Cincinnati: University of Cincinnati Department of Art History, 1973.

"Bahnhof in Cincinnati; A. Fellheimer und S. Wagner, Architekten." *Monatshefte für Baukunst und Städtebau* 17:10 (October 1933), pp. 468–72 pl. 20.

Baldwin, A. S. "Factors Governing the Design of Passenger Terminals." *Railway Age* 73:10 (2 September 1922), pp. 429–35.

Baldwin, A. S. "On the Question of Terminal Stations for Passengers." *Bulletin of the International Railway Congress Association* 3:10 (October 1921), pp. 1483–1526.

"Black Lines and White (Red) Lines." *Trains* 32:10 (August 1972), pp. 16–17.

"C. and O. to Renew Bridge over the Ohio River." *Railway Age* 85:4 (28 July 1928), pp. 139–43.

"C. & O. to Spend $12,000,000 at Covington and Cincinnati." *Railway Age* 82:29 (18 June 1927), p. 1980.

"Carew Tower, Cincinnati, Ohio." *Architecture and Building* 63:34 (February 1931), pp. 46–49.

"Cincinnati's New Union Railway Terminal." *Engineering News-Record* 111:18 (2 November 1933) pp. 524–26.

"Cincinnati's Union Station Plan Embodies Distinctive Features." *Railway Age* 87:6 (10 August 1929), pp. 375–77.

"Cincinnati, Ohio." Map of railroad facilities in the Cincinnati area. C & O/B & O Map No. 35250, undated.

"Cincinnati to Have Union Station." *Railway Age* 84:7 (18 February 1928), pp. 409–10.

"Cincinnati Union Terminal Company." *Railway Age* 83:21 (19 November 1927), p. 1016; 84:2 (14 January 1928), p. 166; 84:23 (9 June 1928), p. 1359.

Cincinnati Union Terminal, The: A Pictorial History. Cincinnati: Cincinnati Chamber of Commerce, 1933.

"Continuous Truss Bridge 1,575 Ft. Long at Cincinnati." *Engineering News-Record* 103:19 (7 November 1929), pp. 734–37.

Crane, Jacob L., Jr. "Street Development in Relation to Railroad Terminals."

Transactions of the American Society of Civil Engineers 87 (1924): 795-801.

Delano, Frederick A. "Railway Terminals and their Relation to City Planning." *Railroad Age Gazette* 47:26 (24 December 1909), pp. 1234-37.

"Double-Deck Viaduct Built over Cincinnati Terminal." *Engineering News-Record* 108:6 (11 February 1932), pp. 202-5.

Fellheimer, Alfred. "Design of Railway Terminal Stations." *Contract Record and Engineering Review* 37:35 (29 August 1923), pp. 844-46.

Fellheimer, Alfred. "Modern Railway Passenger Terminals." *Architectural Forum* 53:6 (December 1930, Part I), pp. 655-94.

Fellheimer, Alfred. "Principles of Terminal Station Design." *Railway Age* 75:3 (21 July 1923), pp. 109-11.

Fellheimer, Alfred, and Stewart Wagner. "The Cincinnati Union Terminal Co. Passenger Station Improvement. Cincinnati, Ohio." New York: Fellheimer and Wagner drawings, dated 1 June 1931.

Hobbs, D. B. "Aluminum Details in the Cincinnati Union Terminal; Fellheimer and Wagner, architects." *Architectural Record* 74:3 (September 1933), pp. 227-36.

"How Much Moves Where on Penn Central." *Trains* 33:12 (October 1973), pp. 16-17.

Huxtable, Ada Louise. "The Bigger They Are. . . ." *New York Times*, 19 November 1972, section 2, p. 22.

Lacher, Walter S. "Cincinnati's New Union Terminal Now in Service." *Railway Age* 94:16 (22 April 1933), pp. 575-90.

Loweth, C. F. "The Railroad and the City Plan." *Railway Age* 80:27 (5 June 1926), pp. 1475-78.

Maccallini, Louis. "On the Question of Terminal Stations for Passengers." *Bulletin of the International Railway Congress Association* 4:3 (March 1922), pp. 553-73.

McGavren, D. A. "Concrete Rigid-Frame Bridges for Railroad Loadings." *Engineering News-Record* 111:18 (2 November 1933), pp. 526-28.

Morgan, David P. "Cincinnati Union Terminal: A Memoir." *Trains* 33:4 (February 1972), pp. 18-22.

Payzant, O. S. "Long-Span Platforms for Cincinnati Station." *Engineering News-Record* 108:26 (30 June 1932), p. 912.

Payzant, O. S. "Parallel Trusses Carry Dome of Cincinnati Station." *Engineering News-Record* 108:23 (9 June 1932), pp. 817-20.

Pence, Herbert, Jr. "Big Railroad Center." *Cincinnati*, August 1973, pp. 73, 103-05.

"Railroad Terminals." *Proceedings of the American Society of Civil Engineers* 49:7 (September 1923), pp. 1455-1606.

"Railway Station Design Data." *Architectural Forum* 53:6 (December, 1930), pp. 767-68.

"Relation of Railroad Terminals to City Plan." *Railway Age* 68:18 (30 April 1920), pp. 1285-88.

Bibliography

Scott, Mel. *American City Planning since 1890*. Berkeley and Los Angeles: University of California Press, 1969.

Skerrett, R. G. "Seven Great Railroads Build Union Terminal." *Compressed Air Magazine* 38:6 (June 1933), pp. 4134–40.

"Station Dome Gets New Aluminum Cover." *Railway Age* 120:22 (1 June 1946), pp. 1109–11.

Stone, A. H. "Practical Considerations in Design of Large Stations." *Railway Age Gazette* 57:13 (25 September 1914), pp. 555–58.

Track Profile/Western Division/C N O & T P/Cincinnati to Chattanooga/MP 0 to MP 337. Revised 15 March 1972. Atlanta: Southern Railway System, 1972.

Turner, E. K. "Railroad Terminal Stations." *Railroad Gazette* v. 28 (6 November 1896), pp. 769–70.

"Union Terminal, Cincinnati; A. Fellheimer and S. Wagner, Architects." *Architectural Forum* 58:6 (June 1933), pp. 453–78.

Index

Index

Cincinnati Rapid Transit and Inter-urban Railway Company, 170, 171

Cincinnati Street Railway Company, 54, 55, 92, 94, 129 n. 15, 161, 162, 170, 204

Cincinnati Traction Company, 170, 171, 204

Cincinnati Trust Company, 151

Cincinnati, University of, 71, 170, 276, 278

Cincinnati: alluvial plain, 4, 16; canals, 4, 6; city center, 9, 32, 90, 145, 147, 149, 155, 232, 235, 242, 270, 271, 272; elevations above sea level, 42 n. 3; gateway to Pocahontas-Tidewater region, 180; gateway to South, 19, 178, 180; hills, 3, 4, 52, 112; history, 4-5, 51, 71-72; loans to railroad companies, 7, 23, 44 n. 20; locomotive builders, 40-41, 48 n. 44; manufacturing and railroad center, 109; meat-processing center, 5; population of, 299; railroads, 4, 5, 6, 22, 32-33, 34, 38, 51, 55, 78, 91, 113-16, 236, 276, figs. 34, 39, 43; railroad stations, 32-33, fig. 9; riverfront development, 272; rock systems, 3; sports stadium, 272; standard time, adoption of, 109; steamboat construction, 5; steamboat traffic, 5, 7; street railways, 33, fig. 38

Cincinnati (including Hamilton County) parks: Eden, 78, 116; Jackson Hill, 53; Mount Storm, 44 n. 22; Sharon Woods, 44 n. 22

Cincinnati suburbs (within city; for suburbs outside city, see under separate names): Anderson's Ferry, 161, 162; Avondale, 55; Bond Hill, 95, 96, 124, 144, 175; Brighton, 94, 112, 172; Clifton, 55, 94, 117, 257; College Hill, 92, 117, 121, 160; Cumminsville, 55, 94, 116, 144; East End, 124, 143, 150, 239; Fairview, 54, 257; Fernbank, 116, 162; Hartwell, 116; Hyde Park, 169; Idlewild, 95; Ivorydale, 95, 124; Kennedy Heights, 117; Linwood, 239; Ludlow Grove, 20, 44 n. 22; Madisonville, 20, 116, 162; Mariemont, 162, 276 n. 18; Mount Adams, 55, 72, 116, 117; Mount Auburn, 53, 55, 94, 117; Mount Lookout, 92, 117; Mount Washington, 93; North Side, 116, 205 n. 34; Oakley, 116, 144, 167; Pendleton, 7, 9, 92, 117; Pleasant Ridge, 117; Price Hill, 53, 55, 112; Red Bank, 143, 144; Sedamsville, 143; Spring Grove, 20; Walnut Hills, 21, 55, 95, 117, 150, 167, 169; West End, 54, 82, 83, 90, 115, 124, 143, 149, 167, 198 n. 8, 236, 271, 277 n. 21; Western Hills, 257; Westwood, 55, 92, 112, 117, 121; Winton Place, 44 n. 22, 55, 92, 116, 144, 282 n. 43

Cist, Charles, 23

Civil War, 5, 20, 24, 31, 32, 51, 55

Clare, Ohio, 239

Cleveland, Ohio, 32, 42 n. 8, 44 n. 28, 109, 118, 122, 151, 155, 163

Cleves, Ohio, 6, 27, 116

Clinch Mountains, 64

Collinwood, Ohio, 191

Columbia, Ohio, 92, 93

Columbus, Ohio, 7, 43 n. 9, 44 n. 28, 90, 119, 127 n. 1, 130 n. 17, 157, 163, 165, 186, 190, 205 n. 35.

Coney Island (Cincinnati), 162

Connersville, Indiana, 6, 42 n. 6

Consolidated Railway Company, 55

Conway, Thomas, 161

Corbin, Kentucky, 183

Covington, Kentucky, 32, 35, 55, 102, 103, 106, 123, 239, 282 n. 43

Covington Locomotive Works, 48 n. 44

Covington, Virginia, 151, 200 n. 13

Crabbs, George Dent, 216, 217, 276 n. 20

Cret, Paul Philippe, 234-35, 246, 276 n. 18, 278 n. 26

Cumberland Mountains, 64

Danville, Kentucky, 283 n. 45

Dayton, Ohio, 5, 15, 16, 19, 20, 21, 31, 32, 38, 39, 42 n. 5, 44 n. 28, 47 n. 4, 82, 90, 127 n. 1, 157, 160, 163, 274 n. 14

De Coursey, Kentucky, 124

Deer Creek, 11, 15, 42 n. 1, 67 n. 6, 78, 95

Index

Interstate Commerce Commission, 176, 180, 233-34

Italian style, 87

Jacksonville, Florida, 63, 118
Janney, Eli H., 37
Jeffersonville, Indiana, 24, 97, 98
Jersey City, New Jersey, 21, 39, 40
Johns, C. W., 241
Jones, Pusey, 276 n. 17

Kanawha River, 188
Kankakee, Illinois, 31, 132 n. 28
Kentucky coalfields, 103, 183
Keystone Bridge Company, 59, 64
Kiefer, Paul W., 191
Kilgour, Charles H., 92
Kings Mountain, Kentucky, 62
Knoxville, Tennessee, 103, 118, 131, 157
Kreling, August von, 71

Lamb, Thomas, 232
Latonia, Kentucky, 131 n. 24
Lattig, J. W., 38
Lawrenceburg, Indiana, 29
Lebanon, Ohio, 78, 82, 162, 236
Lexington, Kentucky, 15, 32, 47, 55, 58, 61, 67, 103
L'Hommedieu, S. S., 20
Licking River, 3, 4, 55, 58, 200, 210
Lick Run, 42, 112
Linville, Jacob H., 59, 64
Little Miami River, 3, 4, 5, 9, 20, 92, 93, 124, 162, 163, 239
Lockland, Ohio, 116, 282 n. 43
Locomotives: American (4-4-0), 40-41, 124, 138 n. 40; Atlantic (4-4-2), 125, 138 n. 42, 188, 194; Baltimore and Ohio, 125, 188-89, 193, 209 n. 51, 210 n. 57; Chesapeake and Ohio, 125, 138 n. 44, 188, 189, 209 n. 50; Chicago, Saint Paul, Minneapolis and Omaha, 209 n. 51; Cincinnati, Hamilton and Dayton, 40, 41, 124, 125, 138 n. 41; Cincinnati, New Orleans and Texas Pacific, 124, 125, 138 n. 41, 190, 209 n. 53; Cleveland, Cincinnati, Chicago and Saint Louis,
124, 125, 138 n. 41, 188-89, 191, 193, 194, 209 n. 51, 210 n. 56; Consolidation (2-8-0), 40, 124, 125; diesel-electric, 212 n. 59; dummy, 92; efficient use of, 212 n. 59; electric, 212 n. 59; feedwater heater, 125, 191, 193; Hudson (4-6-4), 191-93, 194, 210, 212 n. 59, fig. 42; high-horsepower, 264; Indianapolis and Cincinnati, 41; Little Miami, 40; Louisville and Nashville, 124, 125, 187-88, 190, 194, 209 n. 49, 210 n. 59; Mad River and Lake Erie, 41; Mastodon (*see* Twelve-wheel); mechanical stoker, 125-26; Michigan Central, 193; Mikado (2-8-2), 125, 193, 210 n. 56; Mogul (2-6-0), 125; Mohawk (*see* Mountain); Mountain (4-8-2), 189-90, 191, 209 n. 53, 212 n. 59; New York Central, 188-89, 190, 191, 193, 210 n. 55, 212 n. 59; Norfolk and Western, 190-91, 193, 210 n. 54; Pacific (4-6-2), 125, 187, 188, 189, 191, 193, 194, 209 n. 51, 210 n. 54; Pennsylvania, 125, 138, 187, 194, 208 n. 47; Pittsburgh, Cincinnati, Chicago and Saint Louis, 124, 125; reverse gear, power, 191, 193; Santa Fe (2-10-2), 193, 210 n. 57; Southern 188, 209 n. 50; super-heater, 125-26; Ten-wheel (4-6-0), 40-41, 124, 125, 138, 187, 194, 208 n. 47; Twelve-wheel (4-8-0), 193, 210 n. 57

Logansport, Indiana, 43, 132 n. 28, 265
Lookout House, 53
Lorain, Ohio, 42
Lord, Henry C., 24, 27, 31, 32, 82, 97
Losantiville, Ohio, 4-5
Louisville, Kentucky, 24, 58, 97, 98, 103, 112, 118, 120, 131 n. 24, 194, 195, 283 n. 45
Loveland, Ohio, 7, 20, 117, 239
Loweth, C. F., 229-31
Ludlow, Kentucky, 64, 67
Lynch, Kevin, 132, 270

Mabley and Carew store, 233
McAdoo, William G., 178-79
McCammon, William, 11
McGavren, D. A., 276 n. 16

325

Index

Procter and Gamble Company, 31
Procter, William Cooper, 170
Progressive movement, 227, 274 n. 14
Pullman, George M., 39

Queen Anne style, 83

Railroad companies: Alabama and Vicksburg, 63; Alabama Great Southern, 63; Atchison, Topeka and Santa Fe, 128 n. 1; Atlantic and Great Western, 19, 23, 35, 38, 39, 40, 44 n. 28; Baltimore and Ohio, 20, 21, 22, 39, 44 n. 22, 59, 96, 98, 115, 116, 117, 122, 123, 138 n. 39, 142, 161, 167, 181, 185, 208 n. 46, 217, 236, 239, 242, 257, 259, 260, 261, 266, 277 n. 21, 282 n. 43, 299; Baltimore and Ohio Southwestern, 95, 96, 110, 144, 161, 200, 203, 299; belt and transfer lines, 143; belt line projects, 144, 152, 215; Belt Railway of Chicago, 144; Big Four (see Cleveland, Cincinnati, Chicago and Saint Louis); Boston, 118; Boston and Albany, 37, 189; Burlington (see Chicago, Burlington and Quincy); Central of New Jersey, 38; Central Ohio, 127; Central Pacific, 130; Chesapeake and Ohio, 58, 99, 101-3, 109-10, 112, 117, 119, 123, 130 nn. 17, 21-23, 137 n. 39, 138 nn. 43-44, 142, 143, 145, 150, 151, 157, 200 nn. 12-13, 217, 236, 259, 260, 262, 264, 265, 266, 277 n. 21, 282 n. 43, 283 n. 46, 299; Chesapeake and Ohio of Indiana, 112; Chicago and Alton, 281 n. 38; Chicago and North Western, 184; Chicago, Burlington and Quincy, 37; Chicago, Cincinnati and Louisville, 110-13, 123, 132 nn. 29-30, 299; Chicago, Columbus and Indiana Central, 47 n. 41; Chicago, Indianapolis and Louisville, 132; Chicago, Milwaukee and Saint Paul, 129 n. 12, 186, 205 n. 33; Chicago, Saint Louis and Pittsburgh, 43 n. 18, 47 n. 41, 99; Chicago Short Line, 19; Cincinnati and Baltimore, 44 n. 22, 299; Cincinnati and Chicago Air Line, 43 n. 18, 47 n. 41; Cincinnati and Columbia Street, 91-92, 299; Cin-

cinnati and Eastern, 82, 93, 95, 299; Cincinnati and Hamilton, 16, 299; Cincinnati and Indiana, 27, 45 n. 30, 265, 299; Cincinnati and Indianapolis Junction, 43 n. 18, 47 n. 41; Cincinnati and Indianapolis Short Line, 47 n. 30; Cincinnati and Louisville, 132 n. 29; Cincinnati and Muskingum Valley, 43 n. 10, 77; Cincinnati and Portsmouth, 93; Cincinnati and Richmond, 99, 299; Cincinnati and Springfield, 31, 34, 299; Cincinnati and Westwood, 92-93, 119, 121, 167, 299; Cincinnati Circle Road, 143; Cincinnati Connecting Belt, 95-96, 190, 299; Cincinnati, Georgetown and Portsmouth, 93, 299; Cincinnati, Hamilton and Dayton, 16-20, 21, 23, 32, 34, 35, 38, 39, 40, 41, 43 n. 18, 44 n. 28, 47 n. 41, 92, 96, 108, 109, 110, 112, 116, 122, 132 n. 32, 144, 150, 157, 181, 190, 193, 259, 299; Cincinnati, Hamilton and Indianapolis, 43 n. 18; Cincinnati, Indiana and Louisville, 98; Cincinnati, Indianapolis and Western, 43 n. 18, 181, 299; Cincinnati, Indianapolis, Saint Louis and Chicago, 31, 45 n. 37, 47 n. 41, 68 n. 10, 83, 87, 97, 98, 130 n. 20, 265, 299; Cincinnati Intersecting, 144; Cincinnati Interterminal, 110; Cincinnati, Lafayette and Chicago, 47 n. 41; Cincinnati, Lebanon and Northern, 82, 117, 128 n. 7, 131 n. 27, 149, 239, 299; Cincinnati, New Orleans and Texas Pacific, 62, 63, 106, 108, 143, 145-46, 157, 181, 183, 200 nn. 12, 16-17, 208 n. 44, 217, 236, 262, 265, 267-68, 277 n. 21, 282 n. 45, 299; Cincinnati Northern, 78-82, 93, 128 n. 5, 131 n. 27, 143, 198 n. 5, 299-300; Cincinnati-Northwestern, 92, 121, 160, 300; Cincinnati, Portsmouth and Virginia, 95-96, 144, 300; Cincinnati Railroad Terminal Development Company, 218, 232, 233; Cincinnati Railway Tunnel Company, 128 n. 7, 300; Cincinnati, Richmond and Chicago, 43 n. 18, 99, 143, 144; Cincinnati, Richmond and Muncie, 110; Cincinnati Southern, 61-66, 67-68, 71, 101, 144, 158, 159, 169, 181,

Index

Index

Index